WOMEN OF A LESSER COST

£3 —

Ge

16142

Anthropology, Culture and Society

Series Editor: Dr Richard Wilson, University of Sussex

*Ethnicity and Nationalism:
Anthropological Perspectives*
THOMAS HYLLAND ERIKSEN

*Power and Its Disguises:
Anthropological Perspectives on Politics*
JOHN GLEDHILL

*Anthropology of the Self:
The Individual in Cultural Perspective*
BRIAN MORRIS

WOMEN OF A LESSER COST

Female Labour, Foreign Exchange and Philippine Development

Sylvia Chant and Cathy McIlwaine

Pluto  Press

LONDON • EAST HAVEN, CT

First published 1995 by Pluto Press
345 Archway Road, London N6 5AA
and 140 Commerce Street
East Haven, CT 06512, USA

Exclusively distributed in the Philippines, Brunei, Indonesia,
Malaysia, Singapore, Thailand, and Vietnam, by the Ateneo de
Manila University Press; and in the rest of the world by Pluto Press.

British Library Cataloguing in Publication Data
A catalogue record for this book is available from
the British Library

ISBN 0 7453 0946 1 (hardback)

Library of Congress Cataloging in Publication Data
Chant, Sylvia H.
  Women of a lesser cost: female labour, foreign exchange, and
Philippine development / Sylvia Chant and Cathy McIlwaine.
      p.   cm.
  Includes bibliographical references and index.
  ISBN 0-7453-0946-1 (hardback).
    1. Women—Employment—Philippines. 2. Foreign exchange—
Philippines. 3. Philippines—Economic conditions—1946–
I. McIlwaine, Cathy. II Title.
HD6195.C48   1995
331.4'09599—dc20   94–45270
                                                          CIP

Designed and produced for the publisher by
Chase Production Services, Chipping Norton, OX7 5QR.
Typeset from editors' disks by
Stanford DTP Services.
Printed in the EC by Biddles Ltd, Guildford, England

CONTENTS

List of figures   vi

List of tables   vii

Preface and acknowledgements   viii

1 Introduction: Gender and Development in
the Philippines   1

2 The Philippine Economy: National Perspectives,
Export-oriented Development, and Growth in the
Central and Western Visayas   45

3 Gender, Migration and Low-income Households in
Cebu, Lapu-Lapu and Boracay: An Overview   82

4 Gender and Manufacturing Employment   129

5 Gender and Tourism Employment   172

6 Gender and Sex Work   211

7 Comparative Perspectives on Work and Women's
Status   256

8 Conclusion: Policy Implications and Directions for
Future Research   304

Appendix: Methodology   318

Bibliography   324

Index   358

LIST OF FIGURES

Figure 1.1   Location of study centres and places referred to in text   3

Figure 3.1   Cebu City: location of study settlement and main industrial areas   83

Figure 3.2   Philippines: regions and provinces   86

Figure 3.3   Migrant origins of women by region: Cebu   88

Figure 3.4   Migrant origins of men by region: Cebu   89

Figure 3.5   Lapu-Lapu City: location of study settlement and Mactan Export Processing Zone   90

Figure 3.6   Migrant origins of women by region: Lapu-Lapu   91

Figure 3.7   Migrant origins of men by region: Lapu-Lapu   91

Figure 3.8   Boracay: location of study settlements and main tourist zone   92

Figure 3.9   Migrant origins of women by region: Boracay   94

Figure 3.10   Migrant origins of men by region: Boracay   94

Figure 3.11   Household headship: Cebu   97

Figure 3.12   Household structure: Cebu   97

Figure 3.13   Household headship: Lapu-Lapu   101

Figure 3.14   Household structure: Lapu-Lapu   101

Figure 3.15   Household headship: Boracay   103

Figure 3.16   Household structure: Boracay   104

Figure 3.17   Female occupational groups: Cebu   108

Figure 3.18   Female occupational groups: Lapu-Lapu   111

Figure 3.19   Female occupational groups: Boracay   114

Figure 4.1   Percentage of women in different departments in electronics and garment factories, MEPZ, Lapu-Lapu   140

Figure 4.2   Percentage of women in different departments in rattan furniture and handicraft factories, Cebu   146

Figure 4.3   Percentage of women in different departments in
              fashion accessory factories, Cebu   146
Figure 5.1   Percentage of women in different hotel
              departments, Cebu and Boracay   179
Figure 5.2   Percentage of women employed in subsections
              of food and beverage departments in hotels
              and accommodation establishments, Cebu   183
Figure 5.3   Percentage of women employed in subsections
              of food and beverage departments in hotels
              and accommodation establishments, Boracay   183
Figure 6.1   Hierarchy of sex work in Cebu City   215

LIST OF TABLES

Table 4.1   Product, ownership, size of workforce and number
              of female workers in export manufacturing firms
              interviewed in Lapu-Lapu and Cebu   132
Table 6.1   Male visitors to entertainment establishments,
              Cebu City   223
Table 6.2   Male tourists in Boracay   228
Table 7.1   Key migration characteristics of women in
              target occupational groups   258
Table 7.2   Key household characteristics of women in
              target occupational groups   266
Table A2.1   Worker sample in export manufacturing firms,
              Cebu and Lapu-Lapu   320
Table A2.2   Worker sample in tourism establishments,
              Boracay and Cebu   321
Table A2.3   Worker sample in entertainment establishments,
              Cebu City   321

PREFACE AND ACKNOWLEDGEMENTS

While this is the first piece of work the present authors have jointly published on the Philippines, it is by no means the first time we have worked together. During a period of collaboration stretching back to 1987, when one of us was a student and the other a newly arrived lecturer at the University of Liverpool, we have worked together in a variety of capacities and shared numerous journeys overseas, the first to Costa Rica in 1989. Two years later, our evolving joint and individual experiences of Latin America, our personal and professional concerns with global aspects of gender and development, and an urge, as geographers, to explore contingencies of place, led to the desire to expand our research in a part of the world that would be new to us both. Our reasons for choosing the Philippines included the fact that the country's colonial heritage and contemporary economic and social structure shared various common features with the Latin American contexts with which we were familiar, and that the Philippines was known to have an extremely active women's movement, even if there did not seem to be much literature available at an international level on other aspects of gender in the country. This is important, in that while this book is mainly concerned with exploring the interrelations among women's employment, migration and household organisation in the Philippine Visayas, the findings are evaluated in the light of wider debates on gender and economic change in the developing world.

The major project on which this book is based lasted 15 months from January 1993 and was funded by a grant to Sylvia Chant from the Economic and Social Research Council (award no. R000234020), for which grateful acknowledgement is duly registered. Thanks are also owed to the ESRC (award no. R000233291), which, along with the Nuffield Foundation, British Academy and Suntory-Toyota International Centre for Economics and Related Disciplines, provided valuable seed finance for a pilot study between November 1991 and April 1992.

The intellectual and methodological aspects of the research also depended in great measure on the generous assistance and collaboration of a wide range of individuals and organisations, foremost among whom are Marilen Dañguilan and Emmeline Versoza (presently with the Office of the Senate President of the Philippines and the Policy Studies Group), to whom we were kindly introduced by Ellen Wratten of the London School of Economics Department of Social Science and Administration. Along with Alice Donald and Maggie Byrne of the Philippine Resource Centre, London (now at the BBC World Service and the Asia Desk of the Catholic Institute of International Relations, respectively), Marilen and Emmeline went out of their way to direct us to material and to put us in contact with individuals in both the UK and the Philippines who could help with our research. They have also, on numerous occasions, shown many other aspects of friendship and support for which we are deeply indebted, especially during our visits to Manila.

Other Manila-based individuals who made much-appreciated sacrifices on our account and to whom we would like to record thanks are: Aida Santos and Lynn Lee of the Women's Education, Development, Productivity and Research Organisation (WEDPRO); Elizabeth Eviota and Emma Porio, Ateneo de Manila University; Sister Mary John Mananzan, Institute of Women's Studies, St Scholastica's College; Reena Marcelo and Florence Macagba Tadiar, Institute for Social Studies and Action; Princess Nemenzo, Womanhealth Phil Inc; Lorna Makil, Philippine Social Science Council; Amar Torres, Rosalinda Pineda-Ofreneo, Rosario del Rosario and Aurora Perez, University of the Philippines; Ruth Ruiz, Philippine Volunteer Programme; Fe Mangahas, Women's Desk, Cultural Center of the Philippines; Luisa Engracia, National Statistics Office; Ampy Pinlac, Bureau of Women and Young Workers; Hilda Sumabat, Export Processing Zone Authority; Aleli Lopez-Dee and Sally Almendral, National Economic and Development Authority (NEDA); Paul Moselina, UNICEF Philippines; Gigi Francisco, Women's Resource and Research Center; Raquel Tiglao, Women's Crisis Center; Beth Encilla, Remedios Training Center; Nancy Garcia, KMK; Corazon Buenaventura,

National Statistical Coordination Board, and Rene de los Santos, Adel Carmen and Ramona Pi of the Department of Tourism.

Our first visit to the Visayas in February 1992 was aided in numerous ways by Allyson Thirkell, a PhD student at the LSE who was conducting her research on housing in Cebu at the time. Others who were particularly helpful include: Rey Bernil, Urban Poor Development Center; Glofe Calinawan, SAMAKANA; Carlos Allones, KMU Visayas; Father Wilhelm Flieger, Father Thomas Murnane and Erlinda Alburo, San Carlos University; Joel Yu, Department of Trade and Industry Region VII; Rogelio Balajadia, Mactan Export Processing Zone Authority; Gwen Ngolaban, FORGE; Ester Espinosa, Women's Resource Center of Cebu; Raymond Fonollera, NEDA Region VII; Alex Umadhay, NEDA Region VI; Boy Homicillada, PROCESS, Iloilo; Fely David, Central Philippines University; Edgar Decena and Judith Icotanim, Boracay Island Tourism Administration; Adolfo Mameng, Association of Small Fisherfolk and Farmers of Malay, Aklan (AMMASMA), and Sofia Logarta and Mads de la Cerna, UP Cebu College.

Many of these individuals also assisted us during our extended period of fieldwork in 1993, especially Father Wilhelm Flieger of the Office of Population Studies, San Carlos University, who kindly arranged for two of his field officers, Tessie Sato and Ging-Ging Uy, to help with household surveys in Cebu, Lapu-Lapu and Negros Oriental province. Along with Emma Galvez, Tessie and Ging-Ging gave unfailing assistance and companionship. The same is true of Lisa Tarectaran of KMU, Visayas, and Ami Garcia, Rodrigo Navarro and Armand Alforque of the National Federation of Labor, who were instrumental in helping us make contact with manufacturing workers and union officials in the Central Visayas, and Beng Lao of MEPZA and Vicky Diaz of DTI Region VII, who provided considerable assistance in arranging introductions to employers. Gloria Abbu, Eva Pinat and Gloria Paz of the Cebu City Health Department Social Hygiene Clinic gave much-appreciated insights into the health aspects of employment in the local hospitality industry; while in Boracay Nonoy Gelito's assistance in household interviews, as well as in worker contacts, was indispensable. The residents of Rubberworld in Cebu, Pusok in Lapu-Lapu and Manoc-Manoc and Balabag in Boracay, together with workers and employers in all three centres who gave generously of their time and patience, deserve special gratitude:

without their contributions this book could not have been written, nor would we feel such immense enthusiasm for returning to the Visayas at the earliest opportunity.

Back in the UK our gratitude extends to Penny Page for help in inputting our computer data, to Jane Pugh and Mina Moshkiri for drawing the maps, and to Carlo Faulds and Karl Fulton for their photographic assistance. We would also like to thank Peter Krinks, Macquarie University, New South Wales, Australia, who directed us to some of our first reading and who has subsequently provided helpful follow-up advice and contacts. We are indebted to LSE colleagues James Putzel (Development Studies Institute), Jim Thomas (Economics) and Hazel Johnstone (Geography), who were kind enough to read various draft material, and to others – John Gledhill, University College London; Nici Nelson, Goldsmiths College; Bryan Roberts, University of Texas at Austin; Thea Sinclair, University of Kent at Canterbury; Peter Wade, University of Liverpool; Paul Cammack, University of Manchester, and Bob Bradnock, School of Oriental and African Studies – who gave further advice and support at various stages of the project. Thanks are also owed to Pluto Press in expediting the final product, and particularly to Anne Beech, Editorial Director, and Richard Wilson, editor of this series, for their time and effort expended in reading the manuscript and suggesting ways to trim excess fat!

Our families and friends were there, as ever, with love and kindness, especially during the painful times which followed the death of Sylvia's 18-month-old nephew, Cameron, in December 1992. It is to his short but profoundly significant life that we dedicate this book.

Sylvia Chant
Cathy McIlwaine   August 1994

I am Maria
taught to cook and wash
to be bought
not to remain
He is Pedro
left to play
morning till noon
because he's male
and would lose nothing
So what if I play
and Pedro is taught to cook and wash
please tell me
what would be lost.

Ruby Enario, 'New Generation'
('Bag-ong Tubo')

Hush now my littlest one, do not be troubled
I shall be back in the afternoon, I promise.
I have to work in the factory of the foreign boss
To earn money with which to buy your milk.

Eat now, my littlest one, do not mind the meal of dried fish
For this is all my pocket could afford
In spite of my whole day's labour
No matter how best we try, our resources never last.

Sleep now my littlest one, move to the side a bit
So we can both fit. Curve your body a moment more
Compared to the cold streets, this little shanty is better
Out there are the street-children and beggars.

Wake-up now, my littlest one, it is morning
Study well to fulfil your dreams
For the darkness now will be replaced by hopes
We shall have equality.

Arni Mercado, 'There is Hope'
('May Pag-asa ang Bukas'),
translated by Marjorie Evasco

1 INTRODUCTION: GENDER AND DEVELOPMENT IN THE PHILIPPINES

AIMS AND OBJECTIVES

As Thea Sinclair notes in her introduction to one of the first books dealing with gender and labour ideology from an international perspective (Redclift and Sinclair, 1991), 'women and men participate in the paid labour market on a very different basis'. Nowhere is this truer, perhaps, than in cases where promotion of the export sector has been central to strategies aimed at wresting poor countries from the grips of external debt, recession and a weak position in the global order. While women in postwar developing societies have often been situated on the so-called margins of economic activity, the last two decades of rapid expansion in export-oriented development have seen their massive incorporation into mainstream niches of the international division of labour, usually under the aegis of transnational capital. Third World women are cheaper to employ than their counterparts in the advanced economies (and than men in their own countries), and their 'lesser cost' is a crucial pivot around which enquiry into the feminisation of labour has revolved. Yet while export manufacturing, for its high visibility and its key role in economic growth, has been the main focus of attempts to analyse this phenomenon, other activities characterised by similarly high levels of multinational investment, foreign exchange generation and use of female workers have received relatively little attention (see below). Although patterns of female employment even within the manufacturing sector itself cannot be generalised within countries, let alone between them (see, for example, Pearson, 1986:68; Sklair,1991:93–101), similarities do exist and their comparative analysis is vital in assessing the role of economic internationalisation in the contemporary 'global feminisation of labour' (see Joekes, 1987;

1

Moghadam, 1994; G.Standing, 1989). While the empirical base of this book is in the Philippines, therefore, its conceptual scope is wider. In considering female insertion into three branches of activity – manufacturing, international tourism and sex work[1] – in three localities – Cebu, Lapu-Lapu and Boracay Island (Fig.1.1) – the intention is not only to examine the causes and consequences of women's involvement in the export sector[2] in a comparatively little-studied region (the Visayas),[3] but to use the insights to illuminate discussions of gender and development at a broader level.

Central concerns are the extent to which current economic strategies are exacerbating or lessening inequality between the sexes, and their effects on women's lives and status. Given mounting recognition that female labour force participation (and its outcomes) depends on a broad range of economic, demographic and social factors, and that these require detailed exploration in a more comprehensive array of locations (see, for example, Blumberg, 1991b; Palriwala, 1990; Stichter, 1990), the study pays particular attention to the multiple and interacting links between women's employment, migration and household organisation, with the further aim of aiding their conceptual integration. In accordance with these objectives, we draw on extensive primary data gathered from low-income households, target groups of workers, employers and other relevant parties in the Visayas (see Appendix),

---

1 Sex work is more usually referred to in the Philippines as the 'entertainment' or 'hospitality' industry, with the latter officially classified as consisting of nightclubs, dance halls, cabarets, cocktail lounges, massage parlours, steam and sauna baths, soda fountains, restaurants, beer gardens and discos (see Perpiñan, 1983:12; also NCRFW, 1989:138). It is tempting to speculate on whether this very broad brush has been in some senses a deliberate move to 'bury' the more explictly sex-oriented businesses within a spectrum of more straightforward leisure, tourism and recreational facilities and in so doing to play down and/or legitimise commercial sex as an acceptable form of enterprise. Similarly, many have noted that the term 'hospitality industry', along with its military counterpart 'Rest and Recreation' (R&R), tends to neutralise and/or sanitise the naked facts of sexual commodification (see, for example, Azarcon de la Cruz, 1985; Moselina, 1981).

2 While international tourism (and its attendant sex industry) are not export activities *sensu strictu*, the fact that tourists bring foreign exchange into the Philippines to purchase goods (food, souvenirs and the like) and services (hotel rooms, transport, tour guides' time, sex and so on) is equivalent to exporting these goods and services, even if they do not actually leave the country (see, for example, Harrison, 1992:13–14; W.Lee, 1991:79; McKercher, 1993:13).

3 Most studies of gender and development in the Philippines to date have focused on Manila or other major cities in the northern island group of Luzon, as opposed to the Visayas and Mindanao (see Fig 1.1).

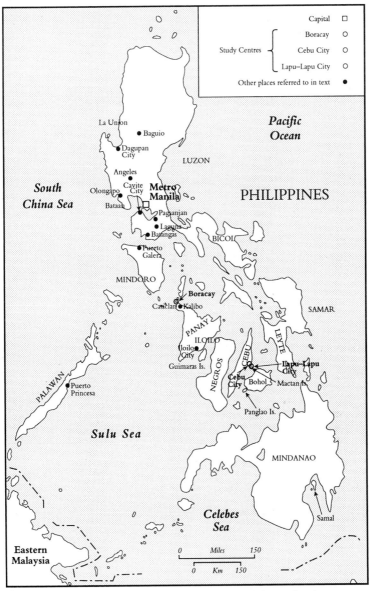

Figure 1.1: Philippines: Location of study centres and places referred to in text

both to identify the impacts on women of export-oriented develop-ment and to assess (and inform) broader approaches to the analysis of gender-selective migration, household evolution, female labour force participation and the relationships between them.

With this in mind, the present chapter provides a brief synopsis of current debates surrounding the core themes of the book, notably gender and the household, employment and migration. These sections review the existing literature, first in relation to developing countries in general and then in relation to the Philippines, where most studies to date have not been particularly accessible to a wider international readership. The discussions are intended not only to provide a backdrop to the detailed case study material in subsequent chapters, but to clarify and contextualise the more specific questions examined in the book. The different sections on the Philippines, together with an overview of the women's movement and gender policy, are also intended to give the reader a general impression of Filipino women's lives and ex-periences. The chapter concludes with a synthesis of the key issues and a guide as to how these are explored in the body of the text.

GENDER AND DEVELOPMENT: CURRENT RESEARCH AND PHILIPPINE PERSPECTIVES

Gender and the household

In considering gender and the household, it is necessary first to give a definition of what is usually understood by the latter (increasingly controversial) term. While some authors, for example Pepe Roberts (1991:64), claim that households often take on such different forms in different societies around the world that we should abandon searches for universal definitions, it is generally agreed that a household is a group of people who share the same residence and participate collec-tively, if not always cooperatively, in the basic tasks of reproduction and consumption (see Brydon and Chant, 1993:8–10).[4] In addition

---

4 Interestingly the Philippine Census uses the same criteria for defining households. The National Statistics Office specifies households as collections of people who:

• sleep in the same housing unit, and
• have a common arrangement for the preparation and consumption of food.

It is also noted that in most cases households consist of persons who are related by kinship ties (NSO, 1992a:xiii).

to the fact that households are usually viewed as residential and con-sumption units, they are generally observed to contain members who are related by blood or marriage. Households are accordingly seen to embrace various aspects of family and kinship ideology and to be important mediators of social and cultural values which may change through time and across space in line with wider structural shifts in the mode of production, evolution of the state, economic growth and so on (Kuzesnof, 1989:169). Households are also viewed as embodying norms which govern divisions of labour and differences in power and status between the sexes and between different age groups. The frequent identification of household with family has meant that within gender analysis the household is taken as a critical, if not primary site of women's oppression (Kabeer and Joekes, 1991:1; see also Townsend and Momsen, 1987:40). However, as with most definitions which aspire to universality, it is often difficult in practice to encapsulate, let alone explain, the wide-ranging heterogeneity of household forms and organisation both within and among countries and over time.

Within recent academic work on gender and the household, therefore, one important area of enquiry has revolved around analysing the diversity of household forms in different geographical and historical contexts, and exploring the ways in which these may impact upon gender roles and relations at domestic and wider societal levels (see, for example, Chant, 1991a; McIlwaine, 1993; Moore, 1988:112–19; Nelson, 1992; Palriwala, 1990; Smith and Wallerstein, 1992). Another important development has been increased recognition of the fact that whatever form household structure might take, households do not nec-essarily have a 'joint utility' function, but are often characterised by inequality and conflict. This has led to identification of the household as an arena of what the economist Amartya Sen (1987,1990) has termed 'cooperative conflicts'. In turn this has provoked interest in the ways in which power relations are generated and sustained within households (Radcliffe,1991; Safilios-Rothschild, 1990; Stichter, 1990; Stolcke, 1991; White, 1992; Wolf, 1990a), as well as the more practical ways in which these often have very serious resource implications for women and children (see Blumberg, 1991b,1991c; Dwyer and Bruce, 1988; Hoddinott and Haddad, 1991; Young, 1992). More recently, interest has also been shown in the manner in which life-cycle changes affect the roles and resources of women within households (see, for example, Katz and Monk, 1993). In short, discourses on the subject of gender and the household have increasingly begun to embrace notions of difference, and to put paid to the idea that women everywhere, of different cultures, classes, ages and ethnic origin, as well as household type, will necessarily share commonalities of experience. The call for appreciation of difference is perhaps nowhere more relevant than in countries such as the Philippines, where it has long been recognised that in many respects households do not appear to be the constraining structures for women that they often are in other places.

Gender and households in the Philippine context

Gender divisions of labour

Bearing in mind the difficulties of making generalisations about gender in a society as diverse as the Philippines (Banzon-Bautista, 1989), Filipino women are often seen as having a stronger position in society than their counterparts in other cultures, mainly as a result of their prominent role within the household and a relative fluidity in the domestic allocation of productive and reproductive tasks.[5] While in many developing countries there is quite a marked normative divide between men's and women's familial responsibilities, in that men are expected primarily to fulfil breadwinning functions and women to adhere mainly to housework and childcare, these gender role expectations are often seen to be less rigidly demarcated in Philippine society (see, for example, Illo, 1988; Illo and Veneracion, 1988). Although Filipino women still have to shoulder the bulk of domestic duties, among lower-income groups in particular, women who take on remunerative work are generally accorded 'approval and prestige' by their male and female peers (Hollnsteiner, 1991a:266; see also Bucoy, 1992; Sevilla, 1989). Thus Filipino wives and mothers often have higher rates of labour force participation than their counterparts in other cultures, and this is often construed as leading to higher levels of domestic decision-making (see below). Just as both women and men may share

5 Discussions of gender in the Philippines in this chapter concentrate mainly on lowland Christian groups from Luzon and the Visayas, rather than on highland tribes such as the Igorots of northern Luzon's Cordillera region or the Muslim population of the southern island group, Mindanao. This reflects both the fact that over 90 per cent of Filipinos identify themselves as Christian, and that less has been written about ethnic minority groups within the country (although see Anti-Slavery Society, 1983; Goodno, 1991: Chapter 21; Industan, 1992; Johnson, 1994; Le Guen, 1994; Loyré, 1994; Pineda-Ofreneo, 1991: Chapter 9; Schneider, 1994; Stanyukovich, 1994).

in the task of generating household income, it is also observed that even if Filipino men do not help out to a great extent with housework, it is not uncommon for them to wash clothes or to sweep up, and they do play a role in looking after children (see Aguilar, 1991:159; Illo and Polo, 1990:101; PROCESS, 1993:32; Sevilla, 1989:4). Indeed, Lucia Pavia-Ticzon (1990:117) notes that men put in almost one-third of the time that women do to household chores. In this respect, gender divisions of labour are arguably less rigid than in other places and to some degree are reflected in the relatively equal treatment of male and female children. For example, Medina (1991:24) notes that parents are expected to maintain 'impartiality in extending favours and privileges to sons and daughters' (though see also Ramirez, 1984:32). This is manifested in the fact that all children, regardless of sex, have equal rights of inheritance (ibid.; see also Church, 1986:57). Moreover, boys and girls usually receive similar opportunities for schooling (see King and Domingo, 1986:16; Licuanan, 1991:15; Villariba, 1993:8).

Another factor identified as critical in enhancing women's status in Filipino households is their strong role in household financial management (see Church, 1986; Illo, 1989; Medina, 1991; Ramirez, 1984). It has been observed not only that Filipino women are often in charge of the family 'purse strings', but, as such, that they are more often 'co-managers' than 'implementers of their husbands' wishes' (Castillo, 1991:250). Indeed, a strong thread running through much writing on gender and the family-based household in the Philippines is that of egalitarianism in domestic relations and democratic consultation between spouses on matters of expenditure and labour allocation (see Medina, 1991; Miralao, 1984; Sala-Boza, 1982; Sevilla, 1989). Many of these features are viewed as having roots in pre-Hispanic patterns of gender roles and relations, common not only to the Philippines but other parts of Southeast Asia where principles of 'human sameness and complementarity' arguably prevailed over structures of hierarchy and difference (Blanc-Szanton, 1990:346; see also Cruz, 1991; Mananzan, 1991a; A.Santos, 1991; Steinberg, 1986:32–3; Villariba, 1993:7).

Challenges to the 'egalitarian household' model

Having said this, three sets of factors caution against uncritical acceptance of this rather positive view of household-level gender equality and its

implications for Filipino women's status. One is the persistent association of women with the domestic sphere, which inevitably impinges
on their involvement in wider political, economic and social life. As
Raul Pertierra (1991:194) points out: 'despite the autonomy that
women exercise in certain domains, such as religion and the economy,
Filipinos generally concede that the ultimate orientation of women is
to domestic matters'. Second, all too often the position of Filipino
women is viewed out of context and evaluated against notionally
universal norms of 'female status'. This is inappropriate for a number
of reasons, usefully summarised by Elizabeth Eviota (1991:157):

> There is no denying the social visibility of some Filipino women, but to infer
> that this visibility is an indicator of high status is incorrect. Many point out
> that, relative to women in other countries, Filipino women have high status
> ... However, if Filipino women's status is to be assessed in a meaningful way,
> it should be assessed within the society relative to the status of Filipino men.

A final point is the widespread existence of alternative, and perhaps
rather more critical, analyses which demonstrate quite significant
evidence of female subordination and/or disadvantage. Indeed, as
Carolyn Israel-Sobritchea (1991:90) observes, several studies carried
out on women since the inauguration of the UN Decade for Women
in 1975 suggest that 'the majority of Filipino women today are not
exactly on an equal footing with their male counterparts'.

One factor emphasised by critics of the 'egalitarian model' is the
rather limited extent to which gender roles between the sexes are actually
mutable in practice. For example, although Filipino men probably do
spend more time 'helping their wives' with domestic labour and
childcare than is the case in other cultures, it is undoubtedly women
who bear the more fundamental and regular responsibility for reproductive work (Bucoy, 1992:36; Miralao, 1984:380; Pavia-Ticzon,
1990:117). As regards male involvement in childcare, for instance,
Hollnsteiner (1991b:278) points out this does not necessarily involve
routine engagement in chores such as dressing children or putting them
to bed, but is likely to be sporadic or to take the form of more pleas-
urable activities such as taking them for walks, amusing them or
playing games with them. Moreover, in a study of women workers
in multinational factories in the Export Processing Zone of Bataan,
Luzon, Zosa-Feranil (1984:399) found that only 3 per cent of the
married women in her sample could delegate childcare to husbands;
in most cases older children had to look after younger siblings while

their mothers were at work. Indeed, men who do too much to help their wives in the home may earn the pejorative label of being *ander di saya*, or 'under their wives' skirts' (ibid.).[6] As a result of the greater physical and emotional investment of women in reproductive tasks, it is also the case that female labour force participation, particularly that of married women, is often limited compared with men's. As Raul Pertierra (1991:195) points out, 'the emphasis on domestic responsibility clashes with their public and communal duties'. The fact that women tend to be found in lower paid and less prestigious jobs than their male counterparts relates very much to the practical constraints imposed by household divisions of labour, as well as to the fact that, at a normative level, employers tend to regard women as secondary workers who are merely supplementing their husbands' wages (Aleta et al., 1977; BWM, 1985; Eviota, 1986, 1988,1991; Licuanan, 1991; Pavia Ticzon, 1990; Zarate, 1990; see also the later section on employment in this chapter). Popular expressions such as the Cebuano saying *Way batasang asawaha magpunay lang ug make-up ug suroy-suroy* ('A good wife stays at home to attend to the needs of her family') tend to reinforce this syndrome (see Buenaventura-Ojeda, 1973:106). As Belen Medina (1991:131) sums up: 'despite changes taking place in Philippine society, husband and wife role expectations have remained basically the same as in previous generations. The traditional segregation of roles where the husband is the breadwinner and the wife the homemaker is still the ideal.'

Another caveat to the egalitarian household model relates to the power imagined to accrue to women in their roles as 'family treasurers'. While it is often the case that men hand their wages over to their wives, who in turn manage and distribute household income, this by no means implies that women are able to take major decisions (see, for example, Eviota, 1988; Israel-Sobritchea, 1991; Miralao, 1984; Sevilla, 1989). Indeed, the amount of income held by women in poor households may only be just enough to cover basic needs; this may not merely mean very little in terms of opportunities for personal power or autonomy (Aguilar, 1988; Angeles, 1990; Illo and Veneracion, 1988; Licuanan, 1991), but can also impose the unenviable problem of struggling with money shortages (Banzon-Bautista,1989). Moreover, while women may well be 'keepers of the family purse', they are not

---

6 Unless otherwise stated, all Filipino terms in this chapter are in the national *lingua franca*, Tagalog.

normally able to refuse their husbands' requests for gambling and drinking money (PROCESS, 1993:510). Studies have also revealed that while women devote all their wages to the household budget, men withhold some of theirs at the outset to spend on so-called vices (Illo and Lee, 1991:70). In the final analysis, Elizabeth Eviota's (1986:194) point that men's relationship to economic assets is direct, while a woman's access is 'indirect and mediated through her husband', is suggestive of certain constraints on what is ostensibly a strong managerial role for women in the realm of household finances.

Power relations

Moving beyond these material considerations, it is important to acknowledge the existence of factors of a more ideological nature which also shape gender differences. Much debate, for example, has centred on the issue of the differential levels and manifestations of power among men and women in Filipino households. Several writers have been keen to stress that women have power within the household, even if this is not immediately obvious to the outside observer or indeed to the members of a woman's own family. For example, Elizabeth King and Lita Domingo (1986:12) liken the situation of Filipino women to an 'underworld matriarchy', where although there is the appearance of a 'man's world ... women rule without anybody but themselves knowing it'. Raul Pertierra (1991:195) also points to the fact that women often use 'individualised and covert strategies to accomplish their ends', and Mary Hollnsteiner (1991a:260) identifies a myriad 'indirect means' through which women try to influence their husbands, including crying, sulking, going home to their parents, physical self-abuse and/or diminished care of spouses. However, while recourse to manipulative, non-confrontational tactics may have earned many women the place of 'silent but influential' partners (Medina, 1991:156), the question remains as to whether this 'behind-the-scenes' power can actually compete with authority of a more formal and visible nature. Why, for example, does the headship of households automatically fall to the oldest male (see Medina, 1991:24; also Illo, 1989)? Why do fathers and husbands remain as authority figures (Buenaventura-Ojeda, 1973:131)? Why are women so 'protective of male egos' as to 'take pains not to appear dominant in the household or public affairs' (Sevilla, 1989:16)? And why have some viewed the family–household as a conflictive, hierarchical unit where 'men unambiguously exercise direct power over women' (see Eviota, 1992:113)? Part of the answer may lie in the fact that even protagonists of the egalitarian model themselves concede that 'near equality' in domestic relations is perhaps a more accurate term than full equality (see Medina, 1991). In this sense we might infer that some of the more optimistic readings in the literature have been somewhat overdrawn and/or overstated.

Gender identity

Beyond the question of power relations per se, it is also important to consider the ways in which images and constructions of masculinity and femininity result in differences in behaviour and opportunities for men and women. At a general level, maleness or masculinity (*pagkalalaki/pagigingtunay na lalaki*) is popularly equated with men being breadwinners, being able to conquer women and to sire children (Ramirez, 1984:32). Feminine identity, on the other hand, tends to be predicated on mothering and caring roles in the domestic arena (ibid.). Lutgarda Resurrecion-Elviña (1990:86) notes that in media channels (novels, newspapers, magazines, TV programmes, pornographic films and so on) women are portrayed as passive, inferior, intellectually and physically dependent upon men as wives and mothers, and as objects of male sexual gratification.

These general ideas are borne out in more detailed case studies, such as that by Carolyn Israel-Sobritchea (1991) on gender ideology in a farm and fishing community in the town of Kalayaan, Laguna province. Israel-Sobritchea (p.100) found that, in physical terms, the ideal feminine person was regarded as one who was weaker (*mas mahina*), shorter (*mas maliit*) and smaller in bodily stature (*mas maliit ang katawan*) than a man, and that very negative assumptions were made about women whose appearance was regarded as male (*parang lalaki ang katawan*). In practice these ideals translated both into women's non-participation in masculine activities (avoiding the carrying and pushing of heavy objects, for example) and onto their receiving lower wages for agricultural work, owing to their perceived lack of strength and lower productivity (ibid.).

The importance of confining women to a narrow sphere of influence is also apparent from another angle in Raul Pertierra's paper, 'Viscera Suckers and Female Sociality'. Pertierra's discussion concentrates on the phenomenon of the Philippine *asuang*, perhaps best translated as 'vampire', a creature with strongly feminine connotations which in many ways encapsulates the pervasive notion that women who lie outside male control are both deviant and destructive. *Asuangs* are most commonly found in the Central Visayas and Bicol (Southern Luzon) and, like women, they 'insinuate themselves into the privatised areas of life in order to wreak havoc, largely through covert means' (Pertierra, 1991:195).

A further discussion of ideology is found in A.Timothy Church's book, *Filipino Personality: A Review of Research and Writings*, in which he claims that the dominant 'ego-ideal' for women continues to retain various elements of the so-called Maria Clara syndrome whereby women are meant to be reserved, soft, yielding, loyal and enduring (Church, 1986:6). While Church himself recognises that these norms may be somewhat diluted in contemporary social practice, he does argue that women are still encouraged to be 'maternal, actively supportive and permissive with husbands'. Women are also expected to adopt an attitude of reservation in terms of their own sexuality, with virginity remaining 'the most highly valued male criterion for marriage' (ibid.).

Sexuality and violence

The sphere of sexuality is undoubtedly one where there is clear evidence of male–female differentiation. While active (and promiscuous) sexual behaviour among both single and married men is widely tolerated, women are expected to be chaste spinsters and faithful wives. This system of 'sexual double standards' or the 'double standard of morality' (see Eviota, 1991:166; Hollnsteiner, 1991a:253; Medina, 1991:99; Ramirez, 1984:32) is by no means unique to the Philippines, where, in fact, prior to the Spanish conquest there were relatively tolerant attitudes towards sexual freedom for both men and women, even among deities and other religious figures (see Blanc-Szanton, 1990; Daño, 1990; Mananzan, 1991a; Veneracion, 1992). However, Hollnsteiner (1991a:252–3) argues that the aggressive imposition of Catholicism, with its glorification of the Virgin Mary and its prohibition on divorce, forced a situation in which men sought an 'informal adaptation' to safeguard their privileges. In the contemporary context, wives are generally faithful to husbands, whereas the latter will often have mistresses (*kerida* or *kabit*), in addition to casual sex with other women (see Eviota, 1991:166; Medina, 1991:107-8; Ramirez, 1984:30; Yu and Liu, 1980:179 et seq.). James Goodno (1991:259) sums up the rather contradictory juxtaposition of these different elements of women's situation as follows:

Women in the Philippines find themselves in an odd position. Many doors are open to them and they can enter virtually every profession and respon-sible position in the public and private sectors. Yet society expects them to manage a house, maintain their virtue and provide their men with sexual grat-ification. Among Catholic Filipinos, who are not allowed to divorce, there is a flourishing macho tradition in which men pursue their sexual fantasies, have extra-marital relations, and often keep two families.[7]

Other institutionalised aspects of male superiority within the Filipino household include the practice of wife-beating. Domestic violence is viewed as 'ordinary' and 'normal' within the context of marriage and stems from the polarised socialisation of men as aggressive and assertive, and women as passive and submissive (Unas, 1992:7). In her case study of Kalayaan, for example, Israel-Sobritchea (1991:102) found that 'reprimands and an occasional beating are considered necessary for the wives', especially in cases of infidelity and 'wilful disobedience'. This is echoed by Nagot's research, which records conflict over husbands' unfounded jealousy and resistance to their wives' decision to separate, along with unwanted pregnancies, money shortages, male drinking and womanising, as giving rise to domestic violence (Nagot, 1991:118; see also de la Cerna,1992:54 on Cebu). Wife-beating is so common in some low-income communities that Hollnsteiner (1991a:263) reports that lack of domestic abuse is construed as positive affirmation by women that their husbands love them. Even without domestic violence, marital conflict is far from rare, and Yu and Liu (1980:153) point out that husband–wife relationships face constant competition from the male *barkada* system. The *barkada* is a male drinking group or 'gang' and may demand much of a man's time – and resources (see also Hollnsteiner, 1991b:282; IACDVC, 1992:14).

---

7 While the widespread phenomenon of male involvement in extra-marital household arrangements might conceivably have led to a major body of research into 'second' households, as well as high figures of female-headed units in census and survey data, this does not appear to be the case. With one or two exceptions, female-headed households are conspicuously absent from statistical, academic and policy material in the Philippines.

Marriage, fertility and household stability

In the face of the underlying tensions and inequalities which have been
widely noted as undermining not just women's status, but the very
fabric of the family life, it is perhaps surprising that households in the
Philippines appear to be rather stable groupings. Although difficult to
estimate from official figures, most partnerships seem to stay intact (see,
for example, Clarke, 1981; Medina, 1991; Nagot, 1991; Sevilla, 1989).
As of 1990, excluding single women who represented 46.6 per cent
of the population aged ten years or more, the Philippine census records
only 1.3 per cent of women as separated or divorced, as against 7.4
per cent widowed and 91.2 per cent married (NSO, 1992a:xxix). The
stability of formal marriage is undoubtedly due in part to the fact that
Philippine law makes no provision for absolute divorce (see Pineda,
1991:95–6); even though legal separation may now be granted on certain
grounds, such as physical violence and incest (Sempio-Diy, 1988:73),
neither party is entitled to remarry since the marital bonds themselves
remain unsevered (Medina, 1991:180; Villariba, 1993:33). It should
also be noted that grounds for separation on the basis of sexual infidelity
are strongly weighted in favour of men, in that a wife only has to have
sexual intercourse with another man for this to be granted, whereas
a charge of adultery against a husband has to involve concubinage (see
Nolasco, 1991:82; Reyes, 1992:50).[8] The bureaucratic and financial
difficulties associated with legal separation are such that among low-
income groups with troubled marriages, people are more likely to resort
to informal separation (locally termed *hiwalay sa asawa* – separated from
spouse), or abandonment/desertion (Medina, 1991:182). The latter
usually involves men leaving women (see also Eviota, 1992:153;
Francisco, 1990; Hollnsteiner, 1991a,1991b), although in statistical terms
the proportion of female-headed households seems small in comparison
with other countries: 11.3 per cent nationally according to 1990
census figures (NSO, 1992a:xxxiv).

---

8 More specifically there are two separate articles governing infidelity in the Revised
Penal Code, one pertaining to women, the other to men. Article 333 specifies that
'adultery is committed by any married woman who shall have intercourse with a man
not her husband', whereas Article 334 specifies that concubinage applies to 'any
husband who shall keep a mistress in the conjugal dwelling, or, shall have sexual intercourse under *scandalous* circumstances, with a woman who is not his wife, or shall
cohabit with her in any other place' (CBSI, 1990:167; emphasis added).

   Aside from the legal difficulties of obtaining divorce, the pervasive influence of religion (especially Catholicism) and a strong sense of love and duty towards children have been seen as important in keeping Filipino couples together (see Ramirez, 1984:30). Another likely reason for the endurance of conjugal unions is the prop provided by close (albeit pressurising) kin networks (ibid.). In general terms the Filipino household has been classified as 'residentially nuclear but functionally extended' (see Castillo, 1991:245; Medina, 1991:14–16). Not only do young married couples frequently live in the house of one set of parents until their first child is born, but even afterwards they often endeavour to live either in the same compound or close by (Medina, 1991:17; Shimuzu, 1991:106–9). Kinship ties are extremely important in Philippine society, possibly because so 'few sources of support, material or otherwise, exist outside the family' (Aguilar, 1991:12). Whatever the reason, very distant relatives such as third cousins are often acknowledged, and although it may be impossible in practice to maintain close associations with all relatives, Shimuzu (1991:115) points out that an average Filipino may regard up to 300 people as kin over a single lifetime. In these terms, Filipino couples are rarely isolated and may be constantly reminded of family obligations and/or the importance of not causing shame or disgrace (*hiya*)[9] by giving in to interpersonal difficulties with spouses. The concept of *hiya* also ties in with the importance to social (and ipso facto family) relations in the Philippines of 'smooth interpersonal relations', originally identified by the anthropologist Frank Lynch. Widespread norms of *pakikisama* (concession/pleasing or giving in to the lead of others/ritual politeness), *utang na loob* (inner debt of gratitude), *galang* (respect) and so on are viewed as having their roots in family-based social organisation (Church, 1986:56; Ramirez, 1984:36; Steinberg, 1986:32) and may well act as checks on open confrontation and aggressive behaviour, either within or beyond the family (see Shimuzu, 1991:114–18). As symbolised by Cebuano sayings such as *Bisan mag ka lisud-lisud basta maghi-usa/*'Through thick and thin we'll stay together' and *Sagdi lang ug pobre basta magbinatiay/*'Poverty will not break us apart' (Buenaventura-Ojeda, 1973:104–6), families endeavour, as far as possible, to maintain cohesion and minimise internal dissent (see also Mangahas and Pasalo, 1994:258–9; Mulder, 1994). This could well contribute to inhibiting marital break-up.

9 *Hiya* may also be construed as 'not losing face', avoiding guilt and maintaining a sense of propriety (see Enriquez, 1991:99; Shimuzu, 1991:118; Villariba, 1993:20).

Family continuity is also important in Philippine society and high value is placed accordingly on both marriage and children (Hollnsteiner, 1991a; Licuanan, 1991; Ramirez, 1984). This is particularly the case for women, with Hollnsteiner (1991a:254) noting that 'the possibility that a woman might voluntarily choose to perpetuate her single state rarely enters the Filipino mind'.[10] Concern about a woman fulfilling her gender-assigned role and avoiding the unseemly prospect of becoming a *matandang dalaga* (old maid) means that parents with unmarried daughters of 30 years or more will often encourage them to 'lower their sights' in respect of potential partners (Hollnsteiner, 1991a:254). Among other things, the belief that 'children are considered essential to marital harmony and are gifts from God' (Sevilla, 1989:13) also means that newly married women are under pressure to have children as soon as possible. Thus while the total fertility rate[11] in the Philippines is now considerably lower than it once was (3.7 in 1990 compared with 6.8 in 1965), it is still higher than in many other parts of Southeast Asia and the developing world (see World Bank, 1992a:270–1). Moreover, while family planning is available to married couples and an estimated third of married Filipino women in the reproductive age group (15–44 years) are thought to be practising contraception (Department of Health, 1990:2), legal abortion is completely unattainable in the country, even if informal terminations are widely documented (ISSA, 1991; Marcelo, 1991; Miralao, 1989; see also Chapter 2, this volume).[12]

Key questions on gender and the household in the present study

Having drawn a general sketch of gender and the Philippine household, it is important to recognise gaps in the literature and to identify the key issues on the subject to be explored further below.

---

10 The importance attached to legal marriage in Philippine society is evident in the rather pejorative census definition of those not married by law. Those in consensual unions are defined as 'others – a person living consensually together (by mere consent) as husband and wife without the benefit of a legal marriage' (NSO, 1992a:xvi–xvii).
11 The term 'total fertility rate' refers to the average number of children likely to be born to a woman if she survives her childbearing years.
12 In part this is due to the very strong role of the Roman Catholic Church in the country. The 1990 census reports 83 per cent of the Philippine population as declaring themselves Catholics. The Constitution of 1987 also includes a clause protecting the rights of the unborn child (Reyes, 1992:47).

Changing patterns of household composition and gender relations:
the importance of locality-based research

One major question concerns the forms and behaviour which households adopt in the context of changing social, economic and demographic conditions and how these interrelate with changing patterns of gender. Although it is generally agreed that nuclear units are the most common type of living arrangement in both rural and urban areas of the country, it is also recognised, as noted earlier, that many households maintain close links with relatives and, as Hiromo Shimuzu (1991:101) describes, are 'not closed, isolated units consisting of only the married couple and their unmarried children' (see also Peterson, 1993). Despite the strong linkages maintained with kin on an interhousehold basis in the Philippines, one significant trend viewed as associated with urbanisation is the increased absorption of kin within extended households (Castillo, 1991:245). Pineda Deang (1992:26) argues that the 'concentration of many extended family households in Philippine cities reflects deep-seated values among Filipinos to provide help and care to needy relatives', and points to kin ties continuing to flourish despite the distances over which family members migrate (see also Castillo, 1991:247; Church, 1986:57). At the same time, writers such as Yu and Liu (1980:205) have noted that nuclear households are more likely to be the norm in urban areas because dwellings are small and because poor people may not have the resources to support migrant relatives. This tends to corroborate Medina's (1991) argument that kinship ties have weakened in the face of urbanisation and economic change, although, as Peterson (1993:571–4) points out, there may be some advantage (mainly in respect of maintaining a more flexible resource base) in prioritising extended family support *beyond*, rather than *within*, the household. This does not necessarily mean that links diminish in strength, especially in the light of the embeddedness in Filipino culture of what she refers to as 'generalised extended family exchange'[13] whereby kin often help one another in a relatively unconditional manner.

---

13 The term 'generalised extended family exchange', as used by Peterson (1993) is based on a concept originally developed by Claude Lévi-Strauss to describe one type of marriage exchange designed to create alliances among different groups or communities.

Given these varied observations and interpretations, and the relative absence of discussions of gender, one important question concerns the ways in which different types of urbanisation and economic development give rise to changing economic roles for women, and their effects on household composition. Research in other countries has demonstrated interesting links between local economic development, household structure and, in particular, the rise in female employment (see, for example, Chant, 1991a; Fernández-Kelly, 1983b; García et al., 1983; Safa, 1993:28; Salaff, 1990:125–6; H.Standing, 1985). From this perspective, it would seem appropriate to incorporate analysis of household characteristics into the more detailed case studies of (poor) women's lives and realities called for by Filipino researchers (see Francisco and Carlos, 1988:4).

Changing patterns of household headship

Another issue begging exploration is the extent to which urbanisation in the Philippines has led, as some have argued, to a greater incidence of marital instability and thus of 'solo parenthood' in urban settings (Medina, 1991:35).[14] While female-headed households are generally regarded as rare in the Philippines (see, for example, Illo, 1989), there is actually little data beyond that of the census and what there is, is likely to be underestimated due to the informal nature of marital separation. In addition to identifying the actual prevalence of women-headed households it is important to discover whether they are able to survive as independent entities in the sense of maintaining separate residential arrangements with their children, or whether they are submerged for economic or social reasons within larger extended households (see Bradshaw, 1994; Buvinić and Gupta, 1993; Moser, 1993b; Varley, 1993). Related to this, it is important to consider the nature and viability of women-headed units. A general tendency in the literature (including that on the Philippines) is to see women-headed households as victims of widowhood or desertion by spouses, and to emphasise the problems they are likely to encounter (see, for example, Eviota, 1986:203; Medina, 1991:183; Republic of the Philippines and UNICEF, 1990:62)

14 'Solo parenthood' has only relatively recently become a subject of national debate, with experts and the media now drawing attention to the need to recognise such households and give them due claim to state resources (see Rina Jimenez-David 'The Changing Filipino Family', in the *Philippine Daily Inquirer*, 9 May 1993, p.5).

rather than to explore the possibility that they might result from self-determination on the part of women and may also, within the context of supportive kinship networks and growing female job opportunities, be advantageous structures – something that has been suggested for other countries (see Bradshaw, 1994; Bruce and Lloyd, 1992; Casinader et al., 1987; Chant, 1985; Etienne, 1983; Harris, 1982; Safa, 1980). One major concern of the present research, therefore, is to examine the causes, characteristics and consequences of a possible increase in female-headed households in the context of in-migration and economic change in Cebu, Lapu-Lapu and Boracay.

Female labour force participation, household structure and welfare

A final related issue concerns the widely observed phenomenon of increased labour force activity among Filipino women as a result of recession and the debt crisis (see, for example, Chant, forthcoming a; Illo, 1989; Medel-Añonuevo, 1993b; Santos and Lee, 1989; UNICEF, Manila, 1988). To what extent is this likely to provoke changes in household structure and/or further flexibility in gender roles, and to enlarge women's basis of formal power and ability to control their own lives? Embodied in this question is whether particular types of employment are associated with shifts in marital status, fertility and household arrangements.

Gender and employment

Household-employment linkages

Despite the growing presence of women in the labour force on a global scale, and particularly in sectors such as offshore/multinational export manufacturing, relatively little detailed attention has been paid to the household characteristics of female workers, either in the Philippines itself or elsewhere in the developing world. While detailed holistic analyses which try to encompass the intersection between what might be termed the 'demand' and 'supply' elements of female labour force participation are gaining in number and analytical currency (see, for example, Benería and Roldan, 1987; Chant, 1991a; Fernández-Kelly, 1983b; Foo and Lim, 1989; McIlwaine, 1993, 1994a; Palriwala, 1990; Safa, 1990,1993; Salaff, 1990; Stichter, 1990; Tiano, 1990; Wolf,

1990a, 1990b,1991), something of an impasse is presented by the legacy of tending to divide such studies into those with either a 'family' or a 'workplace' orientation. Sometimes this is a matter of time and other practical constraints on individual researchers, but it may also have to do with the complexity of integrating data from different scales, levels and perspectives (see Chant, 1991a:12). Another possible reason for the neglect of workers' household characteristics is that many of the women involved in expanding sectors of production such as multinational export processing are young and single, and are possibly not seen to be as enmeshed in the gender-assigned duties of household reproduction as their older married counterparts are. In other words, young women might be viewed as a 'special' group who escape some of the more conventional responsibilities (childcare, domestic labour and so on) likely to befall women at later stages of the life-cycle. However, while there is a need to acknowledge heterogeneity among women, and to recognise that gender role activities and expectations may change over the course of a lifetime, it is also important to investigate the strands of gender subordination which run through women's lives and which might be held to account as much for the involvement of young women in the workforce as for the relative exclusion of their older counterparts. Accordingly, one of the most important developments in research on gender and employment in recent years has been to conceptualise young women's employment in these terms and to document their particular roles within households and families – whether as 'surplus' labour better deployed away from the home setting, as altruistic and self-sacrificing contributors to family welfare, or as outright financial supporters of parents and siblings (Lim, 1983; Ong, 1987; Pearson, 1986:71; Salaff, 1990; Zosa-Feranil, 1984). At the same time, and despite the fact that young women may seek employment as a means of contributing to the welfare of their families of origin, it is also valid to explore the extent to which personal aims and objectives override those related to the support of the natal family (see Foo and Lim, 1989:219–21; Wolf, 1990a:54), as well as to investigate the ways in which new forms of employment might be leading to more independent forms of living arrangement and/or postponement of marriage and childbirth (see, for example, Buang, 1993; Phongpaichit, 1984; Salaff, 1990).

Aside from the new enquiry on gender and employment which seeks to locate women's labour force participation within a more comprehensive spectrum of productive and reproductive dimensions of society and economy and to differentiate between women of different ages, classes, ethnic origins and so on (see also Redclift and Sinclair, 1991), another relatively recent development has been to deconstruct the fairly persistent assumption that women are necessarily 'marginalised' by capitalist economic development.

The 'female marginalisation' debate

Marginalisation has generally been viewed as encompassing a range of elements. These are itemised by Alison MacEwen Scott, in her seminal critique of the female marginalisation thesis, as follows: first, marginalisation as exclusion from productive employment; second, marginalisation as concentration on the margins of the labour market; third, marginalisation as feminisation or segregation; and fourth, marginalisation as economic inequality (A.M.Scott, 1986:653–4). In brief, it is argued that women are progressively squeezed out of production as capitalist economic development proceeds, and that when they do work, they are confined to peripheral, low-prestige sectors or to occupational segments where the rest of the workforce is predominantly female. In addition, the benefits accruing to women from their employment in terms of wages, fringe benefits, security and so on are vastly inferior to those accorded to men.

Alison MacEwen Scott (1986) not only questions the bases on which these assumptions are made and the criteria used to interpret trends over time, but also considers the problem of causality, which is deemed by the marginalisation thesis to lie overwhelmingly in capital's need to maintain wages at low levels. With reference to case study material from Peru and Brazil, she shows that female marginalisation may only apply to certain kinds of employment and that the *selective incorporation* of women in other occupational segments is not adequately addressed. Her conclusion is that the female marginalisation thesis is too broad to be of any real use in the analysis of specific examples and that its unilateral emphasis on notions of wage surplus and competition excludes consideration of the fact that 'gender plays a role in structuring labour markets not just as cheap labour, but as subordinate labour, docile labour, immobile labour, domesticated labour, sexual labour and so on'. In this respect, 'it is not just dimensions of marginalisation that need to be distinguished, but dimensions of gender', since 'the use made of these different aspects by employers extends far beyond pressure on wages' (p.673). Notwithstanding the difficulties intrinsic to developing comprehensive conceptual frameworks on the subject, Scott still feels that the search for a general theory of female employment is desirable, provided it is grounded in rigorous micro-level analysis and is open to the notion of multiple causes (ibid.).

Scott's ideas have been followed up by various authors, most notably Anne Faulkner and Victoria Lawson (1991), who not only attempt to reorient the female marginalisation thesis to encompass so-called selective incorporation, but also raise the question of whether women's employment contributes to greater equality between men and women. Although their own case study of Ecuador yields some insights on this, Faulkner and Lawson (pp.40–1) identify the need for further detailed case studies to explore more fully whether 'economic power in the workplace translates into new family power relations, or more generally the way in which workforce differentiation restructures or reaffirms existing gender inequalities in society' (see also Blumberg, 1989:163–7,1991b; Moghadam, 1994:99–101; Moore, 1988:109 et seq.; Safa, 1990,1993; Safilios-Rothschild, 1990; Sinclair, 1991; Ward, 1990; Wolf, 1991). These issues are crucial to the present research.

Women's employment and economic restructuring

A final focus of contemporary debate, mentioned earlier and highly relevant to the present study, is the way in which recession impacts upon female labour and whether, through analysis of this issue, we can more clearly decode the complex picture of gender segmentation in employment. Much recent research on recession and structural adjustment in a range of developing countries has indicated a rise rather than a fall in female employment, despite general job losses, particularly in the formal sector (see, for example, Chant,1993a,1994a,1994b; Dierckxsens, 1992; González de la Rocha, 1988; Moser, 1989; Prates, 1990; Santos and Lee, 1989; Spindel, 1990). In the Philippines, for instance, female labour force participation rates rose from 60 per cent to 64 per cent between 1982 and 1984 alone (Stewart, 1992:27), while women's share of total employment is estimated to have expanded from only 23.1 per cent in 1980 to 37 per cent in 1990 (Moghadam, 1993a: Table 3). More recent research in low-income communities in various parts of the country indicates that for most poor families, women's income-generating efforts are now crucial to household livelihood (Chant, forthcoming a; Medel-Añonuevo, 1993b). This tends to challenge the assumption that as capital's 'reserve army of labour', women are necessarily withdrawn from the workforce in times of slump; it could have to do with women's overall segregation into less dynamic but more stable segments of the labour market (see de Barbieri and de Oliveira, 1989 on Mexico).[15] Another possible reason is that with the opening up of developing economies to foreign investment during economic restructuring, female labour is likely to be sought by competitive multinational enterprises (see Benería and Roldan, 1987; Chant, forthcoming a on Mexico; Cleves Mosse, 1993:123; Eviota, 1992:124 et seq. on the Philippines). One crucial question here concerns the extent to which the segments of employment currently absorbing women will, in the long run, prove sustainable. It is also important to examine the longer-term implications of the work allotted to young women for their effect on employment trajectories over a lifetime.

Gender and employment in the Philippines

Female employment patterns

Female employment is relatively high in the Philippines, with women forming 37 per cent of the total labour force in 1990 (Moghadam, 1993a: Table 3). Approximately half the economically active Filipino population are engaged in rural employment, but while women make up 29 per cent of the rural labour force, they account for only 8 per cent of farmers, fisherfolk and forestry workers, and levels of female unemployment in the countryside are much higher than those for men (17 per cent as against 5.9 per cent). In urban areas women comprise 39 per cent of the total employed (NSO, 1992a: Tables 16 and 18).

While many female workers, especially in Philippine towns and cities, are young, employment is by no means uncommon among older age groups. Abenoja (1982:50) points out that Filipino women's labour force participation tends to be characterised by a 'double peak': the first occurs when women are in their early 20s; the second when they

---

15 Although there are few detailed explorations of this issue in developing countries, some work has been done in advanced economies such as Britain and the US (see, for example, Bruegel, 1979; Milkman, 1979; Walby 1992 for discussions and references).

return to work in their early 40s, after the care of infants is over. While tertiary occupations absorb the majority of female workers (women make up 44 per cent of service and shop/market salesworkers, for example), increasing numbers of young women are engaged in multi-national manufacturing, especially in the country's export processing zones (see Chapters 2 and 4).[16] Since the early 1980s in particular, there has not only been significant expansion in the numbers of foreign man-ufacturing firms in the Philippines which recruit young women into factories producing garments, electronics and so on, but an increase in industrial subcontracting where women workers perform labour-intensive tasks on a piece-rate basis in their own homes (see Aldana, 1989; CAW, 1991; Donald, 1991; Eviota, 1992; ILMS, 1984; Pineda-Ofreneo, 1987, 1988; Rosario, 1985).

Among the service occupations employing women, one major activity (also associated with the new international division of labour and relevant to this book) is sex work. This has been spurred on by the growth in international tourism in the Philippines, especially during the Marcos period (see Chapter 2). Although there is a small gay male sex industry (see Goodno, 1991:263) and a growing amount of child prostitution (see Fernandez-Magno, 1991; HAIN, 1987; de Leon, 1991), sexual services have overwhelmingly relied on the com-moditisation of women to cater to a predominantly male clientele from the advanced economies (see Azarcon de la Cruz, 1985; also Chapters 2 and 6 this volume). In a Catholic country, this sets entertainers apart from the rest of society; as Goodno (1991:259-60) points out:

Economic pressures can push poor unskilled Filipino women into prostitu-tion. With a ready market of foreign tourists, US servicemen and Filipino beerhouse patrons, prostitution flourishes and with it women's alienation from her community, separation from her family, bouts of severe depression and loss of self-respect.

The vast bulk of workers in both multinational manufacturing and sex tourism are young and single and many writers have noted that they are usually unable to continue their employment after their mid-to-late 20s, which may be a time when they get married and/or have their first child. For example, Shivanath (1982:20) notes that in the

16 Data for 1990 show that although manufacturing employment occupies only 10 per cent of all female workers, women still comprise 46 per cent of the industrial labour force as a whole (ILO, 1992:94).

Bataan Export Processing Zone there is discrimination against married women and women are forced to remain single if they wish to keep their jobs. Additionally, Elizabeth Eviota (1992:125) claims that 'this type of paid work provides no prospects for alternative employment when the allowed age of productivity is past, and so women are pushed back into the traditional hope of home and marriage'. There is clearly little career mobility within these sectors; following retirement from their jobs, women in need of cash-generating opportunities may find few other alternatives than informal occupations. As Delia Aguilar (1988:15) notes:

the international division of labour has effectively multiplied the points of antagonism in the class and gender struggles, in this case assigning to Filipino women the role of highly expendable gendered and race-typed workers in the export and sex industries as well as in agri-business.

Tourism employment is of course broader than the sex trade per se, and women workers in this domain are to be found in various informal niches, such as beachfront vending (see, for example, Chant, 1993b, forthcoming b; Olofson and Crisostomo, 1989). At the same time, the pervasive association of women in tourism with sexual services has led to the foreclosure of certain formal sector jobs, such as hotel-room cleaning and bedmaking, due to potential harassment of female staff (O'Grady, 1983; see also P.Lee, 1981). Other more conventional service jobs for women include domestic service, petty retail and trading, home-based manufacturing and craft production, and laundrywork (Bucoy, 1992; BWYW, 1988; Fernandes, 1991; Eviota, 1986; Francisco, 1990; Republic of the Philippines and UNICEF, 1990; Rutten, 1990).

Key questions on gender and employment in the present study

The nature of female labour demand in export employment

One important question surrounding export employment in the present study is the nature of female labour demand in different sectors. Why do employers in multinational manufacturing, tourism and entertainment establishments so often recruit women workers? What kinds of rationale influence their recruitment decisions? What particular types of female employees do they look for in terms of age, migrant status, education, skills, previous work experience and the like, and to what degree do these vary according to different types of export-oriented work? Bearing in mind that recruitment patterns will play a major role in filtering women into particular segments of the labour market, what other factors shape what we might call the 'supply' of female labour to various occupational niches? For example, are there any consistent features among women who seek work in the entertainment sector (in respect of migration history, levels of income in natal families, previous experience of sexual abuse and/or illegitimate childbirth and so on) which distinguish them from female workers in more 'conventional' tourism enterprises, or indeed in export-manufacturing plants?

Interactions between different types of export sector work and the household characteristics of women

Another related and critically important question is the extent to which different types of female employment interact with the marital and household characteristics of women. Women workers in export manufacturing, international tourism and sex work are widely observed to be young and unlikely to be married. But what other reasons might explain the predominance of single women in these occupational niches? In some instances, for example in factories or in entertainment establishments, employers have been noted to specify that female applicants are single, and should remain single if they wish to continue in employment (see Shivanath, 1982). But is this always the case, and is there perhaps something intrinsic to the nature of the jobs women do that actually causes them to avoid marriage or at least put it off for longer than they would in other circumstances? In her study of female factory workers in Java, for instance, Diane Wolf (1990a:53) found that women are now postponing wedlock and are beginning to break with the tradition of arranged unions by choosing their own spouses. While Wolf argues that this is in part due to increased education, another reason offered is that industrial employment grants women greater independence through providing them with a personal income (ibid.). Another conceivable reason is that long, heavy and disciplined factory work schedules deny women time to seek a spouse (see Donald, 1991). Beyond this there may be other reasons associated with the nature of the households from which women workers come which play a decisive role in maintaining single status. For example, young women in the Philippines may only give substantial financial help to their parents until they themselves get married: to what extent, therefore, can parental pressure be as much an influence on the postponement of marriage as employment per se?

It is also important to consider how different types of export-oriented employment might impact upon decisions on fertility and household organisation. Not all women in export employment are single; for those who are married and/or who have children, what kinds of household arrangements evolve to fit in with full-time formal sector work? In the Bataan Export Processing Zone, for example, migrant women workers from outside the area often have to resort to fostering out their offspring in their home villages (Zosa-Feranil, 1984). Are there also cases where women team up with other women, or develop extended household or family arrangements wherein co-resident parents/parents-in-law or other relatives look after their children (see, for instance, Salaff, 1990:125–6)? In identifying patterns of marital status, fertility and household characteristics among women in particular types of employment and in explaining more fully how these evolve, further dimensions are added to the broader question of export-led development's impacts on women's lives and status.

Implications of export-oriented employment for women's roles and status

For women, the general consequences of export-led development have often been viewed in a negative light. In the sphere of export manufacturing, for example, attention has frequently been drawn to health problems associated with maintaining high production quotas in ill-equipped, unsafe and often insanitary working environments (see, for example, Heng Leng and Ng Choon Sim, 1993:14–15; Matsui, 1991a: Chapter 3; M.Santos, 1988; A.Santos and Lee, 1989:34; Zarate, 1990). At another level, emphasis has been placed on the insidious ideological, political and economic corollaries of the transfer of low-skilled, inherently unstable jobs to Third World countries and in particular the 'feminisation' of labour in world market factories (Buang, 1993; Eden, 1990; Grown and Sebstad, 1989:938; Safa, 1993:29). In writing of the global expansion of electronics assembly operations, for example, Karen Hossfeld (1991:13) claims that the international high-tech boom brings a 'very unrevolutionary division of labour based not only on nationality, class and race, but on gender'. Elizabeth Eviota

(1992:125) expands on this in the Philippines case by claiming that 'as industry requires specific groups of women because of their submissiveness, docility and other perceived gender traits, male-dominant and authoritarian structures are reinforced'. She goes on to suggest that:

> young women are confronted with specific definitions of what masculinity and femininity are within the workplace, and which sex is superior in skill and confidence, and which sex has authority and the power to discipline. These definitions then shape women's attitudes and expectations and institutionalise gender differences. (ibid.)

The extent to which these observations pertain to all types of export manufacturing, however, is a point of some debate. Challenging the idea that export-manufacturing employment necessarily reinforces and intensifies the subordination of women, Diane Wolf's (1990a) research on factory workers in Indonesia and Taiwan finds that 'changes in the international division of labour have not greatly changed female status within the family' (p.59). Other authors have even argued that industrial expansion can go some way to improving women's domestic position. Helen Safa's (1990) work on export factory workers in Puerto Rico and the Dominican Republic is instructive here. Although she notes (p.92) that 'by taking advantage of women's inferior position in the labour market, export manufacturing may reinforce their subordination through poorly-paid dead-end jobs', Safa also claims that industrial employment has offered women an important new means of contributing to family income which in turn 'may challenge traditional patriarchal authority patterns and lead to more egalitarian household structures' (see also Safa, 1993). A key paper on female factory workers in Southeast Asia by Gillian Foo and Linda Lim (1989) also questions various assumptions of the 'negative' literature, such as the idea that the majority of export-manufacturing workers are poor (p.213), again venturing to propose that the corollaries of expanded female labour demand in multinational factories may be rather positive for women:

> In short, the ideology of women workers which so conditions their employment in export factories in Asia is a product of gender inequalities within their societies. Factory employment does not create or worsen such inequalities, nor does it destroy it. It does, however, alleviate, at least temporarily, the subordination that women suffer as a result of gender inequality. But these 'liberating' effects are the combined results of education, migration and wage employment *per se*, rather than of export factory jobs in particular. Factory

employment contributes by making available the wage employment, necessitating the migration and motivating the education. (Foo and Lim, 1989:228)

Given the differing interpretations of the direct and indirect implications of factory employment for women, one major aim of the present research is to explore the various dimensions of female involvement in manufacturing in the two study centres, Cebu and Lapu-Lapu, which have strong export-oriented industrial sectors. Attention is paid to the extent to which recruitment patterns, the nature and conditions of work, pay levels and so on are similar to those in other places, and to what degree and in which ways different types of export-manufacturing employment affect women's lives and status.

As noted earlier, the study is also concerned with broadening out the scope of general research on export-oriented employment by taking into consideration women workers in other sectors, notably international tourism and sex work. These are explored in the context of Boracay and Cebu, again from the perspective of the extent to which gender stereotypes play an integral part in recruitment, and how, in turn, female involvement in the various service activities expanding under the umbrella of international tourism are leading to gains or losses in women's status. An integral part of this analysis is to examine women's own opinions of their work, what levels of satisfaction or contentment are associated with different jobs, and whether they would, in other circumstances, prefer to earn their livelihood in different ways.

Female employment trajectories

A final related issue concerns the potential employment and household trajectories of women with experience of export-oriented jobs. Most export-related jobs are regarded as relatively short term insofar as they tend only to occupy women in their youth, so what types of income-generating activities, if any, do women move into once their spell in the sectors under study are over? To what extent do different kinds of export-related employment equip women with skills and assets they can use for financial gain in later life? To what degree does involvement in different kinds of work affect the likelihood of women getting married and/or having children? It is hoped that answers to these questions will shed light on the longer-term corollaries of women's involvement in export-led economic change.

Gender and migration

Conceptual approaches to gender-differentiated migration

In considering migration in developing countries, it is important to stress that while sex-selectivity has long been recognised in the literature, it is only recently that more systematic attempts have been made to theorise the phenomenon (see Radcliffe, 1991; also Chant and Radcliffe, 1992:19). Broadly speaking, four main conceptual frameworks can be identified for gender-differentiated migration: neoclassical/equilibrium approaches, behavioural approaches, structuralist approaches and the household strategies approach. The first tends to emphasise the role of wage rates in stimulating movement from one area to another, and for women 'adds in' the phenomenon of marriage. While useful, it has been criticised on several fronts, most notably because it does not differentiate between women of different classes, ages and so on; because it takes factors such as marriage as 'givens' without considering how marriage relations are structured and may impact differentially upon men and women; and finally, because it treats women as a 'special' group while male migrants are seen as the 'norm' (see Chant and Radcliffe, 1992:20).

An overemphasis on employment and denial of the reproductive relations which so often affect mobility can also be seen as characterising structuralist approaches. These tend to emphasise mode of production over individual agency, but in so doing tend only to recognise capital's direct requirements for female labour (in multinational factories, for example), rather than considering the ways in which domestic divisions of labour may also condition female movement – or lack of it (ibid.:21–2). Behavioural approaches, on the other hand, do take on board reproductive dimensions in explaining differential male–female mobility and are particularly concerned with the ways in which these are structured in different cultures.

However, by far the most comprehensive framework is the household strategies approach, which not only takes into account the intersection of gender-selective mobility and gender-differentiated involvement in production and reproduction, but is also concerned with the power relations that give rise to and sustain gender differences (ibid.:22–3). In this respect, debates on gender and migration in developing countries are moving in a similar direction to those on the household and employment. In other words, they are becoming more comprehensive and open to recognition that both reproductive and productive elements of society and economy are critical in understanding gender-differentiated migrant flows (see also Chant, 1992b).

Impacts of gender-selective migration

Another critical challenge in the analysis of gender and migration is the implications of female out-migration for men and women in source communities. To date, and to some extent reflecting the greater mobility of men in various parts of the developing world, studies have tended to concentrate on the consequences of male movement for women left behind (see, for example, Chant, 1991b,1992a; Connell, 1984; Gulati, 1993; Hetler, 1990; Nelson, 1992; Rahat, 1986). Relatively little, however, is known about what happens when women form the greater number of migrants: an issue which is particularly relevant to the Philippines, where many kinds of contemporary migration flows are female-biased (see Eviota and Smith, 1984; Jackson, 1994; Zosa-Feranil, 1991).

Gender and migration in the Philippines

Rural–urban migration

As far as the rural–urban movement of Filipinos is concerned, women have constituted a significant proportion of migrants since the 1960s (see Engracia and Herrin, 1984; Eviota and Smith, 1984; Trager, 1984; but see also Findley, 1987:139 on Ilocos Norte). Women's disadvantaged position in agriculture in terms of landownership, jobs and wages, frequently aggravated by agricultural mechanisation and male-oriented rural development projects, has meant that they have dominated movement from countryside to city – 'primarily because males have more reason to stay behind' (Eviota, 1986:200; see also Illo, 1988; Illo and Pineda-Ofreneo, 1989; S-H.Lee, 1985: Chapter 5). In the early stages of female migration, movement was mainly directed to the metropolitan region of Manila, but increasingly women have started moving to secondary urban centres in the country (see Miralao et al., 1990; Perez, 1992; Trager, 1988; Zosa-Feranil, 1991). As of 1980, women heavily outnumbered men in towns and cities in the Philippines, with only 95 men per 100 women; 38.3 per cent of the total female population lived in urban areas as against only 36.3 per cent of men (see UN, 1990:191–208, Table 6). Census data for 1990 suggest that this trend continues: while in the country overall there are 101.1 men for every 100 women, in Cebu City in 1990 there were only 94 men per 100 women (or 108 women for every 100 men), and in Lapu-Lapu City there were 103 women for every 100 men (NEDA Region VII, 1992b:4; NSO, 1992b:xxvii; see also Zosa-Feranil, 1991). To a large degree this reflects the female bias in migration to urban areas: for example, women represented 58.6 per cent of all migrants who moved to Cebu City between 1985 and 1990; in Lapu-Lapu City in the same year, they accounted for 54 per cent.

The vast majority of Filipino female migrants are young, single and move primarily for employment, especially to places where there is burgeoning demand for female labour in multinational manufacturing production and in the service sector – domestic service, sex work and so on (see Engracia and Herrin, 1984; Eviota and Smith, 1984; Miralao et al., 1990). Indeed it has been widely noted not only that Filipino female labour force participation tends to be higher in urban than in rural areas, but that women migrants generally have higher levels of workforce involvement than non-migrants (Perez, 1992; Zosa-Feranil, 1991). For example, two-thirds of female workers in Metro Cebu's manufacturing and service establishments are estimated to be migrants (Zosa-Feranil, 1991). In many respects, migration for marriage, as predicted by the neoclassical theoretical approaches, would not seem to be particularly relevant; indeed, in the short term labour migration among young Filipino women may provide an alternative to early wedlock (see Eviota, 1992:172; Zosa-Feranil, 1991). However, while migration is directed to the search for employment and often takes place on an individual basis in the sense that women move alone, the extent to which this movement can be described as 'autonomous' (see Chant and Radcliffe, 1992:14–15) is questionable, since women may move primarily at the behest of their families of origin. For example, most migrants to Metro Cebu, especially those from outside Cebu province, come from large families with six or more siblings (Zosa-Feranil, 1991: Table 2.6); as the majority migrate for work-related reasons (ibid.: Table 2.9), it is highly likely that female migrants in particular view urban employment as a means of helping their families. With respect to the migration of young women to Dagupan City in Luzon, for instance, Lillian Trager (1984:1,273–4) points out that fathers often decide on the migration of daughters, and daughters who move are frequently expected to provide substantial financial assistance to their homes. In a later piece of work, Trager notes that there are important gender differentials here, in that young women are often expected to and do provide more help than migrant sons:

> While both male and female migrants do remit money and otherwise aid their natal families, at least until marriage and sometimes afterwards, parents may expect daughters to be more obedient and less likely to spend money on themselves. It is daughters, for example, who sometimes choose not to marry and instead continue to live with and/or aid their parents and siblings. (Trager, 1988:83)

In their paper on export factory workers in Southeast Asia, Foo and Lim (1989:219) also note that while 'the ideology of "parent repayment" is not peculiar to women only ... they appear to adhere to it more strongly than men' (see also Mather, 1988 on Indonesia; Porpora et al., 1989:281–2 on Thailand; Wolf, 1990a on Taiwan). This kind of observation has led Zosa-Feranil (1991:13) to the conclusion that 'female migration is actually a complex interaction of patterns of economic transformation, cultural traditions, societal perceptions of the role of women, and female responses to social forces'.

Overseas migration

It is not only rural–urban migration in which women may engage in the Philippines, but also overseas or international migration, on either a short- or long-term basis. International migration is absolutely critical to the Philippine economy, with overseas contract workers (OCWs) being required by law to remit between 30 and 70 per cent of their earnings (depending on job and location) through the state and commercial banks (see Villegas, 1988:72).[17] While international

---

17 The Philippine state also benefits from the receipt of consular and passport fees (which range from US$14 to $72 per overseas worker), income taxes and OCW contributions to the Overseas Worker Welfare Authority. In 1992 the government collected at least US$9.6 million in passport fees alone (based on legally deployed OCWs, in the *Filipino* VI:1 [February/March 1994], p.9 numbering 687,457 in that year) and a further $8.2 million in airport taxes (see Arnel F. de Guzman, 'A Filipino "Hero" in Every Corner of the World' also note 18 below). Richard Jackson (1994:78) points out that during the 1980s 1 per cent of the Philippine population left the country each year either as 'short-term' or 'permanent' migrants.

migration was largely male-dominated between the mid-1970s and mid-1980s, nearly half of overseas migrants since this period have been women (see Eviota, 1992:142–4).[18] Many work as domestic helpers in Hong Kong, Singapore, Malaysia, the Middle East and Europe (see Alcid, 1989; CIIR, 1987a; Dioneda, 1993; Eviota, 1992:144–5; Francisco, 1989; Medel-Añonuevo, 1992; Medel-Añonuevo et al., 1989; Tharan, 1989; Tornea and Habana, 1989; Villariba, 1993:24–5). At the same time, various women have also left the Philippines as contract entertainment workers – often a euphemism for prostitutes (Eviota, 1992:144; Santos and Lee, 1992:65; see also De Stoop, 1994; Medel-Añonuevo, 1992; NCRFW, 1989:21). The latter type of movement has been mainly to Japan, where women who move to perform in bars, nightclubs and so on are referred to by the rather pejorative term of *Japayukisan* (see Javate de Dios,1989,1990). In addition, there has long been in existence an active mail-order bride business which has drawn Filipino women abroad (see Matsui, 1991a: Chapter 5, 1991b; Matthei and Amott, 1990; Santos and Lee, 1989:40–1), though this was officially outlawed in 1992 (see Reyes, 1992).

The complex nature of female migration both within and from the Philippines is suggestive of a number of intersecting gender inequalities in terms of labour market segmentation in source and destination areas, and of domestic divisions of labour and status based on age and gender which impact differentially on men and women in terms of control over their lives and command over resources. These complexities indicate that the household strategies approach is probably the most useful tool for analysis.

Key questions on gender and migration in the present study

Bearing in mind the comprehensive nature of the household strategies approach, most of the questions posed here are integrally linked with those identified in our sections on the household and employment.

---

18 Excluding 2.5 million Filipino immigrants in the United States and Canada, 49 per cent of the estimated current total of 4.5 million OCWs (including undocumented and illegal as well as offically processed workers) are thought to be women (de Guzman, 'A Filipino "Hero" in Every Corner of the World': see note 17 above). In 1987 there were officially estimated to be 259,000 Filipina workers overseas, who between them generated US$463 million in remittances that year (NCRFW, 1989:121).

Characteristics of female migration to the study centres

Recognising that some women in export-oriented employment in Cebu, Lapu-Lapu and Boracay are likely to be native to the localities, one core question concerns the characteristics of migrant women who move into the three areas. Do different types of export sector work attract different kinds of migrants in terms of age, area of origin, household characteristics and so on? Here the authors' empirical survey work with low-income households and target groups of workers is critical, since Philippine census tabulations only record the number of people in a given area who were living elsewhere five years beforehand. The census does not specify the localities from which extra-provincial migrants come (or the municipal origins of intra-provincial migrants), nor does it give any indication of the personal characteristics of migrants other than their sex.[19] Through analysis of the primary data on migration collected specifically for the present study (see Appendix), it is hoped to piece together a detailed profile of the kinds of migrant selectivity to which different kinds of export-oriented employment give rise and thereby to assess more accurately the demographic and social impacts of development in the Visayas. For example, are women who move to different kinds of jobs likely to come alone or with other members of their families? Are they usually single when they leave their home areas? Are their decisions to move made personally, in conjunction with other household members, or primarily by parents? Do different kinds of export sector have different levels of drawing power in the sense of pulling migrants over different geographical distances? Do migrants from, and in, different areas regard their movement as permanent or as temporary (i.e. do they intend to return home at a later stage)? What explains possible variations?

---

19 Although there are various detailed academic studies of migration in the Philippines which provide information not included in the census, there are few on the Visayas per se, and these tend to concentrate on Cebu rather than smaller centres such as Boracay. Moreover, with the notable exception of the work of Imelda Zosa-Feranil (1991) and Aurora Perez (1992), few Cebu-based analyses of migration focus on women or issues of gender-selective mobility. For example, the study of five intermediate cities carried out by Michael Costello, Thomas Leinbach and Richard Ulack (1987), which includes Cebu and Cagayan de Oro in the Philippines along with three Indonesian cities (Medan, Pematang and Tebing Tinggi), provides a wealth of useful detail on migrant origins, characteristics, motives and activities in the city, yet concentrates almost exclusively on men on the basis that they are (a) the majority of household heads and (b) the principal breadwinners (see Costello et al., 1987:37).

Gender, employment and source-destination linkages

A second and related question of the research is the extent to which women (and men) moving to the study centres continue to retain links with their areas of origin. As noted earlier, Filipino women are likely to stay more closely tied to home areas than their male counterparts are (Hart, 1971; Trager, 1984,1988). Why is this the case; what form do these linkages take in the Visayas (for instance, financial remittances, personal visits, help with bed and board for migrant relatives, fostering children), and are there any systematic differences related to specific types of migration and employment? For example, where women have moved over long distances, does this scale down the frequency of their visits home? Are certain kinds of employment associated with different types of source-destination? For instance, even if women working in factories or in entertainment establishments earn relatively high wages, are their work schedules too heavy to allow them to make personal visits as well as to send money? Do sex workers feel too much 'shame' to go home and confront their parents and siblings in person?

Another question here is the way in which female out-migration impacts upon household organisation and welfare in places of origin. While at a national level single males in the 20–24 age group outnumber women by around half a million (NSO, 1992a:xxix), and in general there are 100.9 men for every 100 women, in certain parts of the country the ratio of males to females is extremely high: for example, in the Eastern Visayas there are 104.4 men for every 100 women (NSO, 1992a:xxvii). What does this mean for marriage, fertility and household structure in rural areas? Light on this question will be shed by a small survey of households in two migrant source areas in the Central Visayas (see Chapter 3 and Appendix).

Migration, employment and household formation

Given that the interactions of female migrants with their home areas may well condition their behaviour in the places to which they move, what kinds of household emerge around women in different types of employment in Cebu, Lapu-Lapu and Boracay, and are there any consistent differences between migrants and those who are native to the localities? This analysis allows an appreciation of the roles played by contemporary economic development in household formation and diversity in the Philippines.

Export-oriented employment and international migration

A final major question concerns whether different types of export-oriented employment represent avenues for international migration. Overseas migration is regarded as one of the most certain routes out of poverty in the Philippines and it may well be that particular kinds of job are viewed as 'stepping stones' to going abroad. This is perhaps particularly true of tourism and entertainment work, where people are likely to have the greatest contact with foreigners who, via business or legal connections, may be able to facilitate women's passage out of the country.

WOMEN'S MOBILISATION AND GENDER POLICY IN THE PHILIPPINES

Before summing up this chapter, some discussion of the recent history of women's mobilisation and gender policy in the Philippines is important, since this further highlights gender inequalities in the domains of employment, migration and the household, as well as shaping women's roles and status.

Women's mobilisation, from Marcos to Aquino

After gaining the vote in 1937 (following a 20-year struggle, mainly by upper-class women), it was not until the late 1960s that Filipino women resumed organisation in any concerted way. This took the form of a nationalist and progressive women's group calling itself MAKIBAKA (Malayang Kilusan ng Bagong Kababaihan/Free Movement of New Women), whose aims were to advance the struggle for national democracy and to assert women's position in all aspects of economic, social and political life. MAKIBAKA held the view that women's oppression resulted from imperialism, feudalism and bureaucratic capitalism (Espinosa, 1993; A.Santos, 1991). Regrettably, the movement was forced underground when Marcos instituted martial law in 1972. His only real concession to women's needs was to create (in 1976) the National Commission on the Role of Filipino Women (NCRFW, then the NCW – National Commission on Women), although this was largely a response to international pressure arising out of the UN Decade for Women. According to more cynical commentators, it was also a means of deflecting attention from his military dictatorship. Imelda Marcos headed the organisation (Medel-Añonuevo, 1993a:2).

Between 1976 and 1985 the NCRFW engaged in various kinds of projects to 'integrate' women into development, with key interest in the education of rural women (Eviota, 1992:155) and the development of livelihood projects for low-income groups (Enrile and Illo, 1991). At the same time, Marcos's population control campaign, while largely insensitive to the notion that women should have rights over their own fertility, did at least improve female access to contraception. However, in other ways women's position under Marcos deteriorated gravely, not least on account of the regime's aggressive promotion of sex tourism and the attendant exploitation of young females (see Azarcon de la Cruz, 1985; A.Santos, 1991).

In the early 1980s discontent with Marcos in general, and his treatment of women in particular, saw the emergence of a wide range of women's political and opposition groups (see Lanot, 1991), the biggest of which was the General Assembly Binding Women for Reforms, Integrity, Liberty and Action (GABRIELA), established in 1984 (see below). The aims of the various groups ranged from dismantling the Marcos dictatorship, to the alleviation of poverty, to raising female political representation, to obtaining state recognition of women's needs and rights, to incorporating women's concerns into development policy and planning.

When Cory Aquino came to power in 1986 it was difficult to ignore this visible and organised female presence. Proclamations of gender equality were accordingly, for the first time, written into the new Constitution of 1987, with Article II, Section 14 declaring: 'The state recognises the role of women in nation building and shall ensure the fundamental equality before the law of women and men' (Quisumbing, 1990:44). Two main legislative and planning changes for women to emerge during Aquino's term were the revision of the Family Code and the inauguration of the Philippine Development Plan for Women (Espinosa, 1993:11).

The Revised Family Code of 1988

The Family Code had originally been incorporated into the Civil Code of the Philippines in 1949. Although the revisions to the Code enacted in 1988 still aimed to strengthen family and marriage relations, the new format was much more egalitarian in terms of gender (see Republic of the Philippines and UNICEF, 1990; Sempio-Diy, 1988). One of the new provisions was that a woman no longer had to have her husband's permission when applying for credit (Illo, 1991:44). Second was that the family home became the common property of husband and wife (Quisumbing, 1990:45). Another was that the management of the household was recast as the right and duty of both spouses (Sempio-Diy, 1988:100). Moreover, whereas previously husbands had been designated as bearing the 'burden' of financial support of wives and children, this was restated as being the duty of both partners (Pineda-Ofreneo, 1991:118). While many of these changes represented at least a nominal improvement in women's status, various elements of the Code remained staunchly patriarchal. One of the more insidious was that concerning marital rights and obligations, with Article 55 of the Family Code specifying that:

the infidelity of the wife poses more danger than the infidelity of the husband. The reason for this is that it seriously injures the honor of the family, impairs the purity of the home, and may bring children not of the husband, who due to his lack of awareness, may regard them as his own and dutifully support them yet are alien to his own blood. (Pineda, 1991:116)

The Philippine Development Plan for Women

The Philippine Development Plan for Women (PDPW) was instituted by the National Commission on Women directly under the Office of the President and was integrated into the Medium Term Development Plan of the Philippines. The plan set out a series of proposals for the incorporation of women's issues into development activities between 1989 and 1992 (Espinosa, 1993:11; Mangahas and Pasalo, 1994:245–6; Medel-Añonuevo, 1993a:1; Santos and Lee, 1989:58–9).

The aims of the PDPW were to 'alter the traditional concept of a woman's self-worth as being subordinate to a man' (NCRFW, 1989:8), with goals for equality and development in six major spheres: individual, family, socio-cultural, economic, political and legal (ibid.). More specifically, the plan identified key problems experienced by women in these spheres and made various recommendations. In the field of employment, for example, calls were made to reduce the exploitation of women as cheap labour, especially in export-oriented factories; to upgrade women's skills and management capabilities; to develop equal opportunities, and to institutionalise social security benefits for women workers in the informal sector (NCRFW, 1989:49). The updated plan for women (1991–2) echoed all the original prescriptions, but also gave greater emphasis to AIDS and STD risks associated with prostitution (see NCRFW, 1991).

In addition to these major initiatives undertaken during Aquino's term, a number of individual pieces of legislation were passed in the interests of women. These included Republic Act 6725, which strengthened laws against the discrimination of women in respect of terms and conditions of employment; Republic Act 6949, which made 8 March an annual holiday for women (National Women's Day); Republic Act 6955, which outlawed the mail-order bride business; Republic Act 6972, which called for the establishment of day-care centres in all *barangays* (the smallest administrative units in the Philippines – see also Chapter 3); Republic Act 7322, which extended full maternity-leave payments for workers in the private sector from 45 to 60 days, in line with provision for government employees; and Republic Act 7192, which called for the 'integration of women as full and equal partners in nation building'. There were two main parts to this last initiative: first, a legal obligation on the part of the National Economic and Development Authority (NEDA) to transfer a 'substantial portion of official development assistance funds from foreign governments and multilateral agencies and organisations' to support programmes for women; and second, the equality of women with men before the law in terms of entering into contracts, becoming members of clubs and enrolling in military schools (see Mangahas and Pasalo, 1994:245–6; Reyes, 1992:45–6). In addition, at the time of writing, increasingly radical initiatives are being espoused by female members of Ramos's government, with Senator Gloria Macapagal Arroyo having introduced a motion to raise the earning capacity of women, enabling them to hire paid help in the home and alleviate their 'double burden'.

Although these various measures have placed gender on government agendas in a hitherto unprecedented manner, several issues remain to be addressed. Possibly the most important is that of reproductive rights. Abortion in the Philippines is classified along with murder, drug trafficking and so on as a 'heinous crime'; not only do practitioners face life imprisonment, but certain senators have called for reinstatement of the death penalty (see Miralao, 1989). Another major issue in need of attention is that of divorce and the continued sexual double standard in terms of different specifications of marital infidelity among men and women as grounds for legal separation (see note 8 to this chapter). Another problem is that although women now have recourse to legal protection from 'habitual' wife-beating, sporadic domestic violence is still unlikely to bring its perpetrators to justice (see Reyes, 1992:47–8). Moreover, in terms of the general formulation of legislative recommendations under the Philippine Development Plan for Women, Eviota (1992:155) notes that as an explictly 'companion piece' to the Medium Term Philippine Development Plan, the PDPW was basically a 'corrective measure of state strategy', leaving largely unquestioned the role of the state as 'embodiment of gender hierarchy'. Besides this, even if recommendations reach the statute book, there is no guarantee that women will experience benefits in practice. As a result, the mobilisation of non-governmental organisations for women is vital in the continued fight for gender equality.

Grassroots mobilisation

Outside the formal state apparatus, the largest legal coalition in the radical women's movement in the Philippines is GABRIELA. Its aims are to have women's rights recognised in the context of democratic and participatory governance free from neocolonial influence and foreign intervention (Tiglao-Torres, 1990:15). More specifically, GABRIELA focuses on women's concerns such as female exploitation in bars and brothels, mail-order brides and the cost of living. It also tackles broader issues such as the national debt, nuclear power and the environment (García-Moreno, 1991:99; Goodno, 1991:157). One of the organisation's most recent initiatives (1993) has been to hold a national forum on Ramos's 'Philippines 2000' plan, which identified the plan's strategies for continued export orientation and accelerated growth as extremely negative for women (see Israel-Sobritchea, 1994; Taganahan, 1993; Chapters 2 and 8 this volume).

Although the concerns of many Philippine women's organisations overlap, the women's movement as a whole is widely noted as fragmented (Israel-Sobritchea, 1994). A major attempt to forge greater consensus and collective action has been launched by DIWATA (Development Initiatives for Women and Transformative Action), funded by the

Women's Programme of the Canadian International Development Agency (CIDA). DIWATA consists of two major networks: the 'Group of 10' (G-10/Lakas ng Kababaihan), comprising women's groups such as GABRIELA, KALAYAAN, KABAPA and Womanhealth Philippines, and WAND (Women's Action Network for Development), a coalition of development NGOs working on matters relating to women (Israel-Sobritchea, 1994; St Hilaire, 1992:12). The objectives of DIWATA (which has a total of 230 women's groups under its wing) are basically threefold: (1) to support projects leading to gender equality; (2) to promote and encourage the development of policies, programmes and services benefiting women; and (3) the consolidation of networks of women's organisations (Israel-Sobritchea, 1994).

Whether this kind of initiative will help to forge greater unity among Filipino women remains to be seen. One historical point of divergence has hinged upon the relative association of different women's groups with state and nationalist projects (see ibid.). Another is the inevitable diversity of 'women's interests', where class, among other factors, emerges as significant. While there is no doubt that many middle-income groups have a strong commitment to working with and alongside the grassroots, and that there are various organisations such as SAMAKANA and AMIHAN[20] which specifically represent low-income women, all too often it is poor women who suffer most from gender oppression and who are in the weakest position to defend themselves. Through analysing the experiences of women in expanding sectors of feminised employment, the present study hopes not only to pinpoint the manner in which women in the Visayas are affected by various forms of class and gender inequality, but where possible to suggest ways of tempering, if not eliminating, the more negative outcomes of export-led development.

SYNTHESIS OF IDEAS AND ORGANISATION OF THE BOOK

The present chapter has attempted to give a broad sketch of the parameters of the research and to locate them within the context of

---

20 SAMAKANA (Samahan ng Malayang Kababaihang Nagkakaisa/Organisation of Free and United Women) is a mass-based organisation of low-income women which was founded in 1983. AMIHAN (National Federation of Peasant Women) is the main association of Filipinas in the countryside.

current debates on gender and development. The study's aim to provide an overview of the implications for gender roles and relations of export-oriented development in the Central and Western Visayas, and to explore key linkages between rising female labour demand, female labour migration and household organisation, responds to a need identified in the contemporary literature for micro-level analysis that acknowledges the diversity of women's experiences of development and which attempts to move away from monocausal explanations. In revealing the multiple interrelations between different aspects of women's lives in Cebu, Lapu-Lapu and Boracay, the study hopes not only to clarify a series of two-way interactions between, for example, female employment and household structure, or between migration and household evolution, but also to approach a more integrated picture of the interlocking and fundamentally dynamic ways in which gender roles and relations affect and are affected by different social, economic and demographic dimensions of export-led development. Recognition of dynamism is crucial to the study, since while demand for female labour in export-oriented activities seems to rely heavily on traditional gender stereotypes, and indeed may in several respects reinforce them, there would also appear to be a series of associated factors – new patterns of female labour migration, new household arrangements, new relationships to wage income and so on – which generate changes in women's lives. In other words, while the form that export-oriented development takes is often predicated on notions of a status quo in gender roles and relations, the very process of female labour absorption may conceivably modify various of the structures which have given rise to and sustained gender inequality in the past.

With this in mind, the analysis is organised with the aim of highlighting the experiences of women in the target sectors of export-oriented employment against those of low-income women in general. After the next chapter, which provides the context of economic development in the Philippines and the Visayas in the postwar period and which introduces basic information on Cebu, Lapu-Lapu and Boracay, Chapter 3 gives a general overview of migrant characteristics, employment, gender roles and relations and household organisation among the poor in these centres, drawing on household surveys carried out in low-income communities (see Appendix). This in turn acts as a backdrop to discussions of female (and male) workers in the three core export sectors in the study centres: manufacturing (Chapter 4), tourism (Chapter 5) and sex work (Chapter 6). Data sources for these chapters include interviews with workers, employers, and organisations and individuals who either promote the activities, promote the interests of labour and/or consume the services which women provide. The penultimate chapter identifies key variations in migration and household organisation among the different occupational groups and the wider female population, and explores their consequences in the context of a holistic analysis of the outcomes of employment for women. In evaluating the findings in relation to broader conceptual debates on female labour force participation, migration and household formation, the insights are used to suggest future approaches for the comparative study of gender and development. This international perspective is carried through into Chapter 8, where directions for research and policy are identified with a view to ways in which some of the more negative aspects of women's involvement in export-oriented development might be modified, if not transformed, by challenges to some of the global inequalities which underlie them.

2 THE PHILIPPINE ECONOMY: NATIONAL PERSPECTIVES, EXPORT-ORIENTED DEVELOPMENT, AND GROWTH IN THE CENTRAL AND WESTERN VISAYAS

This chapter provides background to the growth and development of the study centres, Cebu, Lapu-Lapu and Boracay, within the context of economic and political change in the Philippines since independence in 1946. We begin with an overview of the Philippine economy, focusing on the evolution of development strategies and their economic, social and demographic consequences in the postwar period with especial reference to the administrations of Ferdinand Marcos (1965–86), Cory Aquino (1986–92) and Fidel Ramos (1992 to the present). Particular attention is paid to the growth of the export-oriented sectors of industry and tourism which have been of special relevance to the Central and Western Visayas. The chapter goes on to comment on the position of these regions vis-à-vis national development and provides a brief introduction to each of the three study centres.

ECONOMIC DEVELOPMENT IN THE PHILIPPINES: AN OVERVIEW

As of 1990, the Philippines had one of the lowest per capita GNPs (US$760) in the East Asia and Pacific region and was one of the most heavily indebted countries in the world (ADB, 1993:114). Although the country became nominally independent in 1946, its 'double dose' of colonialism over four centuries (controlled first by Spain, and from 1898 by the US) left an invidious legacy of aid, trade and capital dependence. This, coupled with the fact that the Philippines is still a predominantly agricultural country,[1] has undoubtedly contributed to its weak position in the international economic order. Compared with fellow states in the Association of South East Asian Nations (ASEAN)[2] and other neighbouring countries, the Philippines has clearly lagged behind in the general economic expansion experienced by the region over the last 30 years (IBON, 1992c:1; World Bank, 1993c). The Philippines not only missed out on Asia's 'first wave' of growth in the late 1960s when the 'Gang of Four' or 'Four Little Tigers' (Singapore, Hong Kong, Taiwan and South Korea) underwent rapid industrial transformation, but also failed to be incorporated in the 'second wave' of the 1980s which began to reshape Indonesia, Malaysia, Thailand and southern China in similar ways (Frankel et al., 1993:23; see also Drakakis-Smith, 1992:10–11, Table 1.1). Per capita GNP in the Philippines is scarcely a tenth of that of Taiwan (IBON, 1992c:1), and the World Bank fears that the performance gap between the Philippines and its neighbours may continue to exist for some time to come.[3] While to some extent all East Asian countries have been affected by global recession in the 1990s, the Philippines is generally regarded as among those which have fared the worst (see World Bank, 1993b:115). External shocks affecting the country since the beginning of the decade have included the Gulf War, which not only raised the country's bill for oil imports by about US$400 million and displaced migrant Filipino workers (and their valuable remittances) from the Middle East (World Bank, 1992b:123), but also threatened to stir unrest among the Muslim population of the country and in turn contributed to a dramatic fall-off in receipts from international tourism (EIU, 1992:20). Other setbacks to Philippine economic development

1 The agricultural basis of the economy is clearly reflected in the fact that the Philippines depends on primary exports for around 30 per cent of its GDP and 40 per cent of its export earnings (see Hodder, 1992:122).
2 The Philippines joined ASEAN in 1967. The original aims and objectives of the Association as set out in the Bangkok Declaration of that year were to promote 'active collaboration and mutual assistance on matters of common interest in the economic, social, cultural, technical, scientific and administrative fields' (see Rigg, 1991:209). ASEAN has six member countries: the Philippines, Thailand, Malaysia, Indonesia, Singapore and Brunei. Currently the Philippines is lagging behind the rest, but the Economic Intelligence Unit (1993a:23) suggests that it could benefit from a comprehensive free trade-agreement, which was first discussed at the beginning of 1993 when a consensus was reached on a 15-year tariff reduction schedule.
3 See World Bank 'The Philippines: An Overview for Sustained Growth' in *Philippine Daily Inquirer*, 15 May 1993, pp.21–2.

came from a series of natural disasters in 1990 and 1991, such as a major earthquake in Baguio and the eruption of Mount Pinatubo (see de Dios, 1992:98–101; World Bank, 1992b:123).

Despite a brief upturn in the economy in the late 1980s, and the implementation of a stabilisation programme in 1991[4] which went some way to reducing the country's financial deficit and managed to halve the rate of inflation by the following year (EIU, 1993a:1; World Bank, 1993b:117), recent economic growth has been slow (only 0.7 per cent in GDP in 1991 and zero in 1992); serious problems of foreign debt, domestic debt and widespread rural and urban poverty remain (ADB, 1993:258; World Bank, 1992b:123). Indeed, while GDP growth averaged 5.7 per cent per annum between 1965 and 1980, between 1980 and 1990 it reached only 0.9 per cent (World Bank, 1992a:220). Total external debt in 1991 stood at US$29.8 billion, with debt servicing claiming as much as 37 per cent of the national budget. This has serious implications for further borrowing; one forecast of the World Bank suggests that total external debt may rise to $40 billion by 1997 (ibid.:6).

Economic development in the postwar years

In order to understand the contemporary situation of the Philippines, it is helpful to go back to the immediate postwar period when the country became an independent republic – not because independence meant the advent of self-determination, but because relations of dependence on former colonial masters were, if anything, intensified (see Estanislao, 1986; NEPA,1992). In return for assistance to patch up the economic and infrastructural ravages of the Second World War, during which time the Philippines had not only been under Japanese occupation but had also suffered huge destruction when the United States regained the country (Miranda, 1988:19–20; Steinberg, 1986:50), Congress was forced into granting 'parity rights' for American businesses (Collins, 1989:14; Pineda-Ofreneo, 1991:4).[5] This allowed US firms

4 The Philippines has introuduced several stabilisation programmes since the onset of the current 'crisis': in 1979, 1980, 1983, 1984 as well as 1991. Most have involved IMF loans (Cruz and Repetto, 1992:52). The major structural adjustment programmes (funded by the World Bank) were implemented in 1980–3 (SAL I) and 1983–5 (SAL II) (ibid.:54).
5 The US Parity Rights (or Laurel-Langley) Agreement did not expire until 1974 (Estanislao, 1986:202).

effectively to enjoy the same status that they had previously held, including power to exploit the country's natural resources and to repatriate export earnings. Other privileges accruing to the United States included the Military Bases Agreement of 1947, which provided for 15,000 troops being stationed permanently in the country (Cammack et al., 1993:69; Goodno, 1991:214–15).[6] Foreign influence in the early part of the postwar period was intensified as a result of free-trade policies which saturated the domestic market with US products and in turn gave rise to serious balance-of-payments problems and a debilitating outflow of national wealth (IBON, 1991b:4; Miranda, 1988:20; Santos and Lee, 1989:4). During the 1940s and 1950s, the Philippines became increasingly reliant on the export of cheap raw materials and agricultural commodities (primarily sugar and coconuts) to generate foreign exchange, while the country's fledgling industrial sector, stretched to compete with foreign producers, became ever more dependent on American technology and managerial expertise. Although in the late 1940s some attempt was made to bolster import substitution industrialisation (ISI) through import and exchange controls, and 1958 saw the adoption of the so-called Filipino First policy by President Carlos Garcia which sought preferential treatment for Filipino companies and restricted imports of finished products, the combination of capital goods (and raw material) dependence with limited domestic markets spelt disaster for ISI. Indeed between the first and second half of the 1950s, manufacturing as a percentage of GNP decreased from 13.5 per cent to only 6.4 per cent (Goodno, 1991:48–9). Moreover, since import substitution industries were predominantly capital-intensive, absorption of the growing pool of labour displaced by capitalist penetration in the countryside was severely limited (CCCI, 1993; CIIR, 1987b:xii).

Another ominous development in the postwar years was the country's mounting external debt. The measures undertaken to promote ISI were revoked in 1961 when Marcos's US-backed predecessor, Diosdado Macapagal, became president and embarked on a new set of strategies to overcome the country's balance-of-payments deficit and to promote agricultural growth (IBON, 1991b:4; Pineda-Ofreneo, 1991:5). Macapagal's abolition of import and exchange controls was largely a response to US pressure. Ostensibly the removal of barriers was

6 The Military Bases Agreement expired in 1992, marked by the final departure of the US Navy from Olongapo in December of that year. The premature closure of the Clark Air Base at Angeles came in 1991 following the eruption of Mount Pinatubo (see Cammack et al., 1993:262–3).

encouraged as a means of reducing corruption and inefficiency in Philippine industry, with underlying motives including easier remittance of profits and capital repatriation by North American business interests (see Miranda, 1988:23). Alongside the removal of controls, Macapagal obtained around US$300 million in public and private loans and, again under US pressure, allowed the peso to be devalued from 2 to 3.9 to the dollar. While benefits accrued to traditional Philippine exporters and foreign investors, consumers and domestic-oriented producers were hit very hard indeed (Goodno, 1991:49). By the end of the 1960s ISI had been thoroughly eclipsed by liberalisation (Cruz and Repetto, 1992:12), with the Philippines firmly entrenched as a net capital exporter and increasingly reliant on foreign loans to counteract the steady diminution of overseas investment (Miranda, 1988:24). From this time on, multilateral financial institutions, notably the IMF and the World Bank, began to take a much more active role in Philippine economic and political life; as Pineda-Ofreneo (1991:5) argues, they set in train the country's 'cycle of permanent dependence on global financial institutions' (see also Miranda, 1988:23; NEPA, 1992).

The Marcos years

When Ferdinand Marcos became president in 1965, policies favouring foreign interests were pursued with equal if not greater vigour than before – symbolised, for instance, by the Investments Incentives Act of 1967, which allowed firms with less than the usual 51 per cent of shares in Filipino hands to operate under certain conditions and which allowed 100 per cent foreign equity in pioneer industries (CIIR, 1987b:33; Shoesmith, 1986:17). This was coupled with further heavy borrowing, part of which was used to furnish a lavish US$50–100 million re-election campaign that in 1969 resulted in Marcos becoming the only Philippine president to be sworn in for a second term. This fuelled a further balance-of-payments crisis, for which Marcos predictably sought another dose of IMF relief. In return the IMF demanded another devaluation of the peso and the end of the decade saw further rises in commodity prices, the closure or takeover of several Filipino industries and further losses in purchasing power (Goodno, 1991:59; Pineda-Ofreneo, 1991:5–6). The degree of openness to foreign money was such that by 1971 only one-third of the country's top 250 business corporations were entirely Philippine-owned, and many of these were actually in the hands of the state or of Marcos's political cronies (Goodno, 1991:106–7; see also Cammack et al., 1993:69; CIIR, 1987b:xiii–xiv).

In addition to allowing foreigners to hold 40 per cent of the shares of companies involved in the exploitation of natural resources, Marcos also tried to keep on the right side of American business interests by waiving legal restrictions on foreign landownership (Goodno, 1991:70). During the 1970s the Philippine countryside became the scene of a massive modernisation programme whereby transnational companies using Green Revolution technologies increased the amount of land under their control, together with their markets for capital goods and inputs, as well as embarking upon the production of new export crops such as pineapple and rubber (see Pineda-Ofreneo, 1991: Chapter 7; Putzel, 1988:52,1992: Chapter 4; de la Rosa, 1993).

Between 1972 and 1981, levels of foreign penetration and external indebtedness escalated as Marcos tightened his hold on the country through martial law, and took ready hold of the petrodollars which foreign banks were then rapidly recycling into the Philippines and other developing countries (Cleves Mosse, 1993:123; Miranda, 1988:25; Montes, 1992b:69–70; Pineda-Ofreneo, 1991:6; Santos and Lee, 1989:5). While external debt had been less than 10 per cent of GDP throughout most of 1950s and early 1960s, from 1967 onwards it increased consistently to an average of 28 per cent during the 1970s (Cruz and Repetto, 1992:15). Supported by a steady flow of money from foreign creditors, Marcos was able to finance the trade deficit and follow a growth policy that furthered the interests of the business community in general and the export sector in particular, the latter benefiting from the creation of free trade or export processing zones (EPZs), bonded warehouses and tax privileges (Goodno, 1991:70). Even then, the Philippines only managed to achieve a trade surplus twice in the whole period of the Marcos regime (Pineda-Ofreneo, 1991:7).

Integral to the negative outcomes of these misplaced economic policies were the corruption and mismanagement of the Marcos years. In addition to furnishing handouts to political allies, the regime proved 'fabulously successful in amassing personal wealth' (Cammack et al., 1993:69). Both these phenomena were due in large part to the diversion of government resources to 'vast patronage machines' (ibid.). One such machine was the Ministry of Human Settlements, of which Imelda Marcos became head in 1981, soon draining the coffers with a lavish programme of buildings and public works. As Pineda-Ofreneo (1991:7) notes: 'The profligacy of the Marcos family was legendary. Luxurious buildings and "white elephants" abound to this day as testimonials to the First Lady's truly impressive "edifice complex"' (see also Villegas, 1986:161–2). The overall effects were to swell Philippine foreign debt twelvefold, from US$2 billion to $24 billion between 1970 and 1983 (FFDC, 1989:190; Miranda, 1988:25; Santos and Lee, 1989:5).

Although martial law was lifted in 1981, the combination of bad management, debt accumulation and corruption had pushed the economy to a state of such severe crisis that Marcos's standing both in the US and in the Philippines had plunged to unprecedented depths (Goodno, 1991:78; see also Canlas, 1988:79–80; CIIR, 1987b:xi; McCoy, 1987:12–13). Despite appeals to the IMF and World Bank for further funds and a resolute commitment to export-oriented free-market strategies, economic collapse seemed certain and challenges began to confront Marcos from all sides. As Kerkvliet and Mojares (1991:6) point out:

As the Philippine economy deteriorated in the 1980s and the government became increasingly immobilised by internal contradictions, Marcos's patronage system, which had been a key instrument for mustering support, became ineffective. Too little was distributed or done so very unevenly: too many people remained disenfranchised; the arrogance and deceit of Marcos and others became transparent. (see also Cammack et al., 1993:69)

In short, despite Marcos's belief that he still had wide support, disenchantment with his regime was so deeply embedded that people began to overcome their fear and to resort to active expressions of protest. Among a growing wave of resistance from groups such as peasants, students, tribal minorities and the urban poor (see CIIR, 1987b:xi), May Day 1980 saw the formation of the KMU (Kilusang Mayo Uno /May First Movement), which attempted to provide wage labour with an alternative to the US-backed, pro-government TUCP, or Trade Union Congress of the Philippines (Goodno, 1991:78; R.Lee, 1987:103). The more conservative TUCP had originated in 1975 (Amnesty International, 1991:2), traditionally receiving money from the US government via the National Endowment for Democracy Fund (Aguado, 1988:9). The formation of an opposition union grew, somewhat inevitably, out of a general trend of what Elias Ramos (1987:175) calls a 'radicalisation of the labour movement' that in turn had burgeoned in response to restrictions on the right to strike and mounting joblessness from 1972 onwards. Despite representing a minority of wage-earners, the KMU until very recently has been one of the two largest labour alliances in the Philippines, alongside the TUCP (see Goodno, 1991:156).[7] In Marcos's time, it was significant not only in acting as a magnet for other unions, but also in bolstering 'organised labour's attempt to establish closer alliances with various community organisations for political purposes' (Ramos, 1987:175; see also R.Lee, 1987). Left-wing party political resistance to Marcos also began to mount in the light of the growth of the National Democratic Front, or NDF, and the New People's Army, or NPA, (CIIR, 1987b:xi; Lande, 1986:129–34).

It was, however, the assassination of Marcos's main political rival, Benigno ('Ninoy') Aquino, in 1983 that really set the seal on the president's demise, bringing large numbers of the middle class and a prominent segment of the Catholic Church into vocal opposition. The incident also provoked international condemnation, with banks closing credit to the Philippine government. As Santos and Lee (1989:9) point out: 'By the end of 1985 the political crisis was coming to fruition. Years of resistance to authoritarian rule by the nationalist movement underlay the strengthening anti-dictatorship feeling.' The scene was ripe for political change.

The Aquino era

When Ninoy Aquino's widow, Cory, was swept into Malacañang Palace in February 1986 by the 'People Power Revolution' and Marcos's last-minute defection to the United States, the catalyst for Philippine society's long-overdue transformation was widely and optimistically thought to have arrived. While 'Aquino had an unrepeated opportunity to lead her nation in bold reform' (Collins, 1989:3), however, the overthrow of Marcos was 'not a social revolution which uprooted the evils of US imperialism and did not mean an end to fundamental problems of the people and the crisis of the social system' (Sison, 1988:23;

7 In August 1993 a leadership squabble within the Communist Party of the Philippines led to the break-up of the KMU, along with other left-wing groups such as the KMP (Kilusang Magbubukid ng Pilipinas – a military peasant group) and the League of Filipino Students (a radical youth group). See Christine Avedaño, 'KMU, Other Left Groups Break up' *Philippine Daily Inquirer*, 27 August 1993, pp.1 and 6 (see also EIU, 1993c:9-10; Putzel, 1994).

see also Canlas, 1988). As had been the case with previous administrations, the bulk of Aquino's cabinet members were drawn from among the elite and the private business sector: groups which tended to favour privatisation and be deeply suspicious of state intervention. Despite the fact that neighbouring countries such as Taiwan and South Korea had achieved their economic success with considerable help from the state (in the form of highly protected domestic markets, large-scale agrarian reform and a huge export drive to take advantage of the United States's relatively open market in the 1960s and 1970s – see Bello, 1993; World Bank, 1993c), Filipino business organisations were (and continue to be) opposed to public investment in anything other than infrastructure development. As James Goodno (1991:107) points out:

Collectively the elite expressed concern about economic recovery, not redistributive justice. With some exceptions, the pro-Aquino elite spoke of justice in the old and largely discredited trickle-down manner. The basic economic reforms demanded by all factions of the elite failed to address the serious problems facing the majority of Filipinos.

Aside from conservatism, intransigence and/or inertia on the part of cabinet members, the Aquino government faced several problems as a result of inheriting what O'Brien (1990:7) terms 'a very sick economy' from the previous administration. The Marcos legacy included a national debt of over US$26 billion, landlessness and rural unrest, labour militancy and a conflict of interests between emerging export-oriented producers of electronics and garments on the one hand, and traditional commodity exporters and domestic manufacturers on the other (Goodno, 1991:107; see also Krinks, 1987:35). Much investment in the new industries was foreign, and came particularly from the US, which well into the 1980s remained the country's leading foreign equity investor by a substantial margin. Even if Japan, and more recently Britain,[8] have now supplanted the US in this position, the Philippines's historical lack of diversity in trade and

---

8 According to 1993 data from the Bangko Sentral (the central financial authority in the Philippines), of US$327.9 million foreign investments in the country, 33 per cent ($108.6 million) was from British investors. Japanese investments in 1993 were only $46.2 million (down 70 per cent on 1992), and US investments only $35.6 million (37 per cent below 1992). See Jose Galang, 'UK Investors Lead Manila Inflow', *Financial Times*, 8 March 1994, p.4 .

investment has undoubtedly been a source of its poor economic health (see, for example, NEDA, 1992).

In addition, there remained the problem of how to address the profound and widespread poverty of Filipino citizens. In 1988 the World Bank reported that between 1975 and 1985 a further 12 million people had swelled the ranks of the absolute poor in the Philippines, and that the country had developed one of the most unequal patterns of income distribution in the world (Goodno, 1991:110). In 1985, for example, the richest 20 per cent of the population owned over half the country's wealth (having increased their share from 53 per cent to 59 per cent between 1971 and 1983), whereas the poorest 20 per cent held only 5.2 per cent (Eviota, 1992:81; O'Brien, 1990:7). Problems were especially apparent in the countryside, where Marcos's rural modernisation programme had not only widened differentials among the peasantry but had also led to deteriorating conditions for many landless peasants and tenant farmers (Putzel, 1992:156). During the period 1971–85 the proportion of rural households living in poverty had risen from 48 per cent to 64 per cent (Collins, 1989:4). Despite Aquino's implementation in 1988 of the Comprehensive Agrarian Reform Programme (CARP), the poorest sectors still tended to lose out to the elite, to foreign corporations and to landed interests (see Collins, 1989:6–10; Putzel, 1992: Chapters 9 and 10 for further details).

Thus although Aquino's accession to the presidency initially raised hopes of a break with the past, little in the way of real transformation occurred. One of the major problems was the administration's resistance to popular demand to cancel payment on debts incurred during Marcos's period in office, and its apparent enthusiasm to seek new loans from the IMF and the World Bank (Santos and Lee, 1989:11). Through Proclamation no.50 the government formally assumed an 'honest debtor policy', whereby the liability of government-owned and controlled corporations became the financial responsibility of the 'common Filipino taxpayer' (Dioneda, 1993:6). By 1988 the Philippines owed money to over 400 private banks and foreign government agencies as well as multilateral institutions, and its total debt had climbed to US$29 billion (Cleves Mosse, 1993:123; Goodno, 1991:222). According to Mariano Miranda (1988:35), Aquino's policy reflected her belief that 'any disruptive action on the debt issue would damage the massive flow of foreign aid and investment and endanger the rescheduling of maturing loans'. Whatever the outcome of an alternative approach might have been, under these conditions the economy continued to spiral downwards, with debt servicing placing such huge demands on the Philippines's budget and foreign exchange earnings that the government was constantly having to hunt for new funds, in turn backing it further into the position of making 'countless concessions to its creditors' (Goodno, 1991:222).

Aquino's determination to honour all national debts was reinforced in early 1989 when she signed the now-famous 'Letter of Intent' to the IMF in which she agreed to an array of stringent conditions, such as reductions in public expenditure, wage freezes and improvements in incentives and conditions for export-oriented producers (Pineda-Ofreneo, 1991:11). Following public outcry and a general strike which forced the government to back down on its pay policy, mid-1989 saw a consortium of advanced economies and international financial institutions (including the US, Japan, the European Community, World Bank, Asian Development Bank and IMF) pledging aid of US$2.8 billion for the fiscal year 1990. Becoming known as the Multilateral Assistance Initiative (MAI) or Philippine Aid Plan (PAP), this initiative was similar to a mini-Marshall Plan implemented by the US in Europe after the Second World War, with growth and modernisation the key objectives (Goodno, 1991:130; Shibusawa et al., 1992:27). Fuelled by underlying concern over the essential 'fragility' of Philippine democracy (O'Brien, 1990:19), related aims included the tackling of the country's continuing problems of insurgency and rural unrest (Santos and Lee, 1989:14), and assuring the country's capacity to uphold its debt repayments. The latter concern was to the undoubted benefit of donor nations, especially in the context of rising interest rates.

The Ramos administration

Despite the declared intention of the current administration of President Fidel Ramos[9] to wean the Philippines off IMF medicine, a new three-year facility worth US$650 million was secured at the start of 1994.[10] This will play a major role in underpinning the Medium Term

---

9 Ramos became president in June 1992, winning 24 per cent of the vote (see Cammack et al., 1993:112).
10 See 'RP Gets New $650m Loan', the *Filipino* VI:1 (February/March 1994), p.3 .

Philippine Development Plan – Philippines 2000 – which aims to bring the country up to 'newly industrialising country' (NIC) status by 1998 (EIU, 1993b:13). Strategies to raise growth rates and create a more attractive climate for foreign investment include the curbing of wage increases[11] and the privatisation of key industries such as steel, copper-smelting and shipyard engineering. A central component of the package is the Philippine Export Development Plan (PEDP). Part-funded by the United Nations Development Programme, the PEDP is the first export plan drawn up with full private sector participation.[12] Working on the assumption that 'exports provide a fast-track way of achieving the country's economic goals' and are the 'primary means to earn foreign exchange to pay for the country's foreign debt obligations' (DTI, 1993:3; see also Villariba, 1993:15), the targets set by the Plan include a 15 per cent average annual increase in exports up to 1996 and a rise in the export sector's share of GNP from 19 per cent to 30 per cent between 1993 and 1998. These targets are to be achieved by making exports a more profitable business in the Philippines and by raising levels of foreign direct investment (DTI, 1993:4; see also DTIITG, 1993). The products designated by the PEDP to become more competitive include garments, furniture, subcontracted electrical components and gifts and houseware (including jewellery), all of which have an important export-manufacturing base in Cebu and Lapu-Lapu, as discussed later in this chapter.

Although to some extent the export sector, especially in the Philippines's export processing zones, has been less affected, one of the major barriers to industrial expansion is the current power crisis, with so-called brown-outs of up to six or seven hours at a time crippling production and business services (ADB, 1993:113). The situation has been particularly bad in Metro Manila, where manufacturing output fell by 5 per cent in the first quarter of 1993 compared with the same period a year earlier, and unemployment reached 18.3 per cent: more than twice the national average (EIU, 1993c:18). In an attempt to sort out the power problem, in April 1993 Ramos signed into law the Electric Power Crisis Act (Republic Act 7648), giving him special

11 Although wage rises of between 8 per cent and 24 per cent (an extra 8–25 pesos per day) were granted by the bulk of the Philippine regional wage boards in late 1993, these are minimal in the light of considerable losses of purchasing power in the last decade (see the *Filipino* V:6 [December 1993/January 1994], p.1).
12 'Primer on Philippine Export Development Plan', *Sun Star Daily*, 20 August 1993, p.S3.

powers to intervene in the distribution of limited electrical supply and
to counter possible abuse by the emergency authority. One of the less
explicit, but extremely significant, provisos of this measure was also
the authority to legislate power rate increases (WRCC, 1993a:3).[13]

Crisis and adjustment

Raising user charges for public services such as electricity is just one
of a whole gamut of debt-related initiatives which have combined to
squeeze the poorest and most disaffected sectors of Philippine society
since the mid-1980s. As Wilfrido Cruz and Robert Repetto (1992:47)
note: 'the worst effects of the debt crisis and the contractionary policies
adopted under the stabilisation programme carried out from 1983 to
1985 were their adverse effects on unemployment, poverty and income
distribution'. For example, real per capita GDP fell dramatically
between 1982 and 1985, with average real wages by the latter year
having declined to 30 per cent below their 1982 level (Stewart,
1992:26). Overt unemployment increased from 4 per cent in 1979 to
7.1 per cent in 1985, and underemployment (classified as applying when
people work less than 40 hours a week) became a way of life for one-
third of the labour force during the crisis (Cruz and Repetto, 1992:47;
Montes, 1992a:49). By 1988 it was officially estimated that 50 per cent
of the Philippine population was on or below the poverty line (Pineda-
Ofreneo, 1991:13).

One of the major corollaries of IMF- and World Bank-inspired
restructuring has been a redirection of subsidies away from basic commodities and social spending towards debt servicing (Montes, 1992a:53).
For example, between 1979 and 1983 the Philippines experienced severe
cuts in per capita GDP (–2.7 per cent per annum), together with reduced
expenditure on health (–1.3 per cent per annum between 1979 and
1982) (Stewart, 1992:28, Table 2.5). Indeed, in 1990 health services
were only allocated 3.2 per cent of the national budget, as against 37
per cent for the debt (Pineda-Ofreneo,1991:17). Although central
government expenditure as a proportion of GNP increased from 15
per cent to 16.1 per cent between 1980 and 1991, the amount spent

---

13 'Things to Watch out for in the Use of Special Powers', *Philippine Daily Inquirer*,
6 July 1993, p.6, editorial. Indeed the day after the Electric Power Crisis Act was signed,
the Energy Regulatory Board raised the limit of the increase allowable by the National
Power Corporation (NAPOCOR) to 57 centavos per kilowatt hour (see *Sun Star
Daily*, 6 April 1993, p.1).

on housing, amenities, social security and welfare declined from 6.6 per cent to 3.7 per cent over the same period (World Bank, 1993a:258). Another major change has been the removal of food subsidies, with concomitant escalation both in the difficulties for small farmers and in prices to consumers. For example, 1984 saw a 27 per cent increase in the prices of rice, tinned fish and canned milk (Cleves Mosse, 1993:124; Vickers, 1991:89), while 1989 witnessed further rises of 20 per cent in the cost of canned milk, along with that of eggs, sugar and cooking oil (Santos and Lee, 1989:46). The debt crisis is perhaps felt particularly by women, who not only have to 'pick up the tab' for shortfalls in basic service delivery, for rising prices of consumption and so on, but who also have to increase their load of paid labour to generate income for their households, often in the highly competitive arena of the informal economy (see, for example, Chant, forthcoming a; Dioneda, 1993; Santos and Lee, 1989,1992; Taganahan, 1993; Taguiwalo, 1993:49–50).

Dissatisfaction with the manner in which restructuring was conducted during the 1980s also reached the higher echelons of government administration, with the head of the National Economic and Development Authority (NEDA) and Secretary of Economic Planning, Solita Collas-Monsod, actually resigning from the cabinet on the grounds of 'irreconcilable differences' with Aquino and her colleagues over the handling of the debt – Monsod had advocated selective debt repudiation, whereas Aquino had sought further loans (Santos and Lee, 1989:19; see also Krinks, 1987:41; Miranda, 1988:35). Monsod has continued to criticise the government since her resignation, maintaining that the

Philippine economy is experiencing a vicious circle whereby budget deficits lead to larger borrowings which in turn lead to higher interest rates, which lead to a combination of heavier debt service expenditures and lower than expected revenues which lead to growing budget deficits and an increase in inflation. (Collas-Monsod, 1991:6)

The adverse effects of economic restructuring on the poor have recently led to a proposal by NEDA for 'safety nets' to protect those on the lowest incomes, including proposals for the retraining of displaced workers, the implementation of food subsidies and targeted livelihood programmes for vulnerable groups.[14]

---

14 See Rita Villadiego, 'NEDA Lists Safety Nets to Protect Poor Sectors' *Philippine Daily Inquirer*, 7 September 1993, p.17.

Negative popular reaction to the debt has crystallised in the founding of the Freedom from Debt Coalition (FFDC), which since 1988 has grown to incorporate 144 organisations including Church groups, community organisations and a range of academic and professional bodies who wish to bring a 'human face' to the forefront of debt policy. The main aims of the FFDC are threefold: (1) that the government should declare a moratorium on foreign debt service payments until levels compatible with the recovery of the Philippine economy are reached;[15] (2) that the government should eschew repaying loans involving fraud or relating to private sector borrowing; and (3) that foreign debt service should not exceed 10 per cent of export earnings (Pineda-Ofreneo, 1991:78).[16]

Before turning to look at some of the social and demographic consequences of Philippine development in more depth, it is useful to take a brief glance at two key sectors of export-oriented growth – export manufacturing and international tourism – which have traditionally been regarded as vital in steering the Philippines out of economic crisis, and which have also played a major role in the evolution of the Visayan localities at the core of this study.

Export manufacturing

As noted earlier, export manufacturing has been one of the main arms of Philippine development policy since the late 1960s, when concerted attempts were made to switch orientation away from the export of primary products towards that of manufactured goods such as garments and electronics – the so-called non-traditional exports (Eviota, 1992:80; IBON, 1991b:4). Indeed, garments and electronics between them now constitute 50 per cent of Philippine exports by value (EIU, 1993c:3).

15 It should be stressed here that the IMF and the Philippine government have had frequent disagreements over growth rates. During talks with the IMF in February 1993, for example, the Philippines declared its preference for a 4.5 per cent economic growth target, whereas the IMF felt that 3–3.5 per cent was more realistic (see *Philippine Daily Inquirer*, 19 April 1993, p.17; see also EIU, 1993a:4). Nonetheless, although it was widely felt that the IMF would press the Philippine government to accept lower targets as a condition for further funds, especially as growth was only 2.5 per cent in 1992, agreement was reached on 4.5 per cent for 1994 (see 'RP Gets New $650m Loan', the *Filipino* VI:6 (February/March 1994), p.3).

16 While lower than in previous years, foreign debt service in 1993 was still around 20 per cent of export earnings (see *Philippine Daily Inquirer*, 19 April 1993, p.21).

The legislation supporting these objectives includes the Investment Incentives Act of 1967, the Export Incentives Act of 1970 and the Republic Act 5490 of 1969 which provided for the creation of a Foreign Free Trade Zone (or Export Processing Zone) Authority – EPZA (CIIR, 1987b:33; Tanchoo-Subido, 1979:27) – see below. Export manufacturing follows two main forms: that taking place within the 'export processing zones' (EPZs), and that taking place outside them.

Export Processing Zones

Three years after the passing of Republic Act no. 5490, and coinciding with the implementation of martial law, the first Philippine export processing zone was established in Mariveles, Bataan. Presidential Decree no.66 set out the aims of EPZA as including the development, establishment and maintenance of an effective and efficient management of export processing operations in the designated zones (EPZs) and in industrial estates (IEs) in strategic areas of the Philippines for local and foreign investors to pursue and promote foreign commerce (EPZA, 1991:1; see also IBON, 1990). The benefits to companies operating in these zones include 100 per cent foreign ownership; the waiver of minimum registered investment; no duties, taxes or licence fees; priority in foreign exchange allocations; speedy administrative procedures; the right to borrow money within the Philippines with government guarantees, and unrestricted repatriation of profits (CIIR, 1987b:34; Shoesmith, 1986:43; see also Dicken, 1990:214). Other benefits consist of strict clampdowns on unionisation and collective wage bargaining (see CIIR, 1987b:xii; also Sklair, 1991:95).

There are currently four main export processing zones in the country: Bataan, Baguio City and Cavite in Luzon, and Mactan in the Visayas (see Fig. 1.1). With nearly 200 firms between them, the largest zone is Cavite with 90 plants, and the smallest Baguio City, with twelve (EPZA, 1993). All have been crucial to Philippine economic recovery: in 1992, for example, when national export earnings rose by only 10 per cent, total earnings from the four zones registered an increase of 30.9 per cent to US$666 million (see EIU, 1993a:22). Part of the reason for this buoyancy is due to preferential treatment from regional electricity companies whereby the zones have escaped the power shortages affecting most other enterprises in the country.

Electronics

The firms operating within the EPZs are predominantly producers of garments and electronics. While garments have traditionally been the Philippines number one dollar earner, the growth of the electronics industry has been especially marked since the late 1980s. By 1991 electronics made-up one-third of total principal exports from the Philippines (excluding tourism) and nearly one-fifth of all exports, generating US$1.75 billion in 1991 alone (NSO,1992c:v). By 1992 semiconductors had become the country's leading export product, with sales between the first quarters of 1992 and 1993 registering a 31 per cent increase to $326 million.[17] The bulk of companies producing micro-electronics are foreign; as with other producers in EPZs, the main attraction of locating in the Philippines is cheap labour. As Elizabeth Eviota (1992:119) notes:

the establishment of the electronics industry in the Philippines was part of a worldwide movement by electronics companies in the West to cut down on labour costs. For the world is one global assembly line where, by means of job fragmentation, labour surplus economies perform the labour-intensive operations in production.

Garments

Although the garment sector has been badly affected by power shortages in the last few years and the Department of Trade is concerned to bolster the industry's global competitiveness,[18] garments were still the top Philippine export in 1991, generating US$1.86 billion and representing 34 per cent of the top ten exports by value (excluding tourism) and 21 per cent of total exports including tourism (NSO, 1992c:vii, Table 1). Even if 1992 saw electronics moving into first place, the value of garment exports had risen by 16.7 per cent (as against 13 per cent in manufacturing exports as a whole) since the previous year, and garments represented a healthy one-third of all manufacturing exports (EIU, 1993b:23). Nonetheless, while garments might appear on the surface to be very valuable to the Philippine economy, production is

17 See 'Trade Gap Widens to $1.94B', *Philippine Daily Inquirer*, 26 July 1993, pp.17 and 21.
18 See Ayen Infante, 'Garment Sector Pushes 5 Measures to Stay Afloat', *Philippines Times Journal*, 23 July 1993, p.9.

so dependent on foreign capital and imports (including raw materials), and technology transfer is so minimal, that expansion may ultimately prove to be damaging (see, for example, Espiritu, 1988). As the Cebu Chamber of Commerce and Industry (1993:3) puts it, in both garments and electronics, as well as other manufactured products, 'Philippine industry essentially adds a thin slice of value-added to imported components, then re-exports them. Thus the export sector is in effect an enclave with surprisingly little linkage to the domestic economy' (see also Chant and McIlwaine, 1994).

Non-EPZ export manufacturing

While the vast bulk of export-oriented plants inside the export processing zones are multinational, foreign ownership outside the zones is also on the increase.[19] Since the time of Marcos, up to 100 per cent foreign equity has been allowed in pioneer industries[20] and in export-oriented manufacturing firms – defined as those where more than 70 per cent of output is exported (EIU, 1991:43). The Foreign Investments Act of 1991 has further reduced export qualification (to 60 per cent), even if it is required by law that those industries exploiting natural resources have a paid-in equity capital of at least US$500,000 (BOI/PITO-P, 1991:11). Foreign investors are also now entitled to full and immediate capital repatriation/dividend/interest remittance privileges without prior approval by the Central Bank; it is hoped this will bring the pace of foreign direct investment more in line with that of other Southeast Asian countries.[21] Further incentives for domestic and export-oriented producers have been provided by

19 This seems to be part of a general trend in developing countries for declining differences between zone and non-zone foreign investments (see Sklair, 1990:110).
20 'Pioneer projects' are eligible for an additional two years' income tax holiday compared with non-pioneer projects (see Republic of the Philippines, 1993:1). 'Pioneer' status is accorded to economic activities where one or more of the following criteria apply:

- manufacturing or elaboration of a product never produced in the Philippines before on a commercial basis;
- use of a new technology or product process never tried in the Philippines;
- introduction or expansion of a product or service which is 'highly essential to the attainment of national economic goals';
- an activity which entails substantial investment, 'outside normal risks' (ibid.).

21 See Mario Lamberte, 'Attracting Foreign Investment to RP', *Philippine Daily Inquirer*, 21 June 1993, pp.20 and 26.

the 1993 Investment Priorities Plan and the Philippine Export Development Plan, especially for those locating in less-developed areas of the country (Republic of the Philippines, 1993). Tourism projects are also included in the drive to encourage export-oriented development, with incentives again applying to the sector as a whole as well as to key areas outside the National Capital Region.

International tourism

The promotion of international tourism in the Philippines stems from the industry's proven, and longstanding, importance as a source of foreign exchange. Despite having dropped from its position as the country's top generator of dollar income in the 1970s, tourism still ranks in third or fourth place in foreign exchange earnings (WRRC/PSC, 1990). The events leading to a fall-off in the last twelve or so years have included public outcry against foreign sex tours to the country in the early 1980s (see below), an attempted coup in 1989, fears of Muslim unrest in the wake of the Gulf War and a swathe of natural disasters (see above). These factors combined to affect the industry particularly severely at the beginning of the 1990s: although receipts from international tourism amounted to US$1,306 million in 1990 (WTO, 1992b:108–12), numbers of foreign-visitor arrivals had actually fallen below 900,000 from over 1 million in the previous year (WTO, 1992b:97–9). Efforts to overcome these difficulties have been sharpened in the wake of the 1992 withdrawal of US naval installations from Subic Bay in Luzon. Indeed, in Subic Bay itself tourism is being actively promoted in attempts to convert the former base into a 'Hong Kong' style duty-free area aimed particularly at the Taiwanese market – the fastest growing source of foreign tourists to the Philippines (see IBON, 1992b; EIU, 1993c:16–17).[22] Other strategies to increase international visitor traffic include Department of Tourism travel incentives, which since 1990 have been provided for Filipinos residing abroad, while in the same year the DOT instigated an International Travel Programme to host selected foreign groups connected

---

22 See Ernesto Hilario, 'Gordon's Black Comedy', in *Philippine Daily Inquirer*, 6 April 1993, p.7 on the conversion of Subic to a major free port. There are also plans to convert Subic into a light manufacturing zone. To this end the Taiwanese government is lending US$20 million to private Taiwanese companies in their joint venture, Century Development Corporation, to industrialise 300 hectares of undeveloped land (EIU, 1993b:17).

with the travel trade and the media (NEDA, 1991:242). The government is also trying to develop new beach centres, particularly northern Palawan off the southwest coast of Luzon, Boracay in the Western Visayas, Panglao Island in the Central Visayas and Samal in Mindanao (see Fig 1.1).[23]

One feature that international tourism has in its favour is that, unlike many other countries heavily reliant on the industry, such as Mexico, which depends on a narrow range of sources of foreign visitors (over 90 per cent of tourists to Mexico come from North America – see Chant, 1992c:86–7), the geographical base of tourism to the Philippines seems healthily diverse. For example, in 1990 23.9 per cent of visitors came from the US and Canada, and nearly as many from Japan (19.7 per cent), while there were also substantial numbers from Hong Kong (6.9 per cent), Taiwan (5.5 per cent) and Australasia (5 per cent) (WTO, 1992a:201–2; see also Chant, forthcoming b). In addition, there is quite a large business element in tourist composition: in selected parts of the country such as Cebu, the breakdown is 40 per cent businesspeople as against 60 per cent 'pure' tourists. This is seen as very positive by the regional office of the DOT and the local chapter of the Hotel, Restaurant and Resort Association (HRRA), which feels that a substantial business component tends to act as insurance in an industry otherwise prone to considerable vagaries.

What is undoubtedly less healthy about international tourism in the Philippines, however, is its historical reliance on the country's so-called hospitality industry, aptly summarised by Aida Santos's (1991:48) statement that Philippine tourism 'has had for its main attraction and commodity the Filipino woman'.[24] As discussed in Chapter 1, this was especially marked during the Marcos years, particularly the 1970s, when desperation for foreign exchange meant that 'prostitution was not only allied with tourism, but did in fact support the industry' (Eviota, 1992:137; see also Raquisa, 1987:218). In the early 1980s adverse publicity about sex tours, especially from Japan, which resulted in civil protest and a petition to Prime Minister Zenko Suzuki, caused an interim tapering off of the phenomenon, or at least a decline in its visibility

23 See also 'Samal: The Next Destination', the *Filipino* VI:1 (February/March 1994), p.4.
24 Alongside female prostitution, there is also a considerable amount of child prostitution, especially in Manila and Pagsanjan, a scenic waterfall area in Luzon (see Bagasao, 1992; de Leon, 1991; Fernandez-Magno, 1991; HAIN, 1987; WRRC/PSC, 1990).

in Manila and a shift towards lesser-known centres such as Cebu (see Azarcon de la Cruz, 1985:25–6; Matsui, 1991a:71–2). Nonetheless, sex-oriented male holidays, if not formal tours, are still very much in evidence, and advertising of the latter continues in foreign men's magazines and specialist publications.[25] In addition, even regular tourism literature within the Philippines contains more than oblique references to 'entertainment' attractions, such as the opening lines of an article in a magazine published by the Department of Tourism's Regional Office in Cebu in 1991: 'Mention Cebu and warm vivid images instantly fill one's mind. Fine sandy beaches, fantastic diving sites, five-star resorts, beautiful Cebuanas,[26] friendly hospitable people ... sunny days and sultry nights' (see Javier, 1991:1). The article concludes with the statement that: 'Cebu is many things – spectacular beaches ... exciting nightlife with dozens of modern discos, hotels, restaurants and other entertainment facilities rivalling those found only in Manila and other key centres of the world' (ibid.:4).

The reference to Manila is more than incidental since, along with Bangkok, the Philippine capital has a longstanding reputation as an 'International Sex City' (Matsui, 1991a:70). Although the advertising and promotion of sex have been played down since the demise of Marcos, with the Department of Tourism now adopting a formal stand against sex tours (NCRFW, 1989:67) and current programmes attempting to promote the image of the Philippines as a 'wholesome travel destination' (NEDA, 1991:242),[27] it seems hard to wipe out the historical legacy of the industry. Indeed the persistent male bias in foreign tourist composition (83 per cent of visitors coming to the country for pleasure) undoubtedly reflects the 'sex tourism stigma' of the 1970s and 1980s (Republic of the Philippines et al.,1991:142).

Whether or not a 'toned-down' form of sex tourism will persist in underpinning the Philippines's relative popularity as a travel destination within Southeast Asia, estimates suggest that tourism receipts are likely to maintain their strong growth (EIU, 1993b:5). Tourist arrivals

25 For example, in 1992 feminists attacked a Japanese publishing house (ICK Booksellers) for the publication of *Southeast Asia for Men Travelling Alone*, a guide indicating where to obtain the best sex in the region at the cheapest prices (see 'Japanese Feminists Hit Sex Tour Guide of Asia', *Philippine Daily Inquirer*, 4 April 1992, p.8).
26 A Cebuana is a girl or woman native to Cebu.
27 One example of the attempt to combat the negative imagery of the Philippine sex trade is reflected in the much-publicised March 1993 'clean-up' of Manila's sex district, Ermita, by Mayor Alfredo Lim. See for example Rina Jimenez-David, 'The Condom and Major Dirty Harry', *Philippine Daily Inquirer*, 7 June 1993, p.5; and 'Man with a Mission', *Asiaweek*, 2 June 1993, p.28 .

were up 19 per cent in the first quarter of 1993 compared with the same period in 1992,[28] and if the trend continues, tourism's contribution to GDP will increase from 4.9 per cent (as of 1990) to 6.9 per cent by the year 2010 (Republic of the Philippines et al., 1991:4).

Despite the isolated (and often dubious) successes of export-oriented development, however, we have already seen the generally deleterious effects of economic change in the postwar period on the bulk of the Philippine populace, especially in terms of the debt burden. Before moving on to look at the Visayan region, therefore, it is useful to provide a brief summary of the major social and demographic consequences of the last 50 years of Philippine development at a national level.

Population and urbanisation

One major result of the country's gradual shift towards a more industrialised status is the rise in urbanisation. While in large part this is due to the movement of people from the countryside to towns (see Chapter 1), it is also due to high rates of natural increase in urban areas, which in turn reflects high growth rates at a national level.

The total population of the Philippines was 60.5 million in 1990 and 64.3 million in 1992. It is expected to reach 75 million by the year 2000 and to exceed 120 million by 2020 (IBON, 1991a:3; SGV/PITO-P,1992:7). With a demographic growth rate of 2.3 per cent per annum, the Philippines has one of the fastest growing populations in Southeast Asia (Jackson, 1994:79) and is the fourteenth most populous country in the world.[29] As the country's first Protestant president, Fidel Ramos does not subscribe to the Catholic doctrine of restricting contraception to natural methods and, in viewing over-population as a major obstacle to economic development, is trying to step up the birth control campaign originally introduced by Marcos and to force the overall population growth rate down to 2 per cent per annum by 1998 (EIU, 1993c:7).[30] Marcos's population programme had also strongly advocated limiting births (to two per couple) and

28 See 'Tourist Arrivals up Slightly', *Philippine Star*, 29 August 1993 pp.1 and 9.
29 See Christine Avedaño, 'Sin Dares FVR on Birth Control', *Philippine Daily Inquirer*, 26 July 1993, pp.1 and 7.
30 Despite Ramos's personal beliefs on the acceptability of contraception, opposition from the Catholic Church could pose certain political difficulties: see, for example, Avedaño, 'Sin Dares FVR on Birth Control', cited in note 29 above; 'Ramos Urged to Review Government Population Control Programme', the *Philippine Star*, 26 July 1993, p.1; and Tony Clifton with Marites Vitug, 'Between a Woman and her God. The Philippines: a Bitter Debate over Birth Control', *Newsweek*, 25 August 1993, p.26.

had actively promoted articificial contraception, achieving a reduction in population growth from an average of 3 per cent in the 1960s to 2.7 per cent in the 1970s (EIU, 1993c:7). Given the Roman Catholic Church's opposition to this campaign and its alliance with Marcos's political opponents, Aquino took a much softer approach to family planning. The number of population control workers dwindled from around 10,000 under Marcos to only 200 under Aquino,[31] and between 1986 and 1991 the demographic growth rate dropped by only 0.1 per cent from its 1985 level of 2.4 per cent (IBON, 1991a:6).

Regardless of whether population growth per se hinders economic progress, however, there is no doubt that it has exacerbated problems of poverty in major urban areas, especially Manila. Urbanisation in the Philippines has proceeded steadily since the 1970s, with only 31.8 per cent of the population living in urban areas in 1970, compared with 48.7 per cent in 1990 (NSO, 1992a:xxvi, Table A). By the end of the century it is estimated that over 50 per cent of Filipinos will live in towns and cities.[32] Despite some increase in levels of urbanisation outside the National Capital Region since 1975 (see Jackson, 1994), Metro Manila, the hub of the nation's employment and resources, still contained 14 per cent of the national population and 32 per cent of the urban population in 1990 (World Bank, 1992b:278). Among other things, urban population growth has caused serious strains on existing urban housing supply. In the late 1980s it was estimated that 7.4 million out of 11 million poor urban dwellers in the country as a whole lived in slums (Santos and Lee, 1989:25). In Metro Manila alone, half the inhabitants are classed as poor and at least one-third are squatting the land on which they live (IBON, 1991a:5). Although the government has introduced various housing projects and slum-upgrading schemes, these usually fall woefully short of demand, especially among those on the lowest incomes (see Ramos-Jimenez et al., 1986; Santos and Lee, 1992:60; Thirkell, 1994: Chapter 3).

Welfare

Social security

As indicated by previous discussions in the text, social welfare for the majority of Filipinos is also very limited. The two main forms of social

31 See 'Cory now Blamed for Overpopulation', *Philippine Daily Inquirer*, 20 July 1993, pp.1 and 8 .
32 See Rina Jimenez-David, 'Who are the Urban Poor?', *Philippine Daily Inquirer*, 26 July, 1993 p.5.

security available to the working population are GSIS, or Government Service Insurance System, and SSS, or Social Security System (see IBON, 1992d). GSIS was created in 1936 by Commonwealth Act 186 and aimed to promote the welfare of government employees and so improve the efficiency of the Philippine government.[33] SSS was not set up until 1957, under Republic Act 1161 (the Social Security Law). This aimed to provide private sector workers with social insurance (IBON, 1992d:2). Employers bear 50–60 per cent of the total contributions of SSS members, and SSS offers death, disability, maternity, sickness and funeral benefits, as well as administering Medicare, a health insurance programme covering hospital charges and medicines (ibid.:3).

Despite the apparent advantages of SSS coverage, there are numerous problems. One is that compulsory wage deductions for SSS members eat heavily into the limited earnings of lower-income workers; another is that most benefits do not meet people's needs. Further difficulties arise from the fact that claims take an inordinately long time to process. Moreover, several employers do not uphold their commitments, either by not paying their own contributions to the fund or by retaining those of their employees (IBON, 1992d:3–4).

Health and nutrition

Health and nutritional status are also important indicators of the way in which development has neglected popular well-being. In 1988, for example, a survey conducted by the National Nutrition Council and the Philippine Food and Nutrition Programmes found that 54 per cent of people suffered from protein deficiency (Santos and Lee, 1989:26). It is also estimated that between 70 per cent and 80 per cent of children under six years of age display varying degrees of malnutrition, and that nearly 50 per cent of pregnant women are affected by nutritional anaemia (ibid.:27; also Cleves Mosse, 1993:124; Montes, 1992a:51; Ramos-Jimenez et al., 1986:26–7; Santos and Lee, 1992:61). In 1988 life expectancy was only 64 years for women and 60 for men (Villariba, 1993:14).

Diseases of poverty and poor environments such as tuberculosis, bronchitis, pneumonia and gastro-enteritic infections, are rife, which is not surprising given that only 15 per cent of Filipino households are provided with sanitary sewerage facilities and only 60 per cent have

33 See 'Government Financing Institutions: Priming the Country's Economy', *Philippine Times Journal*, 23 July 1993, pp.11–12 .

access to a piped water supply (Pineda-Ofreneo, 1991:20). While the satisfaction of basic environmental and housing needs and the provision of primary healthcare facilities would undoubtedly help to reduce the incidence of ill-health among the population, instead 60 per cent of the government's health budget goes to hospitals and health personnel (Santos and Lee, 1989:27). Even so, the Philippines has one of the worst levels of health staffing in the developing world, with only one doctor for every 8,120 persons: less than one-third of the average coverage in other lower-middle-income economies (World Bank, 1993a:292).

Education

Education tends to receive a higher slice of government expenditure than health (14 per cent as against 3.2 per cent in 1990), which partly reflects the 1987 Constitution's declaration that 'the State shall assign the highest budgetary priority to education and ensure that teaching will attract and retain its rightful share of the best available talents through adequate remuneration and other means of job satisfaction and fulfillment'. Nonetheless, debt service has eaten heavily into resources. The ratio of primary pupils per teacher rose from 29 to 33 between 1970 and 1990 (World Bank, 1993a:294), and classrooms are increasingly shabby and overcrowded, lacking both equipment and teaching aids (Pineda-Ofreneo, 1991:24–5). More costs are being passed onto parents and pupils, and educational careers are becoming progressively less alluring to qualified personnel, greater numbers of whom are either having to take on extra jobs to make ends meet or seeking alternative employment overseas, even as domestic servants (ibid.:25; see also Santos and Lee, 1992:59; Vickers, 1991:90; Villariba, 1993:15). Notwithstanding these difficulties, the proportion of the population enrolled in institutes of tertiary education (27 per cent in 1990) is nearly twice that of other lower-middle-income economies (16 per cent) (World Bank, 1993a:294), even if the quality of education provided often leaves much to be desired (see Tacoli, 1994).

Employment and incomes

As suggested earlier, employment and incomes for the majority have also suffered in the postwar period, with the crisis since the mid-1980s giving rise to exceptionally high levels of un- and underemployment.

By 1989, official sources estimated the national rate of unemployment at 8.4 per cent and the number of underemployed (those working less than 40 hours a week or seeking additional work) at 32.4 per cent of the labour force (IBON, 1992a:4; Pineda-Ofreneo, 1991:28). Even for those in work, relative wage levels have steadily eroded over time (see also Montes, 1992a:49–50).

In terms of the sectoral composition of employment, the proportion of the economically active population working in industry actually declined from 16 per cent to only 13 per cent between 1970 and 1983. While agricultural employment remained broadly constant, the proportion of the population working in services expanded to over 32 per cent by 1983 (Ramos, 1987:187). By the second half of the 1980s, 49 per cent of the working population were employed in services, 42 per cent in agriculture and only 10 per cent in industry (UNDP, 1992:158).

Retrenchments in the formal sector have not only led to the expansion in services per se, but also to the burgeoning of the informal sector where people work in an unregistered capacity and often on their own account. While the informal sector was estimated to be contributing 26.7 per cent of GNP in 1960, by 1988 this had risen to 48.2 per cent, with between 60 per cent and 70 per cent of the population employed in this sector by the latter year (Santos and Lee, 1989:35). Accompanying this trend has been a progressive 'informalisation' of industrial employment, with an increased tendency for manufacturing firms to farm out jobs through subcontracting agents to home-based workers who are paid by piece-rates and have no recourse to legal protection or conventional employee benefits (Pineda-Ofreneo, 1991:29–31).

Regional inequalities

In addition to these problems, the Philippine economy suffers from spatial imbalance. In recognition of the heavy concentration of resources and population which had accumulated in the National Capital Region (NCR) by the end of the Marcos dictatorship, there has been some attempt since then to promote regional development. In part this has been motivated by a genuine desire to disperse economic activity for the benefit of the regions themselves; although, tellingly, the National Economic and Development Authority professes a need to accelerate 'positive economic gains' in regions outside the NCR 'to support the national economic recovery' (NEDA, 1990: 16). In other words, national interests would still appear to take precedence over local ones.

Having said this, some hesitant advances in regional development have been made since the mid-1980s, with the Omnibus Investments Code of 1987 granting incentives for firms to locate in less-developed regions and clamping down on the award of tax holidays and capital equipment incentives in the Metro Manila area (see Republic of the Philippines, 1993:15). Yet while investment in the regions increased by 76 per cent between 1989 and 1990 to represent a total of 70 per cent of all new investments, the National Capital Region still managed to come second out of the country's total of 14 planning regions in terms of the capture of new investment capital (NEDA, 1990:81). The prominence of the NCR is also reflected in the allocation of public investment: discounting nationwide and interregional projects, which accounted for 70 per cent of total public investment expenditure of US$567 billion in 1990, the NCR still received 29.3 per cent: by far the largest single regional share and contrasting very markedly with, for example, the Central Visayas, with 5 per cent, and the Western Visayas, with 1 per cent (NSCB, 1991:Table 15.7). Not surprisingly, the period 1987–89 saw the NCR continuing to have the highest growth rate in gross regional domestic product (GRDP), at 8.2 per cent, even if the Central Visayas was one of four other regions which managed to achieve growth rates above the national average of 6 per cent (NEDA, 1990:15). Regions outside the NCR seem to struggle with limited funds and bear the heavy burden of the centralisation of data, expertise and priorities in Metro Manila. Plans for the regions are ambitiously prognostic, yet much in the way of vital diagnostic information can only be found in national headquarters. Except for wealthier centres such as Cebu, which to some extent has been able to fund and shape its own expansion, the usual pattern is that only isolated pockets within the lesser-developed regions, notably those with endowments of strategic importance to national interests, are able to tap development funds. Such areas tend to receive sectoral, rather than regional investment; and since sectoral investment is motivated by national goals, it often has little relevance to local needs, let alone to those in outlying parts of the respective hinterlands. Bearing in mind these contradictions, the following sections take a closer look first at development in the Central and Western Visayas, and then at the three study centres – Cebu, Lapu-Lapu and Boracay – where national interest in expanding export-oriented development has often been critical in shaping their evolution.

ECONOMIC DEVELOPMENT IN THE PHILIPPINE VISAYAS

The Visayas comprise three planning regions as defined by the National Economic and Development Authority: the Eastern Visayas (Region VIII), the Central Visayas (Region VII) and the Western Visayas (Region VI). Together these form a strategic 'growth triangle' within the central/southern (and national) Philippine economy. Of these latter two regions (where the study centres are located), the Central Visayas is by far the more prosperous. It consists of the provinces of Cebu (home to Cebu City and Lapu-Lapu City), Bohol, Negros Oriental and Siquijor (see Fig. 3.2). Government aims in the medium term are for the region to consolidate its position as a major site for new investment in the Philippines and second gateway for international travel and trade (NEDA Region VII, 1993a:2). Although lagging behind the NCR, growth in recent years has been extremely healthy, especially when set against national trends; between 1988 and 1991 the economy of the Central Visayas grew by 2.4 per cent.[34] At the same time, even in Cebu, which is the richest province in the Central Visayas and alone contributes 10 per cent of the nation's wealth, prosperity is largely confined to the major industrial cities (Cebu, Lapu-Lapu, Mandaue); several smaller towns and villages lack not only a healthy job market but many basic services.[35] In other words, while the Central Visayas has distinctive pockets of wealth, there are notable intra-regional and indeed intra-urban inequalities, as discussed later in the text.

As for the Western Visayas, which comprises the provinces of Iloilo, Capiz, Antique, Guimaras, Negros Occidental and Aklan (the latter is home to the third study centre, Boracay), growth in the period 1988–91 was only 1.4 per cent; according to the National Economic and Development Authority, development in the region has always

---

34 Marites Villamor, '120 has to be Turned over to MCIAA within this Month', *Sun Star Daily*, 10 May 1993, p.B1 .
35 See Michelle So, 'Prosperity in Cebu Confined to Cities, Towns with Industries', *Sun Star Daily*, 27 August 1993, p.11.

been limited. The main immediate concern for the Western Visayas, therefore, is to initiate sustainable economic growth and to alleviate poverty (NEDA, 1990:28). Indeed, although the incidence of poverty has declined – it affected 73.4 per cent of the Western Visayan population in 1986, compared with 61.8 per cent in 1988 – the region is actually the second poorest in the country after Region V (Bicol), with poverty levels far in excess of the national average of 49.5 per cent (NEDA Region VI, 1993:1). Although much of the region has fertile soils and considerable fishing potential, its areas of growth remain largely limited to tourist spots such as the Guimaras Islands, and more particularly Boracay (the latter is discussed below).

Cebu City

Dubbed variously the 'next great economic miracle', 'Asia's newest boom town' and 'Queen City of the South', Cebu is actually the oldest city in the Philippines. It is the point where, in 1521, Ferdinand Magellan first set foot on the shores of the Philippine archipelago, and the site of the first permanent settlement of the Spanish under the leadership of Miguel Lopez de Legaspi from 1565 (Bucoy, 1992:34; CCCI, 1992:7). Cebu City is capital of Cebu province and the second most important city in the Philippines, after Manila. Cebu is primarily an industrial, shipping and commercial centre, but is also an increasingly important destination for international tourism (see Costello et al., 1987:31–2; DTI Region VII, 1992:7; NEDA Region VII, 1992a; Mangahas and Pasalo, 1994:252; Republic of the Philippines, 1990). Growth of the city really took off in 1986, when Emilio ('Lito') Osmeña embarked on a six-year term as provincial governor and his brother Tommy became mayor (the Osmeñas are one of Cebu's oldest and richest families). Interestingly, then, the expansion of Cebu originated largely because of local initiative rather than national intervention (Reyes Churchill, 1993). The Osmeña strategy was to increase Cebu's historical distinctiveness within the Philippines as a thriving centre of trade, production and commerce, and to target investment in export-oriented manufacturing from other parts of Southeast Asia (principally Japan, Taiwan and Korea). Growth was so remarkable in the second half of the 1980s, especially in terms of exports, which rose by an unprecedented rate of 15 per cent between 1986 and 1988, that the phenomenon became known as 'Ceboom' (see Thirkell, 1994: Chapter 2; also Ballescas, 1993:2–3).

Demographic increase has inevitably followed on the heels of economic growth. The population of Cebu province grew by 2.3 per cent per annum between 1980 and 1990, largely due to in-migration to Metro Cebu. The latter is an agglomeration of over 1 million people which has developed around Cebu City and has grown to encompass Mandaue City (now Cebu's main industrial suburb), Lapu-Lapu City (see below), Toledo and Danao. In the same period, the population of the city of Cebu itself swelled by 2.9 per cent a year (NEDA Region VII, 1992b:3). Having almost doubled in the last two decades, Cebu City's population is now around 650,000 (accounting for about one-quarter of provincial inhabitants). During the day, the influx of workers and students from neighbouring towns and villages are estimated to increase Cebu City's population to 1 million (MCDC, 1991:2).

Rapid economic and population increase has not, however, been matched by adequate provision of goods and services for low-income groups. For example, a 1992 survey conducted jointly by the Mayor's Office and the City Commission for the Urban Poor revealed that half the population of the city were living in slums and squatter settlements (see Thirkell, 1994: Chapter 3). The city also has inadequate water and power supplies, while other basic services, such as sewerage and rubbish collection, are poor too (UPDC, 1992:3). As Thirkell (1994: Chapter 2) points out, the social consequences of 'Ceboom' have been equivocal. Rapid demographic growth in an economy built on low wage structures where the bias of the local state has been towards services targeted for economic production, such as transport infrastructure, instead of healthcare, housing and social welfare, means an inevitable 'proliferation of urban poverty'. In 1988, 65 per cent of the city's income was in the hands of only 29 per cent of the population (Ballescas, 1993:6), while in the early 1990s the incidence of poverty in Cebu City was over 50 per cent (UPDC, 1992:3). In addition, large numbers of the city's inhabitants have no access to formal employment and are confined to what is referred to locally as 'underground' (i.e. informal) activities such as street vending and personal services (see Ruiz, 1993; also Costello et al., 1987: Chapter 5; Mangahas and Pasalo, 1994:253).

Industry

Much of Cebu's industry consists of export manufacture in the hands of Philippine nationals or joint venture companies, and is registered with the Board of Investments (BOI) as opposed to the Export Processing Zone Authority (EPZA).[36] The major products are indigenous goods such as rattan furniture and wood products (even if no rattan pole is grown locally), as well as fashion accessories that include shellcraft jewellery and other handicrafts. In fact two-thirds of all rattan furniture in the Philippines is manufactured in Cebu, which accounts for 80 per cent of the value generated by rattan exports at a national level (Pineda-Ofreneo, 1991:35; see also Costello et al., 1987:31). The woodcraft and furniture industry in 1991 was the fifth most important dollar earner in the country, after garments, electronics, tourism and coconut oil. Excluding tourism, woodcraft and furniture represented 5.4 per cent of the value of total principal exports (the top ten commodities) and 3.3 per cent of total exports (NSO, 1992c:vii, Table 1). The woodcraft and furniture industry at a national level generated US$291.8 million in 1991 (although this was down on its 1990 level of $303.5 million); in Cebu province, rattan furniture alone earned $75.8 million in 1992, making it the second biggest export from Cebu province.[37] Indeed, until 1991 rattan was Cebu's number one industry; however, in the wake of rising competition from countries such as Indonesia and Vietnam, fashion accessories have come to overtake it.

In terms of the structure of export production in Cebu, while some furniture and fashion accessories plants are large, many production units are small- or medium-scale and service the larger companies.[38] This reflects a general tendency observed earlier to minimise labour costs and thus increase the competitiveness of the export sector (see also Chapter 4). Although Cebu produces a number of other manufactured goods for the local market, the export sector is the main arm of growth; indeed between 1989 and 1990 the increase in BOI investment in the Central Visayas was dominated by the two sectors for which Cebu is renowned: export processing and tourism (NEDA, 1991:100).

---

36 Board of Investment registration allows firms to export but generally gives fewer entitlements to export-oriented producers than the Export Processing Zone Authority registration, where costs of affiliation cover all service installations, land charges and so on, and where membership applies mainly to firms which are 100 per cent foreign-owned and which produce exclusively for the export market (see DTI Region VII, 1991:46; also CCCI, 1992:14–15 and DTI Region VII, 1992:34–6 for further details).
37 See 'Cebu Outpaces RP in Exports', *Sun Star Daily*, 7 April 1993, pp.C1 and 12.
38 See Belinda Olivares-Cunanan, 'Cebu's Fashion Jewelry Props up Economy', *Philippine Daily Inquirer*, 22 August 1993, p.5.

Tourism

The origins of tourism in Cebu date back to the early 1980s and the industry has grown steadily since then, with Cebu City earning a national Tourist Destination Award in 1989 and presently being the second tourism centre in the country after Manila (NEDA Region VII, 1992c:15). The tourist infrastructure of Cebu consists not only of establishments in the city itself, but other beach resorts both on Cebu Island and the adjacent island of Mactan which forms part of the Cebu metropolis (see Fig. 1.1). In 1991 Cebu boasted a total of 35 establishments accredited by the Department of Tourism, nearly half (15) of which were large hotels (DOT, 1991c), with a total capacity of 2,108 rooms (NEDA Region VII, 1992b:6). Much investment in tourism infrastructure has been multinational and at least one-third of all tourists to Cebu are foreigners (131,859 out of 340,859 in 1992). Around 40 per cent of visitors are business travellers with manufacturing, real estate and other interests in the locality. As stated earlier, this is viewed as extremely healthy by the Cebu Chapter of the Hotel, Restaurant and Resort Association (HRRA), because business travel is in the long run far less likely to fluctuate than 'pure' tourism.[39] The vast bulk of visitors are from Japan (50,000 in 1991), but those from the US, Taiwan and Hong Kong also figure prominently – 13,000 US visitors came to Cebu in 1991, together with 10,000 from Taiwan and 8,000 from Hong Kong (Mackie, 1992:80). In the first six months of 1993 as many as 23,269 visitors came from Taiwan – the second largest group of overseas visitors after the Japanese, 24,430 of whom arrived during the same period.[40] The flow of tourists from Japan has been enhanced by the introduction of a direct flight between Tokyo's Narita Airport and Mactan Island International Airport.[41] Indeed, many Japanese men come to Cebu just for a weekend, as it is actually cheaper to take a golfing package deal to Cebu than it is to play at home (ibid.).

39 Interview with Alfonso Elvinia, vice-president of the Hotel Restaurant and Resort Association (HRRA) – Cebu Chapter, Cebu City, March 1993.
40 See Irene Sino Cruz, 'DOT Sees Bright Prospects for Tourism Industry', the *Freeman*, 22 August 1993, p.20.
41 Other direct international flights to Mactan Airport include those from Hong Kong and Singapore, and there are link flights via Manila to Taipei and Seoul where all luggage-handling, customs and immigration are dealt with in Cebu. Mactan Airport is also to undergo expansion as a result of a new P441 million (US$17.6 million) project funded by the national government in conjunction with the private sector (see 'Lito Osmeña to Oversee Government Flagship Projects', the *Filipino* VI:1 [February/March 1994], p.6).

While some of Cebu's attraction for foreign tourists revolves around beach resorts and sports facilities, however, its 'entertainment industry' is critical to the area's growing prominence as an international tourism destination. The Women's Resource Center of Cebu Research Collective (1992:10) notes that 'part of selling Cebu to foreign investors and tourists is the prostitution and trafficking of women'. Between 1987 and 1991 the number of amusement clubs, bars and cocktail lounges rose from 47 to 135 (see Thirkell, 1994: Chapter 2), and the local entertainment sector is likely to expand further with the projected (and actual) influx of sex workers displaced from US base areas in Luzon. For example, a national newspaper has noted that between 1990 and 1991 alone, the number of registered sex workers in the city increased by as much as 20 per cent;[42] and in 1992 the Cebu City Health Office reported a total of 1,557 commercial sex workers attending for compulsory routine check-ups, although this by no means included all women working in the trade (de la Cerna, 1992:53; see also Chapter 6, this volume).

The expansion of industry and tourism in Cebu has been associated with an increased influx of female migrants to the city, with female labour force participation in Metro Cebu as a whole growing faster than that of men during the 1980s (Zosa-Feranil, 1991). According to census data, the female share of the Cebu City workforce in 1990 was 42.8 per cent (higher than the national urban average of 39 per cent), and in 1992 the National Labor Force Survey estimated it had grown to 45.4 per cent (NSO, 1992d:Table P1). As the Women's Resource Center of Cebu Research Collective (1992:5) points out, women's participation in Cebu's labour force has 'increased as Cebu's local government pursues an export-oriented industrialisation program'. Moreover, the proportion of households headed by women in 1990 was 14 per cent: higher than the national average of 11.3 per cent. The extent to which this may be related to female labour demand is discussed later in the text.

Lapu-Lapu City

Lapu-Lapu City in Mactan Island, Cebu province (and part of Metro Cebu), is one of the fastest growing cities in the Central Visayas

---

42 Edmund Coronel, 'Sex Tours Enjoy Cebu Revival', *Philippine Daily Inquirer*, 16 February 1992, p.12.

because of the Mactan Export Processing Zone (MEPZ), which was established in 1978 and is currently the second largest of the four Philippine EPZs in terms of numbers of firms, levels of investment, economic performance and numbers employed. MEPZ accounts for nearly half of Cebu province's entire export sales; it is targeted as one of the key regional industrial centres of the Visayas and the focus of industrial investment in the Visayas Area Development Investment Programme (VADIP).[43] As of 1992, 15,038 workers (77 per cent of whom were women) were employed in the 42 factories operating in the 119-hectare zone – 53 factories were actually registered but eleven had either closed down or not yet started production (EPZA, 1992). By March 1993, 43 firms were operating (MEPZA, 1993), while in May 1993, by which time approval had been given to a further seven firms, plans were under way to accommodate new plants by leasing an additional 120 hectares from the Mactan-Cebu International Airport Authority, or MCIAA (see also DTI Region VII, 1992:27).[44] Nearly half the factories are Japanese, but other countries which have invested in the Zone include the US, the UK, Germany, Taiwan, South Korea and France (Vitug, 1993:24), with prominent companies including General Motors, Timex, NEC, United Technologies, Pentax, Maitland-Smith, Taiyo-Yuden, Muramoto Audio-visual and National Semi-Conductors (ibid.; also EPZA, 1993; MEPZA, 1993; Reyes Churchill, 1993:6). The growing importance of MEPZ to Cebu province is reflected in the fact that in 1992 the Zone was responsible for 42 per cent of all exports from the entity (NEDA Region VII, 1993b:3), having risen from 38 per cent in 1991 (DTI Region VII, 1992:27).

While the largest single employer of people in MEPZ is Timex (classified by EPZA under 'other equipment and instruments'), which had a workforce of 3,416 in December 1992 (87.1 per cent of whom were women),[45] most people in the Zone are engaged in the assembly of electrical machinery (5,333 in December 1992), with plants such

---

43 Marites Villamor, '120 has to be Turned over to MCIAA within this Month', cited in note 34 above.

44 Ibid.

45 Timex is also the leading generator of income in the Mactan Export Processing Zone, achieving export sales worth US$80 million in 1991, which represented 10 per cent of the total export earnings of Cebu province (see Germilina Lacorte, '22 MEPZ Firms Make it to Top Exporters List', *Sun Star Daily*, 15 April 1993, pp.C1 and 14).

as those of National Semi-Conductors (US) and Taiyo Yuden Corporation (Japanese) employing over 2,000 people each. A further
2,257 workers are engaged in wood and wood products industries (2,490
of whom are employed by the British furniture company, Maitland
Smith) and 2,253 in garment production (EPZA, 1992; MEPZA, 1993).
Labour recruitment and labour relations in Mactan, as in other EPZs,
are structured so as to cause the minimum disruption to production
schedules. Job applicants are carefully monitored (see Chapter 4) and
it is virtually impossible for people with a history of union activity to
obtain employment in the Zone (VLDC, 1993). Although some
attempts (mainly by KMU) have been made to organise women
workers in MEPZ, strict labour policies have consistently blocked them
(WRCC Research Collective, 1992:10; also Ballescas, 1993:5; Bucoy,
1993:10).

Although firms generally pay the minimum wage, provide other
benefits required by law and even give additional perks such as family
planning and dental services (see Tiukinhoy and Remedio, 1992:5),
problems frequently arise over delays in payment of weekly salaries,
together with leave and '13th month pay': an annual bonus of one
month's wages, stipulated by law (ibid.:7). Despite these difficulties,
employment in the Mactan Export Processing Zone is generally better
paid than jobs outside; not surprisingly, Lapu-Lapu's population has
grown dramatically since the 1970s. In 1970 the population was only
48,546, but by 1980 it was 98,723 and by 1990 it was 146,194 (NSO,
1992b:1, Table 1). Women accounted for 54 per cent of total migrants
in 1990, and for 38.9 per cent of the labour force. In the same year
the proportion of households headed by women was 11.6 per cent.
Again, it is probable that there is some relationship between female-
selective migration and the high demand for female workers in the
Zone, as explored further in subsequent chapters.

Boracay Island

The third and final study centre, Boracay in Aklan province, Western
Visayas, is the fastest growing tourist resort in the Philippines. From
humble beginnings as an area of 'backyard tourism' in the 1970s , since
the mid-1980s the area has seen medium-sized foreign investment
mounting steadily (Santa Maria, 1991). In 1991 Boracay had a total
of 1,423 hotel and other rooms in 168 establishments (DOT, 1991b).

Boracay is also the most important of the four destinations targeted nationally by the Department of Tourism for priority investment; it has been the object of active government promotion since 1983 and of major public funding since 1986 (Chant, forthcoming b). Recent funding initiatives (1993) have included a US$23 million project backed by the Philippine and Australian governments to improve water supply, communications, sewerage treatment and telecommunications (see NEDA Region VI, 1992). Tourist numbers to Boracay have increased steadily over the years, reaching 47,000 in 1990 and 79,974 in 1991; 32.6 per cent of the latter were foreign (DOT, 1992b). Most foreign tourists come from Europe (70 per cent), with a further 11 per cent from the Middle East, 10 per cent from North America and 6 per cent from Australia (DOT, 1991a:104). According to the Tourism Secretary, Vicente Carlos, and the director of the National Economic and Development Authority, General Cielito Habito, Boracay is the 'centrepiece' of the Philippines's tourism development programme, purportedly illustrating a successful example of the Medium Term Philippine Development Plan's aim to marry global competitiveness and human development/people empowerment.[46]

Considerable emphasis is placed on protecting the environment in Boracay and on preventing the development of high-rise buildings and overcrowding on the beachfront area. There is concern to maintain the survival and integrity of indigenous groups such as the Atis, as well as the values of the island's youth, who are sometimes lured away from school and church by the local nightlife (see DOT, 1991d). Unlike many other tourism destinations in the Philippines, the Island Tourism Administration is also doing its best to promote the image of Boracay as a 'family resort' (DOT, 1992a:8). One strategy is to prevent the opening of 'girlie bars' (establishments with semi-nude entertainment and so on – see Chapter 6); another is to resist adoption of the health-certificate qualification for bar workers. The latter involves carrying official documentation indicating proof of freedom from HIV infection and other sexually transmitted diseases; this is mandatory in places with registered hospitality establishments, such as Manila and Cebu. The fear of the Island Tourism Administration and other influential bodies in the locality is that issuing health certificates will encourage and legitimise sex work (Chant, 1993b:8). The other main force in keeping

---

46 See 'Boracay: Centerpiece of Philippine Tourism', *Philippine Times Journal*, 23 May 1993, p.11 .

Boracay 'clean' is the local detachment of the Philippine National Police (PNP), which monitors and clamps down on potentially illicit behaviour via police visibility, night patrols and community relations activities such as meetings with church leaders and *barangay* captains. Having said this, monitoring and controlling small-scale/individual prostitution on the island is difficult. Although there are known 'pick-up' spots (notably two bars and a disco), the police find it effectively impossible to apprehend women unless they see an actual exchange of money, and must usually be extremely cautious in approaching Filipinas in the company of foreign males in case these are 'genuine' relationships.[47]

Despite the absence of formal commercial sex work, many other types of employment (for both men and women) have grown alongside the increased numbers of visitors to the island in recent years. In turn, in-migration to Boracay has risen rapidly since the late 1980s, with migrants representing around 30 per cent of the island's 8,000 inhabitants in 1993. Women make up over half the migrants to Malay, the municipality to which Boracay belongs, and represent around 45 per cent of the local labour force. In 1990 the proportion of households headed by women was 13.9 per cent. Both these latter figures are higher than in Cebu and Lapu-Lapu, which, along with the larger proportion of women in work, is suggestive of an interesting set of interrelationships between female labour migration, household structure and employment.

Prior to exploring these relationships in detail, the following chapter provides a basic overview of people's lives and livelihood in Boracay, Lapu-Lapu and Cebu, with reference to primary data collected from low-income households in the three centres.

47 Interview with Captain George Dadulo, station commander, Philippine National Police, Boracay, July 1993. (Attached to the Boracay PNP is the Balikbayan Tourist Security Unit, whose main objective is to protect the lives and property of local and foreign tourists. Both work closely with the Island Tourism Administration, part of the Philippine Department of Tourism – see Chapters 5 and 6).

3 GENDER, MIGRATION AND LOW-INCOME HOUSEHOLDS IN CEBU, LAPU-LAPU AND BORACAY: AN OVERVIEW

This chapter presents an overview of low-income households interviewed in Cebu, Lapu-Lapu and Boracay, with the aim of providing a general picture of migrant status and origins, household organisation and employment in poor neighbourhoods. This in turn will act as a basis of comparison with economic, demographic and social patterns surrounding female involvement in specific occupational sectors, discussed in subsequent chapters. We begin with a brief description of the study settlements in the three localities and general characteristics of the sample populations, and go on to examine in greater detail household patterns, the income-generating activities of women (and to a lesser extent men), the migrant origins of the poor, and linkages between rural and urban areas. There is also a short section reviewing principal aspects of gender roles and relations in the communities with reference to such factors as household decision-making and domestic divisons of labour. The data in the chapter are drawn primarily from a settlement survey of 240 low-income households, with additional information provided by in-depth interviews conducted with 30 women in the study areas (see Appendix).

CHARACTERISTICS OF THE STUDY SETTLEMENTS

Cebu: Rubberworld

In Cebu City a survey of 100 households was carried out in a settlement called Rubberworld, so named after an adjacent rubber shoe factory.

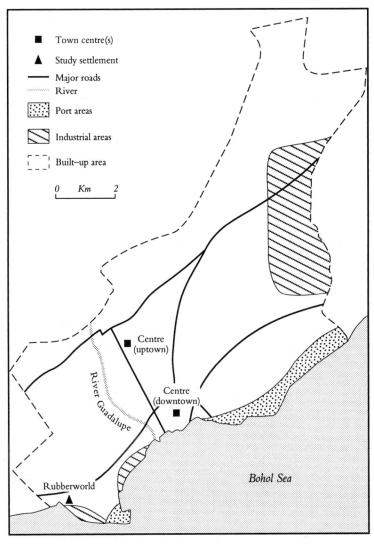

Figure 3.1: Cebu City: location of study settlement and main industrial areas

Rubberworld is one of around 35 low-income settlements in Cebu, located in the southern part of the city in an area called Mambaling, forming part of Barangay Basak San Nicolas (see Fig. 3.1).[1] One of the older settlements in the city, formed in 1972, Rubberworld is typical of most low-income residential areas in Cebu. Out of a population of around 2,800 inhabitants (approximately 500 households), the majority (70 per cent) are in the process of obtaining legal title to their land, while the rest are either squatting or renting rooms. As with most reasonably long-established settlements in the city, the bulk of households have electricity, although only a small number have a piped domestic water supply. For those without an internal tap, the alternatives include drawing water from a deep well, using a standpipe shared among various families, or buying water from suppliers or neighbours (the latter is also an ingenious form of income-generation). While there are fairly wide variations in housing types in Rubberworld, with concrete structures standing cheek by jowl with *nipa* palm huts, general dwelling conditions are poor and overcrowded. Narrow, unpaved passageways make access to certain parts of the settlement difficult, and open sewage ducts become treacherous in the rainy season, as well as posing serious health risks.

As for the inhabitants of Rubberworld, the overwhelming majority of households are headed by men (82 per cent) and are most commonly nuclear in form.[2] While household size varies from one to 16 members, the average is 5.7. Rubberworld is also characterised by a large migrant population, with over three-quarters of women respondents and their male partners (77 per cent and 78 per cent respectively)[3] having been born outside the city – mainly in other parts of the Central Visayas, and more usually in Cebu province itself. In the case of female migrants, for example, 74 per cent were born in the Central Visayas, with 84 per cent of these from various rural municipalities in Cebu province, particularly from those close to the city, such as Naga, Carcar, Barili and Dumanjug (see Figs 3.2, 3.3 and 3.4).

---

1 A *barangay* is the smallest political unit in the country, usually consisting of around 1,000 households and equivalent to an enumeration area in the national census – or part of an enumeration area in the case of larger *barangays* (NSO, 1992a: xii–xiii).

2 As noted in Chapter 1, nuclear households are those consisting of one set of parents living with their children. See Appendix for full details of household type and classification in the settlements.

3 Percentages referring to the sample surveys are rounded up to the nearest whole number.

Employment rates in Rubberworld are high for both women and men, especially when compared with census figures (see Chapter 2). Among male heads, 90 per cent are in full-time employment; only five of the 83 men are unemployed, two are retired and one, interestingly, is a house-husband. More than half the women interviewed are working full-time (59 per cent) with a further 6 per cent involved in part-time income-generation or what is known locally as having a 'sideline' or *negosyo-negosyo*. Common sidelines in Rubberworld are livestock-rearing (mainly involving pigs, or 'hog-raising'); cooking and selling food such as 'banana-cue', or *kamote-cue* (deep-fried sweet potato served on a skewer); or buying and selling clothes ('RTW', or 'ready-to-wear'). In addition, 12 per cent of women are engaged in more than one form of income-generating activity – for example, a woman may rent out rooms as well as run a small *sari-sari* store (grocery shop). These patterns of livelihood in Rubberworld are discussed in more detail later in this chapter.

Education levels in the district are the highest of those in the three settlements, probably because Cebu, as the largest urban area outside Manila, offers the best educational facilities in the Visayas.[4] Although overall levels are high, men's educational attainment appears to be slightly greater than women's (male heads have an average of ten years' schooling, whereas female heads and spouses have nine). It seems this is largely because a smaller proportion of women in the sample have had the opportunity to commence secondary (high-school) education (67 per cent of women compared with 91 per cent of men); moreover, men are more likely than women to have completed this schooling (23 per cent of all men in the sample have graduated from high school, compared with only 16 per cent of women). Gender differences in higher education at vocational colleges and universities are minimal, although more women (18 per cent) have attended vocational school than men (13 per cent), while men are more likely to have been to university (14 per cent) than women (12 per cent).[5]

---

4 Reyes Churchill (1993:7) points out that the island of Cebu boasts 6 universities, 39 colleges and nearly 1,200 private and public elementary schools.

5 Most poor Filipino children enter elementary education without the equivalent of kindergarten schooling (which is generally the preserve of the middle and upper classes) at the age of six or seven years. Elementary schooling usually lasts six years, at which stage a proportion proceed to high school. High school is based on a grade system, similar to that in the United States, with students having to pass exams in each of the four years in order to move on to the next grade. *Note continues on p. 88.*

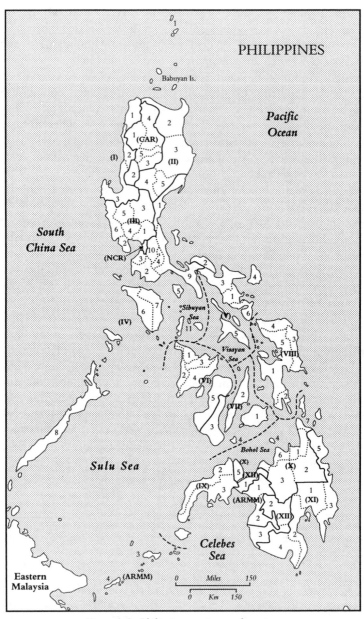

Figure 3.2: Philippines: regions and provinces

Key to Figure 3.2

National Capital Region (NCR)
Cordillera Autonomous Region (CAR)
1 Abra
2 Benguet
3 Ifugao
4 Kalinga Apayao
5 Mountain Province

Ilocos (I)
1 Ilocos Norte
2 Ilocos Sur
3 La Union
4 Pangasinan

Cagayan Valley (II)
1 Batanes
2 Cagayan
3 Isabela
4 Nueva Vizcaya
5 Quirino

Central Luzon (III)
1 Bataan
2 Bulacan
3 Nueva Ecija
4 Pampanga
5 Tarlac
6 Zambales

Southern Tagalog (IV)
1 Aurora
2 Batangas
3 Cavite
4 Laguna
5 Marinduque
6 Mindoro Occidental
7 Mindoro Oriental
8 Palawan
9 Quezon
10 Rizal
11 Romblon

Bicol (V)
1 Albay
2 Camarines Norte
3 Camarines Sur
4 Catanduanes
5 Masbate
6 Sorsogon

Western Visayas (VI)
1 Aklan
2 Antique
3 Capiz
4 Iloilo
5 Negros Occidental

Central Visayas (VII)
1 Bohol
2 Cebu
3 Negros Oriental
4 Siquijor

Eastern Visayas (VIII)
1 Leyte
2 Southern Leyte
3 Eastern Samar
4 Northern Samar
5 Western Samar

Western Mindanao (IX)
1 Basilan
2 Zamboanga del Norte
3 Zamboanga del Sur

Northern Mindanaos (X)
1 Agusan del Norte
2 Agusan del Sur
3 Bakidnon
4 Camiguin
5 Misamis Occidental
6 Misamis Oriental
7 Surigao del Norte

Southern Mindanao (XI)
1 Davao
2 Davao del Sur
3 Davao Oriental
4 South Cotabato
5 Surigao del Sur

Central Mindanao (XII)
1 Lanao del Norte
2 North Cotabato
3 Sultan Kudarat

Muslin Mindanao (ARMM)
1 Lanao del Sur
2 Maguindanao
3 Sulu
4 Tawi Tawi

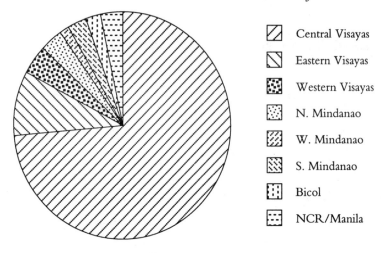

Legend:

- ▨ Central Visayas
- ◩ Eastern Visayas
- ▦ Western Visayas
- ▨ N. Mindanao
- ▨ W. Mindanao
- ▨ S. Mindanao
- ⬚ Bicol
- ⬚ NCR/Manila

Figure 3.3: Migrant origins of women by region: Cebu

Lapu-Lapu: Pusok

The study settlement in Lapu-Lapu, where interviews were held with 80 households, is located on the outskirts of the city in the northwest of Mactan Island, adjacent to Mactan Export Processing Zone, or MEPZ (see Fig. 3.5). Formally, the settlement is referred to as Sitio Pusok Seaside and is part of Barangay Pusok, although residents and locals usually refer to it simply as 'Pusok', using the names 'Pusok Seaside' and 'Pusok Roadside' to refer more specifically to parts of the settlement. Pusok is a linear development on a narrow piece of land between the coast and the Mactan circumferential road. Formed in 1988, Pusok's rapid growth has reflected the expanding need for housing by factory

---

Note 5 continued. Post-high-school courses range from short technical or vocational diplomas, usually not exceeding two years, in such subjects as secretarial work, mechanics and hairdressing, to short- or longer-term academic specialisms. The latter include business management/commerce and hotel and restaurant management, as well as engineering, English and so on. Two-year college courses are roughly equivalent to 'A' levels in the UK, whereas a degree equivalent to a BA or BSc in a British university would normally take five years in the Philippines. Grants are extremely scarce and few low-income people ever start, let alone complete, a university-level degree course (the small minority who do so have to fund themselves). However, it is relatively common for low-income people to follow vocational courses, which are shorter and more affordable (see also Tacoli, 1994).

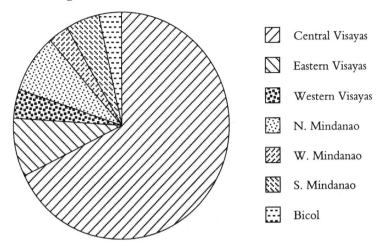

Central Visayas

Eastern Visayas

Western Visayas

N. Mindanao

W. Mindanao

S. Mindanao

Bicol

Figure 3.4: Migrant origins of men by region: Cebu

workers in the export processing zone. Out of a total of 850 inhabitants (approximately 150 households), three-quarters are squatters, 10 per cent are legal owners and the rest either rent or board (the latter are often factory workers). Pusok is a relatively well-serviced settlement; all residents have electricity and around 75 per cent have their own water connections. While parts of Pusok are overcrowded, there tends to be less pressure on land than in Cebu's settlements, with several houses being larger and interspersed with areas of scrubland. Around half of the houses are constructed with *nipa* palm, often on stilts because of flooding.

Households in Pusok follow broadly similar lines to those in Cebu: the majority are headed by men (89 per cent) and are nuclear in structure, with an average size of 5.7. Pusok also has the largest migrant population of the three study localities. This is probably because not only is it the youngest settlement, but its proximity to the export processing zone has undoubtedly attracted those in search of work. Among women, only 9 per cent were born in Lapu-Lapu itself; most of the rest were born in other areas of the Visayas, although a substantial minority (11 per cent) have come from more distant places, such as Bicol and Mindanao (see Figs 3.2 and 3.6). While the proportion of male migrants is also high (82 per cent), men are more likely to come from

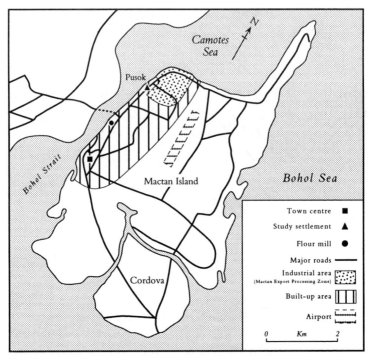

*Figure 3.5: Lapu-Lapu City: location of study settlement and
Mactan Export Processing Zone*

less further afield than women – over 60 per cent hail from Cebu
province and nearly 20 per cent from the other Central Visayan
provinces of Bohol and Negros Oriental (see Fig. 3.7).

The nature of employment in Pusok is, not surprisingly, heavily
influenced by the nearby export processing zone, and labour force participation rates for both men and women are higher than in Cebu. As
many as 92 per cent of men are employed full-time, with only 4 per
cent unemployed, 3 per cent retired and one man studying at university,
while two-thirds of women in Pusok work on a full-time basis (66
per cent), with one-quarter remaining in the home as housewives and
6 per cent currently looking for a job. Although no women work only
on a part-time basis, there are five who combine a full-time job with
another 'sideline' such as selling clothes (RTW) or Avon products,

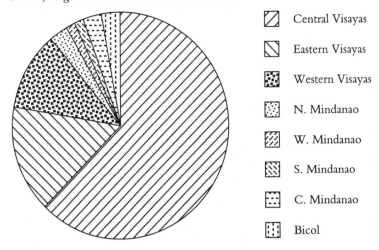

Figure 3.6: Migrant origins of women by region: Lapu-Lapu

or making and selling food such as *puso* ('hanging rice': a mixture of rice, milk and sugar wrapped in banana leaves).

Levels of education in Pusok are slightly lower than in Rubberworld, but again men's attainment appears to be higher. Although male and

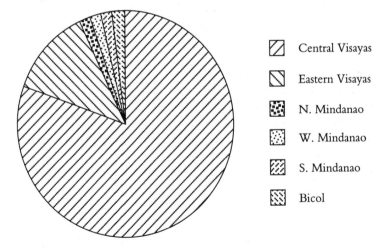

Figure 3.7: Migrant origins of men by region: Lapu-Lapu

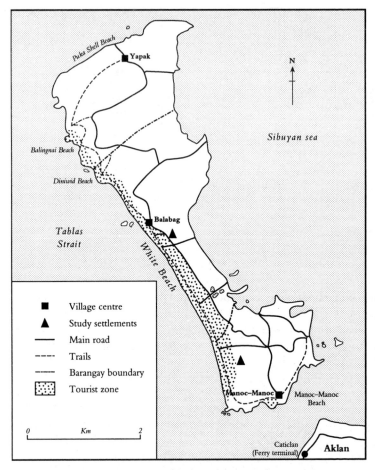

Figure 3.8: Boracay: location of study settlements and main tourist zone

female heads and spouses in Pusok have an average of eight years' schooling, disparities are marked in the sphere of higher education: 11 per cent of men have attended vocational college, compared with only 7 per cent of women, and 16 per cent of males have been to university, compared with 9 per cent of their female counterparts.

Boracay: Manoc-Manoc and Balabag

In the third study centre, Boracay, a survey of 60 households was carried out in sections of two of the island's three *barangays*: Manoc-Manoc and Balabag (specific settlements are not clearly differentiated on the island, hence portions of two *barangays* were chosen in the most urbanised area near the main tourist zone, 'Long Stretch', which lies behind White Beach – see Fig. 3.8). Both *barangays* are very similar in terms of general conditions and are therefore discussed as one. There are around 600 households in the area as a whole, with an approximate population of 4,000. Roughly 70 per cent of the households 'own' their land and the rest are renting, although the issue of land title tends to be contentious and many owners only have informal title, usually inherited from parents.[6] Three-quarters of the households have electricity, although frequent power cuts mean that everyone must depend to some degree on kerosene lamps. Most households also rely on deep wells and standpipes for water, with only 15 per cent having a domestic piped supply. The vast majority of houses are made from *nipa* palm and/or bamboo, with many raised slightly from the ground to guard against flooding. Living conditions are generally poor and overcrowded, with the average household size 6.6. While households in Boracay are also mainly headed by men (85 per cent), these are more likely to be extended than nuclear in form. Moreover, the migrant status of people is considerably different from that in the other two study centres, in that most men and women are natives of the island. Among women who have migrated (38 per cent), more than half are from the Western Visayas, mostly from Aklan province where Boracay itself is located, with a number from Antique and Iloilo (see Figs 3.2 and 3.9). Male migration patterns are broadly similar, with 43 per cent of men born outside Boracay, mostly in the Western Visayas (see Figs 3.2 and 3.10).

Employment in Boracay is heavily influenced by the tourist industry. Interestingly, men have the lowest participation rates of the three

---

6 Before the advent of tourist development on Boracay, no one had legal title to land. However, with mounting demand for plots on which to build hotels, restaurants and so on, land began to be sold on an informal basis. While plots are now bought and sold freely on the island, there are frequent disputes over title, usually involving various parties laying claim to land for which there is no legal documentation. However, natives of Boracay generally have recognised rights where they have not parted with land to commercial developers.

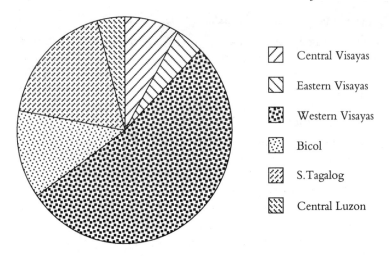

Figure 3.9: Migrant origins of women by region: Boracay

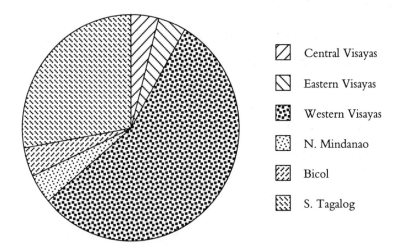

Figure 3.10: Migrant origins of men by region: Boracay

localities (84 per cent), while women have the highest (77 per cent), with a further 8 per cent working on a part-time basis – for instance, doing laundry. Indeed, the overall impression is that men here have much greater difficulty finding work than women do; even when men are employed, it is often the woman in the household who is the main breadwinner.

In terms of schooling, female heads and spouses are slightly better educated than their male counterparts, having an average of nine years' at school as against eight. Not only have a greater proportion of women (69 per cent) than men (62 per cent) gone on to high school, but of those who have, 59 per cent have graduated, compared with 57 per cent of men. Although the attainment of vocational diplomas is similar for both women and men, more women have been to university (9 per cent as against 6 per cent).[7]

Having outlined the basic characteristics of the settlements in terms of their physical structure and amenities, and general patterns of household organisation, migration and employment, the discussion now turns to examine the latter phenomena in more detail.

HOUSEHOLD CHARACTERISTICS IN CEBU, LAPU-LAPU AND BORACAY

Household Organisation in Rubberworld, Cebu

Marriage patterns in Rubberworld display high rates of legal unions; the vast majority of women in male-headed households are formally married (85 per cent). While this broadly corresponds with general norms in Filipino society (see Chapter 1), the proportion of women in consensual unions (15 per cent) is relatively high. Among those in informal partnerships, the main reason cited for not marrying legally was lack of funds (usually for the financing of a party/*fiesta*), although in a few cases women or men had been married before and, given the absence of legal divorce, had not been able to remarry. Among the women in legal unions, the importance of religion is underscored by

---

7 The overall proportion of the population with tertiary education is probably lower in Boracay than in Cebu and Lapu-Lapu because the island has no institute of further or higher education. Those wishing to study beyond high school must go to Kalibo in mainland Aklan (see Fig. 1.1).

the fact that 81 per cent had married in church (4 per cent of this number had also had a civil ceremony). The average age at which women married or began living with their partners is relatively young (22 years), although this is actually the oldest figure for the three study localities.

As for fertility, women have an average of 3.5 children each, although this includes women at early stages of their childbearing years who are likely to have more children in the future (indeed, a number of older women have had as many as ten children). Moreover, at least half of these women have lost one or more children in the past (mainly as infants). Obviously, the number of co-resident children in households in the sample is lower (2.8), since some have left home, although it is not uncommon to find households with four or five co-resident offspring.

As noted previously, the vast majority of households in Cebu are headed by men, with more nuclear than extended forms (see Figs 3.11 and 3.12). However, when female heads are considered too, extended households appear to be as common as nuclear homes (43 per cent and 44 per cent, respectively). The other 13 households in Rubber-world consist of female-headed one-parent structures (five cases), couple households, women living alone or with other childless women, brothers and sisters living together, and one case of a grandfather-headed household (see Fig. 3.12).

Considering extended households, one of the most striking observations is not only their large size (up to 16 people in some cases), but the wide range of additional members, including nephews, nieces, cousins, brothers, sisters and grandchildren. In instances where nephews and nieces are incorporated into households, they have invariably migrated from the home villages of either the male or female head or spouse to attend secondary school or college in the city. Not only are educational facilities better in Cebu City, but migrants can usually expect to receive some degree of financial support from their relatives. Fraternal kin (whether male or female), on the other hand, are usually migrants who come to Cebu in search of employment and on arrival are taken in because they cannot afford alternative accommodation. Once a job is secured, they may start to contribute to household finances, although this does not seem to be obligatory or expected. The shortage of affordable housing also accounts for household extension via the absorption of newly married couples who move in with parents and usually wait until after the birth of their first child before trying to find

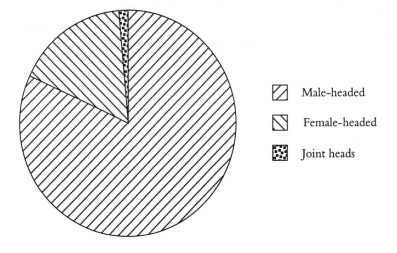

Figure 3.11: Household headship: Cebu

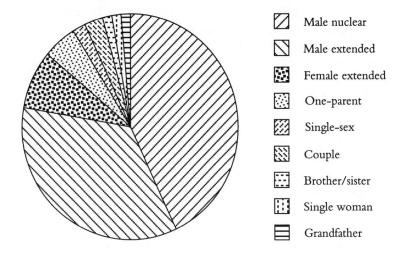

Figure 3.12: Household structure: Cebu

another place to live. In addition to this, the incorporation of grand-children into households is widespread in Rubberworld, even when their own parents do not live there.[8] The latter reflects a tradition of fostering in the Philippines whereby mothers or mothers-in-law are frequently asked to bring up children whose parents do not have the financial capacity to maintain them (see Chapter 1). It is also common for grandmothers to take in grandchildren when a daughter, or in some cases a son, has separated from a spouse, and is unable to support the offspring (see below).

Whatever the particular reasons for kin being incorporated under one roof, the driving force behind household extension in Cebu is that families invariably feel an obligation to help relatives who are worse-off, even if this means that they themselves are placed in tighter economic straits (see also Chapter 1). Having said this, it must also be recognised that household extension in Cebu is not always a drain on resources, and can ultimately bring benefits to host relatives. The example of Fernanda, who lives in a male-extended unit of 14 members, illustrates this point, highlighting how what may first appear to be one-off acts of goodwill are often part of a wider, on-going system of reciprocity. Fernanda is a migrant from Sibonga in Cebu province who lives with her husband, four children between the ages of 14 and 23 years and eight other household members, including a son-in-law, two grandchildren, four nieces and a nephew. Fernanda's husband is a *jeepney* driver[9] and she herself works part-time rearing pigs in the backyard. Apart from Fernanda and her husband, only their son-in-law contributes to the household expenses. While Fernanda admits that it is very expensive to support so many relatives, she observes there is little choice since she is the only family member from Sibonga living in the city; besides, it is only 'natural' for her to help out. Fernanda also claims, however, that benefits (or what she calls *utang na loob* - inner debt of gratitude) arise from helping relatives in that she receives around US $400 a month from a niece in Japan whom she supported to go to college eight years previously. Ironically, perhaps, Fernanda uses this additional income to finance the bed and board of other

---

8 The reason that more grandparent-headed households do not show up in the statistics is because extended households (where there may be grandchildren without their own parents) often include other parents and their children (see Appendix 1).
9 *Jeepneys* are converted 1950s US Army vehicles. They carry around 20 passengers and are the most common form of public transport in the Philippines.

nephews and nieces who are presently living with her, suggesting a certain continuity and self-reinforcement of this system over time. In the light of the previous discussion, it is perhaps not surprising that extended households tend to be more common among migrant households than those native to the city, although it must not be forgotten that even if kin do not actually live together, ties of reciprocity frequently extend beyond the boundaries of individual dwellings and, indeed, across considerable distances (see also below).[10]

Looking at households headed by women, which represent just under one-fifth of the total (see Fig. 3.11), two-thirds are de jure female heads who reside permanently without a male partner and one-third are de facto female heads who are temporarily separated from their menfolk. Of the de jure heads, just under half (five) are widows, four have never had a resident partner and two are permanently separated from their husbands. The women in de facto arrangements are those whose partners are usually working abroad, mainly as seamen, but in some instances in construction jobs in other parts of the Philippines. Although the overall number of female heads may appear to be relatively small, the percentage (17 per cent) is actually higher than that found in census figures for Cebu (14 per cent – see Chapter 2). Apart from this, there are a number of cases where 'solo parents' and their children reside within a larger extended unit and are effectively 'disguised' or 'submerged' (see Chapter 1; also Bradshaw, 1994, forthcoming; Buvinić and Gupta, 1993; Moser, 1993b; Varley, 1993). In many ways, the existence of embedded heads arises for the same basic reason as that which pertains to extended households in general: namely a sense of duty to support relatives in need. For example, just as newly wed couples often move into their parents' homes for reasons of economic exigency, lone parents whose financial position may be even more tenuous also turn to their natal home or that of other relatives if they are unable to survive as independent units. However, in the case of female lone parents, who are often referred to as 'unwed mothers', there is an

---

10 As noted in Chapter 1, inter-household kin ties are very strong in the Philippines. With reference to her work on highland communities in Benguet province, for example, Jean Peterson (1993:572–5) suggests there may be certain advantages in favouring extended family exchange *beyond* the household rather than extending household membership *per se*. The former allows people flexibility, whereas the latter can render the household vulnerable to shared failure (on account of being an isolated unit), as well as giving rise to conflict in interpersonal relations and inequalities in inputs and benefits that might have negative psychological and material consequences.

additional social stigma attached to bringing up children alone. As such, a single parent may be incorporated into an extended household so as to avoid becoming the subject of gossip, or what is referred to locally as *tsismis*.[11] In relation to these embedded households, it is also important to refer back to our earlier point about the incorporation of grandchildren into extended households: given the economic and social difficulties single parents face in surviving alone, fostering out to other relatives (usually their own parents) is the main alternative to actually moving back home themselves (see also Peterson, 1993). Whichever path is chosen, these practices may explain the relatively low incidence of independent one-parent households in Cebu and indeed in the settlements in the other two study localities too (see also Chapter 7).

Household organisation in Pusok, Lapu-Lapu

Marital status in Lapu-Lapu follows similar lines to Cebu in that 86 per cent of women in male-headed households are formally married, with 14 per cent living in informal partnerships. Those in consensual unions tend to be found among the poorest households in the sample, with financial stringency cited as the principal reason for lack of legalisation. Four-fifths of those in formal unions were married in a religious ceremony (8 per cent of whom had also had a civil wedding). Average age at marriage or cohabitation (21 years) is slightly younger than in Cebu. Women in Rubberworld have an average of 3.4 children, with 2.7 children actually resident at home, although again these are probably conservative figures given that many women have not yet completed their childbearing years.

As for household headship and composition, half of the 80 households interviewed in Pusok are nuclear and more than one-third are extended

11 The Cebuano term for gossip, *tsismis*, is derived from the Spanish word *chisme* meaning the same.

Social stigma also appears to apply to lone parents in other parts of the world. For example, Celia Mather (1988:150) shows in her work on Tangerang Regency of West Java, Indonesia, that women bearing children outside wedlock are perceived as 'immoral', which also helps to account for the fact that female heads had all been married at some point. She also observes that divorced or separated women are considered 'unfortunate', and that if they head their own households when still young, they are thought to be in a 'transitory state: "between husbands"' (ibid.:151). See also Casinader et al., (1987), on Sri Lanka, and Vera-Sanso, (1994), on Madras, India.

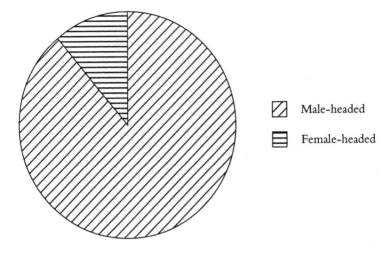

Figure 3.13: Household headship: Lapu-Lapu

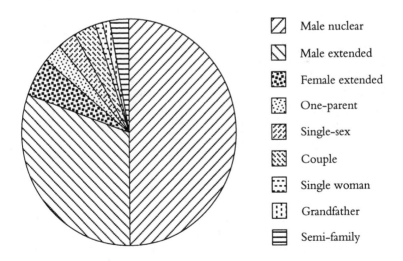

Figure 3.14: Household structure: Lapu-Lapu

units, of which only a small minority are headed by women (see Figs 3.13 and 3.14). A further 11 per cent of households are either female-headed one-parent structures, single-sex households, women living alone, couples, or grandfather-headed arrangements (see Fig. 3.14). The remaining two households in Pusok take the form of a 'semi-family' unit, whereby at least one member of the extended component is unrelated by blood or marriage (see Appendix).

The nature of extended households in Lapu-Lapu is characterised by similar levels of diversity as in Cebu, although for different reasons. The main one is that household extension in Pusok is almost invariably associated one way or another with employment connected to the export processing zone. For example, one-third of extended units in Pusok consist of relatives working in MEPZ factories. These are mainly young female relatives such as nieces or sisters who have migrated in search of employment, or who have already secured a job and prefer to live with relatives rather than rent a room in a boarding house. While male relatives such as nephews and cousins are also present in some extended households for similar reasons, they are more likely to work in a nearby flour mill rather than the export processing zone. The other most common form of household extension is where female kin join nuclear households to help with domestic responsibilities and childcare in cases where the female head or spouse is herself working, usually in factory employment. Indeed, a common pattern is where a young female relative comes to live in a household, ostensibly in the first instance to help with domestic chores, but with the additional intention of looking for factory work at a later date. The system of recruitment in most MEPZ factories (by recommendation or having what is referred to as a 'backer' – see Chapter 4) further encourages this type of household extension, in that friends or relatives of existing employees are often favoured. It is also interesting to note that household extension is only found among the migrant population in Pusok.

The proportion of households headed by women is relatively small in Pusok, with only nine women (11 per cent) living without male partners. Of this group, two are widowed, three have never been married and the rest are de facto heads (three have male partners working overseas, in Kuwait, Saudi Arabia and Japan; the fourth's partner works in another part of Cebu province). A number of embedded female heads also exist, and in these cases the chief rationale seems to be the

rural areas. The final type of extension, most prevalent among non-migrant households, is the incorporation of sons- or daughters-in-law, who cannot afford to rent or buy independent accommodation with their spouses (see also the section on Cebu). This probably explains why the average ages of heads and spouses are higher in extended households (44 and 41 years respectively), than in nuclear structures (35 and 33 years). As in Cebu and Lapu-Lapu, the incorporation of kin may also bring benefits to households. One interesting example in Balabag is the case of Cherry, who has three young children aged between nine months and five years. At the time of the survey, Cherry's husband had pneumonia and had not been able to work for eight months. Although Cherry herself managed to get a temporary job as a waitress during the high season, since that ended, her husband's brother (a labourer constructing tourist cottages) has moved in to help with household finances.

Out of a total of 15 per cent of households headed by women in Boracay (see Fig. 3.15), half the heads are widows, one had left her husband after repeated infidelity on his part and three are temporarily separated from their partners. Of these de facto female heads, two have husbands working in Manila and one has a Swedish husband who has returned to Scandinavia for a while. There are also three embedded female heads, all of whom reside in their parents' homes. Two of these women are de facto heads with partners working in Manila and Singapore, and both have always lived with their parents, even when their husbands return. The other, who has three children by different fathers, is unemployed and unable to survive independently. Perhaps more than anywhere, the difficulties involved in women forming their own households are most strongly emphasised in Boracay. While this may be associated with high levels of formal marriage and reluctance to separate on religious grounds, many women in the interviews gave more specific reasons such as fear of retribution from friends and neighbours, the notion of causing a 'scandal', or anxiety that children would suffer from lack of a father.

These factors obviously also apply in Cebu and Lapu-Lapu and help to explain why the great majority of households in all localities are male-headed. Extended households are also extremely widespread, their high numbers reflecting a general commitment to reciprocity and support of relatives outside the immediate family. While households headed by women represent a comparatively small proportion of the total, the phenomenon of embedded woman heads illustrates that they may be more prevalent than first appears. However, the existence of the latter also illustrates the economic and social difficulties faced by women who might wish to establish independent units (see also Chapter 7).

Having noted these similarities, it is important to highlight the fact that household extension (whether with related or non-related members) is not only more likely in Lapu-Lapu and Boracay than in Cebu, it is also much more directly associated with reasons of employment: this is undoubtedly due to the fact that Cebu is able to offer considerable education as well as employment opportunities (see note 4 above), meaning that people come there with a broader range of motives. Indeed, as we have seen, many of Cebu's extended households contain young school or college age relatives. In Lapu-Lapu and Boracay, on the other hand, household extension either revolves around the search for employment on the part of incoming members, or on the host households' need for relatives to assist with domestic labour where female heads or spouses are themselves working. At this point it is appropriate to turn our attention to details of employment in the localities.

EMPLOYMENT AND INCOME IN CEBU, LAPU-LAPU AND BORACAY

Employment and income in Rubberworld, Cebu

Cebu's position as the most diversified economy of the three study areas (see Chapter 2) is borne out by the variety of occupations in which residents of Rubberworld are engaged. Although a number (eleven) of men and women are employed in the nearby Rubberworld factory (8 per cent of the total working male and female heads and spouses in the settlement), this by no means dominates the local occupational structure: not only are people involved in other types of manufacturing work, they also run *sari-sari* stores, buy and sell fighting cocks, rent out stud pigs and operate small gambling businesses from home. More specifically, for the male household heads in the settlement the most common form of employment is in manufacturing (41 per cent), ranging from salaried work in shoe factories (principally Rubberworld), cement factories, furniture-making and food-processing plants, to involvement in piecework and small-scale manufacturing at home. This is followed by transport work (21 per cent – mainly consisting of *jeepney* and taxi drivers), then retail and commerce (usually white-collar clerical and sales work) and, finally, artisanal enterprises such as carpentry.

Among the female heads and spouses in Cebu, most (36 per cent) are employed in manufacturing (factory and home-based piecework), followed by retail and commerce, which employs almost another third (31 per cent). The remainder are employed in public and private services (17 per cent), or in finance and real estate (14 per cent), the latter consisting mainly of women who rent out rooms. Within these categories, a major distinction can be drawn between occupations which are based at home and extra-domestic paid work. Indeed, the majority of full-time workers are involved in home-based activities (68 per cent), where the single most common job is piecework or outwork (17 per cent of the total of full-time female workers). This type of enterprise involves women making shellcraft items such as hanging baskets, cutting straps for shoes, or stringing necklaces and earrings for local fashion accessory firms (see also Chapter 4). They are paid on a piece-rate basis and the home-based nature of the work affords them greater scope to manage domestic and childcare responsibilities than they would have as factory operatives. Indeed, this undoubtedly explains the fact that piecework is a predominantly female domain: although a few men (5 per cent) do outwork, they are generally older or in the process of searching for another job, and therefore tend to see the activity as a 'stop-gap' only. Given the purported advantages of working at home, it follows that other common female occupations include taking in laundry, cutting hair and giving manicures, running *sari-sari* stores and *carinderias*, and renting out rooms. Only 10 per cent of women are factory workers, with a similar proportion working in white-collar or teaching jobs, and a small number in shops and restaurants (see Fig. 3.17).

Since home-based activities almost invariably generate less income than more formal types of employment, it is not surprising that the earnings of women workers are considerably lower than those of their male counterparts. Average female weekly earnings are less than half of those earned by men (P312 [US$12.40] per week, compared with P696 [$27.80]), and also lower than the general minimum weekly wage of P630 ($25.20)[12] prescribed by law. Having said this, there are extremely wide variations in women's incomes. While *sari-sari* store

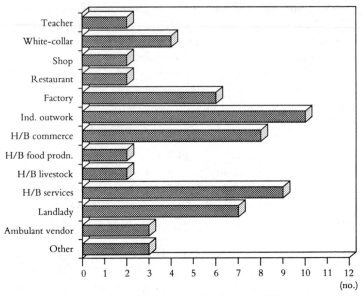

Figure 3.17: Female occupational groups: Cebu

Note: H/B is an abbreviation for home-based. Home-based commerce generally refers to
sari-sari stores; home-based food production to *carenderias* (snack bars/small eateries) or to
neighbourhood selling of cooked foodstuffs; home-based livestock generally refers to pig-
breeding or chicken-rearing, while home-based services usually consist of taking in laundry
or sewing, or providing beauty treatments such as manicures and haircuts.

owners earn an average of only P210 ($8.40) a week, and pieceworkers
as little as P179 ($7.20), female factory workers receive an average weekly
salary of P858 ($34.30).

Regardless of the fact that so many women in Rubberworld are
engaged in low-profit activities, it is important to note that their high
rates of labour force participation reflect a general acceptance that they
should work if they so wish. In the in-depth interviews carried out
with ten women in the settlement, for example, male partners were
rarely noted for restricting women's involvement in the labour force,
especially if additional sources of income were essential to the

12 Peso earnings are rounded up to the nearest whole number and US dollar equiva-
lents to one decimal point. The exchange rate is based on 25 Philippine pesos to US$1.
Although the value of the peso fluctuated during the period of the fieldwork, 25 pesos
is taken as an average.

household's survival. However, there is little doubt that limited flexibility for women, in terms of shedding responsibilities for housework and childcare, impinges heavily on their ability to take paid work, something which is clearly reflected when considering the age differences of women in different types of occupation. For example, the average age of the 17 women employed in factory and white-collar jobs is 34 years, with most between their late 20s and late 30s. In contrast, women running *sari-sari* stores are likely to be older (the average age is 46 years), while those involved in other home-based services have an average age of 40. The work histories which were traced in detail for ten women in the settlement provide a number of explanations for these patterns. A general picture emerges whereby young single women invariably engage in some form of paid employment upon leaving school or college, often in factories, restaurants or commercial establishments. During this time they make significant financial contributions to their parents' households, either directly (in the case of co-resident daughters) or through remittances (in the case of migrant women). Upon marriage, women usually continue working until they have their first child, after which they withdraw from the labour force because of domestic responsibilities. During the period when children are young, however, many women may engage intermittently in piecework as this does not disrupt their domestic routine. Once children have started school, women often take up paid employment outside the home again, not only because childcare becomes less intensive but because money is needed to finance their education. By their 40s, women again seem to retreat to home-based activities, sometimes because they have saved some capital with which to start a small business, but more usually because it becomes extremely difficult to find jobs in the formal sector (see Chapters 4 and 5).

The primary responsibility of women for reproductive work probably also helps to explain why migrant women are less likely to have a job than non-migrants (57 per cent as against 65 per cent). Although much of the literature argues that female migrants are usually more economically active than natives (see Chapter 1), this could relate to the young age structure of target occupational groups in other surveys. In the context of Rubberworld, on the other hand, a relatively long-established settlement with a fairly mature population, many migrant women who perhaps worked when they first moved to the city are now no longer able to do so. For example, after marriage and childbirth it may be more difficult for female migrants to secure jobs than natives because they have fewer relatives or friends to whom to delegate domestic responsibilities. Additionally, migrant women may have fewer contacts through which they can obtain work once their children have grown up (as is the case in the majority of households). Finally, they may have more problems in accumulating capital to set up small home-based businesses because of the constraints of sending remittances to home areas or supporting relatives resident in the household itself.

Employment and income in Pusok, Lapu-Lapu

Given the proximity of Pusok settlement to the Mactan Export Processing Zone, the occupational structure of Pusok is dominated either by factory work itself, or by informal businesses catering for factory operatives. Indeed, a total of 59 MEPZ factory workers (including production workers, guards and janitors) are found among heads, spouses and other household members in the Pusok survey, of whom two-thirds are women (61 per cent). Of the male heads in Pusok, around half (49 per cent) are employed in manufacturing, mainly in the export processing zone, although a large number also work in Lapu-Lapu's flour mill. Aside from factory work, a number of men (11 per cent) are employed in manual jobs indirectly associated with MEPZ, such as construction work (building factories in the Zone, for example). Another common sector of work is transport (14 per cent), usually involving the driving of motorised tricycles which are the main form of public transport in the city, as well as being the only public vehicles allowed inside the export processing zone.

Although a large proportion of women heads and spouses in Pusok are employed in manufacturing (38 per cent), with the majority in factory work in MEPZ, a marginally higher percentage (42 per cent) are in retail and commerce (42 per cent), with the remaining women working in public and private services, or in finance and real estate (see Fig. 3.18). Having said this, many of the commercial occupations are related to factory employment: some women set up *carinderias* inside the zone to serve lunches to factory workers; others work as ambulant vendors, selling snacks and cigarettes to workers as they enter or leave the factories. In addition, many women profit from Pusok's proximity to the Zone by renting out rooms to factory operatives; or, in the case of households in Pusok Roadside, by opening *sari-sari* stores and *carin-*

derias which serve factory workers as well as settlement residents. Although the majority of female occupations are associated in some way with MEPZ, a few women are also employed in unrelated activities such as fish-vending (see Fig. 3.18).

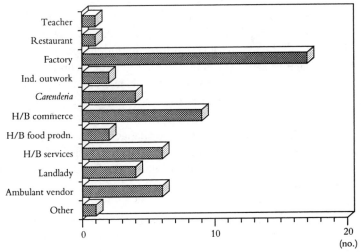

Figure 3.18: Female occupational groups: Lapu-Lapu

While earnings among working women in Pusok are around half the average of men's (P436 [US$17.40] per week, compared with P840 [$33.60]), variations inevitably arise in accordance with occupational branch and category. The highest-paying branch of female employment is manufacturing, where weekly earnings as a whole are P659 ($26.40), and in MEPZ factories, P710 ($28.40). The lowest-paid jobs are, perhaps not surprisingly, those based at home, such as renting out rooms, where average earnings are only P240 per week ($9.60), although earnings from other commercial enterprises such as *sari-sari* stores are considerably higher at P446 per week ($17.80). It is also important to point out that among women working in factories, the majority of those in male-headed households earn more than their partners and hence are the main, and sometimes sole, breadwinners in the home.

As in Cebu, the issue of age is important in influencing female occupational differentiation. For example, MEPZ factory workers are on average 28 years old, while the average age of women involved in home-based activities is 38 years. However, one major difference between the cities is that once factory employment is secured by women in Lapu-Lapu (usually in their early 20s), they continue to work right through until their late 30s, primarily because their childcare and domestic responsibilities are delegated elsewhere. In other words, women in Lapu-Lapu tend to have a much less interrupted run of formal employment lasting up to 15–20 years. The reasons why they eventually withdraw from the industrial labour force in middle age (as in Cebu), is because factory employers tend to prefer younger women and may sometimes encourage (if not explicitly) older women to leave (see Chapter 4), or, more usually, because women themselves have accumulated sufficient capital to set up their own home-based business. The latter is likely to prove a welcome change to the onerous nature of assembly work, although women's generally longer spell of industrial employment in Lapu-Lapu is probably due to the fact that MEPZ jobs are more privileged than those in other types of factories in terms of guaranteed minimum salaries and fringe benefits (see Chapter 4). In other words, the gains from MEPZ employment seem to outweigh the comparative advantages of premature withdrawal to the home.

Employment and income in Manoc-Manoc and Balabag, Boracay

While the economy of Boracay is almost entirely dominated by tourism (see Chapter 2), the employment characteristics of those included in the household survey reflect the informal nature of tourist-related activities rather than formal occupations in hotels, restaurants and so on (see Chapter 5). Among male heads, a relatively high proportion are either unemployed, sick or retired (16 per cent), compared with the other study areas (10 per cent in Cebu and 6 per cent in Lapu-Lapu). Among men in work, the largest branch of employment is transport (40 per cent), with most driving motorbike-taxis, the chief form of public transport on the island for both residents and tourists (see Chapter 5). Other male transport workers are employed on cargo and ferry boats operating between Boracay and Caticlan (see Fig. 3.8). While some men help in family businesses such as *sari-sari* stores, most of the rest are involved in construction (building or maintenance of tourist cottages) and fishing, which again is linked to both the local and tourist markets.

As mentioned earlier, women in Boracay have extremely high rates of labour force participation (77 per cent), of which the majority are involved in some form of commerce (63 per cent). As Fig. 3.19 shows, the latter are predominantly home-based activities such as running *sari-sari* stores (18 per cent) or small *carinderias* (14 per cent). (In Boracay the latter sell such items as *lankuga* [a porridge of bananas and cassava], *bitso-bitso* [deep-fried cassava], and 'sticky rice' [wet rice fried in sugar on skewers].) While these small establishments cater predominantly for the local population, especially the *carinderias*, which mainly serve lunches to schoolchildren, both also profit considerably from tourism. Not only are *sari-sari* stores the principal retail outlets on the island, but both these and *carinderias* provide convenience services for other female tourism workers (for example, food and beverages sold by these outlets often save valuable meal preparation time for women working long hours in hotels and restaurants). Other commercial activities include ambulant vending or ownership of small souvenir shops in the local market, the former including the sale of *bangus fry* (sprats), fruit and vegetables and 'relief clothing' to locals (second-hand clothes sent from developed countries as aid, yet sold to individuals in the Philippines). A number of people also work in local restaurants (see Fig. 3.19). Apart from commerce, other service occupations such as sewing or laundry are common sources of income generation, as well as home-based handicraft production – for instance, making wicker baskets or shellcraft items. As with *sari-sari* stores, these jobs are often associated with the tourism industry: for example, laundry women may receive work from small hotels and cottages, while those involved in handicraft manufacture may sell their produce to tourist shops and hotels, or to beachfront vendors (see also Chapter 5).

Not only are women in Boracay more likely to be involved in paid employment than is the case in the other localities, they have much higher weekly earnings. In addition, their average wage is significantly greater than that of men on the island (P741 [US$29.60] a week, compared with P642 [$25.70]). Commercial jobs are the highest remunerated (averaging P1,334 per week [$53.30], with two women earning as much as P7,000 ($280) – one in a *sari-sari* store, the other buying and selling *bangus* fry. Even in handicraft production (the lowest paying branch of activity), women still earn as much as P350

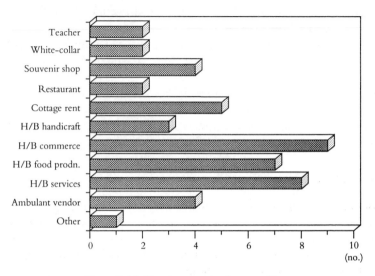

Figure 3.19: Female occupational groups: Boracay

per week ($14), which is higher than in Cebu or Lapu-Lapu for most home-based activities.

Unlike Cebu and Lapu-Lapu, there are few variations in terms of age-employment patterns in Boracay. For example, both housewives and paid workers are on average 37 years old, with no concentration in any particular age group; neither is there any significant difference between workers in home-based activities and those working outside the home (although see Chapter 5; also Chant, 1993b, forthcoming b, on specific occupational groups). The fact that most women are involved in paid employment, regardless of their domestic responsibilities or changing household arrangements, may be due to two things: first, the relatively low employment rates of men in Boracay; and second, the fact that women often earn high wages on the island. Indeed, in more than half the cases of male-headed families women earn more than men; they are the sole breadwinners in eight out of 51 households. In view of the fact that men appear unable to maintain their households single-handedly (or at all, in some instances), it might accordingly be necessary for women to engage in some form of paid work.

Indeed, one feature common to all three localities is that women's employment is rarely predicated on personal imperatives, such as a desire for economic independence or self-fulfilment, or to provide a break from domestic routine. Instead, employment is almost always family-oriented: in the early stages of the life-cycle, single women work to help their natal families; at later stages, employment is taken to supplement partners' incomes and to ensure that children have a 'good education' – something which is always cited as a major rationale for working.

The effects of recession on low-income households in the Visayas

Before going on to consider migration in the three localities, it is important to consider the effects of recession on Visayan households, and the way these might have intensified women's needs to engage in remunerated work (see also Chapter 1). Although the general impression from the household surveys is that economic survival has always been difficult for low-income people in the various localities, most women noted an exacerbation of their difficulties over the previous five to ten years. All 30 female respondents in our in-depth household interview survey, for example, highlighted the rising prices of basic foodstuffs such as rice and milk, the increased costs of utilities (mainly electricity) and education (largely because schools increasingly depend on parents to provide funds for project assignments). Responses by women to deteriorating conditions have involved attempts both to curtail consumption and to increase income. In respect of the former, women have made dietary adjustments such as reducing the amount of meat consumed in family meals, switching to cheaper products like dried fish or vegetables, or missing out breakfast in the morning. They have also tried to conserve the use of water and electricity and to eliminate expenditure on 'luxuries' such as cosmetics and electrical appliances (see Chant, forthcoming a). In respect of attempts to increase income, some women have entered the labour force for the first time or have resumed employment; of those women already in work, many have taken on additional jobs or sidelines. Although respondents usually expressed a desire to secure a formal sector job, especially in Cebu and Lapu-Lapu, most complained of a lack of opportunities, particularly for older women. As a result, most have been forced into creating new sources of income for themselves such

as making and selling food, or renting out rooms (see Chant, forthcoming a). Notwithstanding the difficulties of establishing causality on
the basis of retrospective data, it would appear that recession has contributed to an increase in women's already high labour force participation
in the Visayas, with a 12 per cent rise in labour force participation
between 1986 and 1993 among the sub-sample of 30 women interviewed in the three localities, and 30 per cent of the women already
working having taken on new sidelines in addition to their existing
jobs (ibid.).

MIGRATION AND SOURCE-DESTINATION LINKAGES IN CEBU, LAPU-LAPU AND BORACAY

Having outlined household and employment characteristics in the three
study areas, we now move on to look at patterns of migration in more
detail.

Migration patterns in Rubberworld, Cebu

Bearing in mind that just over three-quarters of all male and female
household heads and spouses in Rubberworld, Cebu, are migrants,
the vast majority of these came originally from rural areas within the
Central Visayas, and more particularly from Cebu province. Among
female migrants, around three-quarters (76 per cent) have come
directly from their birthplaces; of the remainder, one-third were
previously living in Manila, one-quarter in other parts of Cebu
province and the rest in various provinces in the Central and Western
Visayas and Mindanao. Two-thirds of the direct female migrants are
from farming communities, where their families owned smallholdings
of 1–3 hectares. Two-thirds of these cultivated cash crops such as rice,
maize, cassava, bananas and coconuts (the latter sold as copra made
from the fibrous material inside the shell), while the rest were small
subsistence farms growing similar crops, but with the addition of fruits
(for example, star apples and jack fruit) and livestock (mainly pigs, goats
and carabao [water buffalo]). The remaining third of direct migrants
came from tenant farms. Regardless of crop type or landholding, the
general impression given of livelihood in these areas was one of life

conducted very much on a 'hand-to-mouth' basis, with few opportunities to make a decent wage (if any), especially among women. Indeed, nearly half the women who had migrated from rural areas had been involved in unpaid farm labour, either as children or adults, where this was considered part of the daily routine of domestic chores (see also Pineda-Ofreneo, 1985:19–20). Against this backdrop, it is perhaps hardly surprising that rural–urban migration is so prevalent.

While poverty and lack of employment in rural areas certainly contribute to migration, perceptions of what the city has to offer are also highly influential. The average age of female migrants on arrival in Cebu was 15 years, with the largest single group coming by themselves (34 per cent) or with other relatives such as an aunt or a female cousin (15 per cent). A smaller proportion (12 per cent) came with their husbands, usually soon after they had married. The rest came with varying combinations of spouses, children and other relatives. Among women who came to the city with husbands and/or their children, migration was usually a shared decision. Among women who came to the city alone, on the other hand, most stressed that they had made the decision themselves, although the fact that they often sent remittances back to home areas means that parental pressures probably had some part to play (see below). Indeed, in a number of cases respondents stated that a father or mother had encouraged them to find work in the city in order to help support the family. For example, Cristina, a migrant from Naga in Cebu province, came to Cebu at the age of 17 to find a job, primarily to help her mother, whose husband had left home when Cristina was only eight years old. As the eldest of three children, Cristina felt it was her duty to help, and after a childhood selling fruit at the local market in Naga she responded to her mother's suggestion that she go to Cebu City to find a higher paying job. On acquiring a position in a restaurant where bed and board was provided, she sent all but a tiny fraction of her wages back home and continued to do so until she married.

The reasons for moving to Cebu City relate to employment and income in more than half the cases, with educational and family factors accounting for most of the remainder. More specifically, the majority of female migrants had come in search of employment or to take up a job that had already been offered to them (usually through a relative), while others had come to study at high school or college, or to join relatives. Occasionally, women also migrated to find a 'love-match' in the city, to delay the possibility of early marriage, or to remove a spouse from a lover or mistress (see Chapter 1). Overall, however, the general impression is that women had few opportunities for making a living in their areas of origin, and perceived a move to Cebu City as a means of ensuring their own survival as well as that of kin who stayed behind. Once established in the city, most women meet their husbands and decide to remain there to bring up their children, given that opportunities for education and employment are better than in home areas. At this point links with areas of origin tend to weaken (see also Chapter 7).

On the question of linkages between urban and rural areas, we have noted that women are often encouraged by parents to move to Cebu. In these instances, and indeed even when women apparently make an independent decision to migrate, the sending of remittances of some sort is widespread. Women who migrate when still single tend to send the majority of their wages back to home areas and retain only a minimum for basic survival in the city. This is especially the case when they work as *yayas* (domestic helpers) or as restaurant workers, since both are 'live-in' jobs with minimal living costs (see also Chapter 5; the case of Cristina mentioned earlier). Women usually continue to send money to home areas until they marry, after which financial support becomes less regular or stops altogether, due to the economic pressure of raising children. Only 30 per cent of migrant households in Rubber-world send help on anything like a regular basis to other relatives; instead of money, they often send food. This usually means sending sacks of rice (worth P500 [US$20]) back home once a month or so, or taking the rice with them when they visit once every three or four months. The fact that support is more likely to be sent to relatives of women rather than men suggests that women feel a greater sense of obligation to help out (see Chapter 1). Indeed, in in-depth interviews women frequently mentioned that their migrant brothers rarely helped their parents as they did (see also Trager, 1988:83).

Also worth noting is that support may come from relatives in rural home areas, usually in the form of childcare by grandparents. This tends to arise when migrant women in the city work outside the home but are unable to pay childminders and/or do not have any neighbours or friends willing to help out. Alternatively, when women have several children fostering one or more to grandparents may be the only way to ease economic pressure. In a couple of cases too women had sent their children to grandparents because they considered life in Cebu, with its high rates of crime and drug abuse, to be dangerous, and they imagined their children would have a healthier upbringing in the countryside. Although child support is the most important form of help from home areas, it is not uncommon for food, especially vegetables grown on family farms, to be sent to urban relatives.

Migration patterns in Lapu-Lapu

As noted at the beginning of this chapter, Pusok's population is almost entirely made up of migrants (87 per cent), although there are more female migrants than male (91 per cent, as against 82 per cent) and women have come from further afield. The reasons for this are probably related to the fact that demand for labour in the Mactan Export Processing Zone is selective of women (see also Chapter 4). Indeed, over 60 per cent of female migrants came because of employment or income factors, with the rest moving for family reasons (to join either a husband, partner or other relatives). Among more specific reasons for migration, most women came either to look for a job, to take up a position already secured, or to be closer to their place of work. Indeed, with regard to the latter, 55 per cent of female migrants had lived in another place (apart from where they were born) before moving to Lapu-Lapu, with almost half migrating first to Cebu City or Mandaue City (46 per cent), or to other areas near to Metro Cebu (13 per cent). In other words, movement to Pusok is most likely to be part of a process of migrating in stages. Perhaps because of this, migrants to Lapu-Lapu are not only more likely to be older on arrival than is the case in Cebu, with an average age of 24 years, but are less likely to arrive alone (only 14 per cent). Most migrants to Lapu-Lapu tend to come with friends or relatives with whom they have shared lodgings in Cebu City (22 per cent), or with their husbands and children (28 per cent), with the rest accompanied by other combinations of relatives. Migration to Lapu-Lapu is usually permanent, although a significant number of women expressed a desire to move back to Cebu City in the event of losing their present jobs.

Looking at links retained with migrant source areas in Lapu-Lapu, similar patterns emerge to those in Cebu in that around 30 per cent of households send support to home areas, mainly in the form of financial remittances but sometimes of foodstuffs. Similarly, support to home areas comes almost entirely from women, usually those in factory employment (and even where men too have well-paid manufacturing jobs). This again corroborates the idea that women demonstrate greater obligation towards their natal families. Moreover, links with source areas, as in Cebu, are stronger when women are single. Receipt of support from home areas, however, appears to be less common: for example, only a small number of women have sent their children back home. The low incidence of child fostering from Lapu-Lapu is probably because many households have incorporated female relatives to take over childcare responsibilities from working mothers (see above). Related to this, migrant destination and source linkages in Lapu-Lapu are mostly maintained through the incorporation of relatives from home areas, where the provision of shelter and help in finding work is often repaid, if not directly, then by reciprocal assistance in domestic tasks and childraising in situ.

Migration patterns in Manoc-Manoc and Balabag, Boracay

The proportion of migrants in Boracay (41 per cent of the sample population in the settlements) is the smallest among the three study localities and the nature of migration is also distinct. While the number of female migrants who came to Boracay as single women on their own (22 per cent) is higher than in Lapu-Lapu, it is lower than in Cebu. Among this group, most came initially to look for a job or to take up a position in a tourist establishment (where friends or relatives had fixed this up – see Chapter 5). They then met their husbands (often migrants working in the same establishment) and decided to settle on the island. The majority of female migrants to Boracay (61 per cent), however, arrived with husbands and/or children in their late 20s (the average age was 27 years). Of these women, half are married to native Boracaynons, whom the majority had met while working in Manila or other parts of Aklan. The decision to move back to Boracay is usually fuelled by a desire to set up a small business such as a *sari-sari* store in anticipation of profits to be made from the international tourist market, or alternatively because husbands own land on the island which may be sold for further capital or, more commonly, used to build a house. The other half of female migrants to Boracay were accompanied by a migrant partner, again with the aim of establishing a small business.

As for links between migrant households and home areas, the sending of support is the most frequent among the three study localities (43 per cent), with most remitting money every one to three months. As in Cebu, the vast majority of assistance is sent to the home areas of female migrants, with only two men remitting to natal families. While the reasons are undoubtedly due in part to women's greater sense of obligation to kin, their high employment rates and earnings are also important. The receipt of support from home areas, on the other hand, is minimal except in one or two cases of childcare. An interesting example is that of Princessita, a migrant from Numancia, Aklan, who has a well-paid job as a restaurant cashier but, since she works eight hours a day, has little time to look after her only daughter, Juna May, who is one year old. To cope with the situation, she and her mother have developed a very flexible arrangement: every three or four weeks her mother either comes to Boracay to look after Juna May, or takes her back to Numancia, depending on Princessita's work commitments. It is not only the flexibility of this system that is interesting, but the fact that Princessita turns to her mother (rather than paying a local child-minder) despite the onerous long-distance commuting involved. It also suggests to some degree that family ties may prevail over residential propinquity, in that women may prefer to entrust children to family members rather than strangers.

Summarising the main features of female migration to the study localities, most women move to obtain work and/or to improve earnings: in Cebu and Lapu-Lapu, migrants usually seek employment in factories and/or restaurants, whereas those in Boracay tend to be more interested in setting up their own businesses (see Chapters 4 and 5). Variations also apply to the characteristics of movers, with most going to live in Cebu being young and single, those in Lapu-Lapu being older and accompanied by husbands and young families, and those in Boracay being older still. The process of migration is also distinct in each area, with most migrants to Cebu moving directly from rural areas to the city; the majority to Lapu-Lapu coming as part of a stage in migration via nearby centres such as Cebu or Mandaue; and most to Boracay also coming as second-stage migrants, but from places further afield such as Manila. The other distinguishing feature of female migrants in Boracay is that most are accompanied by husbands native to the island. Although husbands have also migrated, when they marry it seems that access to land and other resources associated with kin groups figure importantly in their decision to return. Migration to all areas is usually permanent, whether the women were single or married at the time of arrival. In the case of the former, the meeting of husbands in destination areas usually ties them to the locality, especially when making a living is difficult in their places of origin. As for women who are already married, the fact that migration decisions have usually been taken jointly means that there has probably been a fairly comprehensive range of family-related factors which have stimulated movement. In all localities, links with home areas appear to be maintained via the sending of money or food, by receiving relatives from source areas into the household (and often assuming responsibility for all their living costs) and, in Cebu in particular, through the fostering of children to parents in the provinces. With the exception of incorporating kin, these ties are more likely to be maintained by women than men, notwithstanding the fact that links with natal families often weaken over time as priorities shift towards the needs of immediate dependents.

Migrant source areas: the effects of female out-migration

Although a general impression of conditions in rural source areas was given earlier, a survey of 20 households carried out in Naga, Cebu province, and in Magsaysay, Dauin, Negros Oriental province, highlights the effect of female out-migration on rural communities (see Fig. 3.2 and Appendix). Migration from both Naga and Dauin is strongly selective of young and usually single women, although in both communities married women and men also migrate. The major destination from Naga is Cebu City; and Dauin it is Cebu City and overseas (Canada, the United States and the Middle East), with most migration occurring because of employment. Although the sample sizes are small, household structures in Naga and Dauin appear to follow broadly similar patterns to those outlined for Cebu, Lapu-Lapu and Boracay, although more than half the households are extended in both areas and their members are usually larger in number and older than in the three study localities. For example, average household size is seven in Naga and six in Dauin, while household heads in the former are on average 48 years old, and in the latter 51 years old. The existence of older households suggests that the population in these areas is becoming increasingly elderly as young people migrate elsewhere and rarely return.

Turning to the more specific effects of female out-migration on the communities, the two source areas provide interesting contrasts concerning perceived benefits and/or disadvantages. In Naga, for example, the migration of women is considered largely detrimental to local society, especially where children are left behind. Even if grandmothers play a role in children's upbringing and fathers remain present in the community, boys and girls are seen as suffering from a lack of proper parental guidance. As one respondent noted, 'The man takes the position of the wife ... but men are bad at looking after children.' Indeed, the effects on the male population remaining in the community are generally seen as extremely negative, even when it is single women with no children who migrate. Men tend to remain unemployed and often turn to drugs or drink as a means of assuaging feelings of inadequacy and loneliness. They are also likely to be economically dependent on parents, even if some continue to help on family farms. One respondent noted that when men do find paid employment, they tend to 'show off', boasting to neighbours that they are capable of holding down a job. In terms of dealing with the absence of young women, single men in search of 'marriage partners' either look to other communities, marry later (some female migrants return to home areas), or in certain instances migrate to the city themselves. Perhaps one reason for these predominantly negative attitudes towards female out-migration is that the receipt of remittances or other support from migrants is rather modest. While half the households receive either money, food or clothes, these do not amount to great deal; a number of respondents said they wished they received more, even though they knew that city life was expensive.

In Dauin, by contrast, female out-migration (whether of single or married women) is viewed in a more positive light, largely because many have migrated abroad and are able to send substantial amounts of money back to the community. It is not only individual families that benefit (in two instances, almost 100 per cent of household income comes from remittances), but the community at large: in many cases families have increased crop yields because they are able to buy fertilisers, and donations from migrants have allowed the community to build a new chapel. Although mother-absence, as in Naga, is seen to cause certain problems, families seem to have fewer reservations since children ultimately benefit from a 'good education' financed by remittances. Moreover, the consequences for the male population left behind in Dauin are not perceived as negatively as in Naga. Men continue to work on farms and either wait for girlfriends or wives to return, or, if they desperately want to get married, turn to other communities where female out-migration is not as prevalent. Unlike Naga, however, these issues are not seen as problematic, and indeed one respondent said 'Men forget to marry early because they work hard on the farm.'

The contrasting effects of female out-migration on these two source areas highlights how receipt of financial assistance from migrants to the community colours overall perceptions of whether the movement of women is beneficial or deleterious, although in both areas it appears that the migration of married women with children is seen as more problematic than that of single female migrants. In many ways, the case of Naga reflects more common consequences of this phenomenon, in that throughout the Philippines women are more likely to migrate to cities within the country's borders, rather than abroad (see also Chapters 1 and 7).

GENDER ROLES AND RELATIONS IN CEBU, LAPU-LAPU AND BORACAY

In order to put all this information into the context of the rubric of gender roles and relations in the Philippine Visayas, this last section takes a brief look at the nature of relationships between women and men in the three study localities, focusing on household divisions of labour, relations of power, sexuality and violence. The overall impression of gender roles and relations in some ways corroborates the 'egalitarian model' discussed in Chapter 1, especially in terms of household management and decision-making, yet in other ways inequalities between women and men are glaring, particularly with respect to sexuality, violence and differential entitlement to time and resources for leisure and recreation.

Although women in all study localities have high rates of labour force participation, in-depth interviews with 30 respondents revealed that women still bear a disproportionate burden of domestic work and childcare. Nonetheless, it is significant that in 18 of the 22 male-headed households men undertake some form of responsibility in the home (mainly looking after children), albeit on a sporadic basis. Also worth noting is that both male and female children are encouraged to help around the house, with little distinction between the tasks assigned to boys and girls. Most women stated that they considered it important to teach boys how to do housework, even if the rationale is usually so they will be able to look after themselves in the event that they ever live alone, rather than to ensure assistance of future wives. Overall, therefore, women spend the most time in household chores, as well as shouldering major responsibility for assigning tasks and ensuring that the daily domestic routine is kept in order.

A related point is that women are usually the main decision-makers on domestic and economic matters, with all but one of the 22 female spouses in male-headed households being in charge of finance and budgeting. While women generally welcome this responsibility, it is significant that many stressed the heavy burden involved in trying to make ends meet on limited incomes. In a number of cases, women also complained of additional pressures from their partners' demands for money for drinking, gambling and smoking (see below; also Chapter 1). While women are also invariably charged with the responsibility of deciding issues relating to children and other household members, men often intervene when what they consider 'important' decisions have to be made – in the case of buying major appliances, for example, or moving house (see also Villariba, 1993:8–9). At the same time, a number of women pointed out men's frequent reluctance to enter into decision-making, mainly on the grounds of laziness or lack of interest. Indeed, many men seem to be more concerned with recreational pursuits than with making their voice heard within the home.

Male recreational activities translate into what women call 'vices' (or *bisyos*) and consist mainly of watching cock-fights, playing cards, drinking, smoking, and sometimes indulging in sexual transgressions with what are referred to locally as 'chicks' (mistresses). With the exception of the latter, men usually engage in these pursuits with their *barkada* or gang of male friends (see Chapter 1). In all three areas, women emphasised problems with *barkadas* and, concomitantly, with their husbands being drunkards (known in Cebuano as *pala-hubog* or *lasing*) or wasting money on gambling. While women generally tolerate these particular activities, this does not mean they do not worry about fathers setting bad examples to children, or spending limited household funds. With regard to men having extra-marital affairs, an attitude of resignation seems to prevail, indicating the widespread nature of a 'sexual double standard' (see Chapter 1). Women often admitted that they knew of their partners' dalliances with other women (usually in the past), but that they were willing to forgive them 'for the sake of the children'. One extreme example is that of Armis in Rubberworld, Cebu, whose husband had an affair with a woman in the cinema where he worked as a projectionist. Armis only discovered the relationship when she was told by a friend that her husband had proposed marriage, and that the woman's uncle was checking up on the moral character of his niece's suitor with friends and relatives. When Armis confronted her husband, he assured her that it was just 'a joke' and that he would terminate the relationship immediately. Armis accepted this through fear that her husband might abandon her and leave their two sons fatherless. In terms of vices in general, however, women are more tolerant of drinking, smoking and gambling than of sexual infidelity. As one woman, Eden, put it, 'Better to have cock-fighting than to look at chicks,' the main reason being that cock-fights only tend to happen once a week, whereas womanising is a day-to-day (*adlaw-adlaw*) affair. However, regular expenditure on drink and cigarettes can make women angry: for example, one woman, May, complained that as far as her husband was concerned, it was 'better to lose a thousand women, than a single stick of cigarette, or a single drop of wine' (in other words, he cared more about his vices than he did about her). Especially frustrating for women is when they find themselves subsidising their husbands' activities out of their own hard-earned money, as many do to keep the peace. As for women themselves, vices of any sort are rare, with virtually none having had sex with anyone other than their husbands, let alone indulging in extra-marital affairs.

In terms of the ways in which conflict is played out between men and women at the household level, this is usually verbal rather than physical. Arguments (or what are termed in Cebuano *away-away* or *lalis*) are commonplace, and are usually started by discussions about finances. Although women reported that men would often 'back down' during arguments (possibly reflecting the desire for non-conflictive relationships in society in general – see Chapter 1), the opposite occurs where men resort to physical violence. In nine of the 30 cases, women had experienced domestic violence of some sort in their lives. Abuse is most likely when men are drunk. Attacks range from slapping women in the face, threatening them with knives or even breaking

bones. Women rarely fight back, however, and are often philosoph-
ical about 'boxings', rarely seeing these as grounds for leaving husbands.
Besides, bouts of aggression are normally short-lived: for instance, one
woman, Elvira, now a widow (and thankful to be one), usually found
that running off for ten minutes or so after a beating would tend to
diffuse her husband's violence.

In summary, women in the three study areas appear to have considerable power at the household level in respect of making decisions
and organising daily family affairs. However, this is often undermined
by men's apparent ease in withdrawing from major financial and
domestic responsibilities, and to pursue personal objectives instead:
where the latter involves indulgence in pursuits such as drinking and
gambling, the result is often conflict, and sometimes physical violence.
The juxtaposition of female commitment to family life with men's
seeming disregard for participation in household matters, imposes
considerable emotional, physical and economic strains on women, yet
few seek to break out of their situations. If anything, women pride
themselves on being able to keep their marriages going, even if they
are usually concerned that their daughters pursue their education and
ensure some form of economic independence before having families
of their own. The fact that most state a preference for daughters to
get married later than themselves (at an average of around 23–4 years),
and to have fewer (three to four) children, is possibly indicative of a
desire to protect their young from a range of hardships they themselves
have faced.

CONCLUSION

This chapter has given a general outline of household, employment
and migration characteristics of low-income people in the three study
locations. The most pertinent patterns to emerge are that households
are mainly male-headed, either nuclear or extended in form, with the
latter in particular forming significant proportions in all localities and
highlighting the importance of links with kin beyond the immediate
residential unit. Employment patterns in the three centres indicate wide
levels of female, as well as male, labour force participation, and
underscore the importance of women's income-generation for
household survival, as well as the diversity of activities in which

women engage. Our exploration of migration shows how mobility is frequently bound up with employment and income opportunities in destination areas, whether this is migration to obtain waged work (as in the case of young, single female migrants to Cebu, or their slightly older [and often married] counterparts in Lapu-Lapu), or to maximise the yields from own-account businesses in Boracay. The effects of female out-migration on source areas can sometimes be deleterious, with the greatest impact felt by men left behind with children to care for, or who face limited prospects of marriage in the community. Finally, gender roles and relations in the three localities reflect deep-seated inequalities; one major one is the polarisation between women's heavy responsibilities in income generation, domestic labour, childcare, household financial management and decision-making, and a general disregard and disinterest on the part of men to involve themselves in everyday life in the home.

Having identified these basic economic, demographic and social patterns, the following chapters go on to look at those associated with specific sectors of employment.

4 GENDER AND MANUFACTURING EMPLOYMENT

Our first of three chapters on target occupational groups deals with export manufacturing, one of the main sectors of economic growth in the Visayas. With reference to interviews among employers and workers in Lapu-Lapu and Cebu, manufacturing employment is explored in the context of the types of activities firms undertake, the nature of ownership and production methods, and how these give rise to gender differences in recruitment patterns and working conditions – pay, benefits and so on (see Appendix). Following this, an examination is made of the demographic and household characteristics of male and female factory workers in the two localities. At relevant junctures the discussion also identifies features of export manufacturing in the Visayas which seem to differ from those observed in a range of countries in Southeast Asia and other parts of the Third World where multinational companies have transferred substantial parts of their operations.

MANUFACTURING EMPLOYMENT IN LAPU-LAPU AND CEBU: AN OVERVIEW

Characteristics of manufacturing employment in Lapu-Lapu and Cebu

As noted in Chapter 2, manufacturing in Lapu-Lapu and Cebu is predominantly export-oriented, with the main industrial sectors in both localities producing for the export market. In the 22 firms interviewed in the authors' survey, all but one company export 100 per cent of their goods abroad (with the exception exporting 95 per cent). However, there are distinct differences in the nature of industrial activity between the two localities, which, as we shall see, have significant implications for gender segmentation and segregation among the workforce.

129

As discussed previously, export manufacturing in Lapu-Lapu is overwhelmingly tied to the Mactan Export Processing Zone (MEPZ). As with most zones of this kind, the companies are mainly foreign-owned subsidiaries or branch plants of larger multinational enterprises, and are primarily engaged in the assembly of electronics or garments, with a minority producing fashion accessory components or wood products. The ten firms selected for interview reflect this pattern, with four involved in electronics, four in garments, one in jewellery and one in wood veneer (see Table 4.1).[1] All the companies are foreign-owned, with the exception of one Filipino garment manufacturer (five are Japanese, one American, one British, one Taiwanese and one Italian), and most are classified as having 'non-traditional' or 'pioneer' status (principally the electronics and garments factories – see Chapter 2). In contrast, export manufacturing in Cebu consists largely of traditional or 'non-pioneer' industries producing rattan furniture and wood products, fashion accessories and other handicrafts. These firms are more likely to be owned by Filipinos than is the case in the export processing zone, although foreign or joint ownership of enterprises appears to be increasingly significant in the expanding fashion accessory industry. In the sample of twelve firms interviewed in Cebu, five are involved in the manufacture of rattan furniture and handicrafts (including shellcraft), six in fashion accessories and one in the production of carageenan (from seaweed), which is used as an emulsifying agent in food and cosmetic products.[2] Of these firms, six are indigenous (two

1 More specifically, the four electronics firms included in the survey are involved respectively in the assembly of car stereo components, automotive wire harnesses (casings for car steering wheel shafts), electrical light fittings and the production of binoculars. The four garment factories produce a range of items including women's fashion dresses and suits, Nike and Adidas sportswear and Levi's jeans. The fashion accessory factory makes gold clasps for pearl necklaces, and the wood products firm produces sliced veneer for wood panelling and furniture.

2 Carageenan is made from a red algae known as euchema; once processed it is used as a thickener and gelling agent in food products such as processed meat, ice-cream and so on, as well as in cosmetics, toothpaste and pharmaceutical items (see Reyes Churchill, 1993:7). The carageenan company in the survey is owned by a Chinese-Filipino family and is one of the largest enterprises in Cebu, employing 3,000 workers. Although not a traditional manufacturing firm, it was included because of its importance to the local economy and the fact that it is the largest carageenan producer in Asia. The furniture firms in the sample produce rattan, buri, wicker and bamboo chairs, tables and sofas, sometimes with wrought iron and stone inlay (for tables, for example). Handicraft production mainly consists of making baskets, plant holders and novelty items out of rattan, buri, wicker and cogon (a rough grass), while the fashion accessory firms produce earrings, necklaces and hair-clips out of natural materials such as wood, shells, coconut and stone.

producing rattan furniture, two handicrafts, one fashion accessories and the carageenan factory), two are joint Filipino/foreign ventures (both fashion accessory producers) and the remainder are 100 per cent foreign-owned (see Table 4.1).

Besides these general differences in product and ownership, there are also some more specific variations. One of the more apparent is that factories in Lapu-Lapu are more likely to be capital-intensive than those in Cebu. Having said this, while MEPZ firms use much more sophisticated technology and machinery, especially in electronics production, they nonetheless employ large numbers of workers on their labour-intensive assembly lines. This relates to a second major difference between Lapu-Lapu and Cebu: firms in MEPZ import not only all their machinery from abroad, but also the majority (usually at least 95 per cent) of their materials and components.[3] Firms in Cebu, on the other hand, depend to a much greater extent on indigenous inputs, importing much less equipment and only a small proportion (15–20 per cent) of components (clasps for jewellery, lacquers and varnishes for rattan, for example). Related to this, Cebu-based companies, as independent producers, are involved in the complete production of goods, whereas firms in Lapu-Lapu, as subsidiaries of multinationals, are more likely to be involved in assembly only, even if only three out of the ten firms in MEPZ exclusively assemble components as part of a wider chain of production. In garments, for instance, all firms import materials such as cloth and buttons, yet assemble the complete product within the factory, from cutting to the finishing stage. Among electronics firms, half import all their component parts and assemble the finished item on the premises. This high proportion of firms manufacturing finished products in Mactan is significant, given that historically branch plants in export processing zones around the world have usually engaged only in partial assembly of goods (see Aldana, 1989:3; IBON, 1990:15; Pineda-Ofreneo, 1987:93 on the Philippines; also Dicken, 1990:217; Elson and Pearson, 1981:88; Heyzer, 1986:93; Hossfeld, 1991:14). Recognising that the assembly of imported materials and components continues to underpin the nature of production in

---

3 In the case of electronics factories, components are usually imported from the parent company or from other branch plants, with only packaging and boxes bought within the Philippines. In garment factories, cloth, buttons and trimmings are received either directly from the parent company or from individual suppliers (mainly in Hong Kong, Taiwan, Korea, India and Japan). The only materials bought within the Philippines are threads and packing materials (see also Pineda-Ofreneo, 1988:159).

Table 4.1 Product, ownership, size of workforce and number of female workers in export manufacturing firms interviewed in Lapu-Lapu and Cebu

Product	Nationality	No. of workers	No. of female workers	% of female workers
MEPZ/LAPU-LAPU				
Electronics				
Electric lighting fixtures	Japanese	67	21	31%
Binoculars	Japanese	188	154	82%
Car stereos	Japanese	332	313	94%
Automotive wire harnesses	US	919	753	82%
Garments				
Ladies suits and dresses	Japanese	251	231	92%
Sportswear and jackets	Taiwanese	389	343	88%
Sportswear and jeans	Filipino	425	327	77%
Sportswear and jackets	British	581	429	74%
Other				
Wood veneer	Italian	38	13	34%
Jewellery components	Japanese	78	52	67%
CEBU				
Rattan furniture and handicrafts				
Shellcrafts	Filipino	8	5	62%
Rattan furniture/novelty items	Filipino	48	13	27%
Baskets	Italian	83	33	40%
Rattan furniture/stone inlay	Filipino	190	97	51%
Rattan furniture/wicker items	Filipino	375	60	16%
Fashion accessories				
Earrings/necklaces, etc.	Filipino/Italian	24	17	70%
Earrings/necklaces, etc.	Dutch	86	61	71%
Earrings/necklaces, etc.	French	87	81	93%
Earrings/necklaces, etc.	South Korean	140	85	61%
Earrings/necklaces, etc.	Filipino	170	125	74%
Earrings/necklaces, etc.	Filipino/Italian	204	179	89%
Other				
Carageenan	Filipino	3,000	1,245	42%

Note: Names of firms are not disclosed for reasons of confidentiality.

export processing zones, therefore, it is increasingly likely that finished products will be manufactured in situ (see also A.J.Scott, 1987, who notes how the Southeast Asian semi-conductor industry in particular has become progressively sophisticated and less monofunctional, often involving end products; also P.Wilson, 1992:25). The rationale behind this apparent shift in the nature of production lies partly in rising wage differentials between advanced and developing economies (see Heyzer, 1986:94),[4] and partly in the increasingly high levels of education and training among workers in less developed countries. While education rarely equips workers for carrying out specific skills required in factory production, it is assumed to enhance potential for learning more complicated tasks. In the Philippines in particular, the fact that English is an integral component of high-school education, and is widely spoken, further facilitates the ease of training industrial operatives. However, economic considerations do seem to be uppermost: for example, the manager of the Japanese firm manufacturing binoculars in MEPZ reported that the daily wage in Japan was now so high (US$80, compared with US$4.20 in the Visayas – see also note 4) that the company had decided to transfer the entire production process outside the country, including testing and quality control (see also Heyzer, 1986:93; IBON, 1990:39–40; O'Connor, 1987:259). In order to do this, considerable investment has been devoted to training Filipinos, with most supervisors undergoing intensive six-month programmes in the factory itself, and others being sent to the parent company in

4 One problem in evaluating wage differentials between the advanced and developing economies (apart from the obvious difficulties in standardising the purchasing power of wages) arises from the fact that categories of unskilled and semi-skilled work may cover different types of jobs in different contexts. Another is that there may be wide variations in terms of the hours people work, levels of overtime and the amount of paid holiday (see Addison and Demery, 1988:374–7). Having said this, in the specific case of the Philippines it would appear that wage differentials have risen over time. In 1973, for example, garments and textiles workers in the Philippines earned only 85 per cent of the wages of their counterparts in Korea, and only 15 per cent of those in Japan (Pineda-Ofreneo, 1988:160). Information from our own survey of MEPZ firms indicates that Japanese firms are paying just 5 per cent of the wages to Filipinos that they would pay in their own country (see also Cleves-Mosse, 1993:124, who estimates that wages for women workers in the Philippines are merely 5–15 per cent of those of their counterparts in Japan and the West; and Villariba, 1993:17, who observes that although Filipinas are among the best educated women in Asia, they have the lowest wage rates, at only one-fifth of those in NICs such as Taiwan).

Japan for a further six months (see also Kenney and Florida, 1994:34–5 on Japanese firms in Mexico).

A further difference in the nature of production between manufacturers in Lapu-Lapu and Cebu is the extent to which they engage in subcontracting or outwork. Known locally as 'job-out', subcontracting usually takes the form of sending out parts to agents who in turn recruit people in small workshops or their own homes to assemble semi-finished products on a piece-rate basis. These are then returned to the factory for finishing. In Lapu-Lapu, subcontracting to individuals is not permitted by the Export Processing Zone Authority, although four firms (three garment and one electronics) have obtained approval to subcontract specialised stages of their production processes to other factories since they claim not to have the space or facilities on site; for example, one garment company contracts a firm outside the Zone to carry out intricate embroidery work (see also Chant and McIlwaine, 1994). By contrast, the majority of firms in Cebu subcontract an average of 70 per cent of the labour necessary for their products, predominantly in the assembly stage (for instance, furniture firms often contract out the assembly of chairs; fashion accessory firms may contract out the stringing of beads for necklaces or earrings). The rationale behind subcontracting is partly to reduce labour costs (usually by at least 25 per cent), and partly to allow greater flexibility in production methods in view of changing patterns of demand for goods in a competitive world market (see also Eviota, 1992:112–13; Ward, 1990:2). Other advantages of subcontracted labour for companies include piece-rate payments which often work out cheaper than fixed daily wages,[5] and freedom from compulsory welfare benefits such as social security and Medicare (see also Mitter and van Luijken, 1983:63; Moghadam, 1993a:26; Singh and Kelles-Viitanen, 1987:15). For example, the owner of a shellcraft enterprise which subcontracts 100 per cent of its production to small family-based workshops stated that

---

5 According to our employer survey, piece-rates are usually calculated with the daily minimum wage in mind. For example, in the costume jewellery sector a test is carried out to ascertain how many earrings or necklaces it is possible to assemble in one day, after which the average rate per piece is calculated on the basis of dividing the legal daily minimum wage of P105 by the total number of pieces. Since 'high' totals are taken to represent the norm, piece-rates are usually set at low levels and mean that workers have to maintain extremely high productivity to earn a basic living. This often ends up contravening Article 101 of the Philippine Labour Code, which states that piece workers should not be paid less than the minimum hourly wage for each hour worked (see Nolledo, 1992:34).

this system helped him avoid the 'headache' of paying social security, as well as reducing the costs of employing a large administrative and supervisory staff.

The issue of subcontracting is also important when considering the size of factory workforces in Lapu-Lapu and Cebu. Although in general MEPZ labour forces are larger than is the case in Cebu (at an average of 324 in the former and 129 in the latter),[6] when subcontracted labour is taken into account it is actually Cebu firms which employ more people, albeit indirectly (Cebu companies employ an average of 990 when outworkers are included). However, our main concern here is with in-house employees, and one consequence of different workforce sizes lies in management–labour relations. In the smaller factories of Cebu, managers have frequent and personalised contact with workers, creating what most call a 'family atmosphere'. Although reference was also made to a 'family atmosphere' by managers in MEPZ, this was of a much more formal nature, with managers tending only to come into contact with a handful of supervisors and worker representatives in the context of scheduled monthly meetings.

One final distinction between manufacturing employment in the two localities is that trade unionism is non-existent in Lapu-Lapu, whereas in Cebu four out of twelve firms have unions. While throughout the Philippines it is a constitutional right for workers to establish a trade union, given certain stipulations, firms in both localities actively discourage organisation.[7] This is particularly the case in MEPZ,

---

6 The average for Cebu-based firms excludes the carageenan factory which employs 3,000 workers, as this distorts the general picture.

7 Article 211 of the Philippine Labour Code recognises 'free trade unionism as an instrument for the enhancement of democracy and the promotion of social justice and development' (Nolledo, 1992:74). However, in order to establish a union, at least 20 per cent of a given workforce must desire its formation (ibid.:90), with assessment based on a 'certification' election among workers which must first be approved by the Department of Labour and Employment and company management (Amnesty International, 1991:1). According to branch representatives of federal labour centres, the reluctance of Zone workers in particular to vote for unions is due to fear of being identified as troublemakers by management and/or of losing their jobs. Workers may also be dissuaded from activism by 'incentives' such as additional fringe benefits in the run-up to elections. Although the bulk of firms in Cebu do not allow trade union formation, their universal absence in MEPZ tends to support Diane Elson's (1991:45) observation that workers in export processing zones tend to have fewer rights than non-zone workers (see also Bucoy, 1993; Ballescas, 1993:5–6; and Tiukinhoy and Remedio, 1992, for more detailed accounts of unionism and attempted unionism in Cebu and in the Mactan Export Processing Zone).

where the Zone authority uses industrial peace as a selling point to foreign investors and goes to great lengths to ensure that workers do not seek to establish labour organisations – including the screening of job applicants for previous union activity (see below). However, working conditions are generally better in MEPZ factories, although unionised operatives in Cebu are more privileged than their non-unionised counterparts in the city.

Labour recruitment in MEPZ/Lapu-Lapu

Reflecting the general differences in the nature of industrial production in Lapu-Lapu and Cebu, labour recruitment also varies, with MEPZ firms tending to be much more rigid in their specifications for workers and in the tests to which they subject applicants. Entry requirements for factory employment in Lapu-Lapu follow broadly similar lines to recruitment in other export processing zones in the Philippines (see Eviota, 1992:119–26; Pineda-Ofreneo, 1987; Rosario, 1985) and other parts of Southeast Asia (Armstrong and McGee, 1985: Chapter 9; Elson and Pearson, 1981:71; Foo and Lim, 1989; Fuentes and Ehrenreich, 1983:16-26; Heyzer, 1986: Chapter 6; Ong, 1987:147–8; Yun, 1988). One similarity, for example, is a preference for female workers, who constitute 80 per cent of the total labour force in the firms surveyed (see Table 4.1, and below). Another point of correspondence is a desire for workers in the 18–25 age range. Younger workers are thought to be more productive, to have better health (particularly eyesight) and to be more malleable in terms of adhering to the company ethos, or, as one manager said, 'to be moulded into the company way' (see below). Young workers are also likely to be more educated, with most factories stipulating a completed high-school education, the main reasoning being that a certain level of intelligence is required to understand machine operation and/or to undergo training programmes. In addition, as discussed earlier, high-school graduates are more likely to have an understanding of English, the usual *lingua franca* of training schemes and chief medium of communication between employees and foreign managers (see also Reyes Churchill, 1993:7-8; Shoesmith, 1986:211). While these educational requirements undoubtedly reflect a degree of credentialism, however, they should not be overstated, as a number of employers in electronics firms reported that 'overqualified' applicants (i.e. those with more than two years' college education) are not usually considered because they are likely to have high aspirations and may not remain in their jobs. There are also slight variations between electronics and garments factories, insofar as the latter are more open to workers with only primary-level schooling (see also Fernández-Kelly, 1983b; Tiano, 1990 on Mexico; Reardon, 1991a on South Korea).

In addition to the fact that most firms require educated workers, they also prefer them to be 'fresh' or recent graduates who come direct from school. This is especially the case with electronics factories, who maintain that young inexperienced people are more likely to take orders and embrace company ethics (see also Eviota, 1992:120–1; Heyzer, 1986:101). These workers are also thought to accept lower pay and to be more easily dissuaded from participating in union activity (see also Pineda-Ofreneo, 1987:96). A further factor is that school-leavers are less likely to have picked up 'bad habits' such as tardiness or slacking. This is also relevant insofar as many electronics firms prefer to train workers from scratch, partly because production operations within these firms are so distinct, and also, as discussed earlier, because investment in training is increasingly worthwhile in the light of rising wage differentials between advanced and developing economies. The situation in garment factories is broadly similar to that in electronics firms, with only the British and Filipino garment companies looking for previous machine experience (either in the home or another factory) in order to reduce training costs.

Also related to the desire for young workers, and found in most other studies of export manufacturing, is a preference for single employees. Single people are thought to be more productive, mainly on account of an assumed lack of household responsibilities (Eviota, 1992:120). Having said this, few employers expressed objections to existing female workers getting married or having children.[8] Maternity benefits are not, as might be expected, seen as a major problem (see, for example, ILMS, 1984:12; Safa, 1990:77); moreover, older married women are often thought to be 'workaholics', because they have families to support and are therefore more conscientious (see also Fuentes and

---

8 In one sense this is not surprising, since Article 136 of the Labour Code states that 'it shall be unlawful for an employer to require as a condition of employment or continuation of employment that a woman employee shall not get married, or to stipulate expressly or tacitly that upon getting married a woman employee shall be deemed resigned' (Nolledo, 1992: 49).

Ehrenreich, 1983:13 on Singapore; Hein, 1986:288 on Mauritius; Safa, 1990:77–8 on Puerto Rico and the Dominican Republic).[9] While somewhat contradictory, this challenges the widely held belief that women workers in export processing zones are virtually always single, and that upon marrying they may be dismissed or voluntarily leave the labour force in the context of what Pineda-Ofreneo (1987:96) refers to as 'programmed unemployment' (see also Elson and Pearson, 1981:93; Foo and Lim, 1989:221; Hossfeld, 1991:16; ILMS, 1984:12; Safa, 1990:77). Indeed, eight out of ten employers in our MEPZ survey are so concerned to foster long-term loyalty among operatives that this seems to override any misgivings they may have about marital circumstances at later stages in a worker's career.

Although employers rarely cited migrant status as a condition for recruitment (only one employer stressed a bias towards migrants on the grounds that workers from a wide range of places might be less likely to form a trade union than people from the same area of origin), a preference *was* reported for workers to reside in Lapu-Lapu (as opposed to other parts of Metro Cebu), mainly to guard against late arrival at work. Over and above the personal entry requirements already described, MEPZ firms also operate strict screening systems whereby applicants have to obtain police and/or National Bureau of Investigation clearance, and to provide a residence permit or letter of commendation from a *barangay* captain/leader (often to verify that a person lives in Lapu-Lapu and not another part of Metro Cebu). The American electronics firm in the sample even goes as far as employing a private investigator to check out new recruits in an attempt to by-pass potential corruption and bribery via routine methods. In the few cases where applicants have had previous jobs, former employers are asked to vouch for the character of potential recruits. The initiatives of employers in vetting applicants are often reinforced by the screening service of the Mactan Export Processing Zone Authority.

Other passports to MEPZ employment include a medical certificate (obtained from the Department of Labour and Employment at the applicant's own expense), or a full medical examination by a company doctor. In two electronics factories, women applicants are

9 Ruth Pearson (1986:70–2) provides a useful discussion of the ways in which different groups of women are favoured in different situations, although she concludes that, in general, export factories in Southeast Asia, especially electronics firms, desire young, single (and fairly well-educated) women.

also expected to undergo pregnancy tests, ostensibly on grounds of protecting them from health problems that might arise from the use of certain machinery. In a further two cases (one electronics and one garment factory), height restrictions are imposed (a minimum of 5ft 5in for men and 5ft 3in for women), because machinery and worktables are tailored to taller workers from developed countries. In virtually all factories, applicants also have to undergo some kind of intelligence and/or practical skills test, ranging from assessments of manual dexterity and eyesight, to mathematical and general IQ examinations. In garment factories, potential recruits also have to perform sewing tests.[10]

In spite of these numerous eligibility criteria and screening mechanisms, demand for MEPZ factory employment is high. Most employers reported that they rarely need to advertise positions, since people constantly approach the firms as 'walk-in' applicants and files are held of suitable candidates.[11] A more common method of recruitment, however, is the use of a 'backer' system whereby existing employees recommend a relative or friend to management (see Chapter 3). Given that the reputation of existing employees is on the line, this helps to ensure that firms obtain productive and responsible workers (see also Reardon 1991a:25 on South Korea). Finally, two companies who look for recent graduates recruit directly from local vocational schools and colleges.

Gender segmentation in manufacturing employment in MEPZ/Lapu-Lapu

As mentioned earlier, recruitment in MEPZ factories is highly selective of women. As Table 4.1 shows, the highest average percentage of female employees is in garments (81 per cent) and electronics (76 per cent),

10 One common test is the peg and board dexterity/colour test which involves matching pegs of four different colours with 30 holes in a board within a set time of two to three minutes. Other tests include stringing sequins onto nylon thread (in three minutes applicants have to string at least 24 sequins with their right hand and 17 with their left). Sewing tests usually involve a half-hour stint on a machine doing complicated piping or difficult stitches. All companies except the jewellery component firm carry out one or more tests, with the American electronics company conducting the most, including a 90-minute written IQ and English test, a dexterity and colour-blindness test, as well as a complete physical examination.

11 In cases where advertising is necessary, notice of vacancies is posted at the entrance of the Zone, usually resulting in hundreds of applicants presenting 'bio-data' (curriculum vitae).

although there are some variations between firms. For example, one of the electronics companies has a workforce that is only 31 per cent female, explaining this on account of its use of a higher than average degree of capital-intensive technology (see below). The general dominance of women in the workforce is marked, however; the reasons for this are perhaps best understood through examination of the gender composition of departments or sections within factories, notably administration, pre-assembly or preparation, assembly, post-assembly or finishing, warehousing and packing, and maintenance.

Looking at electronics and garment firms in particular, women predominate in all departments except maintenance. As Fig. 4.1 shows, they tend to be most heavily concentrated in assembly (83 per cent in garments, 94 per cent in electronics), post-assembly or finishing (90 per cent and 63 per cent) and administration (78 per cent and 53 per cent). Although no department in any firm in the sample is exclusively female, there is often strict gender segregation of activity within the departments, especially in Japanese factories, which in the words of one manager is claimed to reflect 'the Japanese pattern' (see below).

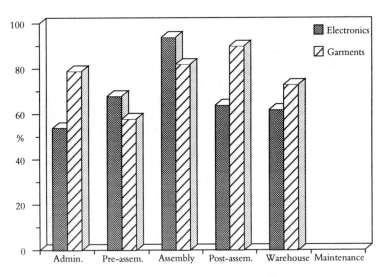

Figure 4.1: Percentage of women in different departments in electronics and garment factories, MEPZ, Lapu-Lapu

On the other hand, maintenance departments, employing janitors, cleaners and engineers, are exclusively male because men are thought to be 'stronger' and more adept at heavy and/or technical jobs. Indeed, preference for males in jobs demanding physical strength or technical expertise accounts for their inclusion in departments otherwise employing a largely female workforce. This is particularly so in pre-assembly or preparation: in garment firms, for example, men make up 43 per cent of preparatory workers, mainly assigned to the machine-cutting and distribution of large bundles of fabric. According to one employer, the mechanised part of this operation requires 'strong hands' and 'presence of mind', with another citing 'masculine strength' as essential for the distributional work (see also Eviota, 1992:115; Heyzer, 1986:103). The majority of women employed in pre-assembly, on the other hand, are involved in more labour-intensive tasks such as sorting material into batches. The grounds for female selectivity are usually that women are 'more meticulous'. While fewer men tend to be employed in the preparation stage of electronic products (33 per cent), the same kinds of reasons are used to justify their concentration in certain tasks. In the electrical lighting factory, for example, the spinning and punching of aluminium disks for bulbs involves the operation of machinery which requires technical know-how as well as physical strength, and only men are thought to possess relevant capacities. In addition to gender-stereotyped assumptions about disposition and skills, most employers state that women never apply for jobs which involve technical expertise or physical strength, even when they are ostensibly open to both sexes.

Women do apply, however, for assembly jobs, which not only employ the majority of workers but also have the highest proportion of women workers (at least 90 per cent in most cases) – see Fig. 4.1. In garment factories, assembly mainly consists of machine-operated sewing, which is almost entirely done by women. Female concentration here is due to their supposed 'dexterity', or, as one employer reported, 'because women have good hands', and because sewing is deemed to be more 'natural' for women owing to their social conditioning in the home. One manager even stated that women were more suitable for these jobs because 'their anatomy and biology allows them to sit in one place for longer than men'. The few men in sewing departments (mainly in the Filipino-owned factory) are engaged on larger machines for specialised tasks such as overstitching (for seams on jeans, for example), which require greater strength to operate. In electronics, assembly usually involves the fitting, moulding and/or splicing of electrical components, which one manager admitted is the 'most tedious' set of tasks in the factory. Women comprise over 90 per cent of operatives here because they are thought to be more patient and able to concentrate than men, and to have a higher boredom threshold. In only two factories are a small number of men employed in electronics assembly, in one because some of the American-made machinery is too high for Filipino women to operate, and in the other because the final stage of assembly requires the use of machines with levers which are deemed 'too heavy' for women to manoeuvre.

The other heavily female-dominated department is post-assembly or finishing (including quality control) and, in the case of garment factories, the trimming of stray threads, washing and pressing. Again, employers consider women to be more adept at these intricate tasks, or, as one employer stated, for 'the obvious reason' that women are more 'meticulous' and 'careful' in selection procedures. Although women constitute a smaller proportion of employees in warehouse and packing departments (see Fig. 4.1), their predominance is due to the light weight of garments and electrical goods and, as one employer asserted, because women are more able to 'withstand the boredom' of repetitive counting and packaging work.

Besides manual work, women are also given preference as administrative employees, although this is more marked in garment firms than in electronics (see Fig. 4.1). The reasons given are arguably based on more positive assumptions about women than those cited with regard to rank-and-file occupations, in that women are perceived as being 'reliable', 'efficient', 'good with figures' and as having sound organisational abilities. Having said this, while all companies employ some women in managerial positions (mainly in accounts and personnel), this is rarely in proportion to the number of women employed in the firms overall, nor does their recruitment in personnel positions have a positive effect on the occupational distribution of other women workers (see also Chant and McIlwaine, 1994; Foo and Lim, 1989:221; Ong, 1987:160). Men tend to remain in senior decision-making posts and key supervisory positions, to the extent that in predominantly female sections nearly half the heads are male (see also Chant and McIlwaine, 1994; Eviota, 1992:115). Moreover, men are usually promoted faster than women.

Labour recruitment in manufacturing employment in Cebu

While labour recruitment patterns in manufacturing firms in Cebu (predominantly furniture and handicraft, and fashion accessory firms)[12] are considerably more relaxed in terms of entry requirements and screening practices than those in Lapu-Lapu, certain similarities obtain. For example, while youth is not a declared prerequisite for most Cebu firms, the majority of workers, as in Lapu-Lapu, are young. Having said this, some fashion accessory firms express a preference for young workers on the grounds of recruiting a 'fresh' workforce with no accumulated 'bad habits', although even so, 20 is usually the minimum age, with one employer suggesting that 17- and 18-year-olds are 'not mature enough' to understand instructions on different designs. Educational requirements are also more flexible, with only three firms (two of which are foreign-owned and prefer their workforce to speak some English) asking for high-school graduates; the rest either request only primary level education or have no stipulation at all. Indeed, in half the factories (mainly the furniture and handicraft firms) work-related skills are considered more important than educational qualifications. Reasons for the latter include, first, that Cebu is a historic centre for furniture and handicraft production and skilled labour is readily available; second, that employers regard those with experience as more likely to have higher productivity levels; and finally, because hiring skilled workers reduces training costs. However, while experienced applicants may have worked in other factories beforehand, firms also recruit employees from their own pools of subcontracted labour as these people are already familiar with the company's output and production methods. Previous experience is not deemed essential by the other half of the companies in the sample (mainly fashion accessory firms), because the products are simple to make and, accordingly, little training is necessary. Where relevant, references from previous employers or subcontracting agents are sought to check up on labour militancy and the character of potential recruits.

The marital status of applicants is not generally important, with most companies engaging a mixture of 'singles and marrieds'. Neither is the migrant origin of potential applicants significant, with most employers

---

12 While the carageenan factory is included in this analysis, another of the twelve firms interviewed in Cebu (a shellcraft company) is excluded as it subcontracts 100 per cent of its production and employs only eight administrative staff.

unaware of the migrant status of their employees, except where workers have been recruited from subcontractors based in specific towns or provinces outside Cebu. Having said this, as in Lapu-Lapu, many employers prefer their labour force to live nearby to minimise tardiness.

The bureaucratic procedures required before appointment to factory positions in Cebu follow similar lines to those decribed for MEPZ firms, although they are generally less stringent. While a medical certificate together with police clearance is required in most cases, few employers demand a reference from a *barangay* captain. In addition, three of the eleven firms require no clearance at all, with one foreign employer stating that he put no trust in any of the usual methods, given their openness to bribery and corruption. Perhaps more notable in terms of requirements for entry into Cebu factories is possession of an 'enthusiastic and dedicated attitude to work', with two firms also specifying that applicants should have a 'pleasing personality' (here referring to a deferential and polite nature, together with good deportment – see also Chapter 5). Reflecting the somewhat more arbitrary nature of labour recruitment in Cebu than in Lapu-Lapu, tests for applicants are not commonplace: only one furniture company requires a skills test for wicker weavers and framers, while two foreign-owned fashion accessory firms request an IQ test, and one stipulates a peg-and-board aptitude test (see note 10 above). The advertising of vacancies is largely achieved through personal recommendations from existing employees (similar to the 'backer' system operating in MEPZ), although recruitment through subcontracting agents and from 'walk-ins' arriving 'on spec', as discussed earlier, are also important. While demand for positions in Cebu factories is not as fierce as in Lapu-Lapu, employers have no difficulties filling posts.

Gender segmentation in manufacturing employment in Cebu

Whereas in Lapu-Lapu demand for female labour is relatively gener-alised, the gender composition of the factory workforce in Cebu is much more dependent on the activity of the firm. Overall, women make up a total of 45 per cent of the workforce in the firms surveyed,[13] although they are a much larger component in the costume jewellery

---

13 This percentage is based on all twelve firms in the Cebu survey, i.e. including the shellcraft firm which only employs eight administrative workers on site (see note 12 above).

companies (77 per cent) than in furniture and handicrafts (33 per cent) – see Table 4.1. Examination of the internal structures of these firms helps to explain these patterns, bearing in mind that it is necessary to deal with different types of firms individually, not only because of huge variations in production processes between, say, furniture and fashion accessory companies, but also because much labour is sub-contracted elsewhere and results in some companies not having certain departments.

Rattan furniture and handicrafts

In the four rattan furniture and handicrafts factories in the sample, women are found almost exclusively in finishing and sanding depart-ments, where they constitute 93 per cent of workers and where tasks include the manual sanding of chairs and sofas, the varnishing and lacquering of furniture and the trimming and lining of baskets (see Fig. 4.2). These are labour-intensive jobs which are perceived as 'female tasks' because they are relatively 'clean' and 'light'. In addition, one employer stated that women have a 'natural talent for intricate jobs', because they have 'good hands and pay attention to detail'. The only other departments where women are employed are in receiving and administration (see Fig. 4.2). In the former, raw materials are sorted and distributed throughout the factory, with the proportion of women in this section varying according to the scale and bulk of the items concerned. For example, in the handicraft factories producing baskets and small novelty items, women are employed as receivers on the grounds that they are 'patient' and 'careful' in sorting materials into bundles, whereas in furniture factories, where raw materials consist of rattan and bamboo poles, the preference for men is due to the fact that physical strength is needed for heavy loads.

Women are often employed in administration for similar reasons as in MEPZ factories, namely that they are thought to be 'reliable', 'numerate', 'responsible' and 'efficient' in comparison with men. Indeed, one female manager in a handicrafts factory described men as 'lazy, irresponsible and likely to spend all their wages on San Miguel [beer]', adding that 'they are only interested in power, not produc-tivity'. Having said this, men are still employed in all the main production operations involved in furniture and handicraft manufac-ture, particularly in highly skilled sections such as weaving (of wicker,

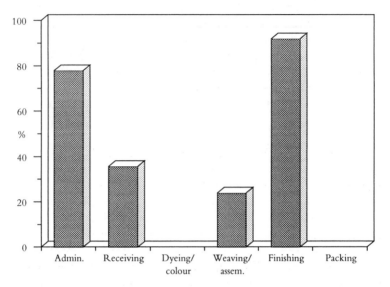

*Figure 4.2: Percentage of women in different departments in rattan
furniture and handicraft factories, Cebu*

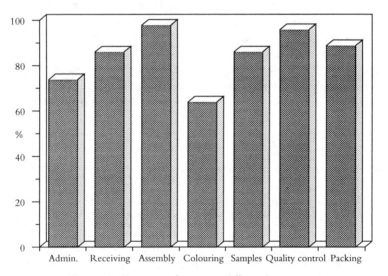

*Figure 4.3: Percentage of women in different departments in
fashion accessory factories, Cebu*

rattan and leather for chair bases and baskets), framing (assembling furniture in jig frames) and sample-making, as well as in colouring departments where hot ovens and boiling dyes are thought to be too dangerous for women. Men are preferred not only because they are thought to have the requisite capacity, experience and training, but also because the materials and tools are heavy.

Fashion accessory firms

In fashion accessory firms, women are preferred in all departments; they are employed exclusively in assembly and almost exclusively in quality control sections (see Fig. 4.3), again on the grounds that they are 'good with their hands', 'patient' and 'notice details'. Similar to the comment from one of the garment firms in MEPZ, one manager also stated that 'women are able to sit for four to five hours longer than men'. Only in dyeing and colouring sections are there fewer women: colouring involves the dyeing of wood and other natural materials for earrings, necklaces and so on; as in handicrafts and furniture production, it requires the use of hot ovens throught inappropriate for operation by women. The owners/managers of foreign fashion accessory firms are the most emphatic about their preference for female workers and reluctance to employ men. The owner of the French firm in the survey, for example, refuses to engage men in any in-house production, stating that he considers them 'inefficient', 'untrustworthy' and 'wont to drink alcohol and gamble on the premises' (something, incidentally, which he blames on a so-called process of 'cultural distintegration in the Philippines'). For the same kinds of reasons, and with the additional factor that men frequently turn up late for work, an Italian owner described men as 'too problematic to employ'. Women, on the other hand, are perceived to be more likely to conform with company rules, to be less disruptive and demanding, and to be less prone to labour militancy.

Although our discussion here is primarily concerned with in-house operatives in Cebu, it is also important to make a brief point about subcontracted labour. As mentioned earlier, 70 per cent of manufacturing production in Cebu is conducted outside the factory. Based on approximate estimations by employers, more than half their subcontracted labour is female, usually comprising very young women with children, operating either from home or from community-based workshops (where children may sit alongside their mothers). Once women have reached their mid-to-late 20 and their children have started school, it is common for them to seek positions in the factories themselves, which is made easier by the fact that employers often recruit from the ranks of their own subcontractors. This is particularly interesting as it is usually assumed that women involved in subcontracting in the Philippines and elsewhere are older women at the end of their working cycle (see Benería and Roldan, 1987; Drakakis-Smith, 1987:81; Heyzer, 1986:98). Although in Cebu women may leave factory employment again in their 30s, it is significant that young women, at an early stage in their family life-cycles, are also involved in outwork (see also Rao and Husain, 1987 on India; F.Wilson, 1991 on Mexico).

To sum up general patterns of labour demand in manufacturing employment, entry requirements in MEPZ factories are considerably more stringent than in Cebu-based firms in terms both of workers' personal attributes and screening mechanisms, not to mention medical and aptitude tests. While MEPZ employers prefer to recruit young, single, high-school graduates with no previous experience, Cebu factories tend to favour skilled workers, regardless of educational qualifications, marital status and sometimes even age. In terms of gender, women form the majority of workers in both electronics and garment firms in MEPZ, although men are employed in more mechanised aspects of production, as well as in heavier tasks in packing and warehousing. In Cebu women have preferential access to most jobs in fashion accessory companies, whereas men make up the majority in furniture and handicraft production in the city, particularly in jobs which are heavy and/or defined as 'skilled'. As such, the activity of the company seems to be more important in determining the gender composition of the workforce in Cebu than in Lapu-Lapu, where women usually comprise the majority labour force in all factories.

The role of gender stereotypes in manufacturing recruitment

Having said this, high degrees of gender-stereotyping pervade factory recruitment in both localities. The so-called female attributes cited by employers in MEPZ and in fashion accessory firms in Cebu in rationalising their preference for women workers reflect a range of assumptions about women, which fall into various categories. One relates to physiological factors, perhaps best encapsulated by the concept of the 'nimble fingers' syndrome (Elson and Pearson, 1981), whereby women are thought to be more dexterous than men and capable of performing manual assembly and finishing work at high speed. Although there seems to be little scientific basis for these assumptions, women's association with jobs requiring a light touch and manual dexterity is reinforced over time, leading to their exclusion from more skilled tasks involving mechanised apparatus (Rohini, 1991; Heng Leng and Ng Choon Sim, 1993). As Elizabeth Eviota (1992:115) observes: 'skill, an objective category, becomes implicated with subjective gender ideology to pre-empt women from higher technology work and higher wages'; she also notes that women's work is defined as low-skilled because women do it (see also Phillips, 1983:17).

Another set of gender biases relates to perceptions about female psychology, foremost among which is the notion that women have a patient disposition and a capacity for high levels of concentration, which equip them for carrying out monotonous, repetitive tasks (Fuentes and Ehrenreich, 1983:13; Sklair, 1991:98). Also contributing to their ability to perform such jobs is their alleged passivity and docility, meaning that they are less likely to be vocal about their rights and/or to cause disturbances. Interrelated with psychological factors are assumed cultural norms seen as conditioning women into accepting subordinate positions in male-dominated society and, ipso facto, male authority on the factory floor (see Fuentes and Ehrenreich, 1983:15; Heyzer, 1986:98; Shoesmith, 1986:87; G.Standing, 1989:1080). Indeed, in firms with a so-called family atmosphere, workers ('daughters') are effectively encouraged to see their bosses as father-figures or patriarchs (see also Armstrong and McGee, 1985:211; Eviota, 1992:120–1; Pineda-Ofreneo, 1987:101).

A final set of ideologies is linked with the prospective increase in women's commitment to reproductive work within their families as they move through the life-cycle. Writers have often stressed that employers prefer young women to young men because the former are likely to leave work voluntarily on marriage or childbirth, thereby contributing to low commitment to labour organisation and/or reduced threats of redundancy payments; in addition, youth is associated with an assumed lack of family distractions (see Carney and O'Kelly, 1990:137; Foo and Lim, 1989:221; Fuentes and Ehrenreich, 1983:12; Hossfeld, 1991:16). Although, to an extent, this is observable in the Visayas in that MEPZ firms in particular recruit young women on the basis that they are likely to be freer of family responsibilities (see also Eviota, 1992:120), one major reason is that their youth is seen as conducive to the inculcation of long-term loyalty, an issue reflected in the fact that once women do marry and have children, they are usually allowed to stay. In other words, young women may encounter preference in recruitment, but not necessarily for the same range of reasons as in other contexts (see Chant and McIlwaine, 1994). In fact, if anything, there is recognition on the part of employers in the Visayas that women have major responsibilities to families *throughout* the life-cycle, which is likely to make them reliable long-term employees.[14] Indeed, regardless of age, women in general are usually thought to be more committed and hardworking than their male counterparts, and to have higher rates of productivity.

Pay and conditions in manufacturing employment in MEPZ/Lapu-Lapu and Cebu

Having outlined the nature of recruitment in manufacturing employment in Lapu-Lapu and Cebu, the discussion now turns to the pay and working conditions of the labour force.

In Lapu-Lapu, workers in all factories in the export processing zone are paid at least the daily minimum wage (P105 or US$4.20), and work a six-day week based on an eight to nine hour day[15] (see also ILMS, 1984:22). The weekly wage of P630 ($25.20) is supplemented by a monthly cost-of-living allowance (COLA), which means an extra US$1–3 every seven days. While this is the basic starting salary, most

---

14 This question of family responsibilities relates to an issue raised in Chapter 1, namely that the *nature* of women's responsibility within the household might change over the life-cycle, but not necessarily the *degree*. This is echoed by Ruth Pearson (1986:71) who, in talking of women workers in Asian export manufacturing, notes that employers may 'select those workers who on the one hand do not have a significant role in reproduction which might interfere with their availability and productivity in production, but on the other hand have a significant role in the subsistence and survival of the families in which they are *daughters* rather than wives or mothers.' (original emphasis) See also Chant and McIlwaine, 1994.

15 Only three of the ten firms work an eight-hour day, while the rest work a nine-hour day. Given that wages are paid on a daily rate, this is obviously a means to have employees work longer for less pay. A nine-hour day actually breaches regulations set out in the Labour Code (Article 83), which states that 'the normal hours of work of any employee shall not exceed eight in a day' (Nolledo, 1992: 28).

workers in the firms included in the sample are paid more, with an average weekly wage of P727 ($29.10), inclusive of COLA. In addition, employees in all but two companies work overtime, paid at the hourly rate of 25 per cent of the minimum wage for weekdays and 30 per cent on Sundays,[16] which brings average salaries up to P893 ($35.70) a week. Variations in wages depend largely on seniority, with most workers awarded annual increments of around P2–3 on the daily wage rate. In addition, three out of ten firms pay productivity bonuses, in one case to all workers where the factory has reached its productivity targets; in the other two, to workers (mainly female assembly-line operatives) who have consistently fulfilled their quotas. While there is little variation in wages between departments, in some cases skilled jobs receive higher rates of remuneration. The men employed in these positions accordingly receive higher earnings than women. For example, in one garment factory the all-male group of skilled sample-makers and utility workers, or 'floaters' (workers who fill in for all the tasks carried out in the factory), earn an extra P5 per day compared with the predominantly female sewers, finishers and so on. Therefore, while it is often said that employers in export processing zones prefer to employ women because they can pay them lower wages than they would men in the same jobs (see, for example, Fuentes and Ehrenreich, 1983:5–6; Gallin, 1990:179; Heyzer, 1986:104; Reardon and Rivers, 1991:103; G.Standing, 1989:1080; Ward, 1990:13), this is not entirely the case in Mactan (see also Addison and Demery, 1988:385–6; Sklair, 1991:96–101). Although some men earn higher wages as they hold jobs regarded as more skilled, all regular workers, regardless of sex, are guaranteed at least the minimum wage; length of service counts in equal favour of men and women in terms of annual wage increments; while productivity bonuses, where relevant, are distributed to both male and female operatives. Having said this, new recruits, known as 'probationary workers' or 'apprentices', may be paid, by law, at 75 per cent of the minimum wage (P78.80 [$3.20]) for a maximum of six months, provided training is given by the company during the period (see Nolledo, 1992: 28 and 189; also Sklair, 1991:100). Most factories do not just take advantage of this provision, but abuse it, either by

---

16 Hourly overtime rates on weekdays (Monday to Saturday) work out at an extra P26 (US$1), and P31.50 ($1.20) on Sundays (see Nolledo, 1992: 28–9).

not giving training or by dismissing workers before their six-months' probation is up, thereby allowing them to keep their wage costs down and in some cases to minimise payment of other benefits such as social security (see also Donald, 1991:199; Fuentes and Ehrenreich, 1983:22; IBON, 1990:50; Ong, 1987:160). Moreover, as Elizabeth Eviota (1992:121) notes with reference to micro-electronics firms in the Bataan Export Processing Zone, six-month apprenticeship periods are way in excess for jobs which can effectively be learned within one or two weeks.

For regular or permanent workers, however, factories usually provide not only legal but other fringe benefits. Statutory SSS benefits (see Chapter 2) include maternity, death, disability, sickness and funeral payments, as well as membership of Medicare (the state health scheme). Seven out of ten firms also pay SSS for their probationary and casual workers. Since the SSS scheme suffers from a series of shortcomings, however, as many as 60 per cent of MEPZ employers provide additional private medical and accident insurance. Other common fringe benefits include free or subsidised meals (in 90 per cent of firms), emergency loan systems allowing workers to borrow at very low rates of interest (50 per cent) and workers' credit cooperatives, again providing low-interest loans (50 per cent). Some companies also offer the services of a company doctor, free uniforms, cakes on employees' birthdays and incentive schemes such as 'Model Employee of the Month', where winners receive cash prizes or household goods like electrical appliances.

One significant omission from this list of benefits, given the high proportion of female workers in the Zone, is childcare facilities. However, since the Philippine Labour Code fails to spell out the precise conditions under which employers should provide crêches or nurseries,[17] and the Philippine state is only likely to enforce the bare minimum of restrictions on foreign companies in the country, it is perhaps no surprise that little cognisance is taken of women's needs. In addition, a large pool of female labour on firms' waiting lists means that mothers are unlikely to be particularly vocal in demanding this kind of support.

---

17 The provision of nursery facilities is a somewhat grey area in the eyes of the law. Article 132 of the Labour Code states, equivocally, that 'in appropriate cases, he [the Secretary of Labor and Employment] shall by regulations require any employer to – establish a nursery in a workplace for the benefit of the woman employees therein' (Nolledo, 1992: 47).

A further negative aspect of working conditions in MEPZ factories is the strict nature of daily work routines and the setting of production quotas to achieve maximum productivity. In the majority of factories, the nine-hour day is broken only by a one-hour lunch period. Although a small number of firms do allow a 15-minute break in the morning and afternoon, most companies permit workers only one three-to-five-minute respite a day, to use the toilets. Moreover, if operatives are behind in reaching their quotas, they may be forced to continue working through their already limited rest periods (see also M.Santos, 1988; Yap, 1989; Zarate, 1990). This has obvious implications for all workers, especially women, in terms of urinary tract infections, kidney problems and menstrual complications. Further occupational hazards such as backache, eye strain, blurred vision and headaches are also encountered by female assembly workers, as a result of having to sit and concentrate for long periods of time, not to mention complaints such as chest infections and skin irritations which arise from the handling and inhalation of chemical substances (see also Donald, 1991; Eviota, 1992:121; Pineda-Ofreneo, 1987; Rosario, 1985; Yap, 1989; Zarate, 1990).

Nonetheless, factory workers in Lapu-Lapu are generally well-protected and provided for in terms of payment of minimum and above-minimum wages and legal and extra privileges (see also Addison and Demery, 1988); their counterparts in Cebu, on the other hand, especially those in Filipino (as opposed to foreign) firms, are not so fortunate. Rank-and-file employees in Cebu usually work at least a nine-hour day, with more than half working ten hours a day, six days a week. Although average weekly wages in the firms included in the sample are about 5 per cent higher than the legal minimum (P671 [US$25.80]), they are substantially lower than in MEPZ and rarely include COLA. Variations exist not only in wage levels between firms, but also in payment methods. For example, all but one of the four rattan furniture and handicraft companies pay the bulk of their workers on a piece-rate basis. While employers claim that piece-workers receive the equivalent, if not more, of salaried earners' money, average wages in these firms are only P650 per week, as opposed to P800 in the firm using a fixed-rate system (a foreign-owned basket-weaving company).[18] Interestingly, the only fashion accessory company

18 Two out of three of the piece-rate employers stated their rationale as lying in the need to increase productivity, or, as one argued, if he paid workers on a fixed rate 'people would use the comfort room [toilet] all day'.

to use the piece-rate system is Filipino-owned, which, moreover, pays the lowest average wages of all jewellery firms (P630). Foreign firms in this sector pay much higher fixed salaries (P763 [US$30.50] per week basic and P1,022 ($40.90] including an average amount of overtime). Also pertinent is that the Filipino-owned carageenan company not only pays the lowest average wage of all firms in the sample (P388 per week [$15.50]), but in giving this as a fixed wage, violates the legal minimum requirements.

In summary, therefore, while wages are highly variable in different types of factories, Filipino firms tend to remunerate their workers at a much lower level than do foreign-owned companies, usually by paying piece-rates. In addition, Filipino firms are much less likely to uphold social security commitments and to provide extra privileges for workers compared with foreign companies, who not only adhere to legal requirements but frequently give fringe benefits as well. While two Filipino firms claim to pay no social security on the grounds that their workers do not want deductions from their salaries (see Chapter 2), the rest only pay SSS for their few permanent workers. Foreign companies, on the other hand, provide SSS for all workers; in addition, over and above the extra benefits characteristic of their counterparts in MEPZ, one provides free transport for workers and another is in the process of building a rent-free dormitory for migrant employees. While some Filipino enterprises provide perks such as subsidised meals, emergency loans and, occasionally, productivity bonuses, these are not very extensive, and one employer in a rattan factory even cited free tuberculosis testing as a fringe benefit, though it is presumably more in the interests of the company than of the workers. In terms of working conditions, foreign firms are more likely to tolerate breaks than Filipino enterprises are (the normal working day in foreign factories includes two 15-minute rest periods in addition to one hour for lunch), although this is complicated by the fact that Filipino firms are more likely to employ piece-rate workers who effectively create their own timetables: since pieceworkers have to put in long hours to attain salaries comparable with those working on a daily rate, they are less likely to use the rest periods advised by management.

With respect to gender, it would appear that women are generally better off than men in Cebu, given their concentration in the high-wage fashion accessory sector where employment is characterised by the receipt of extra privileges. Having said this, women in furniture and handicrafts manufacture receive a rougher deal. Since men are concentrated in skilled positions as weavers, sample-makers and so on, they earn higher wages than women, who are mainly in finishing jobs. Although the majority of tasks are paid by the piece, the rates for skilled jobs are considerably higher: for example, in one furniture company male weavers earn around P100 for a chair, while female workers earn only P20–5 for sanding the same item. In this context, therefore, women have to work substantially longer hours to earn comparable salaries. Also significant is that women in furniture companies are more likely to be employed as casual workers: in one rattan furniture factory, for instance, around 85 per cent of all casual workers are female sanders, who not only earn lower piece rates than regulars but also have little job security.

Bearing in mind these general patterns of labour demand in manufacturing in Lapu-Lapu and Cebu, we now turn to examine more closely the characteristics of the workers themselves, focusing on migration and domestic organisation.

MANUFACTURING WORKERS AND MIGRATION

Migrant origins and source-destination linkages among workers in MEPZ/Lapu-Lapu

Although a preference for migrant workers was not explicitly identified by employers in MEPZ, the majority of people working in the factories are not native to the locality (see also Chapter 3). Out of a total of twelve MEPZ factory workers interviewed in Lapu-Lapu (eight female and four male), nine are migrants (five female and four male) – see Appendix. Of these migrants, the vast majority (eight) were born in the Central Visayas, with five originating within Cebu province itself and three from the nearby province of Bohol. Only one woman was born outside the region – in Samar, in the Eastern Visayas (see Fig. 3.2). While one-third (three) of the MEPZ migrants had lived for a period in Cebu City before making the short step to Lapu-Lapu, the rest had come straight from their places of birth (although one woman had also lived in Manila earning her living in a rattan factory, and one man had lived in Cagayan de Oro in Mindanao working on a relative's farm). Among this latter group, most arrived at a young age (the average was 18 years old), while those who had lived in Cebu City first had arrived in Lapu-Lapu at 31 years of age on average.

All but one of the nine migrants had arrived in Lapu-Lapu for reasons of employment in the Zone. One woman had already secured a position in a factory prior to arrival, three moved from Cebu City to be closer to their workplaces and four came to Lapu-Lapu in the hope of finding a job. While employment opportunities in MEPZ were extremely influential in determining movement, migrants who had come straight from their places of birth also emphasised the lack of work in rural areas as a major factor. All had come from farming areas where subsistence agriculture was the mainstay of the local economy and wage opportunities for young people were extremely limited. In one more extreme case, a woman called Maria was effectively forced to leave her home area in Samar at the age of 18, after a typhoon devasted the small farming community where she lived with her parents and siblings. As one of the eldest children in the family, Maria said she had little option but to migrate to find some means of livelihood. On moving first to Mandaue City, she stayed with relatives until she found a job in a department store, after which she moved to Lapu-Lapu to seek work in MEPZ. While Maria's decision to migrate was largely taken on grounds of necessity and a sense of duty to her parents, the whole family rallied to overcome the situation, with other brothers and sisters moving to Manila at the same time to find ways of supporting those who had remained behind.

Indeed, financial support of parents and siblings was a primary consideration among migrants coming to Lapu-Lapu, with five of the nine migrating with this aim in mind, and another in order to support a wife and two young children remaining in Tuburan, Cebu province. Although most arrived when they were single, and were able to remit substantial amounts of their wages to parents at first, those who have since married still try to transfer support back to home areas. All but two of the nine migrants send financial help to their areas of origin, in most cases representing between one-quarter and one-third of their wages, depending on whether they are married or single: those with their own families send the least and on a more irregular basis than single people, who remit at least one-third of their wages once a month or even every 15 days. The latter applies to Alma, a 21-year-old sewing machine operative. Born in Busay, Cebu province, Alma managed to secure her present job in a garment factory before migrating to Lapu-Lapu, through family contacts and a personal 'backer' (see above). While Alma ultimately wants to continue her studies (in the form of a computer science course), her main rationale for working at the moment is to help her parents. So, besides putting a little money aside for future education and spending a minimum on personal subsistence, Alma sends P750, almost half her wages, back home at regular 15-day intervals. This also used to be the case with Esmerelda, a 28-year-old splicer (cutter) in a wood product factory, born in Inabanga, Bohol. Esmerelda originally came to Lapu-Lapu as a single woman and sent around half her salary back home to her parents. Now she is married with two children, she has reduced this to around one-tenth, remitting only P500 once every two months.

Although most migrants come from areas relatively close to Lapu-Lapu, visits to home areas are usually confined to Christmas and Easter. While single migrants are more likely to make visits than those who are married, journeys are limited by the punishing work schedules in factories, where long working hours and overtime make it difficult to take leave except during statutory holiday periods. While none of the interviewees reported being expressly asked by parents to migrate to Lapu-Lapu to find a job, a sense of responsibility to natal families figures very strongly in their decisions to move (see also Chapter 3), and for many the primary consideration was to help parents and/or siblings.

To sum up the general patterns, it appears that migrants to Lapu-Lapu are mainly young and single on arrival, with the sole intention of securing or taking up employment in the export processing zone. Migration tends to be perceived as permanent, with no interviewees expressing any wish to return to home areas, mainly because of the lack of economic opportunities in rural communities and, in the case of married migrants, because they have now established their family lives in the city and have no desire to disrupt them (see also Chapter 3). Nonetheless, links with home areas remain strong, largely through the sending of remittances and an enduring sense of responsibility to natal families.

Migrant origins and source-destination linkages among factory workers in Cebu

Moving on to migration patterns in Cebu, of the twelve factory workers (eight female and four male) interviewed in the city, seven (four female, three male) had been born elsewhere: in other words, the proportion of migrants is lower (i.e. just over half) than among MEPZ operatives. The majority (four) were born in other parts of Cebu province, with a further two in Misamis Occidental, Mindanao, and one in Negros Occidental (see Fig. 3.2). Only two had lived in other places before coming to Cebu City (one woman in Dumaguete City with her parents as a child, and a man in Cagayan de Oro City who had worked in the construction industry).

Although these general characteristics are similar to those in Lapu-Lapu, reasons for migration to Cebu City seem to be more diverse. While employment factors figure strongly in more than half the decisions to migrate, family and educational issues were also identified as important, especially where people had moved as children or teenagers accompanied by parents (see also Chapter 3). In some cases, idiosyncratic personal motives also featured. For example, one man, Elmo, a 33-year-old sanding machine operator in a rattan factory, who was born in Carmen in Cebu province and had worked for three years in Cagayan de Oro, came to Cebu City at the age of 24 with his *barkada* (see Chapters 1 and 3) as a kind of 'dare', as well as hoping to find a job in the San Miguel beer-bottling plant. While unsuccessful in this latter aim, Elmo soon found a position in the rattan factory, where he has been working for the last nine years. While Elmo's move was thus primarily work-related, it is interesting that male camaraderie and, in some senses, a desire to 'prove himself' also played an important role in the decision. The only woman who migrated specifically to find employment, Glecerie, came from Misamis Occidental when she was 17 years old and still single. With few opportunities in her home area, especially in terms of factory employment, Glecerie was persuaded by her older sister to come to Cebu to look for a job. Soon after arrival, she found work in a garment factory where she remained for eleven years, before taking her present job in a handicrafts firm. This diversity in reasons for coming to Cebu is also reflected in the ages of migrants on arrival: the four who came when single, primarily in search of work, were on average 18 years old, whereas the average age of those coming with parents was twelve years.

As in Lapu-Lapu, migrants to Cebu are not only prompted by the greater opportunities available in urban environments (be these related to their own or other relatives' employment or educational facilities), but by the lack of livelihood options in the predominantly rural areas from whence they come. Even migrants from urban areas complained that there were no factories and hence few jobs in other cities. Unlike the case in Lapu-Lapu, however, none of the interviewees said their movement stemmed from a desire to help or support parents in home areas. Although half the migrants moved when they were still single, mainly to find work, this was primarily for personal motives – to improve their own lives rather than those of their natal families. As a result, the sending of remittances to home communities is extremely rare: only Glecerie takes gifts to her parents once a year when she returns for her annual holiday; and even then, she says that her parents are more likely to help her – usually by sending rice, bananas and other fruit (see also Eviota, 1992:114 and Wolf, 1990b on two-way linkages between factory workers and their home areas). Although in three cases parents are actually resident in Cebu, the main reason reported for lack of financial support to relatives in home areas is that workers are barely able to sustain their own families, let alone have a surplus with which to help others. Two female migrants, Tessie and Jeanette, are both the main breadwinners in the household as their husbands have only casual employment. Financial constraints also explain why workers in general are unable to make regular visits to their home areas. While those living close to Cebu City are more likely to visit, most make trips only once a year, and one migrant (Elmo) has not seen his parents for nine years. Given these weak links between source and destination areas, it is hardly surprising that none of the workers expressed a desire to return to home villages. Overall then, around half the migrant workers to Cebu appear to be independent movers, in the sense that family influences were minimal in stimulating movement and that once established in the city, few have maintained active ties on any consistent basis. The rest moved with parents or partners, where links with home areas are less relevant.

In summary, migration patterns among factory workers in Lapu-Lapu and Cebu are rather different. Migrants to Lapu-Lapu are primarily concerned with securing or taking up employment in the export processing zone, whereas in Cebu motives are more diverse. People coming to Lapu-Lapu are mostly young and single with limited experience of previous employment or migration, reflecting the demand for 'fresh' labour in MEPZ. In Cebu, on the other hand, there is a much greater range of age groups, marital characteristics and work/migration histories. Perhaps the most important variation, however, is in terms of source-destination linkages: these are extremely strong in Lapu-Lapu, yet virtually non-existent in Cebu. While it is difficult to pinpoint why so few migrants to Cebu appear not to have been influenced by parental considerations on first moving, the weak maintenance of ties after migration appears to rest on financial constraints, namely the lower wage levels in Cebu's factories compared with those of MEPZ, as well as higher living costs in terms of rents and so on.[19] In Lapu-Lapu, on the other hand, MEPZ workers have higher earnings; moreover, the extra privileges provided by employers, together with lower rents and transport costs, seem to allow greater leeway to send support to areas of origin, accepting that remittances tend to diminish as marriage and children start to weigh more heavily on household budgets.

HOUSEHOLD CHARACTERISTICS OF MANUFACTURING WORKERS

Given the differences in recruitment patterns in manufacturing sectors between Lapu-Lapu and Cebu, particularly in terms of personal characteristics such as age and marital status, how might these influence or interrelate with the organisation of workers' households in the two localities?

Household characteristics in Lapu-Lapu

In Lapu-Lapu, just under half the workers included in the sample are single (five), while the rest are married (seven), with an average age of 27 years among men and 28 years among women. Of the single workers who have an average age of 22 years, two (one male, one female) live in boarding houses near the export processing zone, one of which is actually a company staff house, where residents live rent-

---

19 Average rents in Cebu are higher than in Lapu-Lapu. For example, the monthly price of a single room in a boarding house is P350, compared with P200 in Lapu-Lapu, and the cost of a cheap one-or two-roomed dwelling in a low-income neighbourhood is on average P500 a month, compared with P400 in Lapu-Lapu.

free in return for guarding the premises.[20] Boarding is usually the domain of single migrant workers, who may not know anyone in the vicinity. As it is, the other single migrant in the sample, Leonicio, a 28-year-old cutter in a garment factory, lives with his brother and family in nearby Pusok (see also Chapter 3). The other two single people in the group, both female electronics machine operatives, reside with their parents, one set of whom migrated several years ago to Lapu-Lapu, while the other is native to the area. The alternatives open to single workers in MEPZ seem, therefore, to depend largely on migrant status, with those who are strangers to the city residing in boarding houses or with relatives, and those native to the locality in their parents' homes.

Boarding houses also provide accommodation for married labour migrants who have left their spouses and children behind in home areas. This applies to 28-year-old Junior, an overstitcher in a garment factory, who shares a small room in a Pusok boarding house with four members of his *barkada*. Among the remaining six married workers (five female, one male), one couple without children live alone, and the other five live in nuclear arrangements with an average of three offspring. The average age of these workers is 34 years, and women in the group have had to devise various ways of reconciling their work outside the home with that of domestic labour and childcare. Both Leonida, a 37-year-old sewing machine operator with three children under eight years old, and Gemma, a 27-year-old recorder[21] in an electronics firm with two children under five years old, are natives of Lapu-Lapu, with mothers living nearby who look after children on a daily basis. This option does not, however, exist for the other working mothers in the sample, Esmerelda, 28, and Maria, 45, both of whom work as splicers in wood factories. Having older children, Maria is able to charge her

---

20 In a small survey conducted among owners of five boarding houses in Lapu-Lapu and Cebu (see Appendix), the two located in Lapu-Lapu were mixed-sex, although men and women were divided into single-sex rooms housing two or three people each. While one establishment, in the centre of Lapu-Lapu, had boarders working in various occupations, the one located adjacent to the Zone exclusively housed MEPZ workers. In the latter, there were 30 women and ten men, all in the 17–25 year age range, who came primarily from Cebu province, Bohol and Negros, and who were all single. The tariff for a room sleeping up to three people is P600 per month, although it is up to the boarders themselves as to whether they fill the room, as only one person is required to register.

21 The post of recorder involves recording the daily output of the factory.

eldest (21 years old) with caring for the two younger ones (twelve and
eight years old). Esmerelda, however, is unable to do this since the
elder of her two children is only four years old. Fortunately, her
husband is a 'job-outer' for a rattan factory who works at home and
is able to mind them. The other married worker, Evelyn, 26 years
old, is pregnant with her first child; her husband, who also works in
the same factory, is presently trying to persuade her sister to come and
live with them to help out (see also Chapter 3). Thus, despite the fact
that over half the female workers in the sample are married with children,
combining employment in MEPZ with having a family is not an easy
task (see also Zosa-Feranil, 1984 on Bataan).

Moreover, married women do not just face problems of childcare,
but must also prove to employers that they are equally efficient as their
single counterparts, especially if they are already married when applying
for jobs. Three of the five married women in the group were actually
in this position when they began their present employment. One
managed to obtain her job in a wood products factory because the
personnel department was not particularly concerned about marital
status. Another, Leonida, a garment factory worker, had had extensive
experience in other MEPZ plants; the fact that her skills were relevant
to the job seemed to outweigh the possible disadvantages of being
married. The remaining case, however, that of Gemma, illustrates the
lengths to which some married women must go if they wish to obtain
work in the Zone. Gemma made a false declaration about her marital
status when she applied to the electronics firm in which she has
worked for the last three-and-a-half years. Six months into the job
when she was made a permanent worker and had to sign social security
documents, she was forced to come clean about her status. As it
happened, several other women were in a similar position, and in order
to keep these trained workers the company compromised by granting
a special 'amnesty' for married women (see Donald, 1991:195 on a
similar situation in Bataan; see also Gothoskar, 1991:101–2 on women's
struggle against the marriage clause in the Indian pharmaceutical
industry).

Household characteristics in Cebu

Manufacturing workers in Cebu are generally older (with the eight
women averaging 31 years old and the four men 36 years) and more

likely to be married than those in Lapu-Lapu, undoubtedly reflecting the different recruitment practices in the two areas. Here, only one-quarter of the sample are single people, all of whom are women working in fashion accessory firms (which tend to be most stringent about marital status). As natives of Cebu, these single women workers all reside in their parents' homes, although one, Veronica, 24 years old, has a four-year-old son, effectively making her an embedded female head (see Chapter 3).

The nine workers who are married (five women, four men) are considerably older than their single counterparts (with an average age of 35 years, compared with 25 years among the latter) and tend to reside in a wide diversity of household arrangements. In the case of women workers in particular, domestic organisation appears to hinge primarily around childcare strategies. Of the four spouses living in male nuclear households, for example, only one is a woman: Jeanette, 41 years old, who lives with her husband and five children. The only reason she is able to work is because her children are grown-up, the eldest being 21 years old and the youngest twelve. While Jeanette feels confident to leave her youngest child alone when necessary, the eldest daughter is given responsibility for the affairs of the house when Jeanette is working. Among the male workers heading nuclear units, all are breadwinners, with their wives taking full responsibility for domestic labour. The remaining five married workers live in extended units (four female, one male). All the female workers living in extended households delegate childcare to other relatives residing in the home, except for Tessie, 36, whose children are old enough to be left alone.

Summing up the major differences between the two localities, workers in Lapu-Lapu are more likely to be young and single, with migrants residing either in boarding houses or with other relatives in the city, and non-migrants living with their parents. Married MEPZ workers, who tend to be younger than their counterparts in Cebu, mainly live in nuclear arrangements where child care strategies among women range from leaving children with nearby relatives, to using other members within the household (husbands or older children, for example). In Cebu, where most workers are older and married, there is a wider diversity of household organisation, with most of the men residing in male nuclear households where their wives adopt a homemaker role, and the majority of female workers living in extended households where female relatives assist with domestic labour and childcare.

Attitudes to marriage and fertility among young, single manufacturing workers

Notwithstanding the difficulties that married women face in combining factory work with their social roles of wife and mother, it is interesting to explore whether single women in manufacturing employment have different views on marriage and children than their older counterparts. Although there are only six women in the Cebu and Lapu-Lapu samples who are still unmarried, it would seem in general that they are likely to marry later and also to have fewer children, albeit for rather different reasons in the two localities.

In Lapu-Lapu, for example, none of the three single women (aged between 19 and 21 years) presently have boyfriends, in two cases because they say that they 'don't have time' due to the long hours they spend on the assembly line.[22] In spite of this, they all expressed the intention to marry in the future, preferably around the age of 25, which is about one year older than the average age of the women workers already married in the MEPZ sample. The main reason for waiting is to have an opportunity to further their studies (in computer science and/or commerce). Since they are presently unable to study on a part-time basis because of long factory shifts, the plan is to save money for a concentrated spell at college between leaving work and starting a family. The longer-term aim of two of the women is to use their education to enter a profession or profitable self-employment which would allow them to buy in domestic help and childcare if necessary. One interesting point is not only that these women wish to embark upon a career prior to marriage, but also that factory employment is conceived as a 'stepping stone' in the process. Certainly, none of the women see their present work as fulfilling career aspirations, especially in the light of limited promotion prospects within the firms.

22 A similar observation has been made in the Bataan Export Processing Zone in Luzon, where older unmarried workers often claim that they 'grew old' working in the factories and missed out on the opportunity of meeting men (interview with Rosalinda Pineda-Ofreneo, College of Social Work and Community Development, University of the Philippines, January, 1992). See also Eviota, 1992:121; Fuentes and Ehrenreich, 1983:25; Pineda-Ofreneo, 1988.

In Cebu, the three single women express somewhat different attitudes to those in Lapu-Lapu. One woman is 24 years old and the other two are 25, which is already older than the average age at marriage of their married counterparts in the worker sample (20 years). Both Gloria and Armi, who are 25 years old, have boyfriends, yet want to 'wait a few years' before getting married on the grounds of wishing to 'enjoy life' before they start looking after husbands and children. According to Gloria this means 'having experiences first', or, as Armi stated, 'to enjoy being a lady'. The case of Veronica, the embedded female head with a son of four years, is somewhat different as she married at 20, yet only lived with her husband for two months before separating because of his 'irresponsibility' and 'argumentativeness'. Veronica is now very reluctant to have another boyfriend, as her perception of men has become tainted. She also admits that she was too young to get married the first time; with hindsight, she should have waited until she was older.

As for children, the married women workers in the Lapu-Lapu sample have an average of four, although this is highly skewed in that the eldest, Maria, 41 years old, has eight, Leonida, 37, has three, and the two women under 30 have only two apiece. While this could simply reflect the fact that younger married women have not had all the children they eventually will, the interviews suggest that younger women are more likely to limit their births, and in many respects this is borne out by the fact that all the three single women interviewed expressed a desire to have only two offspring (usually one of each sex), mainly because they wanted 'to give them a good life' in terms of being able to pay for education and so on. Similar fertility decisions prevail in Cebu, where married women have an average of three children, with the eldest, Jeanette, 41 years old, having five, compared with an average of two among those in their early 30s. Two of the three single women (Armi and Gloria) want two children each, although the third, Veronica, in the light of her negative experience with the father of her four-year-old son (see above), is content to have only one, preferring to give him the best possible future with no help from her estranged partner. Overall then, younger, single and indeed even married women appear to be limiting the number of children they have, or intend to have, and mainly for economic reasons. At the same time, this may also relate to the fact that women generally want to

continue working after having children, and it may be easier to find
alternative childcare for smaller numbers of offspring.

While fertility projections among young manufacturing workers are
slightly lower than among their counterparts in the household surveys
in Cebu and Lapu-Lapu (see Chapter 3), what is perhaps most interesting is that female operatives in Cebu wish to get married later in
order to delay responsibility, and those in Lapu-Lapu in order to
further their studies and careers. These patterns suggest that women
in both Lapu-Lapu and Cebu are in the process of in some way challenging the nature of prevailing gender roles and relations, with
workers in MEPZ perhaps forging ahead of those in Cebu. This leads
us into the final and concluding section of this chapter, which explores
how export manufacturing employment may influence gender
ideologies in more general ways.

PRELIMINARY CONCLUSIONS ON THE GENDER
IMPLICATIONS OF MANUFACTURING EMPLOYMENT

While Chapter 7 deals with these issues in greater depth, the present
section highlights a number of possible impacts of manufacturing
employment on the lives and status of women. As we have seen, recruitment into export-oriented manufacturing employment almost always
involves gender considerations; more specifically, it translates into a
distinct preference for women over men in most rank-and-file jobs,
mainly on account of stereotypical assumptions about 'female' attributes.
While at first glance the prevalence of gender-stereotyping within this
sector may suggest that the implications for women's status might be
overwhelmingly negative, one or two more positive effects must also
be taken into consideration.

Highlighting the negative aspects first, however, the most obvious
is what might be termed the 'feminisation' of manufacturing in the
Visayas, particularly in the export processing zone. This arises from a
range of dubious physiological and psychological stereotypes, such as
women being more manually dexterous, physically capable of sitting
for long hours, being docile and malleable and having a high threshold
for boring, repetitive work. Under these circumstances, women
arguably have few opportunities to break out of the mould imposed
upon them by employers. Indeed, they have little choice but to

conform with expectations and to acquiesce uncomplainingly with the status quo, since if they did not, they would be out of work.

A related consequence of female stereotyping in export manufacturing is that it impedes women's mobility both horizontally and vertically within firms. Because women are perceived to be most suited to labour-intensive tasks, they are mainly assigned to assembly and finishing departments and are overlooked when it comes to more skilled jobs involving mechanised techniques (see also Moghadam, 1993a:25; Rohini, 1991:262 on India). This of course is inherently discriminatory, since in MEPZ in particular workers are rarely required to have any previous experience as they are trained from scratch. Moreover, women's persistent relegation to labour-intensive jobs means that if automation in their departments does occur, then new jobs are likely to go to men (see also Heng Leng and Ng Choon Sim, 1993; O'Connor, 1987:264; Rohini, 1991:262). With regard to vertical mobility, the assumption that women are docile and passive puts them at a disadvantage vis-à-vis men who are thought to have better leadership qualities (see also Reardon, 1991b:155 on India). Moreover, since it is male managers who 'create and implement employment strategies', then male interests are likely to be privileged, even when this goes against the grain of economic efficiency (Eviota, 1992:115). Women therefore usually remain in dead-end, manual occupations, from which ascent to supervisory and especially managerial positions is extremely unlikely; if women do succeed in climbing any kind of career ladder, they usually have to wait longer to do so than men (see also Addison and Demery, 1988:384; Gallin, 1990:179; Ward, 1990:12).[23] Occupational inertia tends to become reinforced over time as women are rarely promoted and so continue to perceive men as having exclusive rights to positions of authority. This has important ramifications for women's social and household roles: psychologically, women's role as secondary workers is reinforced; pragmatically, their earnings often remain too low to assert themselves as individuals fully independent of husbands or fathers (see Chant and

---

23 An additional factor here is that most women in the upper echelons of factory employment (notably administration) are usually recruited from among college and/or university graduates. This further inhibits the upward mobility of rank-and-file workers (see Chant and McIlwaine, 1994).

McIlwaine, 1994; also Chapter 3, this volume),[24] quite apart from the fact that independent women have little social legitimacy (see Chapter 7). As such, patriarchal authority and traditional gender roles may not only remain in place, but even intensify (see Elson and Pearson, 1981:101–4; Eviota, 1992:124–5; Taylor and Turton, 1988:145–6; Ward, 1990:12; also Humphrey, 1985).

A further consequence of women's concentration in low-level assembly work is that tasks require limited training and mean little in the way of learning new skills. Coupled with the fact that most operatives are only high-school graduates (and likely to remain that way, since punishing work schedules do not allow women to pursue further education at night school), options for other (perhaps more fulfilling) careers outside the factories are inevitably limited. The highly specialised nature of the work they do (especially in electronics factories) also means that work experience is not readily transferable to other jobs (see also Eviota, 1992:121; Pineda-Ofreneo, 1987:96), although factory employment in MEPZ does seem to offer some scope to accumulate the necessary capital for further education, retraining, or to set up a small business.[25]

Having said this, in a situation where women have few possibilities for internal career promotion and are confined to carrying out exhausting and repetitive tasks all day, initiative and enterprise are likely to be suppressed. Time constraints arising from long working hours (especially where people do regular overtime) may also leave women with little space to reflect on their position and formulate any positive plans for their futures. In the light of daily drudgery on the assembly line, women's only thoughts may be focused on the receipt of a salary at the end of the week. The cruel irony is that while their wage may be a key to potential economic (and personal) autonomy, they may have little time to spend it or use it for their own benefit, bearing in

---

24 Aihwa Ong (1987:198) notes a similar pattern in the Telok Free Trade Zone in Malaysia, where, she argues: 'Although rural women sought in factory employment a source of independent wealth, in practice their low wages, the unavoidable claims of their families, and insecurity of employment did not provide a sufficient basis for economic independence.'

25 Ong's work on the Telok Free Trade Zone also finds that some women workers view their wages as a means of improving their technical qualifications to allow them to compete for better jobs (Ong, 1987:197).

mind that women of all ages play a major role in supporting their own families as well as their natal kin (see Chapter 3).

The restricted nature of factory employment, especially in terms of long working hours, may also have implications for women's potential for meeting a partner and having children. Indeed, some respondents stated that they did not have time to have boyfriends. While delaying marriage and childbirth may have positive implications for women (see below), the downside is a prospective denial of any experiences and enjoyment which might come from having boyfriends and a social life.[26]

Another serious aspect of factory employment is the exposure of workers to occupational hazards. Many women in assembly and finishing jobs report backstrain and headaches as the result of sitting for long hours performing repetitive tasks. While men also experience these problems, they are less likely to be employed in jobs requiring concentrated attention to detail (Rosario, 1985; Yap, 1989; Zarate, 1990). Some women (especially in MEPZ) also complain of kidney and urinary tract infections as a result of only being allowed to use toilet facilities at scheduled times (see also Fuentes and Ehrenreich, 1983:23). Indeed, in firms where women are not allowed off the assembly line for four hours at a time, menstruation also becomes a major problem. This situation is unlikely to improve, given the obstacles faced by women registering formal complaints about their work conditions.

Despite this, it cannot be denied that export manufacturing employment in the Visayas provides women with relatively privileged jobs in a context of limited alternatives (see also Armstrong and McGee, 1985b:211; Foo and Lim, 1989:213–14; Sklair, 1991:96–8; Wolf, 1990a:52). In both Lapu-Lapu and Cebu, most women earn at least the legal minimum wage (usually more); in MEPZ firms and fashion accessory factories in Cebu, they also receive substantial benefits over and above those prescribed by law. Indeed, if anything, women rather than men seem to be concentrated in sectors which provide the highest wages and most benefits, even if the scope to capitalise on these

---

26 This seems to contrast with the situation of female factory workers in Hong Kong and Taiwan, who have been observed to enjoy greater freedom and more active social lives as a result of employment (see Salaff, 1990:126–7; also Armstrong and McGee, 1985:211; Buang, 1993:206 et seq.; Ong, 1987:200 et seq. on Malay factory women).

in terms of personal well-being is held in check either by the demands of natal kin in areas of origin, or in their own homes, especially where husbands use wives' earnings to justify diminution of their own inputs to family life (see Chapter 3; also Chant, forthcoming b; Eviota, 1992:123). Nonetheless, manufacturing employment at least provides an opportunity to delay marriage and childbirth; although this may be by default in some cases (lack of time to find a husband, for example), the fact that wages are higher than in many other jobs means there is some scope for personal independence and self-determination. Moreover, provided women can maintain productivity, they can often expect to remain in work in the longer term. This is important, since it might provide a rather different range of options than those which present themselves to women in lower-paid or less regular work. Indeed, female factory operatives not only seem to delay marriage and childbirth for longer than other women, but often continue working full-time through the family life-cycle. This modifies certain aspects of their household roles, especially in respect of entitling them to delegate childcare, to exert greater control over household expenditure and to play a larger role in determining their children's futures (see also Heyzer, 1986:110; Safa, 1993; Wolf, 1991:141). Thus, despite the gender-typing which leads to the absorption of women into factories in the first place, young women in particular seem to be making decisions that are different to those of some of their older counterparts in manufacturing firms in Cebu and Lapu-Lapu, and to women in the localities in general (see Chapter 3). Over time, these tendencies may afford certain opportunities to challenge the inequities of marriage, if not to deviate from the usual role of wife and mother (see also Foo and Lim, 1989:215). Thus, while factory employment itself may not provide much in the way of satisfaction per se, it could conceivably act as a 'stepping stone' to positive, if gradual, changes in the personal and household circumstances of women.

Silver linings aside, in general terms women employed in export manufacturing find themselves in an ambivalent position. While they are given preferential access to jobs, compared with men, the reasons are ultimately exploitative of existing gender inequalities and do relatively little, in a direct sense at least, to empower women. Women face innumerable difficulties in altering gender-stereotypical notions, given their fundamental embeddedness in the nature of manufacturing activity in the Visayas (see also Eviota, 1992:120–6; A.M.Scott,

1986); in Mactan in particular they have little scope to assert their rights through collective bargaining structures. As Eviota (1992:123) maintains: 'while employment in export factories may have expanded the range of women's productive work, it is work that has led to their subordination to a global market and a male-dominated hierarchy of management which has single-mindedly reaffirmed sexual stereotypes'.

A final cause for concern is that export manufacturing employment, particularly in multinational companies, is inherently vulnerable, given competition from other peripheral countries,[27] a changing configuration of the world market through the consolidation of new and pre-existing trading blocs such as NAFTA and the EC, and increased prospects of automation within more advanced economies as technological developments proceed (see Eviota, 1992:125; also Dicken, 1990:221; O'Connor, 1987:258–60; Pearson, 1986:68). As such, any gains made by Filipino women as a result of export-oriented industrialisation may be wiped out at any point. If this proves to be the case, women's options for alternative employment may be at best severely limited, and at worst equally or more exploitative. Indeed, other sources of employment geared to external consumers and the generation of foreign exchange, and which recruit large numbers of women, are also likely to face uncertain futures. International tourism is one such sector, and it is to different types of women's work within this that we turn in the following two chapters.

---

27 In the specific case of the Philippines, threats arise from the fact that neighbouring countries such as Indonesia, Thailand and Vietnam are becoming increasingly attractive to foreign investors in search of cheap labour. More generally, prospects for industrial relocation to Third World countries seem to be stemmed, at least in part, by a tendency for new investment in the peripheral states of industrial Europe (Pearson, 1986:68). The break-up of the former USSR and the Eastern bloc is also likely to have implications for changing patterns of multinational investment.

5   GENDER AND TOURISM EMPLOYMENT

This chapter explores the nature of female recruitment in tourism employment in the Visayas, with particular reference to Boracay Island. The emphasis on Boracay stems from our concern to deal here with what is perhaps most appropriately termed 'conventional' tourism employment, namely jobs in hotels, restaurants and commerce. By contrast, Cebu is given greater prominence in Chapter 6, which concentrates on the other major element of international tourism in the Philippines: the sex industry. While the present chapter does take into account conventional tourism employment in Cebu, the slant towards Boracay stems from the fact that sex work (in a formal sense at least) is not a significant employer of the island's populace, and a notably more elaborate range of formal and informal tourism and tourism-related activities have come to characterise the local labour market. This undoubtedly arises from the fact that tourism underpins Boracay's economy in a way that it does not in Cebu, where a much more diverse economic base, including export manufacturing, large-scale retail and public services, has provided other openings for the workforce. Indeed, aside from the entertainment sector, tourism employment in Cebu is mainly confined to work in hotels and restaurants. Accordingly, fewer interviews with workers and employers in 'ordinary' tourist activities were conducted here in comparison with Boracay (see Appendix).

TOURISM EMPLOYMENT IN BORACAY AND CEBU: AN OVERVIEW

Boracay possesses a wide range of tourism occupations common to most international 'sun and sea' resorts. These include jobs in hotels, restaurants and shops which are normally characterised by registration and contract and to all intents and purposes can be described as part of the 'formal sector'. Formal sector tourism employment of this type is also found in Cebu; analysis of conditions, recruitment patterns and so on will accordingly make reference to both localities. When it comes to more 'informal' tourism occupations, however, such as ambulant vending and home-based tourism-related activities, Boracay is the focus of discussion: the large-scale, business-oriented nature of tourism Cebu, together with the wide range of informal openings in other sectors of the local economy there, seems to have precluded the development of an informal labour market tied specifically to the tourist industry.

Differences in formal tourism employment between Cebu and Boracay

Having made the point that Boracay and Cebu share common ground in possessing a formal tourism employment sector, there are interesting and important differences between the two. For example, while hotels in Cebu tend to be large, high-rise, geared to business visitors and fall in the three- to five-star range, most tourist accommodation in Boracay is in the form of modest, low- to medium-priced beach cottage developments which cater for a wider range of visitors, most of whom are travelling for pleasure. This, as we shall see, goes some way to account for differences in the gender composition of hotel/accommodation staff between the two localities. Differences are also apparent in the nature of restaurants. Restaurants catering for tourists in Cebu tend to be up-market and fairly formal in the sense of dress code and so on. Boracay, on the other hand, has several beachfront restaurants which serve as bars as well as eating places, and where the ambience is considerably more relaxed. Finally, tourist shops in Cebu are mostly found in the foyers of large hotels and tend only to trade in high-value goods such as imported sun preparations, gold and silver jewellery and fine handicrafts. Boracay's retail outlets, on the other hand, sell a wider range of products: alongside souvenirs and clothing, basic consumer items such as mineral water, batteries and shampoo are available, with the result that the shops are often frequented as much by local people as by tourists. In general terms, therefore, Boracay's tourism infrastructure is on a smaller scale, with a wider market and a less elite, business-oriented nature.

In terms of the ways in which these differences impact upon formal tourism employment in Cebu and Boracay, one of the most notable features is that the smaller size of enterprises in the latter mean smaller staff numbers, especially in hotels. Among other things, this means that intra-establishment occupational hierarchies tend to be much less elaborate in Boracay. Whereas the large numbers of employees in Cebu's hotels require more in the way of intermediate supervisory and managerial posts, in Boracay there is sometimes no intermediate layer between workers and management. Moreover, because the workers required to run small accommodation ventures in Boracay are few in number, absenteeism is not easily covered unless people are prepared to move between posts. Thus workers in Boracay often have to 'double up' to perform other functions when their colleagues are away or when there is a sudden influx of visitors. This is rarely the case in Cebu, where hotels are usually divided into a number of distinct departments comprising various ranks and specialisations, and where people generally remain confined to one job.

Another characteristic associated with small workforces in Boracay is that trade unionism on the island is non-existent. In Cebu, on the other hand, most hotel workers are unionised.[1] While unionisation is by no means a guarantee of fair treatment, affiliated members do tend to have a greater awareness of their rights and benefits. Certainly all regular workers in Cebu's hotels are paid the legal minimum wage, have guaranteed overtime rates and receive other entitlements associated with full social security coverage, which is not the case in Boracay.

A third and related feature of different workforce sizes is that management–employee relations tend to be much more personalised in Boracay, whereas senior managers in Cebu rarely interact on a daily basis, if at all, with ordinary workers. The personalised nature of management–employee interaction in Boracay is also associated with paternalistic labour practices. Many workers in Boracay's hotels (and restaurants and shops) are housed on the premises as 'live-ins', much in the style of apprentices or servants. While this predominant pattern of live-in arrangements is due in part to the fact that it is obviously easier to provide accommodation for small workforces, and in part because many of Boracay's workers are young migrants who find it difficult to acquire rented lodging on the island (especially if they have no family contacts in local settlements or are only employed on a short-

---

1 Among three of the four hotels in the authors' employer survey, workers in two were affiliated to the Associated Labour Union, and in the other to the more left-wing National Federation of Labour.

term basis), it is also the case that employers prefer to be able to keep an eye on their staff. Indeed, other benefits to employers include the fact that 'live-ins' can be persuaded to work longer hours than those who live out (known locally as 'stay-outs'), are less likely to be absent for reasons other than sickness, are more isolated from family problems and are more likely to develop a dependence on employers which tends to translate into greater productivity. In addition, deductions for bed and board create scope for reducing wages to below the legal minimum (see also Chant, 1993b).

Labour recruitment in formal tourism establishments

In terms of the patterns of labour recruitment to which these broad differences in the nature of tourism and size of firm-specific workforces give rise, entry requirements for work in hotels and restaurants in Cebu seem to be stricter, more standardised and more credentialist than in Boracay. Employers in Cebu tend to look for at least a completed college-level education for so-called frontline posts requiring direct contact with clientele (waitering and front-desk clerical and reception work and so on), mainly because college graduates are assumed to have a reasonable level of proficiency in English. This sometimes applies to room staff as well, although people with a high-school leaving certificate are also considered for most rank-and-file positions. In Boracay, by contrast, only the larger hotels seem to be particularly concerned with educational qualifications: although high-school graduates are preferred in principle, work experience may be deemed a reasonable substitute for formal schooling in lower-level posts requiring minimum interaction with the public. Moreover, unlike Cebu, none of Boracay's formal sector employers screen prospective applicants by using aptitude tests.

Other entry criteria on which Cebu employers tend to be more rigid include age, marital status and, interestingly, height. The latter seems to reflect the desire on the part of Cebu hotels to present a 'Western' image, with a minimum height specification for women of 5ft 2in, and for men 5ft 6in.[2] This aside, there is a distinct preference for young

---

2 It is not only hotels which specify a minimum height in their entry criteria. We saw in the previous chapter that this sometimes applies to factory jobs (when machinery is tailored to Western operatives, for example). However, supermarkets and chain stores in the Philippines follow a similar practice to hotels in including height qualifications

workers in the 18–25 age range. Young people who are 'fresh out of college' are thought to be more amenable to training in the exacting standards required by international establishments (see also Chapter 4). Being single is also an advantage, especially for female workers: first, because marriage and childbirth are regarded as incurring additional expense for employers (whether on account of the cost of maternity leave and finding replacements, and/or imagined higher rates of absenteeism), and second, because motherhood is seen as incompatible with concentration on the job and working overtime. While Boracay employers also have a preference for young people, especially for frontline posts in shops, restaurants and hotels, they are generally less particular, and in fact sometimes prefer their workers to be 20 years old or more (teenagers are thought to be less responsible and too easily distracted by the island's nightlife). Partly for this reason, perhaps, there is no declared preference for single applicants, even if most formal sector employees are not actually married.

Another interesting difference is that whereas Cebu's employers recruit people native to the locality, employers in Boracay, especially those born elsewhere themselves, almost invariably favour staff from outside the island. Migrant preference is accounted for in a number of ways. Employers in larger establishments in Boracay, who also tend to be more stringent on educational qualifications, maintain that migrants from elsewhere in the Philippines, especially cities, are likely to have better standards of education. This is particularly relevant for administrative staff, who are usually required to possess a college degree in Hotel and Restaurant Management, which is only offered in larger urban centres. Another reason is the belief that people from more urbanised areas have 'better work discipline'. Others prefer migrants for more pragmatic reasons. Migrants are likelier to want to live in, which corresponds with management's ideal of having staff residing on the premises. Some also feel that migrants will not be as distracted by family problems as those native to the island and/or that it is easier to dismiss staff who do not have relatives in Boracay (disputes with local families have been known to break out when native islanders

---

for cashiers and counter staff which have little practical relevance to the jobs in question and stem more from imperatives of image. Having said this, when questioned at length about the extent to which stature counted when applicants were in all other respects well qualified for posts, Cebu's hotel employers said they would sometimes waive the height-bar, particularly in the case of women who could compensate by wearing high-heeled shoes!

have lost jobs). The non-migrant preference in Cebu, on the other hand, is explained in terms of the fact that it is easier to vet staff who are known in the locality, that there is no accommodation problem since people already reside in the area, and that Cebu has a large and highly skilled pool of labour: indeed, given Cebu's position as the best education centre in the Visayas, employers feel they can do no better than recruit locally, except in the case of managers who are sometimes headhunted in Manila. Another important reason for migrant–native recruitment differentials is that Boracay relies almost entirely on straightforward 'sun-and-sea/pleasure tourism', which tends to peak during the drier months of November to May, but drops over the summer period. In the leaner months of the low season, migrant workers, who are usually on contracts of six to eight months, are viewed as easier to lay-off. Moreover, migrant workers themselves tend to see the 'quiet' period as a useful opportunity to return to their home areas, especially as days off in the working season are limited to three or four a month. In Cebu, on the other hand, tourist demand is less subject to fluctuation, since the bulk of visitors are business travellers. Hotels thus need permanent staff (even if 'extras' are sometimes employed for short periods – for trade fairs or Holy Week, for example), and locals are regarded as less likely to leave, since their families reside in the city or its immediate environs.

A final difference, of particular relevance to the present study's concern with women, is that Boracay's employers seem to be less rigid in terms of gender specifications for their posts. This is exemplified both by the gender breakdown of staff in different enterprises and the fact that Cebu's employers often express such definite preferences for placing men in certain jobs, and women in others, that their advertisements often specify the sex of applicants at the outset.

Gender segmentation in formal tourism employment: hotels, shops and restaurants

Hotels and accommodation establishments are usually divided into a series of different departments and thereby offer a useful example of gender-selective recruitment patterns across a wide range of occupations. A total of four hotel managers were interviewed in Cebu and six in Boracay. The four Cebu hotels are large, cater for an international (mainly business) clientele and between them employ a total of

1,261 workers; two of them are owned by Filipino corporations, and
two belong to corporations where there is some multinational involvement.[3] Capacity ranges from 78 and 300 rooms, with tariffs for a
standard double between US$65 and $100. The six hotels in the Boracay
survey employ a total of 226 workers and range from a very small
establishment with only two workers to one of the largest hotels on
the island, which employs 88 persons; the largest three hotels have
between 50 and 60 per cent foreign equity participation (Australian
or British).[4] Room numbers in Boracay range from 11 to 38, with
tariffs starting at $10 per night in the smallest place and going up to
$70 in the largest. Overall, women make up 39 per cent of employees
in the Cebu hotels and 42 per cent of those in Boracay. In the former,
all personnel managers are male; in the latter, two out of six are female
– although this does not seem to make a great deal of difference to
the proportion of female staff recruited, as it often does in other
places (see Chant, 1991a: Chapter 3, for example, on the Mexican
tourist industry).

In terms of similarities between Cebu and Boracay, it is notable that
certain departments in hotels in both localities are exclusively male,
save for one or two female secretarial staff. Departments with an all-
male rank-and-file workforce include porterage and guest transportation,
engineering and maintenance, construction and security (see Fig.
5.1).[5] While all are decribed definitively as 'masculine' domains,
however, employers find this hard to explain except insofar as heavy
and/or technical jobs are regarded as 'men's work'. In contrast, no
department in the sample as a whole is exclusively the domain of
women. Thus although women have definite areas of concentration,
notably in administration and accounts (49 per cent of the administration and accounts workforce in Cebu and 74 per cent in Boracay),

---

3 As in the previous chapter, the names of tourism establishments in the survey are
not disclosed for reasons of confidentiality (see also Appendix 3).

4 The interviews with tourism employers and workers in Cebu were conducted in
April 1993, and those in Boracay during June and July. In the case of Boracay, these
months represent the low season and figures for the enterprises' workforces are accordingly only around two-thirds of what they normally are in the high season. It should
also be noted that the bulk of workers interviewed were also regular and/or long-
term employees.

5 Only a minimum of security staff (generally a supervisor) is actually employed directly
by most hotels. Instead specially trained guards are hired from agencies, which in the
event of conflict deflect problems away from the hotels themselves.

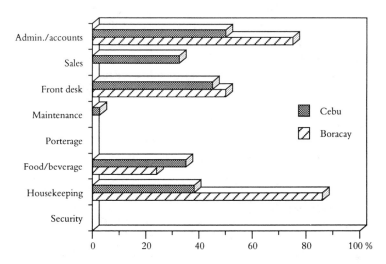

Figure 5.1: Percentage of women in different hotel departments:
Cebu and Boracay

front-desk duties (45 per cent in Cebu and 50 per cent in Boracay) and housekeeping (38 per cent in Cebu, 86 per cent in Boracay), men are still usually involved in these departments in some capacity (see Fig. 5.1).

Within administration and accounts, the large number of female employees is explained by employers on the grounds of their patience, reliability, integrity and skill with figures. While these notions in themselves are obviously heavily gender-stereotyped, they are at least reasonably positive assumptions about women (see also Chapter 4). The same cannot be said of the reasons for placing women in front-desk employment, where considerations of physical and sexual attributes appear to be uppermost. In Cebu, for example, employers unashamedly rationalised their preference for female reception workers in terms of women adding to the 'charm of the hotel' and projecting a 'good image'. One employer said that the majority of his counter staff were female because they had 'beautiful faces' and 'warm personalities'. Another claimed that while he was by no means looking for 'beauty queens' to fill front-desk posts, women would have to be 'beautiful in their manner of speaking, possess charm and a beautiful body, have excellent poise and be graceful in the way they walked'. Another stated that female employees 'add colour' to what is still a predominantly 'male world' (the business world). The importance of recruiting young, attractive women into public liaison positions is further borne out by the fact that photographs of smiling, uniformed, female receptionists are found on virtually all adverts or brochures for major Cebu hotels, alongside lists of 'starred attractions' that almost invariably highlight the establishment's 'charming and courteous frontliners'.

While hotel housekeeping also employs large numbers of women, different sets of gender attributes are identified by personnel managers, which again vary both between the two locations and between sub-sections of departmental activity. While in both Cebu and Boracay laundrywork employs an exclusively female staff, for example, the cleaning of rooms and public areas such as foyers and corridors is another matter. In Boracay women are usually in charge of cleaning rooms and making beds, except in one hotel where wood floors require polishing with coconut husks (an activity thought to give rise to uterine cramps, especially during menstruation). In Cebu, on the other hand, female housekeeping employees either have rather limited responsibilities or are barred altogether from servicing rooms. Although the rationale offered by Cebu employers is that cleaning rooms is 'heavy work', it is difficult to see why the same principle does not apply in Boracay. Indeed, Boracay employers tend to stress a preference for female chambermaids, given that women usually have more domestic experience from their home backgrounds and can be relied upon to maintain high standards. Besides this, female cleaners are usually prepared to double up as laundrywomen, which is all-important to small hostelries where occupational flexibility acts to counterbalance low staff numbers. Apart from the fact that the more sizeable hotel workforces in Cebu render this last criterion unnecessary, one conceivable reason for preferring to employ male cleaners in Cebu is that chambermaids may be prone to sexual harassment, since most clients are lone male businessmen. Indeed, one hotel which does employ female bedmakers has a policy of sending them into rooms in pairs (and separately from male room cleaners), ostensibly for their own protection. Another reason for the use of room boys in Cebu is possibly to facilitate clients' access to sexual companionship, especially as hotels do not wish to be seen openly providing information about 'hospitality' services. Although managers did not explicitly cite this as a reason for male recruitment in room cleaning, it may be a contributory factor: it is widely known that hotel guests use room attendants to provide leads on how and where to obtain women in the city.[6]

Another hotel department in which there are significant, albeit unsatisfactorily explained, differences in the recruitment of men and women is food and beverages. In Cebu an average of 35 per cent of food and beverage department staff are female, most of whom are in posts requiring direct liaison with customers, whether as waitresses, 'food attendants', or cashiers (see Fig. 5.2). Again, this tends to relate to the sexually based 'frontline' compartmentalisation of women workers, with one employer maintaining that 'female food attendants are more pleasing to customers'. At the same time, no women are employed as bartenders, or as stewards who deliver food and drink to rooms. Room service is seen as a male domain, not only because it requires staff who are available to work any shift during a 24–hour period, but also because it is thought unseemly for women to enter a room when guests are present. Again, parallels may be drawn with the situation in housekeeping departments. The other area of food and beverage departments in which women are conspicuously absent is kitchen duties, often on the grounds that men are more adept at operating complicated cooking equipment and large industrial dish-washers. Apart from their supposed technical advantage, men are also presumed to have 'quick and strong reflexes' which enable them to cope with the heavier aspects of kitchen portering.

In Boracay, however, which women do not form such a large proportion of the workforce in hotel food and beverage departments (making up only 24 per cent of employees in this section across the sample as a whole), they do tend to be spread more evenly between kitchen and restaurant work, possibly because the smaller scale of cuisine in beach cottage establishments is more labour-intensive and less demanding of specialised skills (see Fig. 5.3). Indeed, some of the restaurants attached to accommodation establishments are very small and serve only simple food (mainly breakfasts and light snacks) to hotel guests.

---

6 Various women's groups in Cebu and former employees in large hotels claim that, among other individuals, room boys, room service attendants, doormen, male desk clerks, porters (as well as taxi drivers) are commonly asked by tourists not only to provide details of bars with floorshows, massage parlours and brothels, but sometimes to arrange direct meetings with women. This is usually done via networks, and the tips received by individual brokers are shared out among the different parties involved. Tips are also given to doormen, room boys and night receptionists for 'overlooking' the entry of additional 'guests' to clients' rooms (see also Chapter 6).

But although some women may be cooks in Boracay hotels, senior culinary positions such as that of chef, as in Cebu, are invariably occupied by men. Some employers attribute this to the fact that Filipino men are 'good with food' and do a good deal of cooking in the home, even if our own household surveys reveal otherwise (see Chapter 3). However, another employer maintained that it was because only male applicants put themselves forward for this kind of job, and one in Cebu rationalised it in terms of women being 'more changeable and fussy', whereas 'men just prepare the food, and that's that' (failing to explain why he thought women were more 'changeable and fussy', let alone why these supposed character traits did not prevent women from doing several other jobs in his hotel). Another feature peculiar to Boracay is that the larger and more prestigious the accommodation establishment, the greater the likelihood that men will be employed as waiters, mainly because male food attendants are thought to present a more professional and sophisticated image. An employer in one of the larger hotels, for example, said that while it was acceptable for women to serve in the coffee shop, 'only men should be involved in fine dining'.

Although this last point might also be expected to apply to independent restaurants on the island, this is not the case: the four restaurants in the Boracay survey, consisting of three fairly prestigious enterprises (two with the involvement of French capital, another Swiss) and a smaller family-run business, employ a high percentage of women (54 per cent of their joint total of 57 workers). Additionally, women constitute nearly two-thirds (64 per cent) of staff waiting on tables. The main reason for the difference between independent and hotel restaurants appears to arise from the fact that the former usually abut directly onto the beach, and staff are often expected to stand at the entrances and solicit custom (in hotels, by contrast, the restaurants are generally enclosed and out of public view). The rationale for female preference was stated in terms of women being more 'charming' and 'attractive' and thereby able to draw greater numbers of customers. Not all women are eligible for such posts, however; consideration is usually only given to applicants who can speak English, German or another foreign language and have 'pleasing personalities'. The widely used term 'pleasing personality' means, among other things, youth, good looks and grooming, charm, a gracious manner and a 'well-modulated' voice. Employers state a preference for young single

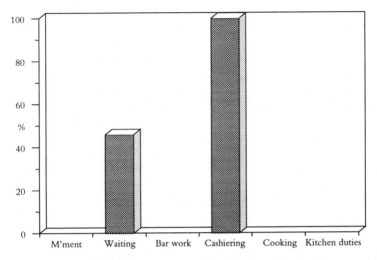

Figure 5.2: Percentage of women employed in subsections of food and beverage departments in hotels and accommodation establishments, Cebu

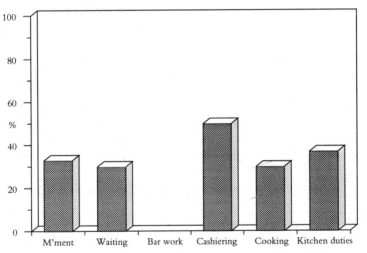

Figure 5.3: Percentage of women employed in subsections of food and beverage departments in hotels and accommodation establishments, Boracay

Note: Not all hotels have all categories of activity; percentages for each category therefore only pertain to establishments where the relevant subsections exists.

women, not only because they are 'prettier' but because they are freer
to work in the evenings and likelier to live in, as 86 per cent of restaurant
workers do. The same kinds of attributes and qualities demanded of
women in customer liaison positions in restaurants also apply to shops.
Women appear to make up the entire contingent of sales assistants in
Boracay, again being preferred for their natural 'way' with people and
their likelihood of attracting custom, as well as being thought more
adept at arranging merchandise.[7]

Summing up the general picture of labour demand in formal tourism
employment, key similarities between Cebu and Boracay include a
preference for youth, single status and a level of education no less than
completed high school, although Boracay employers are less stringent
on the last two counts. As far as gender is concerned, men comprise
the majority in hotel and accommodation establishments and in the
staffing of certain departments: porterage, maintenance and security,
for example, are exclusively male. Women are mostly employed in
administration and accounts, in front-desk duties and in housekeeping,
although there are variations between the localities in the latter area
in particular, with Cebu's employers more reluctant to allocate women
to room cleaning. Women in Boracay, on the other hand, have
greater access to housekeeping jobs and are also spread over a wider
range of occupations in food and beverage departments. Women in
Boracay also seem to have preferential access to restaurant, and particularly shop work, in comparison with men.

While gender is obviously significant in labour recruitment, and a
high level of gender-stereotyping comes across in employer rational-
isations for appointing women or men to particular formal sector
tourism jobs, two features are worth noting. One is that no single
dimension or attribute of gender applies across the range of occupations (with the possible exception of men's assumed technical skills
and/or capacity for strenuous physical work, which gives them sole
access to jobs in maintenance and portering, for example). The second
is that a gendered criterion which might be specified for one job in
one location, might not be relevant in another. These inconsistencies
reveal that different 'gender attributes' are utilised and/or manipulated
in different ways under different sets of circumstances. This suggests

7 Given that during a three-month period in Boracay no male sales assistants were
observed to work in the island's shops, it was not deemed necessary to interview more
than two shopowners/managers in a formal capacity.

that barriers to women's work may be imposed for reasons other than those pertaining to assumed female traits per se, even if gender differences are consistently accorded primary importance in explanations for the barriers. Indeed, while employers tend to share similar conceptions of 'female characteristics', they are highly selective about the ones they choose to emphasise when it comes to justifying the exclusion (or indeed incorporation) of women into certain jobs in certain places. When characteristics deemed intrinsic to sex are used to rationalise gender composition and specialisation in different departments, a situation emerges whereby women are effectively 'blamed' for failing to gain access to particular jobs: in other words, the onus appears to lie with the characteristics of the applicant, rather than the biases and motivations of the employer. A prime example here is the way in which 'physical weakness' is ostensibly the reason why women in some Cebu hotels are not given the task of cleaning rooms, whereas in other hotels in the city, and in Boracay, strength (or rather lack of it) is not an issue and indeed women's purportedly closer identification with the domestic domain is seen to give them a distinct advantage in housekeeping positions. The underlying reasons for Cebu employers' reluctance to recruit female chambermaids, as already discussed, are much more likely to have to do with the fact that in circumstances where the majority of hotel guests are lone male businessmen, room boys may perform certain covert roles in sexual brokerage and/or assist in keeping levels of staff harassment to a minimum.

Notwithstanding the inconsistent (and often contradictory) variations in gender-selective recruitment both within and between Cebu and Boracay, two main sets of supposed 'female characteristics' conditioning women's employment in formal sector tourism appear to stand out. The first is women's greater assumed (and often actual) experience of domestic labour which is seen to equip them for jobs associated with the home (usually laundrywork, bedmaking and cleaning). The second, and probably more widely applicable, set of female attributes drawn on by employers relates to polarised constructions of male–female sexuality whereby women are regarded as ornaments and/or objects of male desire and are allotted to positions where they can be seen, admired (albeit from a distance) and used to increase the flow of custom. This explains the use of women in front-desk work, and as food attendants/hostesses in hotel restaurants in Cebu and in independent beach restaurants in Boracay (see also Adkins, 1993).

Pay and conditions in formal tourism employment

Before moving on to look at employment patterns in the informal sector, it is useful to make a few points about general conditions of formal sector tourism employment in Cebu and Boracay: this not only helps to establish the extent to which gender-selective recruitment impacts upon gender inequalities in pay and other benefits, but also provides a basis for comparing the relative advantages of formal employment vis-à-vis informal sector work. At the outset, perhaps, it should be noted that *within* individual establishments in both localities, there is rarely much distinction in the wage levels of rank-and-file workers; instead, gratuities are what make the difference to take-home earnings.

In Cebu, for example, most hotel employees work an eight-hour day, six days a week, and earn only a minimum wage (P105 or US $4.20 a day). On top of this, however, they receive tips plus a share of the service charge (a 10 per cent tax levied on rooms, food and drink). In firms with strong trade unions, non-administrative workers receive the whole of the service charge; in others the proportion is 85 per cent (with 15 per cent going to management, part of which is used to cover breakages and repairs). The average service charge accrued by workers amounts to P1,000 per week ($40), which is more than one-and-a-half times the average weekly wage of P630 ($25.20). While the service charge is distributed evenly among workers, however, tip systems vary from place to place. Those in food and beverages usually receive the most (ranging between P50 and P500 a day), making up average take-home pay to P2,000 ($80) a week. Those in cleaning, however, receive very little (mainly because Filipino guests do not have the habit of tipping room cleaners), and for most rank-and-file workers, weekly earnings are in the region of P1,700 ($68). Having said this, most hotel workers earn much more than their counterparts in other types of enterprise (factories and shops, for example). As in the main they are permanent employees, they also receive full social security benefits (see also Chapter 4).

While the majority of hotel workers in Cebu earn substantially more than the bulk of other formal sector workers, Boracay's employees are in a different position. Hotel wages are usually much lower than in Cebu, with the highest weekly wage (in the most prestigious hotel) only P,1000 ($40) per week, inclusive of service charge and gratuities. Moreover, in the sample as a whole, average weekly earnings for workers not living on the premises (the stay-outs) are P704 ($28.20), again inclusive of service charge and tips. For those who live in (36 per cent of the survey workforce overall, and 76 per cent in the four smallest establishments), conditions are markedly inferior, with inclusive earnings averaging only P275 ($11) per week. Moreover, workers in the small accommodation establishments, many of whom are employed on a short-term basis, have no social security cover and, in the event of crisis, rely overwhelmingly on paternalistic largesse, which might extend to an interest-free loan, one-off handouts for medical attention and/or (in the case of migrant workers) an occasional fare back to home areas.

Basic weekly wages in restaurants tend to be higher (around P380 [US$15.20]) for stay-outs, and with tips may be nearly doubled to P700–750 ($28–30). The 86 per cent of staff who live in, however, may receive pay as low as P200 ($8) a week, with the average in the region of P275–300 ($11–12). This also applies to shops where, for P250 ($10) a week, live-in staff work days of 12–14 hours and often have only two days off a month.

Conditions of formal sector tourism employment are highly varied, therefore, with Cebu's hotel employees and those in the largest two Boracay establishments having by far the best wages and fringe benefits. Interestingly, it is these enterprises which have the lowest levels of female recruitment, with women accounting for only 39 per cent of staff in the four Cebu hotels and 37 per cent in the top two Boracay establishments. In the four smaller Boracay accommodation establishments, on the other hand, 49 per cent of workers are women. In restaurants in Boracay, where women comprise an even higher proportion of workers (54 per cent), wages and tips combined might constitute an above-minimum take-home pay, at least for the minority of non-resident workers, but are still not on a par with those in up-market hotels. Moreover, most of these employees earn substantially less. In shops, where 100 per cent of workers are women, conditions seem to be even less favourable, with all being live-ins, receiving no tips and ending up with a wage less than half the legal minimum. These general patterns seem to suggest that while women within different establishments are not paid significantly less than their male counterparts, regardless of occupational specialisation, the enterprises in which women make up a greater proportion of the workforce are found lower down the remunerative hierarchy.

However, it is instructive to note that most female (and male) formal sector workers appear to be satisfied with their jobs, regardless of occupational specialisation or wage level. Out of seven workers interviewed in Cebu, for example, only one, a chambermaid, complained that her salary was on the low side, even though she herself said it compared favourably with what she had earned previously in two different factory jobs. As for Boracay, only four out of 16 formal tourism workers identified problems, ranging from boredom (in the case of one very overqualified worker), to minor health ailments and tiredness. For example, one waitress, Leonela, who was working in the restaurant owned by her aunt's British husband, complained that she often got very tired in the high season when there were countless customers. At the same time, she stressed that the advantages of the job far outweighed the difficulties, stating: 'Our boss-uncle is good ... we are mostly relatives here, so it is like one big family.' Several other people identified good staff relations among the high points of their work, as well as the sociability of tourism-related employment in respect of meeting vistors (see also Levy and Lerch, 1991:77 on Barbados). Many also claimed that Boracay's natural beauty, relaxed atmosphere and recreational facilities made work less of a chore than in other places. In general terms, therefore, perceptions of conditions in formal tourism are positive, even when people earn quite low wages and could perhaps make more in informal activities, and certainly in jobs elsewhere. The extent to which openings are actually available to young migrants in the island's informal sector, however, appears to be quite limited, as we discuss below.

Gender and informal employment in Boracay

As stated earlier, formal employment provides by no means the only way of making a livelihood in Boracay, where expansion in international and domestic tourism since the early 1980s has given rise to a buoyant informal economy on the island (see also Chapter 3). Here people tend to work on their own account, so employer recruitment is irrelevant in influencing the breakdown of employment segments in terms of age, sex, education, migrant status and so on, except insofar as personnel decisions in the formal sector will inevitably impact to some degree on the supply of labour for informal activities. For example, the tendency to erect educational barriers to formal employment means that people with lower levels of schooling are more likely to be found in the informal sector. Indeed, while all formal workers interviewed in Boracay have at least a high-school education, this only applies to 43 per cent of our survey of ambulant vendors. Moreover, while the bulk of formal sector employees are under 30 years of age, most in the informal sector are over 30. What is most interesting, however, is that within the domain of informal income-generating activities, gender divisions seem more marked than in formal employment.

For those working outside the formal sector of Boracay's economy, the main areas of activity are fishing, transport, commerce and a range of home-based activities. The first two sectors are exclusively male. In the case of fishing, this reflects the traditional mainstay of the island's menfolk; in the case of transport, the wider association of the male labour force in the Philippines (as elsewhere) with mechanised or heavy equipment. Male transport workers are either engaged as boat hands or operators, ferrying people and freight between Boracay and Caticlan on the mainland (all passengers to Boracay have to come by boat from this terminal), or in the operation of the island's 'taxi-service', consisting of pedicabs, motorised bikes and motorised tricycles, which are again used for merchandise as well as passengers (see also Chapter 3). Commercial operators of boats and other vehicles on the island are required to belong to a local association which attempts to regulate prices and minimise unequal competition and which grants licences approving safety and so on. Many owners have a part share in a boat or motorbike and/or rent out use of their vehicles to other operators or drivers. Those who do not (predominantly young men) may expend up to 50 per cent of their weekly takings on rental charges. For all age groups, however, transport is a fairly profitable business, easily capable of generating an above-minimum weekly wage.

As for commerce, the largest (and sometimes most remunerative) sphere for own-account workers is ambulant vending, where people trade their goods on the beach itself, along the beachfront, or directly to shops and/or restaurants. Although to all intents and purposes this work is 'informal' in the sense that people do not work for an employer and are free to decide the number of hours they devote to their work each day or week, as with transport, association membership and possession of a trading permit are required by law. Although some people trade without a permit, the vast majority belong to the Boracay Island

Vendors and Peddlers Association.[8] As of 1993 this had 247 members, of which 85 per cent were women (including illegal vendors, whose estimated total number in Boracay is around 350).

While women clearly dominate ambulant vending in Boracay, however, they are by no means involved in the sale of all produce or services. Female vendors are concentrated in the sale of massages, manicures, shorts and T-shirts, shellcraft and wickerware, fresh fruit, coconut oil and light home-cooked snacks such as 'sticky rice' and boiled cassava. The sale of fish, ice-cream and newspapers, on the other hand, is completely dominated by men. Fish-selling is a male activity because fish is sold by the people who catch it and, as noted previously, fishing in Boracay is a male preserve, with boys or men working in pairs to sell the night catch first thing in the morning or the day's catch in the late afternoon. Sales are usually direct to restaurants, which provide a guaranteed market for fresh fish. Men make up 100 per cent of ambulant ice-cream retailers because considerable physical strength is needed to carry heavy polystyrene freeze boxes up and down the beach; as for newspapers, the job requires an early start to get to a depot in Kalibo (two hours away by bus and boat), which women find virtually impossible to do: they often need to get their children ready to go to school and to be contactable in the event of a family crisis, and as such can neither commit themselves to starting work too early, or to being off the island for too long. Whatever the reasons for women avoiding the products usually sold by men, it is interesting to observe that demand for the latter is fairly stable and they do not require the 'sales pitch' which characterises many of the women's items. Indeed, most of the goods and services peddled by women – manicures, massages,

8 The Boracay Island Vendors and Peddlers Association was founded in 1987 in response to a directive from the local office of the Department of Tourism to regulate commerce in the resort. From that year onwards, vendors in Boracay have been obliged to obtain an official trading permit and to become members of the association. The association endeavours to regulate prices and to control criminal activity (prior to the inauguration of the organisation there was rumoured to be much petty theft among beach vendors). Initial registration with the organisation requires a mayor's permit, a character reference from one's *barangay* captain, together with a residence certificate (although one does not have to be actually resident on the island), police clearance, a health certificate plus a joining fee and, where relevant, a licence to operate (in the case of masseuses, for example, who must first undergo a short training programme). The cost of a general package is in the region of P350 (US$15), and is followed by an annual renewal fee of P120 ($5) – Interview with Sally Casimero, president of Boracay Island Vendors and Peddlers Association, Manoc-Manoc, Boracay, July 1993.

beachwear, handicrafts and so on – have an arguably less ready market than those sold by the men; even with determined selling, women may come home empty-handed after a whole day's work. The extent to which men have 'pushed' women out of the areas with guaranteed buyers is not clear, although the outcome is that their earnings tend to be more regular and that lower inputs of time and energy are needed to generate income equivalent to a minimum wage (see section below on earnings).

For those women who do not have the freedom (or inclination) to leave their homes, another major area of informal economic activity is the home-based enterprise. In Boracay these tend to fall into three main types, as discussed in Chapter 3: *sari-sari* stores; *carenderias*; and small craft workshops, which may involve women and their children threading shells or beads onto nylon strings to make jewellery, lampshades or door hangings which are then distributed to wholesalers or souvenir shops. Other informal activities oriented to the tourist or tourism worker market may include taking in laundry or minding other people's children.

Having identified the quite significant demarcation of informal sector tourism activities into male and female areas, it is also important to note that in contrast to formal sector tourism employment, most workers are older and a larger proportion are native to the island. In our survey of 14 ambulant vendors, for example, all bar three were aged over 30 years and one was 63. The older age pattern is particularly relevant for women, in that older women do not have the same openings in formal employment as their younger counterparts do. By the same token, women at more advanced stages of the life-course usually have children to take care of, which makes the straight eight-to-ten hour shifts plus overtime common of formal employment extremely difficult (see also Levy and Lerch, 1991). On the other hand, some of the more positive reasons for the movement of older women into independent commerce is that they often have more in the way of resources (savings, property and so on) necessary to set up their own businesses. Native islanders are perhaps especially well placed in this respect, with better access to land and housing and, arguably, the advantage of being in place when tourism started to evolve. Older Boracaynons have probably been able to experiment with different products over the years, to gain experience and to build up long-term contacts with suppliers and relevant local officials. With natives having undoubtedly been in a better position to establish their niche in the market, therefore, it is entirely conceivable that young recent migrants to Boracay are put off by existing competition and, lacking capital and assets, find it easier to work for an employer instead.

Earnings and conditions in informal tourism employment

As for earnings and conditions of informal employment in Boracay, most vendors work a six- or seven-day week, although one or two of the higher earners (notably masseuses) work only on a part-time basis (four hours a day, six days a week). Earnings vary quite substantially between people selling different types of item. Skilled workers with training and qualifications, such as masseuses and/or manicurists (sometimes people offer both services), earn an average of P2,000 (US$80) a week, and indeed one woman who works a 14-hour day seven days a week makes as much as P3,500 ($140). For those in straightforward vending (of T-shirts, shellcraft, wickerware or fruit, for example), earnings are much lower, in the region of P350–400 ($14–16) for a six-day week. It is also important to note that in the case of shellcraft and wickerware, women may not only spend eight hours a day trying to sell their wares, but a further three hours in the evenings making or elaborating their products. For instance, shellcraft vendors often obtain loose shells and/or beads on consignment from a wholesaler or middleman, and then have to thread them into bracelets or necklaces for sale to the public. In terms of hourly returns, therefore, profit margins are low. This contrasts with sellers of newspapers and ice-cream who, while working a shorter day (usually six or seven hours), still manage to earn around P630 ($25) a week.

While some vendors earn as much, if not more, than workers in the formal tourism sector, it is important to remember that their earnings are not guaranteed; quite apart from the inclemency of tropical weather, there is no fixed salary, they do not have fringe benefits and, unlike 'live-ins', they usually have to find subsistence costs for a family as well as themselves out of their wages. The same applies to those in home-based enterprises, where earnings can also be highly variable. Generally speaking, home-based shellcraft businesses are the lowest profit concerns, with average earnings of only around P350 (US$14) a week. Owners of *sari-sari* stores and *carenderias* in Boracay, on the other hand, generate a weekly personal income of around P700 ($128) a week, and one or two very well-stocked *sari-sari* stores with sidelines such as video shows may yield profits of up to P6,000 or P7,000

($240–280), even if to achieve this they have to stay open 16 hours a day and employ more than one family member. The other point to note is that informal workers are probably affected to a greater degree than formal sector employees by seasonal variations in tourist arrivals: permanent formal workers at least receive a basic wage in the low season, even if they obtain less in the way of supplements from service charges and tips. Moreover, native informal workers may have less scope to leave the island to seek employment elsewhere during lean spells. This is especially relevant where people have young families or where they have fixed home-based enterprises that rely on local custom. In the latter case, people cannot afford to lose their regular clientele to other stores or eateries by closing down over the summer.

As for levels of personal satisfaction with informal sector employment, rather more people identify problems than is the case among the formal tourism workforce. For example, vendors often complain about sunburn from being on the beach all day and try to counteract it by carrying umbrellas, wearing hats and covering themselves up with long sleeves and trousers. Others complain of tiredness and aching limbs, and most masseuses mention the frequent hazard of their clients asking for 'special favours' and/or making sexual advances. Another woman said that competition in beach commerce is so strong that fights occasionally break out between vendors. By the same token, the advantages stressed include the flexible nature of the work and its often healthy profit levels, with many women also saying that this is the only income-generating activity they can actually do with children to look after.

Having outlined the broad patterns of recruitment and conditions in formal and informal tourism employment in Cebu and Boracay, we now move on to explore in more detail the personal characteristics of workers with respect to migration and household organisation.

TOURISM WORKERS AND MIGRATION

Migrant origins and source-destination linkages in the formal sector

As identified earlier, whereas formal sector tourism employers tends to favour migrant workers in Boracay, the opposite is true in Cebu. Accordingly, out of a total of seven formal sector tourism workers interviewed in Cebu (in hotels and restaurants), it was no surprise to find

that only two were migrants. These in fact were the only two men
in the sample. One, Rey, a 30-year-old single waiter from Bohol, had
come to Cebu at the age of 20 to further his college education, yet
once he started work his shifts prevented this. Although Rey eventually
hopes to return to study, the prospects are limited. The other migrant
in the sample, 52-year-old Virgilio, a chief bartender, had first come
to Cebu from Leyte in the Eastern Visayas in the mid-1960s and has
been back and forth to the province since that time. Having in the
late 1960s married a teacher from his home town who had a job in
the local school, Virgilio's failure to find employment in the vicinity
forced them to evolve a 'split household' whereby he has spent the
bulk of his married life working in Cebu.

As for Boracay, on the other hand, the vast majority (75 per cent)
of a sample of 16 workers (three male, 13 female) surveyed in formal
tourism establishments are migrants, ten of whom are women and two
men (see Appendix). Of the twelve migrants, half (six) come from other
parts of Aklan province, 13 per cent (two) are from nearby provinces
on Panay Island (Iloilo and Antique), also in the Western Visayas, and
a further 25 per cent (three) are from provinces in the nearby region
of Southern Tagalog: one from Mindoro Oriental and two from
Romblon (see Fig. 3.2). Only one person (a woman) was actually born
more than 200 km from Boracay (in Manila), although a number have
spent time working in the capital. It should also be noted that three
of the four formal tourism workers native to Boracay had spent time
working in Manila and/or Kalibo.

All but one of the six migrants from other parts of Aklan province
came to Boracay with the specific intention not only to work, but
also to help their families in their areas of origin. All stressed the lack
of jobs in their home areas and the fact that their parents either did
not have work (most of their mothers were described as 'housekeep-
ers') or were in precarious or low-paid jobs, such as farm labour or
fishing. Four out of six of these local migrants had fixed up work prior
to arrival through personal contacts, mainly relatives already in Boracay,
and five are transferring substantial amounts of their wages back home.
On average, remittances represent about 30 per cent of an average
monthly live-in salary of P1,000, US$40 (five of the six Aklan migrants
are live-ins). Only one single female live-in does not remit money,
and this is because her elder brother is in a well-paid professional job
and has assumed responsibility for the family. Most make fairly regular

visits home (about once a month), or alternatively relatives visit them in Boracay. Indeed, one possible reason why all but one of the entire group of migrants in formal tourism hail from Aklan or fairly nearby provinces is to facilitate close contact with parents and easy transference of remittances.

Financial support to parents also figures prominently among the extra-provincial migrants in the sample, with four out of six sending regular remittances back home. The two who do not are Teddy, a 29-year-old native of Antique and restaurant supervisor, and Jackie, a 23-year-old waitress whose parents are dead and whose two brothers are able to support themselves. In Jackie's case an additional factor is that as a married woman she now sees her duty as lying with her own household. Another migrant (Oliver, an 18-year-old cook from Romblon), has just got married; while he intends to continue sending money to his parents, the sum is likely to drop from P500 to P300 out of his monthly salary of P2,500 (US$100). When children arrive on the scene he imagines he may have to give up helping altogether.

Both Teddy and Jackie had worked in Manila immediately prior to coming to Boracay and had chosen the area because they found living conditions in Manila so unpleasant. Three of the four remaining extra-provincial migrants had also spent time in Manila: two shop assistants (Lerlyn, 24 years old and a native of Iloilo, who had worked as a maid, and Annalie, a 20-year-old migrant from Romblon who had lived with her aunt in the capital), and a waitress in a beach cottage complex (Josephine, 24 years old, who had been studying in Manila). Josephine's parents live in her home province of Mindoro Oriental and she sends them half of her monthly salary of P2,000 to cover the costs of her two sisters' high-school education. Josephine herself has been unable to complete secretarial college in Manila because of struggles as a self-supporting student, and for this reason she came to work in Boracay. As the eldest of five children, Josephine claims she has a duty to provide for her siblings, especially since her father and brother are only casually employed (*standby-standby/bunjing-bunjing*).

While the Aklanon migrants to Boracay do not have the breadth of migration experience of those from outside the province, one had spent time in Manila and one had even worked in Kuwait for a year. Three of the remaining four had also lived temporarily in Kalibo. This is interesting because it suggests that Boracay is not necessarily a 'first step' for labour migrants and that work opportunities are considered to be at least as favourable in other places (mainly the capital). Having said this, the average age of all migrants in the formal tourism sample at the time of arrival was 20 years old, with six of the twelve younger than that and a further five aged between 20 and 22. These patterns may well reflect the fact that Boracay's employers are known to have a preference for young people with some prior work experience. Indeed, two-thirds of all migrants in formal sector jobs in Boracay had had previous employment, usually in another locality.

In terms of trying to establish the extent to which the migration of young workers to Boracay is based on personal decisions and might be described as 'autonomous', difficulties arise in that no interviewee actually reported having been instructed by their parents to move to the resort. However, there are various characteristics of the sample which suggest that migration has been fairly strongly influenced by family considerations. One significant issue is the young age and predominantly single status of the migrants, which, in a socio-cultural context where people rarely shed major responsibilities to natal households until marriage, implies that duties to parents and siblings have probably played some part in influencing the decision to move (see also Chapters 1 and 3). The relevance of this assertion is clearly demonstrated by the fact that seven of the twelve migrants specified that helping their parents was their main reason for moving to work in Boracay. Lending weight to this argument, is the fact that only three (25 per cent) of the twelve migrants do not send money home (in two cases because relatives are financially self-sufficient). A third point is that the vast bulk of migrants are from Aklan province itself or nearby, which enables more frequent communication and interaction with home areas. A fourth is that over half the migrants had actually been offered work through relatives in Boracay, for instance aunts or cousins, and in this sense a family control of sorts is still exerted, especially when the vast majority of migrants live in and effectively become the charges of paternalistic employers. Indeed, the fact that accommodation is widely known to be provided as part of a formal tourism job in Boracay means that young people (and their parents) might feel more comfortable about an independent move away from home. A final point bearing upon the question of migrant autonomy is that personal considerations for coming to Boracay were rarely identified by respondents. Among the five migrants who did not specify that they were primarily working to help their parents, two were married women who said they were working to support their own families (chiefly because their husbands did not earn enough), and one was the migrant whose brother was taking care of her parents and siblings. This left only two people who voiced what might be described as 'positive' personal reasons for working in Boracay. One was Remmy, a 19-year-old waitress who, while taking money to her parents in Caticlan about once a month, claimed that her prime concern was to build up her own savings and work in an environment where she would meet interesting foreign people. The other was Teddy, the 29-year-old restaurant supervisor, who said he had come to Boracay to escape the pollution of Manila and to initiate a move overseas – currently he is in the process of arranging a permit to go to Hong Kong through a Chinese tourist he had met on the island.

Related to this last point, the low numbers of tourism workers with experience of, or indeed aspirations to, overseas migration may suggest that formal employment in Boracay is not regarded as a 'springboard' to international mobility in the way, for example, that hospitality work is in Cebu (see Chapter 6), although tourism employees are often keen to meet foreigners in the hope of receiving some kind of financial sponsorship. Having said this, migration back to home areas is also low on the agenda of most migrants. Only three mentioned anything that might be regarded as a strong desire to return; all were women who felt that when they had babies it would be better to live nearer their mothers.

Migrant origins and source-destination linkages in the informal sector

Moving on briefly to informal tourism workers in Boracay and concentrating on the survey of 14 ambulant vendors,[9] it is important to remember that migrants form a much smaller proportion of the total (57 per cent of the sample), and smaller still when it is considered that two of the eight migrant ambulant vendors do not actually live on Boracay itself but commute daily from the mainland and a neighbouring island respectively. Discounting these two, only one of the six migrant vendors living in Boracay comes from another part of Aklan province:

---

9 The migration characteristics of other informal sector workers were gathered in the general household survey in Boracay and so have already been dealt with in Chapter 3.

the remaining five are each from different provinces: Masbate (in the Bicol region), Samar (Eastern Visayas), Bohol (Central Visayas), and Romblon and Mindoro Oriental (Southern Tagalog – see Fig. 3.2.

All four married female migrants in this group (with an average age of 36 years) had met and married native Boracaynons in Manila and had moved to the island shortly afterwards (at ages ranging between 17 and 26), mainly because their husbands had land or stood to inherit it. The combined effects of having a territorial base (to build a house, for example), together with small savings from employment in the capital, meant that it was probably easier for these women to set up own-account ventures than it was for younger people with no assets. Moreover, these women had arrived between the mid-1970s and mid-1980s, before the tourist boom in Boracay led to the extreme competition which currently characterises informal commerce. All these women have children and are currently working because their husbands are ill, un- or underemployed and/or earn very little.

As for the other two migrants, these included Dheng, a 34-year-old single woman who worked a 98-hour week giving massages and manicures to tourists. Originally from Mindoro Oriental, Dheng had spent some time working in Cavite as a fisherwoman and had eventually moved her ageing widowed mother and two of her sisters and their children to a house she had built for them in Caticlan, providing them with virtually all their upkeep. Dheng herself had taken the ferry over to Boracay on a daily basis, but a year ago moved to Boracay itself, partly to maximise the working day and partly to gain greater independence from her family. The other migrant, Ricardo, a 46-year-old ice-cream vendor from Numancia, Aklan, had moved to Boracay in 1992, after a three-year factory job in Manila came to an end. Since his wife (a native of Boracay) and ten of their twelve children live with him on the island, none of his income is sent to Aklan in remittances.

In general terms, it is obvious that the migrants involved in beach-vending are of a rather different type to those in the formal sector: they are older, have generally moved with spouses and children, and their main rationale for working is to support their own offspring, rather than their natal families. Indeed, only one of the five married persons, Letty, a 33-year-old T-shirt seller with a second husband, sends remittances back to her home village in Samar. However, three other women in the group mentioned that they had previously remitted money to their parents when they were single. This reinforces the idea that parental considerations are only likely to be prioritised as long as people are unattached. Indeed, the fact that Dheng is a single person means, that regardless of her mature age and the costs associated with living independently, her primary financial allegiance is still to her mother and sisters. In fact, Dheng maintained that she had had to take on so much responsibility for her family that there had been no time for boyfriends, let alone to find a husband. This again reveals a strong element of family influence not only in the labour and migration decisions of young women, but also in their personal lives.

Summing up the principal differences in migration between formal and informal tourism workers in Boracay, it would seem that although migrants outnumber natives in both sectors of activity, the formal sector attracts larger proportions of people from outside the island, and more of the migrants who end up working in shops, hotels and restaurants have moved specifically to Boracay to get jobs. Moreover, even if they come with the main intention of helping their families of origin and have often organised employment in advance through other kin members, their movement is undertaken as individuals rather than as members of households. The fact that many have also migrated elsewhere (and alone) to work before moving to Boracay means that to all intents and purposes this group can be described as independent (if not autonomous) labour migrants. This also applies to the two migrant tourism workers in Cebu, despite the fact that formal tourism employers in the latter tend to recruit natives in preference to outsiders.

Although work is obviously a motive in the decisions of migrants in the informal sector as well, for the bulk of those involved in ambulant vending it is only one of a range of issues stimulating movement. Bearing in mind that the majority of migrant vendors have come to Boracay as older women with spouses native to the island (and often with children as well), considerations relating to family inheritance and resources, mainly land and property, have featured in their decisions too. Differences in the age, marital status and fertility of migrants at their time of arrival in Boracay also play a role in influencing the composition and organisational characteristics of households of people in different sectors, as we discuss below.

HOUSEHOLD CHARACTERISTICS OF
TOURISM WORKERS

Household characteristics of formal tourism workers

Given the differences in formal tourism recruitment in Cebu and
Boracay, especially as regards migrant preference and the fact that
workers tend to live on employers' premises in Boracay, it is perhaps
no surprise that the household characteristics of workers also differ
markedly between the two localities.

In Cebu, where there are no live-in staff in the sample of seven
tourism workers, all four of the female workers reside with parents.
Two of these, Lucy and Thelma, both aged 26, live with their
widowed mothers. Of the other two, one, a 20-year-old cashier called
Elenita, lives with both her parents, while Judy, a 28-year-old chambermaid, returned to live at home when her husband abandoned her and
their two children. As for the three men in the sample, the younger
two, both waiters (Rey, 30, and Bobby, 21), live in boarding houses,
and the 52-year-old bartender Virgilio lives with three of his four
children as part of his widowed sister's household.

In Boracay, by contrast, 69 per cent of the sample of 16 formal tourism
workers live on the premises of their employers, usually sharing rooms
with colleagues of the same sex. The average age of the live-ins is 25,
with only one over 30 years old. Ten of the eleven live-ins are
migrants, and nine are women.

As for the 'stay-outs' in Boracay, whose average age is 26 years (two
are just over 30) and where only three out of five are migrants,
household patterns again differ from those in Cebu. Two (one man,
one woman) have just got married and live alone with their spouses.
The remaining three, all waitresses, have children and two are de facto
female heads. In these latter cases the husbands work in other parts of
the Philippines because they feel they are able to earn more away from
the island. Both women are in fact native Boracaynons, which helps
explain how one of them, Raquel, a 31-year-old mother of five, is
able to cope with full-time formal sector work and childraising: her
mother lives with her and looks after the children while she is out at
work. The other woman, Babes, does not have relatives living in the
home, but because she earns a reasonable wage as a deputy head
waitress (P1,250/US$52 a week inclusive of tips) and because her partner

sends her around $80 a week from his work on a cruiseliner, she is able to pay $15 a week for a childminder. One interesting feature of migrant stay-outs in this group is that all started their working life in Boracay as live-ins, which further indicates the importance of worker accommodation on the island in providing a kind of 'bridge' between leaving a natal household and forming a new one.

In general terms, however, whether people live in or reside away from their work premises, formal sector tourism employees in Cebu and Boracay are predominantly single people without children, which undoubtedly reflects employer preferences for youthful workers who do not have the 'distractions' conventionally thought to accompany married life. Having said this, some people in formal tourism employment *do* have children, or are about to give birth, so what kinds of strategies are adopted to cope with reconciling the demands of full-time formal sector work with childcare?

Out of a total of 23 formal tourism workers interviewed in Cebu and Boracay, six have children and one is pregnant with her first child. Of the six with children, the usual pattern is to make use of relatives who either reside with the workers within an extended household, or who live close by and mind the child (or children) on a daily basis. Cases of extended households include the de facto female head, in Boracay, Raquel, whose mother looks after her five young children, and Judy, the chambermaid in Cebu who moved back with her children to her parents' house on separating from her husband.[10] Virgilio, the 52-year-old bartender in Cebu, also lives as part of a female-headed extended household, although in his case the children are now adults and do not require the same care as they did when they were young: indeed, before reaching college age they lived with their mother back home in Leyte.

Developing a quasi-extended household arrangement is also the way in which a 38-year-old widowed shop assistant, Doloria, manages to work and raise her five small children – except that, in contrast to the above cases, Doloria is actually a live-in. Although most live-ins have to be single, Doloria's aunt owns the shop in which she works and most of the other assistants are relatives. As such, normal regulations are relaxed, and there is always someone around who can mind the children when Doloria is working.

---

10 Judy is of course a clear example of an 'embedded' female head (see Chapter 3).

As for the other two working parents, both in Boracay, the deputy head waitress, Babes, pays a childminder, while Jackie, a 23-year-old waitress, gets her cousin to mind her two young children when she is out at work. This latter strategy will also be used by Donna, a 23-year-old chambermaid pregnant with her first child: Donna will return home to Kalibo for the actual birth, and afterwards leave the baby during the day with a sister who now also lives in Boracay with children of her own.

One very clear pattern in this multiplicity of childcare arrangements is that, for the most part, the care of children is passed on to a female relative, which raises important questions as to whether or not women workers would be able to continue in the formal sector if they did not have relatives in the vicinity or residing as members of their households. This obviously is more likely for natives, who usually have larger numbers of kin on the island. The only other option for mothers who continue working after childbirth is to pay a childminder, but this is something of a luxury; only one, Babes, can afford it.

Household characteristics of informal tourism workers

Among the 14 informal tourism workers, there is much more consistency in household structure, with all bar the two single people living in male-headed nuclear households. The two single people are Gerald, 18 years old and a son in a female-headed household, and 34-year-old Dheng, who lives on her own in rented accommodation.

The average size of the twelve male-headed nuclear households is 6.3, meaning there is an average of four children. Given that the bulk of the informal women workers are in their 30s and 40s, this usually means that they have at least one or two young children still to care for. How is this achieved, especially given that none of them actually have relatives living with them?

Neither of the wives of the two male vendors in this group work, so childcare problems are resolved through the traditional nuclear family pattern of female homemaker and male breadwinner. When it comes to the ten women vendors, however, a much wider variety of arrangements exists. In three cases, women with young children work part-time and leave their children with female relatives who live nearby. In another three cases, where youngest children have reached 11 years of age (and the eldest are boys), mothers try to ensure that they are at least there in the morning to help prepare them for school, even if the children return home in the afternoons to an empty house. As it is, in two of these three cases, husbands are only casually employed and can usually perform the duty of afternoon minding.

Where elder children are girls, however, the situation is different in that those in the 15+ age group are not only given charge of younger brothers and sisters, but undertake a considerable amount of the housework (which obviously frees women workers from something of their 'double burden'). This applies in the case of Gloria, a 36-year-old shellcraft vendor and mother of nine. Gloria's husband is sick and has been unemployed for four years now. To alleviate the problems of being the only earner in the household, Gloria has fostered two of her middle children with an aunt and has her 17- and 18-year-old daughters look after the remaining five siblings, the youngest of whom is only two. A similar pattern is followed by Esing, a 42-year-old fruit vendor whose 16-year-old daughter looks after four younger brothers and sisters.

In the final two cases, that of Rosa, a 25-year-old wickerware vendor, and Veronica, a 31-year-old masseuse, husbands perform the bulk of childcare duties. Rosa's husband is only casually employed; on the two or three days a week he picks coconuts on his father's farm, their three children are taken along and left with his mother. Veronica's partner, on the other hand, is a full-time house-husband. Not only does he take care of their three young children (one is a six-month-old baby), he also does all the laundry, cooking and cleaning. Indeed, while most of the ambulant vendors' husbands are not in regular work and spend considerable amounts of time around the home, Veronica's is the only one who effectively matches the time and labour which his wife expends in making a living for the family.

Attitudes to marriage and fertility among young, single tourism workers

Leading on from this discussion on the household characteristics of tourism workers in Cebu and Boracay, it is interesting to consider the extent to which young, single workers are likely to follow in the footsteps of their older counterparts in terms of getting married at around the same age and having similar numbers of children, and how this might intermesh with people's ideas about future employment. Here we will only consider women, not just because they make up the majority of our survey respondents, but also because women's working lives stand to be much more disrupted by marriage and childbirth than men's. The bases for direct comparison between older and younger workers within particular segments of activity are obviously rather limited. In Cebu, for example, only one woman had experienced marriage and childbirth, while in Boracay five out of 13 of the female formal tourism workers were already married and/or had children. As for the informal sector survey of ambulant vendors, on the other hand, ten out of the eleven women were already married. Despite these difficulties, we can say with some degree of confidence that among single formal tourism workers, the projected age of marriage and intended numbers of children are, respectively, much higher and lower than those of older age groups.

In Cebu, for example, all three unmarried female workers, one aged 20 and the other two 26, are already older than their married counterpart Judy, who married when she was only 15. In fact it is interesting to note that Judy had just one three-month factory job between leaving high school and her wedding, and only went back to work (in her present job as a chambermaid, mainly as a result of financial hardship) at the age of 24, two years before she and her husband split up. Of the three unmarried women, one of the 26-year-olds, Thelma, who already has a boyfriend of two years' standing, expressed a desire to postpone marriage for a further two years. This will allow her and her partner to save for a downpayment on a house. Financial reasoning also lies behind Thelma's intention to have only two children; in her view, money is a critical ingredient to enable them to have a 'more decent life'. As for the other two women, Elenita, 20, said there was no 'right age' to get married and it would depend on whom one met, whereas the other 26-year-old, Lucy, while expressing a strong wish to have a child, was far from keen on the prospect of marriage. At one level, Lucy said that it was extremely difficult to find a man who was both responsible and faithful, claiming that most Filipino men were 'playboys'. At another level, although Lucy has had a boyfriend in the past, her 84-hour week in a hotel shop prevents her from having very much in the way of a social life at all.

As for the formal tourism workers in Boracay, again we find that the projected age of marriage is higher than for those who already have husbands, and the number of children smaller. Of the five women already married, four had done so between the ages of 18 and 21, although only two of the five had been live-in workers in Boracay prior to marriage (live-ins generally have less in the way of time and freedom to meet people). As for those eight who are still single, all expressed the intention to postpone marriage until the age of 25, with most settling on 26 or 27. The average age of this group at present is 22 years, and the reasons offered for delaying marriage vary fairly widely. While some mentioned that they wanted to have more savings behind them, and another that she was too busy in her work to think of having boyfriends, others voiced reasons that had less to do with personal issues than family-related matters. For example, one 26-year-old general helper in a hostelry, Inday, has wanted to get married for over a year, but since her elder brother objects to the fact that her intended is a distant relative, she is wary about going ahead with her plans. Indeed, not only has her brother threatened to disown her personally, but Inday stands to lose contact with the whole family because her brother supports them financially. Another woman, Josephine, 24 years old, claims that she cannot possibly conceive of getting married until she has put her two younger sisters back in Mindoro through high school.

To a certain extent, this latter issue applies to the only single woman (Dheng) among the eleven female vendors. Bearing in mind our discussion in the earlier section on migration, Dheng has basically been the mainstay of her widowed mother and siblings for most of her life. At the age of 34, therefore, she is still single and has effectively lost hope of finding a partner, let alone having children. Indeed, all Dheng's married counterparts in the vendor survey married (or in one case formed a consensual union) much earlier in life (at an average age of 21). Three of these ten women are already in a second partnership.

As for fertility, this is very high among the informal sector workers, with those in the 30+ age group having an average of five children each. Two of the three formal tourism workers in the same age group also have five children; the other has two. The two married women in the formal sector aged under 30 also intend to stop at two children. The fertility decisions of these younger women correspond almost exactly with the general wishes of those who are still single. The maximum number of children desired by the unmarried formal tourism workers is three, with most expressing a wish for two or three. Many of these women have come from families of nine or more children, and their goal of having fewer is to have greater resources and thereby give their children a 'better future'. Indeed, one 19-year-old chambermaid said that she had very dismal memories of her own childhood – along with her eight brothers and sisters she was constantly shuffled from one relative to another when their parents had 'no money to put food on the table'. Although as people want smaller families, however, it is instructive that not one single woman in the Boracay and Cebu surveys is considering *not* having children (even Lucy, who is reluctant to get married), or indeed having only one child. This is partly due to the notion that it is 'sad' for children to be on their own, but it also relates to the desire for greater assurance that they will be cared for in later years (much as the interviewees are doing now with their own parents). Besides this, two births mean the possibility of a child of each sex, although daughters are often preferred because of their greater sense of responsibility and willingness to help out around the home.

As regards the potential effects of fertility on future employment, most women seem to want to go on working and think they will be able to do so, provided they have relatives to whom to turn for help in childcare. Interestingly, however, no one mentioned that having fewer children would help to solve childminding problems, or that fewer pregnancies might extend their term in formal employment. Yet formal sector employers are unlikely to take kindly to repeated periods of maternity leave, and this is largely borne out by their preference to employ single people. Indeed, this could well be another reason for the fact that women with large numbers of children are found disproportionately in the informal sector. Although most interviewees expressed a desire to stay in their present jobs, imagining that in the course of time they might move up the career ladder into supervisory or even managerial positions, some also voiced the intention to set up their own businesses after marriage.

The most interesting points to emerge from this discussion perhaps include the fact that while single people in formal tourism employment generally wish to get married and have children (indeed, some have already done so), contrary to what happened with many of their mothers, and indeed with women in the local population (see Chapter 3), they want to get married later, to have fewer children and to continue working. Obviously there are important interlinkages here, in that marriage at a later age means having more resources to pay for childcare if necessary and/or that small numbers of children may be more easily taken care of by other people. Moreover, in the context of a fairly competitive labour market, it would be unwise for people wishing to retain formal sector jobs to have too many extended absences from work. The extent to which these patterns can be attributed to general social changes occurring in the Philippines, or to the nature of tourism employment per se, is explored more fully in Chapter 7, but in the next, and final, section, certain aspects of conventional tourism employment which might have some bearing on shaping gender roles, relations and ideologies are highlighted for consideration.

PRELIMINARY CONCLUSIONS ON THE GENDER IMPLICATIONS OF TOURISM EMPLOYMENT

As with export manufacturing, tourism employment, in both Cebu and Boracay, entails a diverse and often contradictory mixture of implications for women's status and for patterns of gender roles and relations.

One major factor in tourism employment's favour is that, unlike certain other types of export-oriented activity in the Visayas (see Chapters 4 and 6), the sector as a whole is less obviously 'feminised', which is not to say that there are not significant areas of gender concentration within it, nor that gender-stereotyping is non-existent. The fact that conventional tourism employment recruits a healthier balance of male and female workers, however, means that in financial and status terms, women may suffer less devaluation and exploitation. In formal establishments, for example, minimum wages are generally paid to all rank-and-file workers and there is equal distribution of service charges, if not gratuities (see below). In this context, women at least know that they can command the same remuneration as men, and may be employed on similar terms. In sum, male and female tourism employees may regard one another on a more equal basis than is the case, say, in factories, where men tend to occupy higher ranking positions and/or are employed in skilled segments of production with higher wage rates (see Chapter 4).

A related advantage of formal tourism employment, especially in large hotels in Cebu, is that the existence of the service charge system means that pay can often amount to twice the legal minimum wage. For women in particular, this grants financial power which many other jobs do not permit. Even if women do not necessarily use this for their own ends, the fact that many pay towards the schooling of younger brothers and sisters means that the next generation of women may well benefit in terms of furthering their professional prospects.

Tangentially related is the fact that although the educational requirements for jobs in many formal tourism establishments are often higher than the work demands, there is possibly slightly less credentialism than in export-oriented multinational factories where very repetitive jobs requiring little in the way of initiative could probably be done just as well by people with primary, rather than secondary, schooling (see Chapter 4). Moreover, since language skills (notably English) are used to a greater degree in tourism than in factory work, the mismatch between education and occupational status is perhaps not *felt* to be marked in the former.

In a more general sense, tourism development also seems to offer scope for women (and men) to develop remunerative informal activities. In Boracay, for example, many women vendors (especially masseuses and manicurists) have very profitable concerns which allow them not only to be their own boss but, where relevant, to have a family as well. In the course of this work, they also benefit from learning foreign languages that are picked up over time from conversations with clients and customers. Moreover, the fact that various formal sector workers express a wish eventually to run their own businesses (restaurants, for example) perhaps indicates that skills learned in the tourist industry translate more easily into other income-generating activities than, say, those acquired on a factory production line (see Chapter 4).

At a more ideological level, it could also be argued that in situations where tourism markets comprise a mixture of nationalities, sexes and ages, female workers might expand their knowledge of gender roles and relations in other societies. In countries such as Mexico, which has a large international tourist trade, local women seem to enjoy observing the customs of their North American counterparts, being particularly impressed by their control over money, their greater assertiveness with men and their freedom to travel alone (see, for example, Chant, 1992c: 98; also Badger, 1993:3). While it is not intended here to suggest that exposure to women from other cultures is unequivocally, or even necessarily, positive (especially given the context of unequal status between customer and employee), Filipina workers in conventional tourism at least have the chance to meet foreign *women*. In factory employment or the hospitality industry, on the other hand, the only foreigners they are likely to meet are males who, in their positions as managers or as sexual clients, are unlikely to display particularly forward-thinking attitudes in respect of gender.

A final factor relevant to tourism development in Boracay is that the institution of live-in arrangements, while in many respects conservative and paternalistic, can at the same time be regarded as a potentially positive feature in the life-course trajectories of young women. For example, live-in quarters usually comprise single-sex dormitories where women may live alongside colleagues whom they have only come to know in a work environment. This introduces a new feature to the normal pattern of women moving from the home where they have been daughters, to one in which they are wives, primarily in the sense of providing an opportunity to live independently of kin and without the immediate presence of men. At one extreme, female-only lodging arrangements may perhaps give rise to freer dialogue among women and a sense of solidarity with each other as women as well as workers. More pragmatically, it at least introduces women to the experience of an alternative type of household organisation.

Many of the 'positive' aspects of conventional tourism employment described above naturally have their downside and could be interpreted in a more negative light. For instance, one problem of women's relatively privileged position in income-generation in Boracay is that they are often the major breadwinners in their households: men may use this as justification to work only on a part-time basis themselves and/or to withdraw financial support, if not to spend more money on their own pleasures (see Chapter 3). The opportunity to interact with foreign people is also double-edged. Decidedly negative aspects of exposure to tourists from other countries may include awakening feelings of dissatisfaction, growing desires to leave the country, the belief that foreigners are wealthy (which most are in comparison to the local populace) and that they and their home countries are in some respects role models for Filipino citizens (see also Harrison, 1992 for a broader discussion of these kinds of hazards in international tourism). These problems appear to be intensified in the Philippines by the large number of *balikbayans* (Filipino emigrants) who, on returning to the country, often holiday lavishly in Boracay and other destinations and boast to fellow nationals of their lives abroad.

A final, and perhaps most destructive, feature of tourism development is that a large number of the posts into which women are slotted, both in Cebu and Boracay, are either servile and/or frontline in nature – that is, women are employed in jobs where they will provide a 'pleasing sight to customers' and thereby increase business. The use of female sexuality as a marketing mechanism is found at all levels of tourism promotion, from national advertisements to hotel brochures, to the attraction of customers into restaurants on Boracay beach. However 'discreet' this may be,[11] the end result is that tourism to the Philippines is still accompanied by notions of the availability of Filipinas as sexual commodities, with consequences ranging from the vulgar harassment of beach masseuses for 'special favours', to the exclusion of women workers from chambermaiding or room service in business-class hotels. The idealisation of all things foreign, together with the idea that women's sexuality is something to be traded to advantage, offers little scope for running down the country's hospitality industry, as we examine in the next chapter.

---

11 The use of female sexuality in tourism marketing is rarely blatant to the extent of displaying women naked or in revealing swimwear. However, the question remains as to why women, and not men, repeatedly figure in advertisements and/or are placed in the front line of customer interaction. Moreover, the images of women projected in tourism promotion leave much to be desired. Women are usually portrayed in a highly feminine and ornamental manner: wearing sarongs, flowing cotton dresses or evening gowns, with their hair bedecked with flowers, smiling Filipinas are set against an array of scenic backdrops (lagoons, mountains, forests and so on) which only emphasise the inappropriateness of their clothing. One Philippine Airlines poster widely displayed in national airports, for example, advertises a range of destinations to which there are flights from Manila (Boracay, Baguio, Palawan and so on), with at least one young woman in every picture of the local landscape or other tourist attraction (golf course or historic monument, for instance). Another common image in tourism advertisements is where Filipino women appear alongside foreign men, serving them as waitresses or hotel receptionists, chatting to them in hotel foyers, sharing meals or drinks with them in plush restaurants and sometimes booking them into hotel rooms. In a climate where the country is ostensibly trying to play down the image of the Philippines as a sex tour haven, it is arguable whether the continued use of women in such advertising campaigns will achieve the desired objective (see also Badger, 1993:2; W.Lee, 1991:91; Truong, 1990:177–8 on the representation of women in tourism brochures, advertisements and promotional literature in other developing countries).

6 GENDER AND SEX WORK

The emphasis in the previous chapter on Boracay now shifts to Cebu as we examine the 'hospitality' dimension of international tourism in the Visayas. Although a small-scale, informal sex trade is evident in Boracay, and so given some attention in the discussion, Cebu City's established entertainment industry is much more significant in terms of female employment. While Cebu's entertainment infrastructure is highly diverse, this chapter focuses primarily on its registered hospitality establishments, notably 'girlie bars', karaoke clubs and massage parlours. The analysis begins with an examination of the main characteristics of sex work in these places, and the types of jobs women do. By examining the attitudes of male consumers of sexual services, the discussion is also concerned with exploring the ways in which demand for particular types of female worker is created.[1] After assessing working conditions in the industry, we look at the migrant and household characteristics of the women involved and their main reasons for entering this employment. The conclusion provides a brief analysis of the material, ideological and social implications of sex work for women in the Visayas and in the Philippines more generally.

SEX WORK IN CEBU AND BORACAY: AN OVERVIEW

Characteristics of sex work in Cebu

As mentioned earlier in the text, the growth of a sex industry in the Philippines is largely due to the historical presence of US military personnel and to ex-President Marcos's concerted drive to promote

---

1 Unlike export manufacturing and conventional tourism, it was not possible to interview employers in sex work establishments. For this reason, male clients were used to provide a benchmark for employer attitudes, but the dangers of equating consumer preference with formal labour demand should be borne in mind (see Appendix).

international tourism in the 1970s (see Chapters 1 and 2; also APHD, 1985:45; Azarcon de la Cruz, 1985; Eviota, 1992:137–40; Moselina, 1981; WEDPRO, 1990a). Despite adverse publicity about sex tours since the early 1980s, the closure of the major US bases (Clark and Subic), in 1991 and 1992 respectively, and renewed attempts (in 1993) to clean up Manila's red light district, the industry continues to thrive, with a noticeable shift in concentration towards the Visayas and, more specifically, to Cebu City. Developing alongside the export manufacturing sector, international tourism in Cebu is mainly business-related, and while several visitors make use of beach resorts in the metropolitan hinterland, a primary attraction in the core of the urban environment is the city's 'nightlife'. Although Cebu's status as a port has always meant that some prostitution existed, the market received a major boost in the early 1980s when, in the wake of widespread sex tour protests, Japanese visitors made a conscious attempt to avoid the spotlight of Manila. Since then, Cebu's position as an international sex centre has been furthered by improved airlinks to the capital, the development of supporting tourism infrastructure in the city, such as major international hotels, and, more recently, the displacement of sex workers from the former US base areas in Luzon (see Chapter 2; also Chant, forthcoming b).

Cebu's sex industry encompasses a wide range of activities, establishments and modes of operation, yet while it is known to incorporate some trade in men and children (see, for example, DSWD/ NCSD/UNICEF, 1988; HAIN 1987), women are by far the most significant set of workers. This is very obviously the case with formal hospitality establishments,[2] geared to the international tourist market,

---

2 The term 'hospitality worker' resulted from the reorganisation of the Bureau of Women and Minors (BWM) in 1972 following Presidential Decree no.1, which charged the office with the task of formalising and cleaning-up the sex industry. The main initiatives included changing the name of sex workers from 'prostitute' to 'hospitality girl', to give the latter legal status, and to provide workers with seminars on 'good grooming' and 'strengthening [their] moral fibers' (Azarcon de la Cruz, 1985:5). While on the surface these moves might have had positive effects, mainly in the sphere of protecting workers and raising their social standing, the underlying rationale was to promote international tourism by creating the impression that the Philippine sex trade was safe and wholesome (ibid.). Indeed, while hospitality workers are given legal recognition, prostitution per se is still regarded as a criminal activity, with those working outside designated establishments subject to fines, imprisonment and other forms of abuse (see Sturdevant and Stoltzfus, 1992b:45; see also note 1, Chapter 1 above on officially designated hospitality establishments).

and thus the discussion focuses on this group.[3] Although it is difficult to estimate the numbers of women working in the sex industry in Cebu, a useful starting point is data from the Social Hygiene Clinic (SHC) of the City Health Department, where all workers in Cebu's formal entertainment establishments are legally required to register and to attend weekly check-ups.[4] Those found to be free from sexually transmitted diseases (STDs) are issued with a 'health certificate' which permits them to continue working, while those who are ill must complete a course of treatment and receive full clearance before returning to their jobs. The SHC also provides information on disease prevention and issues free condoms. As of March 1993, 1,705 sex workers were attending the Cebu clinic for routine checks, although staff estimate that at least as many again are involved in the city's non-registered entertainment industry (see also Chapter 2).[5]

Given the large numbers of people conjectured to be working outside the registered hospitality sector, a broad outline of sex work in Cebu is helpful before embarking on a detailed analysis of the formal sex trade per se. Women's occupations in this domain range from high-class call girls, to hostesses and dancers, to masseuses who provide sexual 'extras', to brothel or *casa* workers,[6] and finally to street walkers. These positions may be grouped in a loose hierarchy reflecting varying degrees of status in terms of place of work, level of remuneration and degree of legality, as well as the types of clients serviced and the

---

3 From a practical point of view, it was also more feasible to make contacts with sex workers in formal establishments than with those working on a casual or illegal basis (see note 2 above). However, information on the general nature of the sex industry in Cebu was elicited from discussions with women's groups in the city, and from interviews with male tourists.

4 The origins of social hygiene clinics are closely associated with the establishment of US military bases around the world from 1900 onwards. In 1918 the US government created a Social Hygiene Board to formulate policies to protect troops from venereal diseases both within the country and abroad. These mainly took the form of setting up clinics to monitor women with whom US servicemen came into contact (Sturdevant and Stoltzfus, 1992c:329).

5 Interview with Dr Gloria Paz (Chief Medic) and Staff Nurse Eva Pinat at the Cebu City Health Department Social Hygiene Clinic, April 1993. The March 1993 figures given in the text represent a 10 per cent increase on the figures for 1992 (see Chapter 2).

6 While female brothels in Cebu are referred to by the Spanish term *casa*, male brothels are known as 'greenhouses' (interview with Lihok Pilipina, Cebu City, February 1992).

extent to which the sale of sex is explicitly promoted (see Fig. 6.1; also Heyzer, 1986:58–61; W.Lee, 1991:80-1; Miralao et al., 1990:5; O'Grady 1983:12; Wilke, 1983:16). Groups are not necessarily exclusive, in that workers may sometimes belong to more than one category (depending on their customers at the time), or indeed may move between categories at different points in time (see Heyzer, 1986:59).

Despite this, it is possible to discern a pattern where, at the top of the hierarchy, are those working independently as call girls in high-class hotels and nightclubs which cater for both foreign and wealthy Filipino businessmen (see Fig. 6.1). These women are likely to work on a part-time basis, with most having other jobs such as modelling or promotion work. Given the rather discreet nature of their activities, these women are not usually registered with the City Health Department and instead use private medical centres. Payment at this level is subtle, with money often changing hands in the form of meals, clothes and gifts. However, while call girls operate in a range of establishments (most of which are not geared to the provision of sexual services alone), the majority of sex workers in Cebu are employed in one outlet only. This applies to the second-level group of workers in our hierarchy, where another reasonably 'discreet' form of prostitution is found, notably in karaoke or sing-along bars frequented by male Filipinos and foreign tourists, especially from Japan (see Fig. 6.1). Women here are employed as 'guest-relations ladies', escorts or hostesses and are required to sit and talk with customers, to bring drinks to their tables and even to feed them snacks by hand, as well as accompanying those wanting to sing. Sexual transactions per se are rarely negotiated within the bar itself, but arrangements may be made to see customers after closing time. As such, women wishing to engage in commercial sex are relatively independent, with no commission taken by management.

More explicit in respect of promoting the availability of sexual services on the premises are the 'girlie bars', which form the mainstay of the sex tourism industry in Cebu (see Fig. 6.1). These attract mainly foreign clients, and employ dancers (sometimes referred to as 'back-to-back models' or 'ago-go girls'), together with 'chat-up girls' or hostesses. Even though sex does not take place on the premises themselves, owners take a fee or 'bar fine' from clients who wish to take women out of the club, with sums often varying according to the age of the woman (or women) and their general popularity with

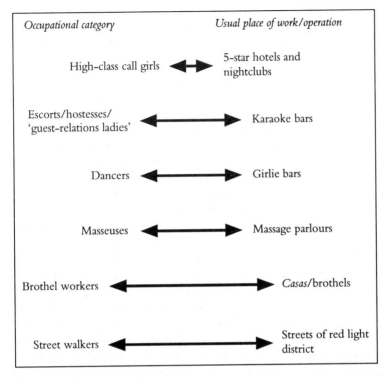

Figure 6.1: Hierarchy of sex work in Cebu City

Note: Length of line indicates relative proportions of workers in each group.

customers, as well as on the length of time a client wishes to spend with them. Following payment of the bar fine, the woman negotiates her own price for sex and is entitled to keep all the money, although a tip may be required to silence hotel workers in the establishments to which customers take them (see Chapter 5 above; also Chant, forthcoming b). Apart from this, sex is aggressively marketed within girlie bars through the deployment of semi-nude females dressed in bikinis or underwear, who dance on stage in front of drinking customers. Dancers perform 'sets' for the duration of three to four songs. In the interim, they change into their normal (slightly less scanty) attire and mingle with the customers along with the regular chat-up 'girls' (who are not normally available for sexual intercourse). Clients wishing to talk with the workers are almost invariably required to buy a 'lady's drink' (normally an excessively priced fruit juice), of which a proportion of the cost (around 20–30 per cent) goes to the woman herself.

Another version of the girlie bar is found in establishments akin to a mixture of disco and music hall which stage thematic floor shows, euphemistically known as 'cultural cabarets'. Women here perform traditional Filipino dances, or choreographed routines to Western pop music. Although not all routines involve the women wearing skimpy costumes, and the nature of the dancing is less blatantly sexual than in the conventional girlie bars, the provocation of arousal is normally central to the displays, and dancers known to accept bar fines are pointed out to male clients by the male or female floor manager (*papasan* or *mamasan*).

Scope for women to resist propositions from male clients is generally less in massage parlours (see Fig. 6.1). Workers in these establishments are controlled much more closely with regard to sexual servicing insofar as they cannot 'choose' their clients to the same degree. The system within massage parlours usually involves a customer selecting from a range of numbered masseuses sitting behind a one-way mirror, often grouped according to the 'extras' they provide (topless massage, hand relief, oral sex and so on). Management collect a fee for the particular service purchased, giving a cut of around 20 per cent to the masseuses concerned, who may also receive extra tips from clients if full sexual intercourse takes place. Since sessions are strictly timed, men wishing to spend longer with workers must wait until after hours when they are free to sell sex on their own terms (see also Heyzer, 1986:60; Moselina, 1981:17; Truong, 1990:186).

At the bottom of the hierarchy of sex work in Cebu are the brothel (or *casa*) workers and street walkers (see Fig. 6.1). Street walkers who work 'illegally' and who are not registered with the City Health Department operate in the downtown district of Cebu, usually under the de facto jurisdiction of pimps. The commission taken by the latter is often high, which, combined with the low prices street walkers have to charge because of their fairly restricted markets (usually local men only), means that they end up with much less in their pockets than their counterparts in girlie bars and massage parlours. Women in *casas* have a similar fate and may fare less well, especially where owners or managers of the brothels require them to reside on the premises. In these instances, deductions for bed and board, together with managerial commission, reduce women's earnings to a pitiful amount. However, depending on the size and formality of the brothel (ranging from small private dwellings with only three or four workers to organised *casas* housing 15–20), some women may be entitled to registered hospitality worker status and the associated medical benefits. Nonetheless, brothel workers and street walkers alike usually face greater exploitation than most of their counterparts further up Cebu's sex work hierarchy, not only because of the employers they serve, but because they cannot command the high prices attached to the international tourist market, even if some foreign businessmen use taxi-drivers and room boys to seek out their services (see also Miralao et al., 1990:6).[7]

The discussion thus far has dealt with a range of prostitution in Cebu, encompassing situations where women are involved (albeit sometimes less visibly than others) in the provision of sexual services. As will be clear, however, the sex industry is not exclusively made up of female workers who sell their bodies. In numerous entertainment establishments, women are also employed as bar attendants, cashiers, receptionists and *mamasans* who, alongside certain dancers and hostesses, do not service clients with sexual intercourse. Having said this, many of these individuals may have just started to work and are 'learning the ropes'; alternatively, they may have previous experience of prostitution but are now too old to attract customers (particularly in the case of *mamasans* – see Azarcon de la Cruz, 1985:9). This does not apply to men, however, whose jobs as doormen, bar attendants or floor managers (*papasan*) rarely involve the sale of sexual favours, even if they are occasionally propositioned (see Chant, forthcoming b). The same applies to the predominantly male 'auxiliaries' of the sex industry, notably the taxi-drivers, private chauffeurs, hotel porters and room boys who, for varying levels of remuneration, often advise foreigners which bars are the 'best' to visit, take them to *casas*, or actually bring women directly to them (see also note 7 above).

The gender inequality apparent not only in the fundamental nature of exchange in sexual services, but also in the character of employment and earnings in the industry (in other words, men's purchase of women's bodies is usually mediated by male auxiliaries who take a slice

---

7 One male taxi-driver interviewed by the authors reported how advising male tourists on Cebu's 'night-time attractions' was a socially expected part of the job, as well as providing a source of additional income through tips (see also Skrobanek, 1987:212 on the Thai sex trade).

of women's profits), is further exacerbated by the fact that overall ownership and control of Cebu's sex industry is firmly in the hands of men. Interwoven in this basic gender hierarchy are the spectres of race, class and nationality. For example, while massage parlours and *casas* in Cebu are usually Filipino-owned, girlie bars tend to be the property of foreigners (especially Australians, Americans and Europeans) who almost invariably have Filipino wives[8] (see also Moselina, 1981:24–5 on Olongapo; Wilke, 1983:16 and WRRC/PSC, 1990:5 on Manila). Karaoke clubs, on the other hand, are usually run by the Japanese, often in association with the Yakuza.[9] In a wider sense, therefore, it is possible to see how the hospitality sector is based on a hierarchy not only among female sex workers themselves (according to the particular type of prostitution in which they engage), but also in terms of all parties involved in the industry, with powerful foreign businessmen at the top of the structure (often assisted by law enforcement agencies) and indigenous women involved in the direct provision of sexual services at the bottom (see also Sturdevant and Stoltzfus, 1992c: 314–15).

---

8 Expatriate men often marry Filipino women to circumvent foreign investment and ownership laws. For example, while the Foreign Investments Act of 1991 allows foreigners to invest up to 100 per cent in export and domestic industries, restrictions are imposed by a so-called Negative List, where between 60 and 100 per cent Filipino ownership is required in various (usually strategic) sectors such as defence, mining, industries using scarce natural resources, and mass media. In the present context, one interesting inclusion on the list (where only 40 per cent foreign equity is permitted) is 'all forms of gambling; bars, beerhouses, dance halls; sauna and steam bathhouses, massage clinics and other like activities regulated by law because of risks they may pose to public health and morals' (DTI, 1992a: 11). As such, a foreigner wishing to open an entertainment establishment must find a Filipino partner, or better, marry a Filipina who effectively acts as a 'dummy', thereby allowing him full freedom and control. While in reality foreigners are able to find loopholes in this system, it is also pertinent that the Philippine state considers the hospitality sector sufficiently important to warrant the imposition of limits on foreign ownership. Although the explicit rationale appears to be concern for the health and moral well-being of the population, it is perhaps more likely that the government is interested in ensuring that the considerable profits to be made from these ventures remain in Filipino hands.

9 The word 'Yakuza', which refers to the Japanese underworld or Mafia, is derived from a card game similar to blackjack and signifies the Japanese words for the numbers 8-9-3. The Yakuza has been in existence since the end of the nineteenth century, although it became particularly active after the Second World War. Like the Mafia, it is involved in prostitution, drugs and the control of labour (Sturdevant and Stoltzfus, 1992a:337).

Before moving on to examine patterns of recruitment in entertainment establishments, which again depend largely on *male* demands in the form of consumer preferences (see note 1 above), the nature of sex work in Boracay is briefly outlined.

Characteristics of sex work in Boracay

As discussed in Chapters 2 and 5, Boracay's active promotion as a 'wholesome' tourist resort has thus far helped it avoid the more formal trappings of an organised sex industry. Yet prostitution clearly exists on the island, even if in the main women work independently and are often sex workers from other parts of the Philippines who have come (or stayed) in the hope of finding 'greater pickings', and/or to get away from middlemen (see below). The usual *modus operandi* of women selling sexual services in Boracay is to promote themselves as 'tourist guides' for foreign men (see also Ploteña, 1987:31). In some cases, these are women who have remained behind in Boracay after being brought for a 'holiday' by men encountered in sex bars in Manila or Cebu: touting for work on the island is conceivably more appealing than returning to jobs in large urban centres where their work is strictly controlled. While the Island Tourism Authority (ITA) and/or Philippine National Police (PNP) can do little to prohibit women from working, or to prevent their arrival by stopping men bringing them to the island in the first place (see Chapter 2), it is interesting that another organisation, the Boracay Multipurpose Cooperative, has initiated the preventive measure of livelihood programmes aimed at alternative sources of female income-generation. Though few in number, and under-resourced, these programmes consist of training in more 'conventional' types of tourist-related skills such as manicures or massages (see also Chapter 5 above).[10]

The situation in Boracay illustrates how the Philippine sex industry often goes hand in hand with international tourism growth, even when there are concerted attempts to prevent it (see also Chant, 1993b). While the efforts of the PNP and ITA might keep prostitution at bay, however, future growth is probably inevitable as long as there is demand

10 Interview with Mila-Yap Sumndad, vice-president of the Boracay Multipurpose Cooperative and president of the Boracay Island Tourism Association (BITZA), May 1993.

from male tourists and a continued flow of women in search of better conditions and earnings than exist in other parts of the country.

Patterns of recruitment in Cebu

Analysing entry into hospitality work is considerably more complex than that involved in other types of employment, mainly because 'morality' and 'ethics' (for want of better terms) become prominent issues. As Noeleen Heyzer (1986:57) points out, the 'voluntary' recruitment[11] of women into sex work must either provide considerable benefits or rewards, and/or reflect a situation where alternative income-earning opportunities are extremely limited. While the reasons behind women's movement into this work are dealt with later in this chapter, it is interesting at the outset to explore the nature of demand for sex workers, something which is rarely touched upon by other studies on prostitution (although see Moselina, 1981:24; Perpiñan, 1983; Sturdevant and Stoltzfus, 1992c:321–7; also Høigård and Finstad, 1992:25–39). Although, as noted earlier, we were unable to interview owners or managers of entertainment establishments, the demand for particular types of female worker can to some extent be gauged by examining the predilections of male clients, especially foreign ones, who have played an integral role in converting Cebu's sex industry into a major generator of income.[12]

Having said this, it is instructive to note the basic prerequisites demanded of staff by entertainment establishments.[13] The main and most common one is a medical certificate from the Cebu City Health Department Social Hygiene Clinic, the cost of which (P250 [US$10])

---

11 This chapter does not deal with involuntary or coerced recruitment into prostitution, although its occurrence in other parts of the Philippines and Southeast Asia is widely recognised, particularly in relation to children (see also Azarcon de la Cruz, 1985: 11; de Leon et al., 1991:56; O'Grady, 1983:11; Srisang, 1991:41). Forced entry into sex work usually happens when female migrants from rural areas arrive in the city and are met by recruiters who trick them into working in prostitution under the guise of helping them find jobs as domestic servants.

12 The names of establishments and male clients in this section of the chapter are not disclosed for reasons of confidentiality. Later in the text, the names of sex workers that appear are pseudonyms ('bar names'), which, along with the fact that none of the establishments are specified, protects the women from identification.

13 Information on basic prerequisites for employment in entertainment establishments was derived from a survey of 16 workers in these places, and from interviews with women's groups and Cebu City Health Department's Social Hygiene Clinic.

is shouldered by the applicant herself.[14] All other criteria, however (with the possible exception of single status – married women are much less likely to have the freedom to sleep with clients), appear to be open to employer discretion and to some degree depend on the nature of the job. For example, education seems to be important when workers need to be able to converse with foreign customers. Indeed, most dancers who end up in girlie bars, where hostessing is an integral part of their duties, must have at least a high-school education in order to possess the relevant proficiency in English. However, workers may be given the chance to acquire a foreign language once employment is secured, as is the case in karaoke bars where Japanese is the main medium of communication (see also Chant, forthcoming b). For jobs with a strong PR component, women may also be required to have a 'pleasing personality' (here embodying notions of charm and deference). It is obvious, however, that youth (and good looks) may outweigh all these considerations. Hospitality workers must have smooth skin, glossy hair and, most importantly, toned, lithe bodies. Although women deemed to be 'well preserved' may be able to continue working into their early 30s (see also Chant, forthcoming b), teenagers and younger women are preferred, which often leads to under-age recruitment (while employers are ostensibly constrained by the fact that the minimum legal age for entertainment work is 18 years, falsification of information is known to occur). Among male workers in entertainment establishments, on the other hand, requirements are much more flexible: although youth, a 'presentable appearance' and high-school education are preferred, none of these is essential.

Visitors to entertainment establishments in Cebu: characteristics and predilections

The conditions described above are very much in accordance with the preferences of male visitors to Cebu's sex centres, about which data were gathered via informal/impromptu interviews with ten men in a range of the city's bars and clubs. While by no means representative, the survey included men from different parts of the world and varied backgrounds, including two Filipinos and a cross-section of foreigners, comprising long-term expatriates, men on business trips

---

14 This applies even to workers who do not engage in commercial sex.

and 'ordinary' tourists (see Table 6.1). The foreign respondents came
from various countries, including the UK, US, France, Canada,
Turkey and Italy; those who were travelling were usually alone,
although they sometimes had male companions (see Table 6.1). The
marital status of these men is also varied, with three single men (two
of whom have girlfriends in their home country), three married (the
Filipino with two wives having married for the second time in Hong
Kong to escape bigamy laws) and four who are divorced or separated
(two of whom have regular Filipina girlfriends) – see Table 6.1. While
nationality and marital status are diverse, however, distinct similarities are found in respect of occupation.[15] For example, the majority
(eight) are involved in business at an executive level, either owning
or managing their own companies (often in the handicraft sector). Two
of these are Filipino, two expatriates (again, businessmen married to
Filipinas)[16] and four foreign businessmen with interests in Cebu (see
Table 6.1). While there is a wide range of ages in the sample (from
25 to 61 years old), a further similarity relates to the distinct clustering
of men in their 40s, with the average age 42.

The most striking similarity of all, however, lies in the sexual
attitudes and predilections of this group of men: despite their different
personal and cultural backgrounds, the vast majority give the impression
that they are in a 'sexual playground' in Cebu, and have every right
to be so. One interesting exception is the 27-year-old Filipino, who
disagreed with the sale of his fellow countrywomen for the pleasure
of foreigners, describing the situation as one of 'old cows on young
grass' (not overly melodramatic, given that the majority are twice the
age of the women concerned). Indeed, most of our male respondents
talked of the availability of young women as a major factor in their

15 In their detailed study of male customers in the Norwegian sex trade, Høigård and
Finstad (1992:28–9) found not only a diversity of age and civil status, but also social
background. The tendency towards greater occupational homogeneity in Cebu may
be due to the fact that the city's formal sex industry caters primarily for foreigners,
many of whom are business travellers.

16 As discussed in note 8 above, marriage to Filipino women is often a means of avoiding
foreign investment restrictions. In the particular case of handicrafts (which applies to
the two expatriates in the male client sample – see Table 6.1), a company can also
qualify for government incentives if 60 per cent of the equity is owned by a Filipino
national (DTI, 1992b:4). Thus foreigners may marry Filipinas and use their name on
all legal documents in order to benefit from state incentives in 'non-pioneer' activities
such as this (see Chapters 2 and 4 above), as well as to maintain full control over business
operations.

Table 6.1: Male visitors to entertainment establishments, Cebu City

Nationality	Age	Marital status	Occupation and residency/visitor status
US	61	Twice divorced/ 24 year-old Filipino girlfriend/mistress	Retired pilot/spends 6 months a year in Cebu
Turkish	40	Thrice divorced/ Filipino wife	Expatriate businessman (handicrafts)
Turkish	25	Single with Turkish girlfriend	Visiting businessman (handicrafts)
British	44	Single with British girlfriend	Visiting tourist (factory worker)
French	41	Divorced (one Filipino ex-wife)	Expatriate businessman (handicrafts)
Canadian	43	Divorced/Filipino girlfriend	Businessman (handicrafts)
Italian	42	Married	Visiting businessman (entertainment)
Italian	49	Separated	Visiting businessman (real estate)
Filipino	27	Single	Local businessman (handicrafts)
Filipino	48	Bigamist (2 wives)	Local businessman (real estate, agriculture)

decision to visit bars and to buy sexual services. Among other things, youth is a novelty when men in their own countries usually have partners closer to their own age. Correspondingly, competition for the youngest girls/women tends to start early on in club sessions. For example, one 44-year-old British tourist, with whom we shared a table at a cabaret, singled out a 14-year-old dancer as his chosen favourite, declaring that he would have to 'make enquiries' to the floor manager before anyone else showed interest. Young women are usually regarded as having the 'best bodies' and to be 'fresh' (in other words less tainted or jaded by extensive sexual activity). Related to this is the supposed 'prestige' of having sex with a very inexperienced girl or, even better, with a virgin. Indeed, one Turkish man now residing permanently in Cebu noted how news of the arrival of a virgin or so-called 'new enter' in one of the bars is passed around the local network of expatriate men known to be interested and willing to pay the high price charged for such a woman (up to US$800). There is also the belief that younger women are 'cleaner' – less likely to have diseases or to be HIV-positive (see also Klouda, 1994:4). Above all, however, it would appear that men's preferences for young women stem from a desire to prove sexual prowess, both to themselves and their peers, as they approach middle age. In reality of course this reflects the potency of money rather than virility, and the fact that being in a foreign land allows men licence to indulge in liaisons for which they would con-ceivably be pitied, ridiculed or outcast in their own countries (see Azarcon de la Cruz, 1985; Chant, forthcoming b).

Over and above the power and prestige men seem to derive from using young women for sexual recreation, the number of such 'liaisons' is also significant and seems to have little to do with questions of what might arguably be regarded as physiological need. Indeed, married men and even those with regular girlfriends appear to be especially concerned to 'chalk up numbers', despite the fact that they presumably experience some sexual gratification at home. For example, one married Italian had bought approximately two women every day since his arrival in Cebu a week and a half earlier, while the thrice-divorced and currently married Turkish expatriate boasted how it was possible in Cebu to emulate a 'harem system' similar to that in his home country. The single British tourist, on the other hand, had only purchased two women during his five-week stay in the Philippines. These differences may to some extent reflect variations in income: the British tourist was a factory worker and had less money at his disposal than most of the businessmen. A further factor is that 'business culture' in the Philip-pines usually incorporates a degree of sexual entertainment (displays of power and wealth, for example, often take the form of lavish parties involving female hostesses and concubines). Nonetheless, the purchasing power of hard currency generally is so high that most foreigners can buy what they want anyway. Indeed, the low cost of Filipino women was cited as a prominent factor in the male travellers' decisions to visit or move to the country in the first place (see also Chant forthcoming b; WEDPRO, 1990a:6).

Even when men had not apparently had commercial sex in mind at the outset, some identified peer pressure as a reason for having taken to visiting Cebu's bars, and especially for indulging in excessive behaviour. For example, one informant told how his friend had bought five women one night in order to 'show-off' to his travelling companions, even if he had only had penetrative sex with two of them. Another factor claimed as responsible for men's participation in buying women was the entertainment industry's ready availability and accessibility to foreigners. Indeed, our British respondent declared that he only bought sex because it was easy to do so in the Philippines, and would probably not have done so if it had involved making an effort (although he also admitted he had chosen the Philippines as a holiday destination *because* of the likely availability of women). Whatever the circumstances of individual cases, most men feel that buying sex abroad is more acceptable than in their own countries: first, because they are away from possible discovery by their womenfolk; second, because they feel liberated from certain moral strictures (see also Abbott and Panos, 1992:7); and third, and pertinently, because there is some illusion that Filipino women are 'grateful' to foreign men for their attentions.

There are several dimensions to this third view. One is that Filipino women give the impression to the vast majority of their customers that relationships may potentially develop into something other than sexual transactions. One Turkish client, for example, stressed that the women he bought told him so often they were in love with him, he would almost forget he was paying them. As negotiations over price often do not take place until after the act, men thus often perceive the women as 'good-time girls' or 'companions' rather than sex workers per se (see also Day, 1988:423; Perpiñan, 1983:18; Sturdevant and Stoltzfus, 1992c: 316–17). Of course, one very good reason for women applying copious amounts of emotion to a basic physical liaison is that the relationship may provide a route to marriage and/or overseas migration. A second, and also strategic, motive is that coquetry and 'sweet talk' can prolong the time a client wishes to spend with a woman and so raise rates of remuneration, as well as possibly reducing the amount of time involved in physical interaction (see Høigård and Finstad, 1992:69). Another possible factor is that sentimentalisation may diminish the disquiet felt by women raised in a culture traditionally antithetical to the deliberate exercise, let alone obvious display, of female sexuality. A final, perhaps less obvious, rationale for the 'love play' of Filipina sex workers is that it feeds a degree of inversion into an essentially racist encounter between First World men and Third World women. In other words, Filipino women may diminish the potential brutalisation of a 'triple weapon' of class, sex and race by cultivating behaviour which makes it difficult for clients to treat them as mere physical objects: offering emotion as well as sex conceivably tempers the degradation inherent in a base economic exchange between people of vastly unequal status[17] (see also Moselina, 1981:15–16).

If nothing else, racial stereotypes of Filipino women as 'affection-ate', 'subservient' and 'loving' are good for business, with many of our respondents clearly of the opinion that Western women were far too 'strong', 'aggressive' and 'authoritarian' for their own good (see also Perpiñan, 1983:18). For example, the Canadian interviewee declared that feminism was one of his country's main contemporary problems, stating that Canada was 'rife' with women who were either 'too demanding' or 'not feminine enough'. Here Filipino women can be seen as having scored a major victory in that their routinised strategies to provide an all-encompassing emotional and sexual experience have clearly caused considerable confusion among their customers as to the motives which so frequently underlie their actions. Male clients seem to forget that the women they meet in bars are working and that it is likely to be worthwhile for them to adopt modes of behaviour, no matter how demeaning, which enable them to maximise their earnings. Having said this, one extremely negative aspect of men's incorpora-tion into more 'rounded' (albeit tactically or illusorily engineered) partnerships with Filipino women is that the latter tell them how much their support means to them and their families in the context of their poverty-stricken existences (see also Moselina, 1981:15 on Olongapo, describing how women often play on men's emotions – and their pockets – by telling them their children are sick). This means that men often end up feeling they are helping the women, rather than exploiting them. However, the fact that on a sexual front Filipino women are often described by men as lacking 'passion' and 'imagination', or more specifically, as one man put it, 'In bed they are nothing ... it's like making love with a piece of ice,' would seem to indicate that emotional posturing (or indeed gratification) is rather emptier than it would first appear (see also Høigård and Finstad, 1992:51).

The fact that men frequently claim not to be completely satisfied with the outcome of buying sex obviously begs the question why they

---

17 'Status' here is used in an economic and ideological sense and refers to the polarised positions of Western men and Filipino women within a highly inegalitarian world system.

continue to do so. One reason is probably male power: in purchasing women, men not only prove their masculinity and virility to themselves and their peers, but their class and economic status as well. Moreover, the conflation of purchasing sexual favours with what they imagine to be a 'winning' of submission as a result of their 'maleness' amounts to an ideological 'trick' whereby three major aspects of a power complex – pyschological, monetary and sexual – are simultaneously fulfilled, at least in their own terms. Objectively of course this combination of male bravado, desire to conquer, to show off and to demonstrate material surplus, could just as easily be regarded as illustrative of deep insecurity and/or inability to sustain relationships with women of the men's own age and status in their home countries.[18] Indeed, the fact that so many of Cebu's male clients are divorced would seem to indicate some difficulty in previous partnerships. Nonetheless, the purchase of young women in economically disadvantaged societies allows men to convince themselves and others, in a superficial manner at least, that they are still sexually desirable and capable of securing relationships, however transitory.

Given the broad similarities in characteristics and attitudes of male visitors to Cebu, i.e. a predominantly business-oriented group who, while not necessarily visiting the city with the primary aim of buying sexual services, at least perceive the availability of cheap sex as an added incentive, it is interesting to consider the attitudes of men travelling to Boracay, where there is no established sex industry.

Male tourists in Boracay: attitudes and characteristics

Our sample of seven male tourists in Boracay is more homogeneous than that of Cebu, mainly on account of the fact that, as a purely tourist destination, the island tends only to attract holidaymakers, rather than people mixing business with pleasure (although some men do visit on breaks from business trips in other parts of the Philippines).[19] Indeed,

18 In their work on male clients of prostitutes in Oslo, Høigård and Finstad (1992:31) found that single men in particular had problems establishing lasting ties with women, suggesting that 'buying sex can be a flight from performance expectations and from confrontations with their own inadequacies and failures'.

19 As in Cebu, the sample of male tourists in Boracay is not only small, but unrepresentative in any statistical sense, consisting as it does of respondents interviewed in a range of tourist establishments (discos, bars, restaurants, etc.) with whom it was possible to converse.

all the men in the survey were visiting specifically for recreational purposes. Two had also come with the intention of taking advantage of the island's diving facilities. In the sample of two British, three Australian, one French and one American male tourists, the vast majority (six) are single (as opposed to the case in Cebu) and travelling alone (except the two British respondents, who arrived together) – see Table 6.2. The average age of the men is also considerably lower than in Cebu (30 years), with more than half in their 20s, which in turn reflects the younger age profile of visitors in general to Boracay (see Chant, 1993b). Occupational differences are also more varied, ranging from students to professionals (see Table 6.2).

While it is entirely conceivable that this group of predominantly single men in their 20s, travelling alone and for recreational purposes only, might be more disposed than those in Cebu to seek sexual companionship, as a general rule they are not. Although all the respondents were aware that some men on the island were engaging in liaisons of a sexual nature, and a number had themselves been propositioned by Filipino women, the majority claimed to have little interest in such matters, with the 26-year-old Australian man declaring that he wanted to 'bring home souvenirs, not diseases'.

Table 6.2: Male tourists in Boracay

Nationality	Age	Marital status	Occupation
British	31	Single	Architect (based in Taiwan)
British	25	Single	Architect (based in Taiwan)
Australian	26	Single	Real estate agent
Australian	29	Single	Traveller*
Australian	43	Divorced	Club promoter
French	21	Single	Student (based in Hong Kong)
US	37	Single	Merchant seaman

* This individual described himself as an 'Asia bum'. He had been travelling around different parts of the region since 1988, returning periodically to Australia to collect a disability pension for a minor recurrent psychological illness.

Having said this, more than half the respondents (four) had some 'interest' in Filipino women. For example, the American merchant seaman admitted that one ulterior motive for choosing the Philippines as his holiday destination was the possibility of finding a spouse, as he had been advised by various friends in his home town of Seattle that Filipinas made 'excellent wives'. In spite of the dubious nature of this quest, he remained apparently uninterested in finding a woman for sex alone, and indeed had come across no potential candidate during his fortnight's stay in Boracay. Two other men, one British and one Australian, also claimed not to be interested in the purchase of sex, despite some involvement with women on the island. Both men were at the time engaged in purportedly 'genuine' alliances with local women, stating that their primary rationale was to learn and understand more about Filipino culture, rather than to pursue romantic dalliances per se. While the character of exploitation in such liaisons is not as direct, or even pronounced, as that involved in formalised sex work, neither of the men's relationships was being conducted on an equal basis: both claimed to be fond of their partners, but expressed no commitment to any long-term contact or communication. They also tended to emphasise the women's 'exotic sexuality' over the kinds of characteristics one would normally associate with a healthy or routine interest in a foreign culture, even going as far as to compare their physical attributes with those of other Oriental and Western women. All these cases are indicative of a somewhat predatory mentality among men who come to the Philippines with no apparent intention at the outset of making use of sexual services.

In many respects this is borne out by the last man displaying an 'interest' in Filipino women, a 21-year-old from France, studying at business school in Hong Kong. This particular respondent was interviewed on three separate occasions, and in the first instance expressed extreme distaste at seeing middle-aged foreign men with young Filipinas. Four days later, however, he himself had 'acquired' two Filipina companions. Although he claimed not to be paying for their services, remuneration came in kind in the form of meals, drinks and a room for the night. We could not find an adequate reason for why the respondent's mind had changed so suddenly, especially given his increased unwillingness to talk, but the pattern suggests some tendency for foreign men to succumb to pairing up with Filipino women if the possibility occurs.

Generally speaking, however, male tourists to Boracay seem to be more aware of the exploitative nature of sex with locals than is the case in Cebu, and are less disposed to become involved. At one level,

this probably reflects the different personal characteristics of visitors
to the two destinations: in Boracay, the youth and single status of most
male tourists perhaps allows them to engage in a range of unpaying
relationships with people from a wider range of national backgrounds,
especially given that many single women from other countries come
to the resort. Middle-aged men in Cebu, on the other hand, especially
those staying on a long-term basis, may feel they have to seek sexual
companionship with local people on a paying basis. At another level,
Cebu is known to possess a thriving entertainment infrastructure and,
as such, is likely to attract those who seek commercial sex as part of
a business or recreational visit. Boracay, by contrast, has more of a
reputation as a quiet 'backpacking' resort and appeals to different
kinds of visitor. Having said this, it is quite possible to procure sexual
services in Boracay, albeit on an informal basis, and the general
perception of the Philippines as an international sex tour haven may
well contribute to eroding the island's traditional resistance to 'moral
decay'. Foreign men coming to the island alone, or with Filipino sex
workers from other parts of the country, act to spread the notion that
demand for this type of companionship exists. In a context where
women stand to gain from participation in the activity (especially in
terms of money and potential overseas migration), it is clear that the
benefits might well be perceived as outweighing the costs. To a significant degree this is apparent in our following discussion of the
financial aspects of registered sex work in Cebu City.

Pay and conditions in sex work in Cebu

Despite the fact that formal hospitality workers have full labour and
wage entitlements under Philippine law (A.Santos, 1992:41), the only
regulation to which their employers uniformly comply is health registration, which of course serves their own and their customers'
interests as much, if not more, than those of the workers themselves
(see below).

Nonetheless, while a basic bar or nightclub salary of P100 (US$4)
for an average shift of seven hours (7pm to 2am) is slightly lower than
the legally prescribed minimum of P105 (based on an eight-hour
day), the vast majority of sex workers earn more than this, even if they
do not provide sexual services. As mentioned earlier, women make
additional money from ladies' drinks, for which they receive an

average of P80 ($3) per night (assuming they have two drinks), in addition to gratuities of around P20 ($0.80). For women not engaging in sex with clients, therefore, a normal wage amounts to just over P200 per night or P1,450 per full (seven-day) week ($58). For those workers who do sleep with customers, a night with one client[20] might bring in anything between P500 and P1,500 ($20–60), or occasionally (especially when clients are Japanese) as much as P4,000 ($160). Most women claim to leave the bars with a customer every three or so days, bringing average earnings for those providing extra services to P3,400 ($136) a week (see also Chant, forthcoming b). In massage parlours, on the other hand, the basic daily wage is lower (P50/$2) for a longer shift (3pm to 1am); even when women provide sexual services, they only receive around P140 ($6) a day commission from management, which, together with gratuities, brings average weekly earnings to a mere P1,700 ($68), although some may be able to procure paying customers after hours.

Indeed, another form of generating income among women in bars, clubs and massage parlours arises through the formation of semi-permanent attachments with male customers, especially businessmen visiting Cebu on a regular basis. When customers return to see specific 'bar girls', they are excused a second bar fine but are expected to provide for all the woman's needs, since the latter do not receive any pay during the time they spend out of the establishments – sometimes up to a month (see Chant, forthcoming b). Women often deem this a preferable way to make their living, particularly if fixed salaries are agreed with clients, who tend to end up being referred to as 'boyfriends' to underline their distinctiveness from normal customers. For example, one masseuse was employed by a foreign businessman for a month-long stint as a 'secretary'; in addition to providing sexual services herself and having to spectate while the man had group sex with other women she was required to procure, she was charged with organising meetings, sending faxes and so on, for a total sum of P10,000 (US$400). While the woman concerned had extra, and often highly unsavoury, duties to perform in this capacity, the package compared favourably

20 Women are rarely in the position of obtaining more than one client per night, except where male visitors to their establishments outnumber the workers available. This tends to apply when men come in large groups to a particular club, which is common when there are major business conventions in Cebu, or when large ships come into port.

with the instability of earnings in the massage parlour and also meant minimising the number of men she herself had to sleep with, at least in the short term.

Indeed, many of the women emphasised how well they are treated by older 'boyfriends', who often supplement their income directly with presents (for them and their children) and/or expensive meals and trips to other parts of the Philippines. Besides this, women have the opportunity to make extra cash through petty theft from men (see also Høigård and Finstad, 1992:45). While the men concerned often only stay in Cebu for short periods at a time, their 'girlfriends' may also be sent money for language training, or alternatively may be 'paid' to stay out of bar work in the interim. In spite of this, most women receiving money from long-term customers continue to work, partly through economic necessity (especially where there are children to support), partly through fear that the flow of money may stop at any time, and, interestingly, partly through feelings of loneliness when contact with other female co-workers is broken (see also section below on households).

On the question of remuneration per se, earnings may appear to be high, especially compared with other tourism jobs (see Chapter 5 above), but it must also be remembered that this is not only extremely unstable and dependent on workers' 'luck' with clients, but may also be eroded through job-related expenses. For example, over and above having to pay for their own health checks and possibly supporting a drug habit as well, women have to invest money in clothes and cosmetics in order to attract customers. Moreover, in some cases costumes or uniforms provided by management and designated as compulsory apparel must either be hired or paid for by workers themselves on an instalment basis. On top of this, a variety of 'penalty systems' operate in establishments, usually consisting of fines for arriving late at work, losing bar property such as cigarette lighters, falling asleep, not wearing the prescribed uniform, or not doing a good job of chatting up customers. Charges range from P10 to P50 for each offence and are deducted from nightly 'extras'. The combined effects of all this mean that the major financial benefits derived by women from sex work actually come from male clients *outside* the establishments, not from their direct employers.

In addition to discriminatory deductions and penalties, sex workers have little in the way of job security. Although women may have worked for long periods in particular establishments, they are rarely given contracts and so cannot demand legal entitlement to social security, sickness pay or holiday leave. While, as mentioned previously, this is largely due to lack of enforcement among employers, it also relates to the somewhat ambivalent legal designation of entertainers as a special group liable to ad hoc provisions.[21] Not only can employers avoid payment of welfare contributions, they are also entitled to dismiss workers who contract STDs without any cost or repercussion, even where retrenchments are of a permanent nature (see also WEDPRO, 1990a:10). The latter perhaps particularly highlights the exploitative nature of an industry where venereal disease is one of the most common, if not inevitable, occupational hazards.

AIDS and sexually transmitted diseases

According to Cebu City Health Department, the most common ailments contracted by sex workers are non-gonococcal infections such as urinary tract cystitis and non-specific urethritis, which may not necessarily be associated with sexual activity but are certainly exacerbated by it.[22] However, several women also end up with diseases directly related to sexual intercourse, including candida (thrush), gonorrhea, syphilis, trichonomiasis, genital warts and pubic lice, as well as fungal infections of the mouth and throat as a result of oral sex. In other cases, women suffer internal bruising and lesions from repeated or aggressive intercourse (often exacerbated by the fact that Filipinas are physiologically smaller than Caucasian men and/or where the former are subject to multiple/group penetration). Despite the psychological trauma accompanying these ailments, in physical terms the majority are fairly responsive to simple treatment (a course of antibiotics, an overnight operation and so on) and routine check-ups in the City Health

21 For example, Article 138 of the Labour Code of the Philippines states that women working in entertainment establishments are only considered full employees if they are 'under the effective control or supervision of the employer for a substantial period of time as determined by the Secretary of Labor and Employment' (Nolledo, 1992:49). As such, employers (and the state) have considerable scope for misinterpretation of, and non-compliance with, workers' statutory rights.

22 The Cebu City Health Department Social Hygiene Clinic sees 250–300 commercial sex workers every day for a one-hour session during which they undergo a swab/smear test to check for a range of non-sexual and sexually transmitted diseases, at a cost of P10 (US$0.40) to the workers themselves (interview with Dr Gloria Paz and Staff Nurse Eva Pinat, Cebu City SHC, April 1993).

Department help to guard against such problems as sterility which might result from diseases going untreated (see also Nichter and Abellanosa, 1994). However, a major practical disadvantage is loss of earnings during recovery periods. Although the City Health Department does not require that women being treated for STDs stop work (only to be extra sure to use condoms), their managers, as noted earlier, are likely to dismiss those found to be infected and to pay them nothing in the meantime (see also Sturdevant and Stoltzfus, 1992b:45).

While condom use is obviously essential to prevent STD transmission, it is even more crucial in respect of HIV/AIDS (*sira* in Cebuano). The City Health Department reported a total of six *known* cases of HIV in Cebu City in March 1993. This may not appear particularly high, especially compared with Manila, which officially has 145 cases of full-blown AIDS and HIV, but Cebu City has two-thirds of all HIV cases in Cebu province and half the total for the Central Visayas as a whole.[23] Furthermore, two of the six persons infected with HIV in Cebu City are female entertainment workers. This is important, since at a national level the Department of Health identifies an overwhelming concentration of HIV and AIDS in the provinces with the major traditional sex centres of the country: the National Capital Region (Manila), and Zambales and San Fernando (home to the former US bases).[24] Moreover, even if the current national total of 408 HIV cases (103 of whom have developed full-blown AIDS, of whom 67 have already died) is nothing compared with Thailand, with well over half a million cases,[25] officially reported numbers are up by 70 per cent on 1990, when total cases were only 239 (Tuazon, 1991). Current estimates suggest that the real prevalence of the disease is in the region of 35,000 people. With tests costing a prohibitive P300 (US$12) outside government hospitals and as much as P100 ($4) within state health institutions, those with limited access to money and information are obviously at risk. Fortunately, for those workers

---

23 See Bobby Timonera, 'AIDS Virus had Spread to 25 Provinces – DOH', *Philippine Daily Inquirer*, 10 March 1993, pp.1 and 10.

24 Ibid.; see also Carol Arguillas and Nico Alconaba, 'AIDS Cases in RP "Still Preventable", Says Flavier', *Philippine Daily Inquirer*, 10 September 1993, p.9. The high incidence of HIV/AIDS cases within the sex trade centres could of course also reflect the more widespread monitoring which goes on in the context of government social hygiene clinics.

25 Arguillas and Alconaba, 'AIDS Cases in RP "Still Preventable" says Flavier': cited in note 24 above.

within the formal entertainment sector in Cebu the state SHC conducts routine HIV tests every six months, issues free condoms at weekly check-ups, gives information and shows educational videos on HIV awareness, and provides regular (and compulsory) seminars for sex workers and bar owners alike. Assessing the efficacy of these preventive measures is extremely difficult, however. While the workers themselves report high levels of condom use, their customers claim it is usually fairly easy to persuade the women to have unprotected sex, particularly if extra remuneration is offered. Moreover, condom use seems to be much more sporadic when women have semi-permanent foreign 'boyfriends' (discussed earlier) or Filipino partners.[26] Also disturbing is the fact that despite the efforts of Cebu's Health Department to show how HIV is transmitted, one of our respondents reported favouring a constant course of antibiotics in order to guard against this and other STDs, rather than practising safer sex (see Nichter and Abellanosa, 1994 on Cebu; also Miralao et al., 1990:42; Tan et al., 1989:189).

While it is essential that preventive HIV/AIDS education programmes be directed towards sex workers, there is in more general terms an obvious danger of creating the belief that women themselves are primarily, if not solely responsible, for disease transmission, or, as the Panos Institute (1990:81) puts it, 'the source of contagion, and not recipients'. Despite the importance of generalised HIV programmes for the national population (see, for example, Klouda, 1994:5–6 on the irrelevance of targeting in Thailand), feminists and other parties in the Philippines who regard foreign men as the primary transmittors feel that instruction and awareness training are vital for these individuals as well (see Maurer, 1991:97; Sturdevant and Stoltzfus, 1992c:310–12; also Day, 1988:421–2).[27] Indeed, considerable controversy has surrounded the dual standard whereby Filipina sex workers must be able to prove they are 'clean' (usually through possession of an authorised medical certificate), yet their foreign clients escape such stipulations (see also Tan et al., 1989:193). While debate on this issue has raged mainly around US military personnel in the Philippines, it

26 Mark Nichter's and Ilya Abellanosa's pilot research on commercial sex workers in Cebu reveals that condom use ranges from 40 to 80 per cent with customers, and only 2–6 per cent with boyfriends or husbands (Nichter and Abellanosa, 1994:4).

27 Interestingly, the chief medic in Cebu's SHC, Dr Gloria Paz, told us how the clinic had occasionally received visits and/or enquiries from foreign men spending extended periods in the city who were concerned about possible risk factors or keen to seek advice on safer sex with 'bar girls'.

can just as easily be extended to include male tourists travelling to the country. A disturbing disregard for use of condoms was certainly apparent among some of the respondents in our survey. Aside from the persistent belief that AIDS is a homosexual condition, the temptation of unprotected sex is often enough to provoke outright risks, whether by avoiding sheaths or by buying women who are likely to be infected. For example, one man boasted how he and three friends had, on one drunken occasion, bribed a bar owner with P400 (US$16) for duplicate health certificates to give to street walkers they wished to bring to their hotel rooms (most hotels which tolerate the entry of female 'room guests' require confirmation that the women are clean – mainly to protect their own reputation and to prevent an influx of lower-status sex workers).[28] Under these circumstances, HIV and AIDS pose the most serious threat to life and health among entertainment workers in Cebu, even if more conventional venereal diseases and abuse-related injuries are those which presently afflict them most on a day-to-day basis.

Fears of infection, and indeed of death, arising from the physiological hazards to which Cebu's sex workers are exposed, act to compound a whole series of social and/or psychological problems related to their jobs, such as low self-esteem, guilt, stigmatisation and a sense of being 'trapped' – often due to perceived inability to get other work or to lead a 'normal' life (see Azarcon de la Cruz, 1985:12; Chant, forthcoming b; Perpiñan, 1983:14). In view of these pressures, it is hardly surprising that a final set of occupational hazards include alcohol and drug use, the latter most commonly involving marijuana, tranquilisers and *shabu*.[29] All are taken in an attempt to block out the denigrating nature of the women's work, and repeated use often leads to dependency (see also Miralao et al., 1990:21; A.Santos, 1992:41; also Høigård and Finstad, 1992:65–6 on Norway). *Shabu* in particular not only depresses the appetite, thereby causing weight loss, but provokes other types of

---

28 Hotels admitting female room guests often charge a tariff or 'joiner fee' for the privilege.

29 *Shabu* is an addictive synthetic drug resembling 'crack' or cocaine, of which Japan is the major supplier to the Philippine market. *Shabu* is a stimulant rather than a relaxant and gives women the necessary energy to dance into the early hours of the morning and, if necessary, stay up all night with clients. A two-day supply (1 gram) costs around P1,500 (US$60), meaning that at least one, if not two customers are needed every other day to support the habit. Mangahas and Pasalo (1994:253) point out that *shabu* has now replaced marijuana as the major drug problem in Cebu City.

physical deterioration too, such as destruction of the nasal cavities. Its highly addictive nature also means that workers may end up having to expose themselves to greater abuse (more sexual activity, less use of condoms and riskier sex acts) in order to support their habit (see also note 29 above).

Given the extremely poor working conditions of registered hospitality women in Cebu City, one can only speculate as to the exploitation suffered by their counterparts lower down the sex work hierarchy. Moreover, although it is possible for formal entertainers to achieve comparatively high earnings (see also W.Lee, 1991:87; Phongpaichit, 1984:254) and not all women (especially those able to be careful) experience the worst excesses of brutalisation,[30] the risks involved may well end up outweighing the advantages. Furthermore, earnings are often eaten into by routine requirements of the job, such as costume hire, cosmetics, beauty treatments and weekly health checks. Having said this, there is little doubt that the prospect of financial reward plays a major part in luring female migrants to sex work in Cebu.

SEX WORKERS AND MIGRATION

Basing the analysis here on our survey of 16 sex workers (two male and 14 female) in Cebu, the discussion, as in Chapters 4 and 5, first considers migratory aspects of the group and then proceeds to examine their household characteristics.

Migrant origins and source-destination linkages among sex workers in Cebu

Out of 16 employees in formal entertainment establishments (see Appendix), seven (all of whom are female) are from other parts of the

---

30 Some women may have a sufficently strong financial position (whether through help from a long-term 'boyfriend', or on account of special physical attributes) to allow them to command a high price for their services, and so to be selective both with their clients and in terms of the frequency and nature of intercourse in which they engage. The likelihood that women with this advantage are prone to succumb to behaviour involving drug or alcohol use or unprotected sex is less than among those whose poverty may provoke greater excesses of self-abuse that not only require the use of artificial stimulants, but in the end may make continuous use of synthetic drugs an integral, or indeed primary, reason for working (see also Høigård and Finstad, 1992:42–5).

Philippines. Of these migrant women, who in turn represent half the female component of the sample, none originate from Cebu province, although one was born in Negros Oriental in the Central Visayas. The rest come from further afield: one from Negros Occidental in the Western Visayas, two from Leyte in the Eastern Visayas and the remaining three from Mindanao (see Fig. 3.2). The vast majority (six) arrived in Cebu directly from their place of birth (mainly in poor rural provinces), with only one woman having lived and worked elsewhere beforehand (notably in Olongapo, the home of the former US Subic naval base). Having said this, another of the migrants had spent time working in Angeles City (the location of the Clark air base) and three of the seven native Cebuanas have extensive migration histories: two of them previously worked as dancers in Angeles and Batangas, Luzon, respectively, while the other had lived in Zamboanga. Therefore, while only half of the female sex workers are migrants in the strict sense, almost three-quarters have lived in other parts of the Philippines.

The vast majority of migrant women (five) came to Cebu in their late teens or early 20s (at an average age of 19 years) to better their economic prospects; four of these had the specific motive of supporting children. Together with two return migrants to Cebu, the latter women were lone parents with sole financial responsibility for their offspring at the time they came to the city. Twenty-four-year-old Marilou from Baybay, Leyte, in the Eastern Visayas, for example, migrated to Cebu shortly after the birth of her three-year-old daughter, Mariel. When the father of the child refused to take any responsibility for their daughter's upbringing, Marilou was faced with the task of finding sufficient income to support herself and her child. With few opportunities in her home village, and aware of the potential returns to be made from sex work, the only option was to migrate to Cebu and leave Mariel in her mother's care (Marilou felt she would rather leave her child in a situation where she would not be exposed to what she herself regards as an unsavoury line of work). Arlene, 27 years old, was in a similar situation after resisting pressure from her boyfriend to abort their child; after coming to Cebu from Negros Occidental, she perceived a sex-related job as the only way to secure an income high enough to support her son Ralph's upbringing. Unlike Marilou, however, Arlene was unable to foster Ralph, as her mother died before he was born. This has caused various problems, with Arlene having to find the resources to pay a childminder. Another of the migrants (also called Marylou but for the sake of distinction hereafter called Mary) who has been able to foster her child, a three-year-old son called Marclint,[31] did so precisely for the reasons described above, even if her rationale for migrating to Cebu was somewhat different and relates more specifically to the closure of the US military bases in Luzon.

The termination of operations at Subic and Clark has affected three women in the survey: Mary, who moved from Olongapo to Cebu for the first time as a result; and two other return migrants (one a native Cebuana, Carmen, and the other, Salome, originally from Negros Occidental), who both came back to Cebu after working in Angeles. All three women had children to support, again stressing the importance of lone parenthood in giving rise to female migration, yet at the same time illustrating the fact that in some cases children are born only once the migration process is set in motion. Twenty-seven-year-old Mary from Leyte, for example, had moved to Olongapo before she became a mother, partly because she could not find work in her home village and partly on account of an offer of a relationship from a US serviceman contacted through a 'penpal' scheme.[32] Unfortunately, the man was killed in service in Panama in 1991, leaving Mary alone with their young son. After turning to bar work in order to provide for the child, her employment was cut short by the closure of Subic. With little experience of other types of work and in the wake of her huge

---

31 Marclint was the product of Mary's relationship with an American serviceman called Clint. It is common practice for first-born children to be named with a fusion or part-fusion of the parents' names.

32 'Penpal schemes' are widespread throughout the Philippines in all strata of society. While ostensibly above board, they are usually a disguised form of the international mail-order bride trade. Filipino women receiving letters may not initially be aware of their correspondent's motives, thinking instead that letter-writing is merely a way of learning about other cultures. Moreover, many are surprised when men make written requests for their 'vital statistics' and 'revealing photographs', not to mention when men actually arrive in the Philippines with marriage proposals. Indeed, a common practice involves the penpals coming to the Philippines with a 'short list' of potential marriage partners who are then vetted until a final choice is made. For example, one professional we knew had such an experience when an American penpal came to visit her in Cebu. Upon declaring this woman his favoured candidate, he laid down a number of conditions, including that she stop working and that she set aside one hour (a 'holy hour') every afternoon for sexual relations. While the offer was in some respects tempting (mainly because the man promised to buy her the house she had always dreamed of, as well as to support her family in the provinces), she politely, but in no uncertain terms, declined.

financial responsibility, she transferred to Cebu, mainly on the basis of its reputation as a growing centre of international sex tourism.

Knowledge of Cebu's expanding entertainment industry was also important in the decisions of the return migrants from Angeles, both of whom had children (one child was born there) and decided to come back for this reason (rather than out of any particular desire to be with kin or to return to a place in which they had grown up and with which they were already familiar). This also applied to another native Cebuana, Crystal, who had moved away from Cebu to Batangas at the age of 22 to become a dancer in a club whose owner promised she would be transferred to Japan. When this did not materialise, she returned to Cebu and began to work in a cultural cabaret. The fact that Crystal had initially moved away to her first entertainment job did not reflect any lack of opportunity in Cebu, but the fact that she felt 'shame' at the idea of doing such work so near to home and family. Nonetheless, once the first step had been taken, and earning power established, it seemed easier to return to the city and continue with hospitality work, even if her parents do not approve and make no reference to her profession within or outside the family. In fact, since Crystal supports them financially, it is rather difficult for them to object openly to her work. Similar situations apply to the other natives and the return migrant initiated into the industry in the Clark air base.

Two features must be stressed here. First, Cebu is an increasingly attractive destination for migrants wishing to secure employment in the sex trade, with six women (three ordinary migrants one return migrant, and two native returnees) having identified the city's openings in entertainment work as a major factor in their decision. Second, it is often necessary for women, whether or not natives of the city, to make their first move into sex work in locations geographically distant from their home contexts. In the latter instance, questions of social stigmatisation figure strongly. In a society where the concept of shame (*hiya*) and pressures to maintain a sense of propriety are major governing principles (see Chapter 1), the social hazards of engaging in sex work (at both a personal and family level) are great. It is thus no surprise that most women in bars, clubs and massage parlours use false names when working and, where possible, move long distances from their home towns (see also Chapter 7; Chant, forthcoming b).

Social stigmatisation is also important when examining migrant sex workers' maintenance of links with their areas of origin, which are significantly less pronounced than among other occupational groups (see Chapters 4 and 5; also WEDPRO, 1990a and 1990b). Although two of the seven migrants (Marilou and Mary) retain ties with home areas through fostering and send substantial remittances in support of this (both remit P3,000/US$120 [around one-third of their average earnings] on a regular monthly basis), these women are the only two who make regular visits to their home provinces. The same women are distinguished from the other migrants in that they are the only ones to have actually told their families what they do in the city. While Mary's family have come to accept her work and give every support to her son, Marclint, they still refer to her as the 'bad one' and are always encouraging her to give up the trade. For the rest of the women, limited ties with home areas minimise the risk of their work being discovered and the attendant humiliation and distress for all concerned. For example Arlene, who has lived in Cebu for three years, has only visited her father once in this time; instead of confessing to working in a girlie bar, she has invented a job as a restaurant cashier instead. While, if nothing else, high earnings among labour migrants would normally lead to financial support to home areas, the fact that three of the five remaining migrant sex workers are supporting children entirely on their own in the city means there is limited cash surplus to send to home areas.

Summing up the general migration characteristics of sex workers in Cebu, the fact that the proportion of migrants in the worker survey (50 per cent of women) is actually lower than among the population in general (see Chapter 3) is perhaps surprising, given the high proportions of migrants among hospitality workers in other Philippine sex centres (see Azarcon de la Cruz, 1985; Miralao et al., 1990; Sturdevant and Stoltzfus, 1992c; WEDPRO, 1990a, 1990b). It is also rather strange insofar as the social opprobrium attached to sex work has played a major role in accounting for the migratory patterns of a number of women in the Cebu City sample. These potential contradictions are in fact reasonably well explained by the specific occupational characteristics of the non-migrants. While we have already seen that in the first instance two of the native Cebuanas actually entered the sex trade in distant locations, the four female non-migrants who have never lived anywhere else do not actually sell sex in the entertainment establishments, nor do they even perform as dancers or masseuses. As waitresses and receptionists, who decline to sleep with customers, these women are able to avoid bringing the same degree of disgrace to their families. Interestingly, the two men in the sample, a choreographer and a cashier respectively, who are both natives, are also able to be completely above board about their work: not only is their flesh neither exposed to public view nor available for purchase, but the sexual double standard whereby Filipino men are entitled to much greater social freedom means that work in entertainment establishments does not pose anything like the moral dilemmas it does for women.

Bearing in mind that female migration to Cebu is often shaped by knowledge or perception that the city's sex industry is likely to provide jobs and, more specifically, jobs which are sufficiently remunerated to support lone women with children, it is also crucial to recognise that an underlying factor of many types of population movement associated with this kind of work is the issue of dealing with social ostracism. These factors are also relevant in our analysis of the household characteristics of sex workers.

HOUSEHOLD CHARACTERISTICS OF SEX WORKERS IN CEBU

While we have already touched upon types of household organisation among sex workers in relation to migration, especially with regard to single parenthood, this section clarifies the picture further. Both men interviewed are young (22 and 23 years old, respectively) and single; one lives with his parents and siblings in a nuclear structure, while the other lives on the premises of the club of which his mother is the owner. As for the 14 women in the sample, their average age is 26 years (ranging from 21 to 37) and, not surprisingly, they display a reasonably wide diversity of household circumstances. Having said this, their marital status is fairly uniform in that only one has a resident male partner and most of the rest, all of whom are single (usually never married as opposed to widowed or separated), have children (see also Miralao et al., 1990; WEDPRO, 1990a, 1990b). Of the four women without dependents (28 per cent of the total), two live with their parents and two live alone (one rents a room in a boarding house, the other resides in the club where she works). While the fact that the childless women living with parents are natives to the city and the other two are migrants may in part explain the nature of domestic arrangements, it is also worth mentioning that the former do not provide sexual services as part of their job. Although they have lower earnings than those engaging in sexual activity and so do not have the resources to set up independent households, it is also the case that their employment in more 'reputable' aspects of the entertainment industry is less likely to prompt malicious gossip or stigmatisation among immediate family and neighbours. This may well mean that their parents are more disposed to let them reside in the family home, particularly in the case of fathers, who are much more likely to put their foot down when it comes to daughters engaging in sex for a living. Indeed, it is pertinent that only three women in the sample as a whole live in households with adult male members, and none of these have sex with customers (the third woman, 29-year-old Carmen, lives with her partner and works as a receptionist, having sexual relations only when she desperately needs the money; even then, this is behind her partner's back). The limited presence of men in households where women engage in full commercial sex is interesting insofar as it suggests that a female-only or female-dominated home is perhaps the only kind of environment where women involved in more extreme aspects of the trade are able to exist. Indeed, with the exception of Carmen, who resides with her partner and ten-year-old son as part of a larger extended structure, including her mother and siblings, the remaining nine women with children live without men: three as independent single-parent households, three as 'embedded female heads' residing in their mothers' homes (all whom in turn were abandoned or widowed), two with other female co-workers in shared lodgings (one of whom has fostered her child to her parents in the countryside) and the other (who has also fostered) living in a self-contained rented room in an aunt's house.

The fact that almost two-thirds of all female sex workers live in some form of female-headed domestic unit, either independently, with their mothers, or with other female companions, is striking, with the proportion of those with resident children in such arrangements (88 per cent of this particular group) considerably higher than that for the population in general in Cebu or for other target occupational groups (see Chapters 3, 4 and 5). Indeed, even when considering only those women who head their own households or live independently (57 per cent of all sex workers), the proportion is still substantially greater than among the population interviewed in Cebu's household survey (where 17 per cent of households are headed by women, and only 5 per cent consist of those living alone with their children – see Chapter 3), not to mention the three (21 per cent) 'disguised' woman heads living in their mothers' homes.[33]

While we have already pointed out that the high proportion of female-dominated living arrangements among sex workers may be partly explained by imperatives of freedom from male control or veto, other factors are equally important, especially those related to lone parenthood. One issue here is economic solvency, in that it is often the case that single parents in other occupations do not have the necessary financial resources to set up independent households and are thereby forced to reside with kin in larger extended units (see Chapter 3). Sex workers, on the other hand, have an earning capacity far exceeding that of other women. Even if this does not lead to their opting for an independent household per se, it usually means that they are able to support relatives rather than vice versa. Indeed, all the 'embedded female heads' in the sex work sample tend to contribute not only to all routine expenses of the wider household, but also to the education of siblings.

Another link in the equation of sex work with female household headship and/or female-dominated living arrangements is social stigmatisation. While we have seen that sex workers are often alienated because of their profession, the same kind of ostracism applies to lone parents (see Chapter 3; also Chant, forthcoming b). Accepting the difficulties in distinguishing whether greater opprobrium accrues to sex work or lone parenthood, it is often the case that once women have experienced the disgrace attached to one state, they have little regard for the other. In other words, if a woman faces condemnation as a sex worker, there is little to lose (and often much to gain) from living independently; alternatively, if a woman has already overcome certain

---

33 It is interesting to note that only four of the 100 households interviewed in Rubberworld contained a female entertainment worker, although a fifth household had recently lost a niece who had gone to work as a 'cultural dancer' in Japan. Two of the four households were headed by these women (one was an extended structure), while the other two consisted of the women concerned residing as part of their parents' or parents-in-laws' household. Of the latter one was a daughter-in-law who worked as a singer in a karaoke bar and did not sleep with clients, while the other was a daughter with two babies who was being supported by a long-term Italian 'boyfriend' whom she had met while working at a club. Unfortunately, she had spent most of the income he sent her on *shabu* (see note 29 above); her mother eventually admitted that she had been addicted for the last year and there seemed to be nothing they could do to help her.

difficulties in living as a single mother, then the move into sex work may be easier from the point of view of dealing with gossip, especially as people will probably assume that she is involved in this kind of activity anyway (Chant, forthcoming a).

Having said this, it appears that the majority (seven out of ten) of women with children entered the sex industry only *after* they had given birth and been abandoned (although one, Carmen, now lives with a partner who did not father her child). Of this group, all had given birth to children of Filipino men who had not only denied responsibility but failed to provide financial help of any type. As for the other three women, who became pregnant as a result of working in the hospitality trade, all had had children by foreign men, two of whom had taken no responsibility for their offspring and one who had died (see the case of Mary above). While this illustrates another occupational hazard of sex work (albeit not particularly common in Cebu), it serves to show how male irresponsibility is central to the continued, if not the initial, involvement of women in hospitality employment.

Summing up the household characteristics of sex workers in Cebu, an overwhelming proportion of women live in female-headed arrangements, whether as heads in their own right, submerged within their mothers' homes, or as co-residents of female companions. Moreover, even two of the four women without children live alone. While the formation of female-dominant households is certainly facilitated by financial solvency, their emergence also appears to be due to social stigmatisation – whether as lone parents, as sex workers, or both. The bottom line, however, is that such alternative domestic arrangements appear to represent an important space for women, free from patriarchal strictures imposed by individual men (fathers or partners) and able to tap critical sources of practical and emotional support from female friends or kin (see also Chapter 7).

Attitudes to marriage and fertility among sex workers

The fact that nearly two-thirds of the female workers in the sample have children, yet remain single, underscores a pattern whereby marriage or even co-residence with men is rarely aspired to, especially since so many have been deserted by boyfriends in the past. A variety of factors come into play here, one of which is that employers are less likely to recruit married women (mainly because this will limit their freedom to have sex with clients). Another is that husbands themselves are likely to forbid it. It may certainly be difficult for women to find partners tolerant enough to allow them to work in the industry, let alone those who accept their sexual histories in the first place. On a more positive (and rather more voluntaristic) note, remaining single may allow women (especially if they live at home) to continue to support their parents and siblings to a greater degree than if they are married, which may assuage some of the guilt or shame they feel about their jobs (see Chant, forthcoming b). For those who live without their relatives, it is also clear that living with friends or heading their own households provides other advantages, such as companionship and/or a sense of self-worth in being able to manage life alone.

Retention of single status could also be important insofar as it might enhance the somewhat remote prospects of marrying a foreigner. Sex workers in Cebu show little interest in marriage to a Filipino, often because their previous experiences (of abandonment, financial irre-sponsibility and so on) have tainted their views of them. Over 50 per cent of the women, however, mentioned that they would not be averse to marrying a foreigner at some stage in the future (one in this group was already engaged to a German 'boyfriend'). Most of these women did not want to get married immediately, but thought that they ought to by the time they were 30 (probably around the time that they would have to leave the sex industry). Apart from economic considerations and those related to overseas migration (see below), women favoured foreign partners because they perceived them as more tolerant than Filipinos of their sexually active pasts, as well as in respect of adopting children fathered by other men. Indeed, in some cases, already having children was seen to further the prospects of a foreign union; men often develop close ties with women's offspring and are possibly able to diminish their own guilt at buying sex by converting themselves (at relatively little cost) into benevolent providers for a whole family.

As for fertility, the mothers in the sample have an average of 1.3 children. The oldest woman, 37-year-old Alice, is the only one to have had three children, which may indicate that younger sex workers will follow suit in due course. Yet while the childless women expressed a desire for two offspring, those with children rarely wanted more than the one or two they already had. Common reasons for this include the fact that, as lone parents, these women are acutely aware of the economic costs involved in childrearing, as well as the problems incurred in having to organise childcare with a third party, especially when they work unsociable hours (although only one actually has to pay a childminder, given the help that usually accrues from female friends and kin in and outside the home). Another important consideration is their unwillingness to have further children while still in the sex industry, mainly on account of the distress and anxiety that this may provoke. For example, one woman, Arlene, had done her best to conceal her activities from her two-year-old son by getting her co-resident female companion to keep him amused, or by not returning to the house until he was asleep. However, her tiny dwelling provided little privacy and Arlene was dismayed when the boy began referring to all the men who entered the house as 'Daddy'. Given the fact that these kinds of problems are likely to escalate as children reach school age and come in for additional abuse or teasing from peers, it is no surprise that women not only declare a preference to curtail their number of children, but express a desire to have stopped working in the bars and clubs by the time their existing offspring are six or seven years old, even if this is unlikely to prove possible economically.

Indeed, the combined forces of shame, guilt and self-deprecation which so often colour sex workers' feelings about the jobs they do and their attitudes to marriage and childbirth are exacerbated by an uneasy sense about the future. Many cannot envisage being able to survive on their own account: by the time they are too old to attract male clients, it is usually too late to move into other types of waged employment such as factory or restaurant work. Their alternatives are further limited by the fact that if they produce employer references, their pasts as entertainers are revealed. One option is to claim they have never worked or worked only in an informal business, but this does not do them any favours in respect of being able to prove they have held regular jobs, or have had any substantial form of work experience. Although some women may be able to move into posts as cashiers or *mamasans* in bars or clubs, such opportunities are scarce. For this reason marriage to a foreigner, as discussed above, comes to represent one of the few ways out (see Chant, forthcoming b; also Moselina, 1981:19).

Notwithstanding the extremely low incidence of Filipino sex workers who actually end up married to men from other countries (see, for example, Miralao et al., 1990: 33–4; Moselina, 1981:16 on the base areas), there is little doubt that in addition to representing a means of avoiding outright destitution, this may also be a method of securing economic betterment, particularly if it results in overseas migration. Given the common belief that life is easier in other countries, international migration is regarded as an opportunity for upward socio-economic mobility. Such considerations often more than outweigh any lukewarm emotions a woman may have towards her betrothed, or indeed any difficulties likely to be encountered later on. For example, 26-year-old Darling, a masseuse, accepted a marriage proposal from an English man and, after a preliminary church blessing in the Philippines, went to live with him in London for two years along with her two children. However, the man was little more than an acquaintance, and Darling found it increasingly difficult to hide her growing disquiet and unhappiness, especially away from the emotional support of her family. Thus, in spite of the economic advantages and the fact that her lover was keen to formalise their union under English law (which again would have strengthened her financial position), Darling left Britain on the pretext of getting a wedding dress made by one of her relatives, and never came back. Despite emotional difficulties and the fact that Filipino women abroad may be treated as skivvies, slaves or second-class citizens, many sex workers still aspire to move overseas via marriage, especially given that the normal routes for international migration, such as possession of a university education or some form of vocational experience (nursing or teaching, for example), are usually foreclosed.

WOMEN'S ATTITUDES TOWARDS SEX WORK

Turning to attitudes about sex work in more general terms, we have already seen that many women consider hospitality jobs 'bad', demeaning or shameful; the sole advantage, aside from the vague possibility of foreign marriage or overseas migration, is economic. Indeed, financial considerations are usually cited as the primary, if not only, justification for work in this business. Few women derive pleasure from their liaisons and, when asked how they feel about sleeping with clients, the vast majority describe sex as a mechanical operation during which their thoughts focus almost exclusively on the money they will receive once the act is over. Some also report how they while away the moments by thinking about what they will buy their children with the proceeds, or even what groceries they need to get the following day.

While sex work is not usually considered strenuous or demanding in the physical sense, it can take a heavy emotional toll; one woman,

Marilou, states: 'It is easy work, but a hard life.' Some claimed that they were frequently 'heartbroken' when clients for whom they had developed emotional attachments abandoned them or failed to respond with similar feelings. Others even declared that their biggest occupational hazard was 'falling in love' and being rejected, yet this must also be seen in the light of the routinised emotional strategies mentioned earlier. For a range of reasons already discussed, women often construct sentimentalised smokescreens around their clients, with one conceivable backlash being that they go some way to convincing themselves that their relationships are meaningful (in other words, they end up 'kidding' themselves). Having said this, it is important to recognise that in justifying their work to us, the women might have felt it necessary to resort (albeit unconsciously) to the same kind of sentimentality that characterises their interactions with clients; this, as we have seen, is a way of stimulating pity (as opposed to opprobrium), as well as veiling their profession with a greater degree of respectability. A second, and probably more relevant, factor is that long experience in this kind of work may have rendered women unable to separate emotional from financial needs. To some extent this probably explains their general preference for older male clients, who are not only perceived as being likelier to want more permanent relationships and to treat them better than younger men, but who are usually financially better-off as well.

While at various junctures in this chapter we have considered some of the reasons why different women enter sex work, it is important to highlight these in more general terms, even if we cannot address the difficult issue of why some women turn to sex work and others do not. Although other researchers have posed the latter question, it has rarely been effectively explained and the present work can only add insights.[34] Bearing in mind Pennie Azarcon de la Cruz's (1985:11)

---

34 Inevitably, any definitive study of factors predisposing women to enter sex work would probably have to entail long-term psychological research on the women involved, together with a 'control group' based on large samples, and examining parent–parent and parent–child relationships, childhood experiences and so on. All of these are obviously beyond the scope of the present study. More work on the backgrounds of sex workers has been conducted in Western countries, with Høigård and Finstad (1992:15) concluding that 'the picture is relatively unambiguous', in that it tends to be working-class women with 'irregular home lives and adjustment difficulties in their working lives' who enter prostitution. It is doubtful, however, that these sets of factors would be particularly applicable in a developing country context, given major structural economic differences, and differences in cultural and social practices.

point that prostitution for most women is a 'forced choice', lone parenthood stands out as having the greatest influence in Cebu. This relates to the fact that not only do few other jobs provide women with sufficient income to raise their children alone, but, as mentioned earlier, considerable social stigmatisation surrounds single mothers: if women are treated as social outcasts because of lone parent status (especially if they live independently), then little may be lost by moving into sex work. Embedded in this is the fact that unmarried mothers are visible to the rest of society as having lost their virginity – indeed, many women are unfortunate enough to get pregnant during their first sexual encounter (see also Miralao et al., 1990:12 and 54 on the base areas). Given widespread condemnation of pre-marital sex among peers, family and prospective marriage partners, it is not surprising that single motherhood's powerful associations with lost virginity and sexual licentiousness result in situations where shame and ostracism make this group (and even their childless counterparts who have 'transgressed' before marriage as well) feel they have little to lose by selling their bodies. This is especially tragic given that so many Filipino sex workers appear to experience 'deflowering' as a result of rape or incest and not through their own volition (see below; also Miralao et al., 1990:11; Moselina, 1981:12; WEDPRO, 1991a:3 on Olongapo; WEDPRO, 1990b:3 on Angeles; and Graburn, 1983 and W.Lee, 1991 on the backgrounds of female sex workers in other parts of Southeast Asia).

Apart from the fact that women often have to turn to sex work to support their children, some are also in the position of having to help parents and siblings as well. Although this concern does not seem to be particularly widespread in Cebu, with many women attempting to minimise their contact with kin and others constraining their professional activities in order to maintain friendly relations, duties to relatives have been seen as a major influence in women's movement into hospitality work elsewhere (see also Moselina, 1981; Sturdevant and Stoltzfus, 1992c). Indeed, a paradoxical situation often arises in which parents encourage their daughters to make contacts with foreigners (through 'penpal schemes' and the like – see note 32 above), yet at the same time condemn them for entering the sex trade.

Although child abuse and rape have been identified as another major set of factors pushing women into sex work (see, for example, Heyzer, 1986:57; Miralao et al., 1991; Sturdevant and Stoltzfus,

1992c), again these concerns did not emerge as important in Cebu. While it might be the case that women were reticent to talk about such issues, or that more in-depth probing over a longer period of time would have revealed an incidence of sexual abuse, it may also be that none of the women had actually experienced this. Nor did education seem important, with most sex workers having at least completed high-school education and being technically able to obtain other kinds of work (although see Chant, forthcoming a), unlike some of their counterparts in Olongapo and Angeles, where lack of schooling is seen as a contributory reason for opting for sex work in the absence of alternatives (see, for example, WEDPRO, 1990a, 1990b). Difficulties obviously remain in evaluating the extent to which the different factors cited here may influence women's decisions to go into entertainment occupations, and there is no doubt that further and more substantial studies of a longitudinal (and comparative) nature are needed (see also note 34 above).

PRELIMINARY CONCLUSIONS ON THE GENDER IMPLICATIONS OF SEX WORK

As for the implications of sex work for women's lives, there is little doubt that compared with export manufacturing and conventional tourism (Chapters 4 and 5), this sector is probably the most explicitly exploitative of all. Women in this industry not only experience outright exploitation as individuals through direct personal contact with male clients, but as workers they face a situation in which male employers and intermediaries take considerable shares of their profits. In addition, patriarchal exploitation is interwoven with a complex array of class and racial inequities which combine to perpetrate both a highly negative self-image among sex workers themselves, and an entire system wherein the rights of privileged groups are exercised in a wide, dangerous and ultimately life-threatening range of ways.

The only slightly redeeming factor is that, compared with their peers, sex workers have relatively high earnings, which confers some autonomy at the domestic level. Bearing in mind that sex workers are not generally admitted to membership of 'normal' Filipino households, at least they are able to afford acceptable alternatives, an important one being the creation of units free from the patriarchal rule of husbands or fathers. Female-only or female-dominant households not only seem to be viable pragmatically, but in many respects provide environments in which female strength and solidarity might be nurtured. This may give women scope to confront gender inequalities at a personal level which in due course may extend to a wider array of societal domains (see Chant, forthcoming b). In the final analysis, the juxtaposition of home lives characterised by an absence of men, and where women seem to have a greater chance to talk freely with one another and assert themselves as individuals, with professional lives which are overwhelmingly dominated by men and patriarchal ideologies, may stimulate some questioning of gender and other injustices in society.

For example, sex work obviously adds to women's experience of men of various backgrounds and nationalities. The fact that so many male clients are married means that one glaring inequality becomes apparent, in that men rarely play by the monogamous rules that women are taught to obey and believe in. This may well engender feelings of mistrust, not only in men but in patriarchal institutions more generally. Entertainers' experiences of foreign males may also dispel certain romanticised, but widely held, illusions about the intrinsic superiority of men from other countries. Sex workers undoubtedly discover in the course of their work that higher economic status is not necessarily consonant with more refined modes of behaviour or more benevolent attitudes towards women. The fact that many are in favour of a foreign marriage is thus much more likely to stem from a realistic assessment of their lack of comparably remunerative long-term career prospects than from clients' personal merits. The downside of this learning process is that male–female (and international) interaction comes to be seen by women as a base for monetary exchange that precludes equality and is bereft of the emotion and sensitivity integral to most other human relationships.

Indeed, having pointed to earnings as one of the compensating factors of sex work, it is also important to stress that this itself is not always in women's every interest, even if it allows them to establish their own households and to raise children single-handedly. For example, women accustomed to large incomes may find themselves unable or unwilling to move into other, inevitably less well-paid jobs, even disregarding the reluctance of most employers to take on former entertainers. In this way, the remuneration attached to sex work may entrench women within a sector from which they are ill equipped to escape. Another conceivably negative consequence of their high earnings is the jealousy it provokes among other women, which may add to the general alienation of hospitality women from society at large. Indeed, although sex workers potentially draw some strength from residence in female-only domestic environments, their effective 'closeting' in these units means they are not only cut off from contact with other women in the community, but often become targets for scapegoating, with their anti-social working hours further reducing the prospects of spending leisure time with (and getting to know) anyone other than co-workers. Women in general may also try to minimise their interaction with entertainers for fear of association or being stigmatised themselves, or because their own personal prejudices neither encourage nor permit them to become involved with this group. Moreover, other women often gossip maliciously about sex workers as a strategy of social distancing: this includes commenting on how they dress, passing on news to neighbours about how many visitors they have had in their homes (and at what hours of the night, how damaging this must be for the children and so on) and speculating as to the lewd acts women must have got up to to be able to afford whatever luxuries they have. Women outside sex work also tend to wear very conservative apparel (long sleeves and hems, high necklines and so on) to distinguish themselves from their 'fallen' counterparts. The sense of 'otherness' to which sex workers often escape in the form of independent or female-only homes, therefore, may actually strengthen discrimination against them, rather than diminish it.

Non-conventional living arrangements may also reinforce the breakdown of family ties and further exacerbate the social isolation of sex workers. Although links with parents and siblings are often severed when women first move into this profession, the fact that the latter usually establish independent households or share with other female companions (often creating a quasi-family situation with co-workers, frequently referred to as 'sisters') may actually distance these women still further from their own families, even to the extent that resumption of contact is impossible.

Additional disdain towards sex workers may accrue from their compliance with stereotypes of Filipino women as passive and subservient. Although we have already seen that this is likely to be part of a wider strategy employed by entertainers to protect themselves and/or to optimise their potential economic gains, it may well be disapproved of by other women on whom the consequences inevitably reverberate. Apart from the implications for other women in society, this adherence to, or rather intensification of, stereotypical female behaviour among sex workers may also reinforce the views held by foreign men (and women) that Filipinas are, at best, willing, compliant and grateful recipients of the attentions of foreign males, or, at worst, calculating money-grabbers, prepared to do anything for a cash reward (see also Sturdevant and Stoltzfus, 1992c:316–7).

As for the broader implications of sex work in the Visayas, all seem unequivocally negative both from the point of view of the parties involved (with the possible exception of male controllers of the industry) and for society in general. One of the most significant outcomes of an entertainment infrastructure is its reinforcement of the notion that women are objects for the sexual gratification of men. Another is its implicit condoning of sexual double standards whereby men have the right to buy sex, while having wives who remain faithful. The latter not only strengthens the polarisation of women into 'virgins' or 'Madonnas' on the one hand, and 'whores' on the other (see, for example W.Lee, 1991:84), but also places women in the humiliating and powerless position of having their status determined by the nature of their sexual relationships with men. The pragmatic (and legally endorsed) availability of commercial sex for men also means that wives have little chance of preventing their husbands from engaging in this activity, let alone of responding with behaviour of a similar nature.

An associated, and especially controversial, issue is the way in which sex work reinforces female dependence on men. Female sex workers are very obviously dependent on both male employers and male clients for their earnings, but to what extent can married women be regarded as being in a similar position? Debates on marriage as an institutionalised form of prostitution become relevant here, and while there is little point in reiterating issues which have been given considerable attention in previous literature, it is important to recognise that sex work has often been seen as simply one of the more visible and extreme forms of male dependence among women, even if at the domestic level (as is the case in Cebu) sex workers seem to have greater financial autonomy than have their counterparts in 'mainstream' society. Indeed, a related and far-reaching implication of sex work is the distance it sets up between one group of women and the rest of the female populace. In the attempt to disassociate themselves from sex workers, most women, as we have seen, must not only dress demurely to be considered 'respectable', but must refrain from smoking, drinking alcohol or changing boyfriends on a regular basis as well. In other words, the wider freedom of women is curtailed in numerous and significant ways by the existence of the hospitality trade (see also Chapter 7).

On a final note, consideration should perhaps also be given to the way in which the sex industry affects its male participants and men in society at large. While on the surface men who pay for sex might regard themselves as privileged and may accumulate certain kinds of social currency by boasting of their encounters with prostitutes, there are also men who do not agree with this behaviour and who not only despise it as weak and/or exploitative, but dislike the manner in which it casts aspersions on male culture as a whole. In the same way, those men who run the industry may only receive support from a relative minority of people. Even if widespread condemnation of such groups tends only to reach major proportions when their activities encompass pederasty or necrophilia (as in so-called snuff movies where women and children are subjected to extreme physical abuse or even killed before, during or after sex acts), or when AIDS cases reach epidemic proportions, and/or when such discoveries hit international headlines, the fact remains that men who exploit the bodies of others are not generally regarded as making a positive contribution to human development. If only for this reason, the sex industry is also damaging to them, even if the major victims remain female. Indeed, Wendy Lee (1991:79) has ventured to comment that women's bodies (in Thailand, South Korea and the Philippines) effectively underpin these countries' balance of payments (see also APHD, 1985:45). Even if our research on Cebu (and Boracay) does not permit us to make similar claims for the Philippine Visayas, there is little doubt that women themselves are usually the last to reap the economic benefits from this otherwise degrading, and increasingly dangerous, activity.

7 COMPARATIVE PERSPECTIVES ON WORK AND WOMEN'S STATUS

As detailed reviews of women's involvement in different economic sectors in the Philippine Visayas have been given, the aim of this chapter is to summarise the key findings of the research and to highlight their conceptual implications for wider debates on gender and development, especially in relation to questions of the direct and indirect impacts of paid work on women's lives and status. In the interests of illuminating current enquiry into the links among female employment, migration and the household, here we assess the extent to which incorporation into different export-oriented sectors is associated with particular demographic and social patterns and how these combine to shape the outcomes of labour force involvement for women. Integral to this analysis is a detailed exploration of the attitudes of women towards their lives and jobs, consideration of the varied dimensions of gender embodied in female recruitment in different types of economic activity, and the degree to which the character of occupations themselves contributes to continuity or change in prevailing gender stereotypes.

With this in mind, the first section of this chapter provides a comparative summary of the key aspects of migration and household structure among women from the different occupational groups and the wider populations in the study localities. It signals the main points of correspondence and divergence and evaluates these in the light of broader conceptual debates on the interactions between social, economic and demographic aspects of women's employment. These findings serve to deepen discussion in the second half of the chapter, which looks more specifically at the varying aspects of gender embedded in female labour demand and the ways in which gender roles and relations may be reinforced or modified by different types of employment in conjunction with attendant and/or 'intervening' factors such as domestic organisation and intra-household relations.

256

WOMEN'S EMPLOYMENT AND MIGRATION: COMPARISONS BETWEEN OCCUPATIONAL GROUPS

Bearing in mind that the small (and uneven) numbers of respondents in our worker surveys preclude anything other than speculative comparisons,[1] one or two differences in migrant status and experience stand out. The first is that formal tourism workers in Boracay (employees in hotels, shops and restaurants) are the only group where female migrants are clearly predominant (77 per cent) – see Table 7.1. Interestingly, perhaps, this represents the most marked contrast with the equivalent category in Cebu, where not one migrant figures among the (admittedly few) women interviewed in the city's conventional tourism establishments (see Table 7.1; also Chapter 5). A second finding (which again distinguishes Boracay from the other localities) is that migrant females form a majority not only among the resort's formal workers, but also among beach-vendors (55 per cent), which is interesting given that only 38 per cent of women in the local household survey were born outside the island (see Chapter 3).[2] The

---

1 In comparing migration (and household) characteristics of occupational groups in this chapter, it is important to bear in mind that we are only considering women, which obviously reduces the size of worker samples (see Tables 7.1 and 7.2). Along with the fact that the numbers of respondents vary from one group to another, this means that differences between groups must be interpreted with extreme caution. However, numerical deficiencies aside, the degree of distinctiveness of certain groups of workers in certain places in terms of their migration or household circumstances was found to be extremely marked, and on these grounds we feel reasonably confident that they provide a basis for exploratory comparative comment. Given the close fusion of *place* of work with *type* of work in terms of women's own perceptions of their jobs, their reasons for migration, the patterns of migration and household structure with which they are associated and so on, it is also important to note that in the present discussion we tend not to abstract the different groups of workers from their localities, or vice versa. This makes comparisons and their explanations easier. Moreover, examinations of place-specific differences for each of the main sectors (manufacturing, tourism and sex work) appear in Chapters 4, 5 and 6 respectively, and various sectoral differences in the context of each locality (Cebu, Lapu–Lapu and Boracay) in Chapter 3.

2 Comparisons between the worker surveys and the household surveys are also likely to be affected (a) by the greater numbers of people interviewed in the latter compared with the former, and (b) by the fact that female migration data in the household surveys only refer to women household heads or spouses, whereas worker samples include daughters and single and/or childless women as well.

worker surveys in Cebu and Lapu-Lapu, on the other hand, reveal lower percentages of migrants than the household samples (77 per cent and 91 per cent respectively), although a proportion of household respondents in all three localities have the same sorts of jobs as those in the target occupational groups.[3]

Table 7.1: Key migration characteristics of women in target occupational groups

Occupational group & locality (no. of women surveyed in brackets)	% of migrants in group	% of migrants from same province	% of migrants from same region[*]	% of whole group with migratory experience	Average age on arrival in in locality (years)(range in brackets)
Industrial workers, MEPZ (8)	63%	60%	80%	80%	19 (5–40)
Industrial workers, Cebu (8)	50%	50%	50%	75%	16 (7–25)
Sex workers, Cebu (14)	50%	0	14%	72%	19 (18–24)
Tourism workers, Cebu [**] (4)	0	n/a	n/a	0	n/a
Tourism workers, Boracay[**] (13)	77%	60%	80%	92%	18 (18–22)
Beach-vendors, Boracay (11)	55%	17%	17%	64%	25 (17–33)

Notes:

n/a = not applicable

[*]   See Fig. 3.2 for Philippine regions

[**]   'Tourism workers' here refers to employees in the formal sector, i.e. hotels, restaurants and shops. 'Beach-vendors', on the other hand, refers to the informal tourism worker survey in Boracay.

A third, and possibly related, feature is that formal tourism workers in Boracay display the highest levels of migratory experience: in other words, natives as well as migrants have often lived in other localities, with 92 per cent of the group as a whole having spent time elsewhere in the country (see Table 7.1). Moreover, many of these respondents

3 This is not to say that any individual in the household surveys 'doubled up' as a respondent in any of the target worker interviews: in order to ensure this, the sample populations were drawn from different contexts: residential communities in the first case, and workplaces in the second (see Appendix).

have resided in distant centres such as Manila,[4] where they have worked in domestic service, factory employment and/or sales jobs. While fewer informal tourism workers on the island have migratory backgrounds, those who do have also tended to spend time in the capital. Indeed, Boracay's beach-vendors, together with Cebu's sex workers (many of whom have lived in other parts of Luzon, such as Olongapo and Angeles – see Chapters 2 and 6), include few migrants from the same provinces and/or regions as their current place of residence (see Table 7.1). Instead, people have come from a wider and more distant range of locations than is the case with other groups of workers (or indeed the bulk of the population in the study centres – see Chapter 3).

Summing up these differences, formal tourism employment in Boracay seems to be distinguished by a high level of migrant prevalence, in relation both to the general population on the island and to other occupational groups here and elsewhere in the Visayas. In addition, and along with local beach-vendors and Cebu's sex workers, formal tourism employees appear to have quite distinctive experiences of mobility in respect of either having been born, or more usually having lived, in places further away from their present destinations (and often home towns as well) than we find among factory workers in Lapu-Lapu and Cebu, or tourism workers in the latter.

Differences in migration among occupational groups: labour market factors

While detailed reviews of migration for each occupational group in each locality have been given in previous chapters, accounting for differences among them is difficult, not least because the differences themselves are only circumspect in nature (see note 1 above). Nonetheless, considering possible reasons for the above-average incidence of migrant women in Boracay's hotels, restaurants and shops, one plausible explanation is that this is the only sector where employers state a distinct preference for workers from outside the locality (see Chapter 5). The importance of employer bias is also evident at the opposite end of the spectrum in Cebu, where the absence of migrant women may reflect the tendency of the tourist industry here to favour native recruitment. Over and above the likely discrimination exercised by Boracay's

---

4 One formal tourism employee had also worked in Kuwait for a year (see Chapter 5).

formal sector management, the small size of the island's population (both in absolute terms as well as in relation to Lapu-Lapu and Cebu) means that posts may have to be filled by migrants for want of local labour. Migrant concentration in Boracay's formal sector may also be due to the specialised base of the economy: those moving to the island undoubtedly seek work in hotels, restaurants or shops since little else is on offer. This is particularly relevant to young single people, since beach-vending, own-account businesses and other types of informal activity are so heavily dominated by natives or longer-established migrants married to indigenous residents (see Chapter 5; Chant, 1993b). The idea that levels of migrant involvement in distinct subsectors of the labour market are linked with the relative diversity of the local economy gains further currency when looking at the three localities as a whole, particularly in respect of their formal activities. Boracay, with the narrowest range of formal employment, has the largest proportion of migrant workers therein; Cebu, on the other hand, with the most diversified economic base, has the lowest levels of migrant representation in all three types of formal employment under consideration (manufacturing, tourism and sex work – see Table 7.1). Given that general levels of in-migration to Cebu, particularly among the poor, are higher than in Boracay (see Chapters 2 and 3), it is possible that people moving to the city are able to become involved in a wider range of economic activities. To some extent this may also apply to our remaining centre, Lapu-Lapu. While dominated by the Mactan Export Processing Zone, Lapu-Lapu is a fairly large city in its own right. In possessing other sources of employment, it might therefore be deemed to have an intermediate level of labour market diversity. This could also be related to the fact that migrant representation among Lapu-Lapu's manufacturing employees stands midway between the extremes presented by formal tourism employment in Boracay and two of the three formal sector activities analysed for Cebu (see Table 7.1).

Differences in migration among occupational groups: migrant perspectives

Having noted the likely influence of a variety of demand-side factors in accounting for varying proportions of migrants in different jobs in the different localities, and in particular the high incidence of female migrants in Boracay's formal sector, it is also important to explore the role that women's own decisions play in the process. While the low numbers of respondents in the worker samples, combined with Boracay's much smaller population compared with Cebu's or Lapu-Lapu's, make it difficult to assert that jobs of a formal nature in the resort are more popular than employment elsewhere, the fact that a larger than average proportion of women have lived and worked in other parts of the Philippines, yet have come (or returned) to the island on a broadly permanent basis, might mean there is a special kind of drawing power for certain types of female labour migrant. It is thus interesting to ask whether, and in what respects, tourism employment in Boracay may be preferred to other forms of livelihood.

In exploring this question, it is useful at the outset to examine factors which, a priori, might make some destinations more appealing to women than others.[5] One plausible factor is a known or perceived tendency for particular employers in particular places to favour female labour, in which case we might expect to find larger proportions of female migrants where women are a major component of the workforce. However, despite the difficulties associated with small worker samples and the different sizes of the study localities, it would seem on the surface that this has little effect. Formal tourism employment in Boracay is actually one of the least feminised occupational domains, even if

---

5 Although use of the term 'a priori' here refers primarily to what might be expected on a logical/first-principle basis, the idea that female-selective migration occurs in centres where women form the major or preferred labour force (or, as discussed later, where women have some guarantee of higher or more regular earnings than in other localities) is, somewhat inevitably, informed by observations made in other literature. At a general level, for example, it is widely noted that female labour migration responds to rural–urban differentials in employment (see Armstrong and McGee, 1985; Brydon and Chant, 1993:125–6; Chant and Radcliffe, 1992:5; Eviota and Smith, 1984; Townsend and Momsen, 1987). More specifically, urban migration among women is often directed to towns and cities where women have above-average access to the local labour market (see, for instance, Fernández-Kelly, 1983b on the industrial border towns of Mexico; Chant, 1991a on women's migration to the Mexican tourist resort of Puerto Vallarta; Chant, 1992a on the temporary migration of young female migrants from northwest Costa Rica to the better employment prospects of the capital, San José; and Singhanetra-Renard and Prabhudhanitisarn, 1992 on Thai women's migration to Bangkok because it offers greater access to service and manufacturing jobs than other cities).

women do form over half the labour force (58 per cent).[6] Much more heavily feminised activities (sex work in Cebu, for example [95 per cent+ female], and export processing employment in MEPZ [80 per cent female]), on the other hand, include lower proportions of migrants (see Table 7.1).

Another, possibly surprising, finding is that wage levels in different types of employment show no consistent or positive set of relationships with levels of migrant representation among workers. While again it might be expected that the greater the remuneration in given kinds of work, the stronger the attraction for migrants, sex work (offering the highest average earnings) is by no means marked by migrant dominance, even if the industry seems to have lured various Cebuanas back to the city after periods away (see Chapter 6). The relative unimportance of wage levels as a predictor of migrant status is perhaps more evident, however, if we recall that most of Boracay's formal workers receive the legal minimum salary or less; this is not only lower than average earnings in factories in the Visayas (see Chapter 4), but also, and interestingly, substantially below those in tourism employment in Cebu (see Chapter 5).

Given the weak explanatory power of both degrees of female recruitment and prospective incomes, it is conceivable that 'non-economic' factors might be more relevant in accounting for Boracay's appeal to female migrants. Indeed, while many respondents admitted that wages were not particularly good, and those without personal contacts in the locality had not been entirely confident they would get jobs on arrival, the *lifestyle* on the island tended both to be anticipated in favourable terms and to prove so in practice. As noted in Chapter 5, most people view Boracay as a pleasant place to live and regard their jobs as sociable and interesting. Although experienced female migrants have often earned more in places like Manila, life in Boracay is perceived as safer, healthier and agreeable enough to compensate

6 The calculation of this figure is based on the numbers of male and female workers derived from the employer survey in Boracay (see Appendix). Although the sample comprised a range of establishments (hotels, restaurants and shops), this was by no means representative and a greater number of shops should probably have been included to provide more of a balance with accommodation and catering establishments. Indeed, given the tendency for shopwork in Boracay to be 100 per cent female, there is a strong possibility that including a greater number of commercial employers would have resulted in a higher overall average figure for female labour in formal tourism employment on the island.

for their drop in income. The fact that the bulk of Boracay's employers provide accommodation probably constitutes an added attraction to young single women worried at the prospect of striking out on their own and/or concerned that their move to a strange new place might generate gossip about their behaviour among kin and friends. Since so many female migrants to Boracay not only move into protected domestic quarters attached to their workplaces, but have jobs arranged for them in the first instance by relatives, these fears are to a large extent dispelled. It is certainly the case that tourism employment in Boracay does not carry anything like the social stigma of sex work in Cebu, or indeed of the wider range of tourism employment in the metropolis, which, by association, might be thought to harbour risks of a socially undesirable nature. In addition, and more pragmatically, a straight-forward tourism job in Boracay does not pose the same kinds of physiological threats as those of sex work, or indeed factory employment where health hazards may combine with strict regimentation, long hours and monotony to make this occupation less desirable than work in a holiday resort.[7] On top of this, neither manufacturing nor sex work offers any possibility of the career mobility that at least a minority of tourism employees can expect (see Chapter 5; also Chant, forthcoming b).[8]

---

7 The argument here is by no means that factory work is not popular among women, since it is often a preferred option in the context of Cebu and Lapu-Lapu, being better paid and more secure and having greater fringe benefits than many other activities in the localities. While the comparative advantages of different kinds of factory work have already been discussed in Chapter 4, it is instructive to recall that one of the main bonuses of employment in the Mactan Export Processing Zone in Lapu-Lapu (as opposed to non-Zone firms in Cebu City) is that pay and, importantly, *working conditions* are usually better. This, along with the fact that firms recruit greater proportions of women, could account for what appears to be a greater amount of targeted labour migration to Lapu-Lapu than to Cebu (see Chapters 3 and 4; also Table 7.1).

8 While we discuss the issue of career mobility in detail later in this chapter, it is important to note here that there are slightly greater prospects for promotion for female employees within formal sector tourism than in manufacturing firms or the sex industry, for two main reasons: (a) because there is less gender segmentation within firms, meaning that women have a wider range of starting points from which to ascend to higher-status positions; and (b) because there is a distinct possibility that tourism workers will stay longer in their jobs, which may lead to promotion on grounds of seniority. We offer the latter argument cautiously, however, because women usually have less chance of promotion than men, whatever their length of their employment or capabilities, and because most of the occupations discussed have a relatively short history in each of the locations under investigation and for this reason do not provide an adequate basis for longitudinal analysis.

If it remains difficult to claim that these factors are responsible for what itself is only a tentative notion that tourism employment in Boracay is more attractive to certain women than other types of work, it is clear why greater levels of job satisfaction are often expressed by the island's formal tourism employees than by those in other occupational groups here and in other places.

Migrant characteristics: differences among occupational groups

Although levels of migrant representation among Boracay's formal tourism workers may distinguish this group from others, the genuine labour migrants among them (i.e. those in the decidedly clear majority who migrate with the specific intention of finding employment) have many features in common with their counterparts in other occupations and localities. Except for informal tourism workers in Boracay and sex workers in Cebu (see below), most female labour migrants are young, single and childless at the time of migration, and move with the primary intention of helping kin. This is mirrored by the high incidence of on-going communication with and support for places of origin, whether through return visits, arranging the migration of other family members and/or sending remittances. For example, even if long hours and limited time off among MEPZ workers mean that home visits are rare, most try to find placements for relatives in the factories and/or send substantial and regular subventions (see Chapter 4). While the economic value of remittances is lower from Boracay (mainly on account of low wages), migrants still send high proportions of their salaries home and maintain more in the way of personal contact, partly because of the proximity of home towns and villages and partly because lay-offs during the low season give them time to return to source areas (see Chapter 5).

As for informal tourism workers in Boracay, where migrant women generally arrive at a later stage in the life-cycle and with husbands indigenous to the island, both remittances to and contacts with home areas tend to be overshadowed by the needs of women's immediate households. This also applies to migrant sex workers in Cebu, where, although the desire to conceal their jobs from kin acts to weaken links with family, the majority come to the city with the aim of fulfilling their obligations as single parents (see Chapter 6). It may be more than coincidental that these latter groups, as noted earlier, are those who also tend to come from areas beyond the immediate provincial or regional boundaries of the study localities. People with children to support might be prepared to move longer distances where this carries the prospect of better jobs or higher earnings, and/or because the wish to maintain links with natal kin is likely to be secondary to the imperatives of providing for dependent children.[9] In other words, although the needs of parents and siblings are an important factor in the mobility of young single women, the onus to provide immediate, regular or all-encompassing financial support is probably less pressing than when there are co-resident offspring to consider. This might go some way to explain why childless people often migrate to areas which are relatively near their home towns and villages: although they clearly move to centres where they are likely to obtain employment, short-distance moves may not maximise income. Women with children, on the other hand, are likely to place their earning potential uppermost among their considerations. Hence single-parent sex workers often come long distances to Cebu City because it promises guaranteed, high-paid employment, especially given the base closures in Luzon and the 'clean-up' campaign in Manila's red-light district (see Chapters 2 and 6). Female beach-vendors married to native Boracaynons may also come to the resort from far afield if their spouses' assets (land, kin networks and so on) can ensure a reasonable level of family livelihood (see Chapter 5). The stakes attached to parenthood may thus provoke more in the way of directed long-distance, place-specific migration at a national level (see note 9 above) than in cases where people's primary, if not exclusive, allegiance is still to parents and family in home areas.

---

9 The argument here is developed in the intra-national context, although it is important to recognise that the majority of overseas female migrants are single and/or childless (see, for example, Birindelli, 1988:393; ILO, 1991:12). However, this does not necessarily contradict our hypothesis that women with children are likely to move further away from home areas than are unwed daughters within the Philippines; only that it is probably more feasible for women without children to move abroad for long periods, whether because of legal aspects of international migration (especially among contract workers) and/or because women's responsibilities for children are usually more than economic: in other words, mothers may also be concerned to play an active part in raising their children and for this reason are likely not to desire the prolonged periods of separation which international mobility usually entails (see, for example, Tacoli, 1994).

WOMEN'S EMPLOYMENT AND HOUSEHOLD STRUCTURE: COMPARISONS AMONG OCCUPATIONAL GROUPS

Household characteristics of workers show substantial diversity both within and among the various occupational categories, but the most distinctive groups by far are the formal tourism workers in Boracay and the sex workers in Cebu (see Table 7.2). The former tend to be single people whose living arrangements are distinguished from the rest of the population in the locality (and from other occupational groups

Table 7.2: Key household characteristics of women in target occupational groups

Occupational group & locality (nos. of women in survey in brackets)	Average age of women in group, and range	Dominant^^ marital status in group	Percentage of mothers in group	Average no. of children per woman* — mothers only	all women	Dominant^^ place in household	Dominant^^ household structure
Industrial workers, MEPZ (8)	28 (19–41)	married	63%	3.8	1.9	spouse	male nuclear
Industrial workers, Cebu (8)	31 (24–41)	married	75%	2.7	2	spouse	male extended
Sex workers, Cebu (14)	26 (21–37)	single	72%	1.3	0.9	head	female-headed (lone parent and extended)
Tourism workers, Cebu ** (4)	25 (20–28)	single	25%	2	0.5	daughter	male nuclear
Tourism workers, Boracay ** (13)	33 (19–28)	single	31%	3.5	1.1	workmate	single-sex/ semi-family household
Beach-vendors, Boracay (11)	35 (25–42)	married	91%	4.5	4.2	spouse	male nuclear

Notes:

^^   'Dominant' here refers to the most commonly occurring pattern in the group; it does not, for example, signify power or authority

*   Includes children who have left home as well as co-resident offspring

**   'Tourism workers' refers to formal sector, i.e. hotels, restaurants and shops

in other places) by the fact that the vast majority live at their place of work in single-sex rooms or dormitories. As for sex workers, most are lone parents who live on their own and/or with their children, female friends or mothers in various forms of female-headed unit. Indeed, 79 per cent of sex workers belong to female-headed households of one type or another, which is a much greater proportion than among any other occupational group or the wider population in the study localities.

The significance of 'alternative' household structures

As discussed in Chapters 5 and 6, female-only or female-dominant living arrangements might be conceived as representing an alternative and potentially liberating domestic space for women in the context of a society where the bulk of households are male-headed.[10] Having said this, few women attribute the absence of men to any deliberate choice on their part. This is clearly the case among tourism workers in Boracay whose bosses generally stipulate residence in female quarters provided on the premises, but even among Cebu's sex workers, who technically have more freedom to shape their domestic arrangements, the reasons given for female households are usually male abandonment on pregnancy or childbirth. Notwithstanding an apparent lack of what we might call 'strategic self-selection' in the formation of female-headed households, the actual experience of residing in these units is usually described positively. Many women seem satisfied with their home lives and rarely express a desire to change their circumstances, whether by getting married or by incorporating male relatives into the household (viz. the relatively late age of marriage aspired to among Boracay's tourism employees [Chapter 5], and the frequent wish to

---

10 When we talk of 'female-only' and 'female-dominant' households here, we refer to the fact that these units do not usually contain adult men (as opposed to other males such as sons). The absence of adult men, particularly partners, is important in the Philippine case, in that conflicts seem more apparent between spouses (and between fathers and daughters) than between women and other male relatives, such as sons. At the same time, it is clear that mother–son (and other male–female) relationships are also gendered (see, for example, Moore, 1994:20). Moreover, the absence of male members in households may not always mean an absence of male influence (see, for instance, Fonseca, 1991 on the interaction of male kin such as fathers, uncles and brothers with female-headed households in Brazil; see also Bruce and Lloyd, 1992 for a more general discussion of the external links of women-headed units).

remain single among Cebu's sex workers [Chapter 6]). In fact, women in female-dominant households, especially those extended units with female relatives, friends or co-workers, tend to stress the advantages of living in situations perceived as giving them valuable assistance with domestic work and childcare, as characterised by 'sisterly' emotional support (among non-kin as well as blood relatives), and which offer congenial company to come home to. Women in male-headed households, on the other hand, especially wives and mothers, speak much more frequently of conflicts, ranging from the difficulties of simultaneously managing childcare and holding down a job, to the onus of providing for families when husbands have no work, to men with 'vices' wasting resources, and/or to the infrequent (and characteristically tense) contact with husbands accustomed to drinking, gambling or spending time with their *barkadas* (see Chapter 3). Thus while the households with female heads are normally described as a locus of refuge and/or support, those with male heads are more usually identified with problems, whether practical, psychological or financial. These disparities assume greater importance when considering what work means for women.

Household structure and women's work

Although we address the broader significance of female employment later in this chapter, it is important to point out here that a distinct sense of pride is evident among women managing their own domestic (and economic) affairs. Female heads of household, women on their own and/or women residing with other women are usually more able than their counterparts in male-headed units to explain why they work and what particular benefits accrue from their jobs, no matter how disagreeable (especially in the case of entertainment work). Many, for example, take pleasure in itemising what percentage of their income goes where (savings, remittances and so on), in demonstrating the sensible, strategically planned (and usually altruistic) nature of their expenditure and in being able to pinpoint the direct outcomes of their earnings. This is particularly apparent among tourism workers in Boracay, whose remittances are often vital to pay for the schooling of younger brothers and sisters (see Chapter 5). In cases where monetary assistance provides for the higher education or vocational training of siblings, and leads to good careers, benefactors not only gain praise and recognition from other family members, but are rewarded by a personal sense of pride and accomplishment. While sex workers talk less frequently or openly of achievements of this nature (often because their jobs have distanced them from their natal kin in the first place), they draw some solace from the fact that their sacrifices have given their children a good start in life and, in the longer term, are likely to mean they will not be forced into similar work.

While much the same concerns and ideals also figure among women in male-headed households, by no means all are able to translate them into practice. It is important to distinguish here between daughters (i.e. single, usually childless, women residing with parents) and wives and mothers. Among the former, who are especially common among formal tourism employees in Cebu (see Table 7.2) and, to a lesser but still significant extent, among factory workers here and in Lapu-Lapu (see Chapter 4), a proportion of earnings is invariably siphoned off to the wider household unit, often for the education and clothing of a specific younger sibling or siblings (much in the way that migrant remittances from Boracay are used). However, women are usually entitled to retain a part (often around half) of their wage. Since the costs of basic reproduction (food, shelter and so on) are borne by the household, working daughters are usually able to glean some benefit from their income in an individual capacity, whether by spending it on personal goods or recreation, or, more usually, by saving it for future studies, business ventures and/or prospective offspring of their own (see Chapter 4). The fact that mothers and/or sisters perform most of the domestic chores also means that young women workers are free to use evenings and Sundays (when not working overtime) for leisure or other activities. Among married workers, on the other hand, time is usually at a premium and few have the opportunity to derive any major individual (or even direct) gain from the proceeds of their work; for this reason, they are also prone to ambivalence when talking about their jobs.

Wives engaged in manufacturing, beach-vending and other occupations in the study localities often see employment as adding stress, time and effort to the already onerous responsibility of running a household, unaccompanied by the independence that perhaps compensates women workers who live alone or with other women, or who are not yet married. More specific factors accounting for half-hearted or negative views of labour force participation among female spouses in male-headed households include their frequently greater burdens of reproductive work compared with women in other domestic positions, such as daughters and female heads. This is partly because the vast majority of women in male-headed units have children (and usually more of them than single parents have), but also because husbands place extra demands on their time and labour (for cooking, cleaning, laundry and so on). While men may assist with childcare or housework, their piecemeal efforts rarely counterbalance the additional work involved. In this manner, the dual toll of women's paid and unpaid work is often heavier in male-headed households.

A further reason for married women's frequently lukewarm attitudes towards employment is that husbands not only tend to contribute less of their income to household use than women do, but they squander money on pursuits which benefit only themselves and which can ultimately prove detrimental to family as well as to personal health and well-being (through domestic abuse and/or costly medical bills arising from alcohol dependence, for example). On top of this, unemployed or low-paid men often ask working wives for additional 'pocket-money'; while such requests are rarely denied (usually to keep the peace), the resultant pressure on income causes anguish among women whose main concern is the survival of their families (see Chapter 3). Allotting their own hard-earned cash to the indulgences of irresponsible husbands can also provoke deep-rooted feelings of resentment and injustice.

A final problem affecting women in male-headed households stems from the fact that although they might have major control over household income, they do not have *sole* control. This, in combination with the previous point, means that it is perhaps harder to plan budgets as effectively as lone women can, and/or to perceive the fruits of their labour in the same range of direct or constructive ways. While by no means all wives suffer negative experiences, for those who do, it is clearly the case that paid work can give rise to greater subordination, with potential gains of a personal nature eroded, if not obliterated, by gender disparities of power and privilege at the domestic level.

Despite the frequent difficulties of wives and mothers in male-headed households, it is also important to stress that most have few prospects of alternatives. As noted earlier in the book, there has traditionally been immense social pressure on Filipino women to get married and have children. Although some mothers are now placing less emphasis on this package for daughters, one part of it (childbirth) is rarely possible in 'decent society' without the other (matrimony). Thus most young female workers continue to aspire to both states, even if they aim to marry later and to have fewer offspring than women in older generations or their peers in the wider population (see Chapters 3, 4 and 5). Sex workers are an exception to the rule in that most cannot expect a conventional marriage in the sense of being accepted by a Filipino husband, either because of their jobs or because they are single parents, or, as is usually the case, both. While it is important to remember that the need or desire to marry may be less where women are financially self-sufficient (as most sex workers are – see Chapter 6), it is also possible that since many already have children, a further incentive is removed, especially as marriage is often valued more as a conduit to motherhood than as an end in itself. In speaking of their future lives, for example, young single workers in shops, restaurants, hotels and factories place much less emphasis on the anticipated characteristics of husbands and the pleasures to be derived from the married state per se, than on the children they hope to have and the sort of upbringing they wish to give them. Indeed, many women respond to the subject of wedlock with distinctly greater resignation and cynicism than might be expected given their enthusiasm when talking of prospective offspring.

One of the main reasons for this apathy towards the marital half of the wife-and-motherhood equation is the already-mentioned fact that men's inputs and commitment to household survival are much less than those of women. Indeed, women wishing to delay marriage often justify this on the grounds that it will bring huge responsibilities which they are not yet ready for, with the responsibilities concerned (usually the economic pressure of raising dependents) tending to be conceived as a personal matter, rather than something which might be alleviated, let alone shared, by spouses.

Moreover, it is commonly stated that finding a 'good man' is difficult, since several treat their wives badly, whether through drinking, infidelity or domestic violence. The case of Lucy, the hotel shop-worker in Cebu discussed in Chapter 5, most forcefully demonstrates the ensuing contradictory bind for women whose distrust of and/or disillusion with men is likely to deny them the fulfilment of motherhood: Lucy desperately wants a child, but because of her own and her mother's experiences cannot envisage finding a suitable partner. Single parenthood, on the other hand, would bring such disgrace to her family that her only alternative is the fate of a *matandang dalaga*, or old maid (see Chapter 1). The barrenness (rather than spinsterhood) which this implies is, in turn, expected to make her particularly 'sad and lonely' in her old age.

Sex workers, on the other hand, have already crossed the boundary between shame and decency (whether because they have become unmarried mothers or have entered the entertainment industry, or both – see Chapter 6). Thus despite the psycho-social costs of their current jobs, and the material uncertainties of their futures, those with children have managed to achieve alone what women in more conventional occupations can only hope to attain via wedlock. This raises the very important question as to whether the price paid for alienation from natal kin on account of sexual transgression may ultimately be worth that of avoiding the enduring difficulties of an inequitable and unhappy marriage, especially given that the latter is possibly less reversible (on legal and/or religious grounds) than parental rejection.[11]

Indeed, in view of the above, it is interesting to speculate as to whether the apparently universal postponement of marriage among single women workers represents the beginning of a longer-term trend towards alternative forms of partnership, parenting and/or gender roles within households and kin groups. Not only do many young women seem comfortable about delaying wedlock, but none envisage a situation where they will not want (or need) to work, even when they have children. And the desire to have fewer offspring is likely to enable them to continue in employment. Therefore, even if women still become wives and mothers, the fact that earning a wage has allowed young women to gain some control over their own lives (in the form of taking a more decisive stance in respect of marriage and fertility) may in time create a situation where they are able to negotiate greater power and equality within other aspects of personal and family life.

---

11 A range of studies point to the distinct possibility that parents will come to accept reconciliation with daughters engaged in hostessing work and/or who have had sex or children outside marriage, although this may take some time (see, for example, Blanc-Szanton, 1990:352; NCRFW, 1989:140; Villariba, 1993:20 and Whitam et al.,1985:149). In other words, ties with natal kin may be mended in time. In the case of marriage, however, there is considerably less flexibility in that once unions are formalised by the state and/or the Church, it is extremely difficult (especially for women) to dissolve them, pragmatically or otherwise (see Chapters 1 and 3; also Chant, forthcoming a).

The significance of wider links with family

For the present, however, those who opt for alternative lifestyles are likely to meet with difficulties. The shame attached to the often twin conjuncture of single-parenthood and involvement in sex work, for example, frequently leads to some degree of rejection by natal kin. Along with their non-conventional household arrangements, therefore, single mothers in the sex industry are likely to face further marginalisation, isolation and vulnerability. Nonetheless, just as alternative domestic environments can be seen to have a number of advantages, so too can the break with wider kin networks, in that the latter gives greater licence for personal and behavioural freedom. For instance, inasmuch as sex workers avoid criticism and disapproval in their home lives through the absence of men from the household, severance of contacts with parents and siblings (particularly fathers and brothers) further diminishes interference and opprobrium. An added, but probably double-edged, advantage in cutting ties with wider family is liberation from a sense of duty and obligation, which in turn may be accompanied by significant financial gains. As noted in Chapter 6, only a minority of migrant sex workers actually remit money to their families in home areas; if they do, it is for the care of their children. Most other migrant women, on the other hand, especially single tourism employees in Boracay and factory workers in Lapu-Lapu, send substantial amounts of support home and receive relatively little, at least of material value, in return (see Chapters 4 and 5). The same applies to factory daughters living in the homes of parents in Cebu and Lapu-Lapu, in that apart from some freedom from domestic responsibilities, the net balance of inputs into household reproduction is usually weighted against them: young women often sacrifice a large part of their wages for household use which might otherwise be used for personal projects.

Having said this, two factors qualify what might be viewed as a one-way flow of resources from single women to natal kin. One is that finance is only one of a range of exchanges that operates within and among households, and considerable satisfaction is gained not only from helping relatives in this way but also insofar as it contributes to maintaining a healthy coherence in family relationships; this in turn may provide significant emotional and psychological support. Second, and in many respects related to the first point, reciprocity is so inscribed within family and kinship networks that at one point or another those who give are likely to become the recipients of assistance themselves (see also Chapters 1 and 3). It is certainly the case among married women in the occupational groups (notably the beach-vendors in Boracay and the bulk of the factory workers in Cebu and Lapu-Lapu), that substantial help in childcare is provided by female kin who reside in the localities. Where mothers of migrants live far away and are unable or unwilling to move, sisters or nieces often step in to fill the breach in households where working women have childcare difficulties. The financial help given to parents and siblings by young single daughters may thus be more than compensated for at a stage when the latter have families of their own.

One abiding question, of course, is why men have greater leeway to evade these financial and pragmatic obligations, yet still benefit from membership of family and kinship networks. In other words, men not only appear to receive much more than they put in to their individual households, but the same applies at a wider scale. The existence of male privilege within Philippine kinship and society is hard to explain without detailed recourse to historical antecedents, but its apparent embeddedness in contemporary culture suggests that regardless of the activities women perform in the context of their *gender roles*, inequality in *gender relations* precludes the reaping of major gains at a micro-level, let alone in any broader sense (see also Chant, forthcoming a).

Wider aspects of the ways in which employment affects female status are dealt with later in this chapter when considering domestic dimensions of gender in conjunction with those operating at the level of the workplace. In order to consolidate the groundwork for this, however, it is helpful to provide a brief summary here of the social and demographic corollaries of women's work in the Visayas and, more particularly, what the links between these factors mean for wider conceptual approaches to female labour force participation, migration and household evolution.

FEMALE EMPLOYMENT, MIGRATION AND THE
HOUSEHOLD: INTERRELATIONSHIPS AND
CONCEPTUAL IMPLICATIONS

Notwithstanding the difficulties in identifying consistent features of migration and household organisation among women in different occupational groups, it is clear that certain types of female employment generated under the auspices of outward-oriented Philippine development strategies are associated with quite distinctive patterns of demographic mobility and domestic formation. These associations arise from the conjuncture of overlapping and multi-directional relationships among the spheres of the *social* (household/family), the *demographic* (migration) and the *economic* (employment), making it necessary to view the causes, as well as the consequences, of female labour force participation in a holistic manner, and to ascribe less importance to factors relating to employment per se (demand for female labour, wage rates and so on) than is often the case in more macro-level analyses of development and the implications for gender.

Systematic three-way relationships between women's work, migration and household formation are more difficult to establish in any definitive sense than bilateral links between employment and migration, and between employment and the household (see earlier). Nonetheless, bearing in mind our analyses of the latter issues, it is interesting to note that the groups which stand out in terms of their migratory origins and/or experience, and those distinguished on account of their household characteristics, are, in two out of three cases,[12] the same groups of people: notably formal tourism employees in Boracay and sex workers in Cebu. This second group in particular highlights a number of factors relevant to the present analysis, especially in respect of revealing the dense and complex range of links between women's migration, their jobs and their relations with household and family. Sex workers, for example, are often migrants from outside Cebu or are natives who have lived elsewhere in the Philippines. That many move (or return) long distances to work in the city's entertainment

---

12 The third case here is the beach-vendors in Boracay. While they are distinguished from most other workers because they often move to this destination from far afield and have more extensive migration histories, their households conform with the dominant male nuclear model. Although the purpose of the detailed discussion of sex workers in the text is to highlight the correspondence between distinctiveness in migration with that in household characteristics and/or employment, this does not rule out inter-relatedness among these elements in other groups. Indeed, the household organisation of female beach-vendors in Boracay is very much up with the fact that they usually move to the island with husbands native to the locality. Their entry into informal vending is facilitated by spouses' contacts and assets, while local kin networks (in combination with the relatively flexible hours of informal commerce) allow women to manage the dual responsibility of paid work and childcare. As with sex workers, therefore, the case of beach-vendors also underlines the multiple and interacting links between social, demographic and economic factors in female labour force participation.

industry seems to be largely due to the fact that they are lone women with children to support. In other words, the likelihood of being able to make a living sufficient to raise dependents single-handedly seems to warrant moves that are often far from home areas or previous places of residence (see Chapter 6).

Although a primary impetus for this labour migration is single mothers' need to maximise earnings (from which conjuncture it is possible to identify the influence of both employment and household factors), it is also important to acknowledge other issues that come into the equation. One is that the lone-parent status of most sex workers affords them the opportunity to take independent decisions on where to move, unlike married women who usually have to follow the wishes of their husbands. Second, and in some respects related to this, as women with major financial responsibilities for children, sex workers are less likely to attach priority to staying close to natal kin, which again poses fewer constraints on their choice of destination. Third, and importantly, the fact of having 'illegitimate' offspring means that the marginal cost of entering or continuing in a 'shameful' occupation such as sex work is relatively minimal; hence women may have few reservations about transferring to places where they can make a reasonable living in this manner. Fourth, and in many ways related to both the last factors, the potential disgrace which the combination of personal and professional circumstances surrounding sex workers is likely to bring upon parents and relatives may urge them to select more remote locations in order to diminish family shame and/or to evade outright social ostracism. Once in the city, barricading themselves in female-only households allows further protection from disapproval and threats to the honour of wider kin groups, as well as facilitating their continued livelihood from the sex trade, which, as one of the few occupations providing women with the means for independent survival, is clearly critical in enabling lone-parent units to maintain their configuration over time.

Effectively, therefore, women's entry into sex work in the particular context of Cebu is only one thread in a large and complex tapestry of interacting influences, where the fundamental interrelations between social, demographic and economic factors make it difficult to isolate one cause or consequence from another, despite the relative homo-geneity among women in the group. Indeed, although patterns of migration and household organisation among women may show less consistency within other occupational categories, it is still possible to discern that the motives and forms of demographic mobility are often closely linked with household and family circumstances and the type of employment women move into, as well as with the organisation of households in destination areas (see also note 12 above). Even if this is not surprising, the fact remains that the varied nature of these relationships lacks empirical verification in many contexts, especially in relation to different types of work.

At the very least, then, the comparative nature of this study is important in pinpointing the specific types of development associated with the greatest departures from the 'normal' contours of women's lives, as well as indicating the kinds of employment that are likely to be accompanied by social (and demographic) stasis. Indeed, while most occupations examined in the Visayas are new (both in terms of individual women entering these jobs for the first time, and in a more general historical sense in that these forms of employment arose because of relatively recent strategies of export-oriented development), the majority seem compatible with existing structures of gender roles and relations. This is clearly the case if factors such as the abiding dominance of male-headed households, the onus on women to devote livelihood efforts to their households or wider family groups and the pressure to uphold the major share of reproductive labour in the home are taken as indicative. Thus while women may find themselves enmeshed in new forms of labour discipline, new types of wage arrangements, new time schedules and so on, considerable continuity is apparent not only in the gendering of the jobs they do (as we discuss later in the chapter), but in the social contexts which surround them.

The value of intra-national comparisons for cross-national research

Alongside the value of the research for indicating the diverse implications of different types of job within the Philippines Visayas, there is undoubtedly relevance for wider international comparisons. As noted in Chapter 1, studies of women's increasing involvement in multinational manufacturing in such countries as Mexico (Fernández-Kelly, 1983b), Puerto Rico and the Dominican Republic (Safa, 1990) have identified that expansion is often associated with new patterns of migration, delayed marriage and stronger and more visible positions for women (both as daughters and wives) within the home. While this is also true to some degree in Cebu and Lapu-Lapu (see Chapter 4), the social 'fall-out', in terms of new household forms, new divisions of labour, new relations of power at a domestic level and so on, seems relatively minimal in comparison with a sector such as sex work (Chapter 6). One obvious question arising from this is whether the impacts of one particular type of employment are mediated by the nature of other jobs in given areas. For example, the comparatively limited changes engendered in women's lives as a result of industrial recruitment in the Visayas might stem from the fact that greater conservatism among women in 'conventional' occupations is necessary in order to distinguish themselves from counterparts on the 'wrong side' of the moral and social fence (principally sex workers). Given a general tendency among women to distance themselves from hospitality workers for fear of being 'tarred with the same brush' (see Chapter 6), female factory operatives may thus be discouraged from fully exercising the freedom and autonomy potentially offered by their own jobs.

Other issues arising from intra-national differences that merit further research on a cross-national basis include the kinds of migration to which different household and employment circumstances give rise, the relative pressure on different types of female labour migrant to retain links with areas of origin, and the acceptability of women's occupations to men (particularly partners). These issues are not only likely to yield advances in international research, they are also useful in examining the utility of existing theoretical frameworks for gender-selective migration and household formation.

Implications for conceptual approaches to female migration and household formation

Migration models

In respect of theories of female migration, our findings clearly indicate that women's mobility is not a simple product of differential wage rates in source and destination areas; even less is it a function of marriage prospects, as posited by the neoclassical/equilibrium approach (see Chapter 1). At the other end of the spectrum, neither can the much more elaborate household strategies framework adequately explain patterns of female mobility in the Visayas. Although the latter encompasses by far the most comprehensive set of precepts necessary for understanding gender-differentiated migration (i.e. gender divisions in reproductive as well as productive labour within households, power relations and decision-making, socio-cultural expectations of gender, and segmentation between the sexes in rural and urban labour markets – see Radcliffe, 1986, 1991), it would appear that certain of these elements need to be more clearly defined and/or disaggregated if they are to be useful theoretical starting points in a range of contexts, particularly if these contexts are to form part of comparative research (Chant and Radcliffe, 1992:24).

While the term 'socio-cultural expectations of gender', for example, inevitably incorporates a broad spectrum of elements embedded in women's normative and actual roles and their relations with men, it would be helpful if the core factors affecting female migration could be more specifically identified – although in order to do this, the household strategies model will need more systematic examination in a range of places (see Chant and Radcliffe, 1992:23). Detailed studies which have adopted this framework to date have nonetheless been useful in identifying the crucial role played particularly by economic, labour and power disparities between men and women in shaping gender-differentiated mobility (see, for instance, Boyd, 1989; Gordon, 1981; Izzard, 1985; Radcliffe, 1986). Questions of kinship obligation, especially in the form of 'duty' and/or 'filial piety' among migrant daughters, have also received attention (see Foo and Lim, 1989:219; Mather, 1988; Radcliffe, 1986:43–4; Trager, 1988:83; Wolf, 1990a). Far less mention has been made, however, of issues pertaining to moral propriety and/or sexuality, which seem critical in a variety of female labour migrations in the Visayas. As discussed earlier, moves made by migrants to Cebu's sex industry are often deliberately undertaken with a view to minimising their families' subjection to shame or dishonour (as well as to protect themselves from ostracism by relatives), while the flow of young female migrants to tourism employment in Boracay is frequently facilitated by the fact that paternalistic employers accommodate them on the premises, thereby helping to allay fears that new-found independence from natal kin will result in moral laxity. In other words, women's moves are often shaped by the concern either to ensure and/or prove their 'good behaviour', or to disguise that which is likely to meet with opprobrium. While these observations display parallels with work on the migration of women in Africa, where historically female migrants (especially those without 'family placement') were regarded with ambivalence and often deemed prostitutes or potential prostitutes (Brydon and Chant, 1993:128; see also Brydon, 1987; Little, 1973; Obbo, 1980; Sudarkasa, 1977), the influences of gender-differentiated social mores (especially surrounding sexuality) are rarely explicitly addressed in the theoretical literature on mobility. Apart from incorporating perspectives on these issues in a more generalised manner, the household and employment features of female labour migrants (which are often critical in determining the relative degree of women's autonomy in migration decisions) are also likely to improve the predictive capacity of existing models (see also Boyd, 1989).

Models of household evolution and survival

Sexuality also appears to be an essential element for advances in theorising household evolution. Existing research on female-headed households, for example, especially those of single parents, has not paid much attention to this or to other ideological or psychological dimensions of male absence from households, except where women are left behind in rural areas or small towns by husbands working in other parts of the same countries or overseas (see, for instance, Chant, 1991b,1992a; Connell, 1984; Hetler, 1990; Murray, 1981; Nelson, 1992; Rahat, 1986). Only a few studies (for example, Chant, 1985; Etienne, 1983; Harris 1982 and Safa, 1980; see also Bradshaw, 1994; Brydon and Chant, 1993:145–51) have pointed to the influence of gender subordination, and female consciousness of this, in giving rise to instances where women themselves opt to break away from men and/or migrate in order to establish their own households. Although the latter is only one of a broad spectrum of factors which affect the emergence of female-headed units (as we have seen for the Visayas, the initial formation of female-headed households is rarely the result of women's own decisions and/or deliberate strategies to assert their independence), the shift in emphasis from women as passive victims of male action to agents of change in their own right is important, given a general tendency to stress limited degrees of female voluntarism in the process (see Chant, 1985; Brydon and Chant, 1993:145–51 for detailed discussions). Indeed, even if women in the Visayas do not necessarily desire to become single parents and/or to leave their partners (especially husbands), the fact that some who find themselves in this position resist submergence within the homes of parents or kin and set up households of their own instead (often in new areas), may well reflect an element of conscious and/or positive self-determination. In circumstances where economic exigency has forced lone parents into sex work, for example, female headship (coupled with migration) may represent a strategy for self-preservation and/or the protection of relatives; in this respect it interacts strongly with sexuality and the taboos around it. As mentioned in our earlier discussion of single-parent sex workers, independent households or those shared with other women create environments which shield these workers from immediate criticism and permit them to pursue their lifestyles in a relatively unconstrained (and more supportive) manner. At the same time (and especially where women move to new places) this also helps to ensure that the name and reputation of the wider family remain undamaged.

However, such factors remain conspicuously rare not only in empirical research,[13] but in more general frameworks of female-headed household evolution. Rae Lesser Blumberg's (1978) seminal model of the prerequisites for the formation of 'mother–child families', for instance, includes only one proposition under which the issue of sexuality and/or social mores could be subsumed (that the interests of the political economy should not be undermined by the existence of women raising children on their own), and even here the emphasis is much more on the state than on civil society or culture, for example. Moreover, the remaining four categories stress essentially pragmatic/material conditions under which female-headed households may emerge, particularly women's earning capacity and their ability to appropriate the income generated by themselves or their children.[14]

---

13 Notable exceptions here include the work of Penny Vera-Sanso (1994) on Madras. See also Chant (forthcoming a) on Mexico and the Philippines, and Bradshaw (1994) on Honduras.

14 Blumberg's other four conditions for the emergence of mother–child households are:

- that the unit of labour, compensation and property must be the individual (as opposed to the kin group), regardless of sex;
- that women must have independent access to the means of subsistence, such as employment, state welfare or inheritance;
- that income generation/subsistence strategies must be reconcilable with childcare;
- that women's subsistence opportunities must not be dramatically fewer or less than those of men.

See Blumberg, 1978; also Blumberg with García, 1977.

Although further factors have been signalled in subsequent research, such as the demographic balance of the sexes in given areas and the socio-cultural legitimacy of female-headed households in different national and regional contexts, owing to historical antecedents, religion and so on (see Brydon and Chant, 1993:145–51 for discussion and references), the present study indicates that concepts of sexuality, shame and honour are critically important in affecting both the formation and constitution of female-headed households (as independent or 'hidden' entities, for instance – see below), as well as underlining the need to explore the intersections between these and the migratory and employment characteristics of women in different settings.

Given the frequent tendency for women heads and other members of their households in the Visayas to draw benefits from these living arrangements (see above), it is also necessary to expand the ways in which we conceptualise the capacity for the survival and longer-term viability of female-headed units. One critical aspect here is to recognise that women's general disadvantage in society does not necessarily translate into disadvantage in the home (Brydon and Chant, 1993:149–51). From our previous discussions of household structures among workers in Cebu, Lapu-Lapu and Boracay, it is clear that female-headed domestic arrangements are often more conducive to women's well-being than those headed by men, and more likely to ensure that they will derive greater personal gains from their work, whether pragmatically or ideologically. Indeed, something of an overemphasis on economic difficulties of female headship in the wider literature (see Buvinić et al., 1992; Buvinić and Gupta, 1993; also Chapter 1 this volume) needs to be tempered not only in view of the comparative financial health of these units (in terms of what women heads earn when they are able to decide upon their own employment, their ability to control their earnings and the minimisation of claims upon income arising from the absence of husbands and/or reduced links with natal relatives), but also on account of social and psychological factors (see also Chant, 1985). As noted earlier, women heads of household (and other women in them) are often under much less stress than those in male-headed units. Moreover, a range of factors such as female companionship and emotional security frequently act to cushion the problems of those in jobs (especially in the sex industry) which may be unpleasant or traumatic. This also raises the issue of needing to look more closely at the outcomes for children raised by female household heads. Although children may suffer from the absence of fathers and of links with wider family, not to mention the difficulties of growing up in a society traditionally antithetical to lone parenthood, it is also the case that single mothers devote considerable effort to providing their offspring with the best upbringing they can, and those in the sex trade usually resolve to extricate themselves before their children are fully aware of what they do. In addition, children in lone-parent households are often brought up in environments relatively free of domestic conflict; those who are not looked after by women's kin when their mothers are working are given over to the care of female companions or co-workers concerned to pull together and help one another. Although the present research cannot address the matter of how different types of household affect the long-term prospects of children, it underlines the necessity for in-depth longitudinal studies to explore more fully whether female household headship is as negative for younger generations as it is often conjectured to be.[15]

Recognising that incorporation within the households of parents is a common option among single mothers in the Visayas who are unable and/or unwilling to establish independent homes, brief consideration should also be made of household composition and how the findings of the study illuminate approaches to the broader changes undergone by household structures in the course of economic development. Bearing in mind that extended households are frequent among women in most occupational groups as well as in the wider populations in the study localities, employment seems to stand out as a major factor giving rise to these arrangements, through people moving either to join relatives in order to seek work themselves or to help out in homes when adult women with children have employment.[16] These factors are embedded within a more general framework of reciprocity within kin groups, especially among female

15 While the general tendency is for studies to emphasise the disadvantages for children of growing up in women-headed households (see Buvinić et al., 1992; Buvinić and Gupta, 1993), there is an increasingly wide body of research on developing countries which has found that children's access to education and nutrition is greater, and their subjection to violence lower, in female-headed units (see Appleton, 1991; Bradshaw, 1994; Bruce and Lloyd, 1992; Casinader et al., 1987; Chant, 1985; Hoddinott and Haddad, 1991; Koussoudji and Mueller, 1983).

16 Cebu City is the slight exception here, in that a much greater proportion of households in our survey of Rubberworld were found to have become extended through young migrant relatives moving to the city to further their education (see Chapter 3).

members (see also Chapters 1 and 3). Considering the role of women's employment in household extension in particular, the fact that rates of female labour force participation in the household surveys tend to be higher in extended units (four-fifths of wives in male-headed extended households in the three localities have some kind of income-generating activity, compared with under two-thirds of their counterparts in nuclear households) suggests that help provided by co-resident kin is important in facilitating female involvement in wage-earning, and in turn that women's entry into the workforce may be an important factor in households' propensity to incorporate relatives.[17]

Having said this, household extension is not strictly necessary in the Visayas, given the wide practice of inter-household exchange: as noted in Chapters 4, 5 and 6, many mothers resort to leaving children with kin in other households during working hours. In addition, the pressures exerted on women's reproductive roles often differ because of factors such as the stage reached in the life-cycle and the nature of the employment. Beach-vendors in Boracay, for example, have more flexibility in their daily routines than, say, factory workers in the Mactan Export Processing Zone, so they can often take care of essential aspects of children's welfare at both ends of the day and do not have to resort to help from third parties either within or outside the home (see Chapter 5). The fact that this latter group consists mainly of older women means too that elder siblings can look after younger ones (see also Miralao, 1984:379). In addition, while household extension might be one of the more convenient strategies for women to reconcile their productive and reproductive activities, the rise in labour force partic-ipation in the wake of recession since the mid-1980s (see Chapter 3) does not seem to have been accompanied by a discernible increase in

---

17 Higher rates of female labour force participation in male-headed extended as opposed to nuclear households have also been observed in other countries such as Mexico (see, for example, Benería and Roldan, 1987:31; Chant, 1991a: 138–9) and Zimbabwe (Kanji, 1994:116 – see also Rakodi,1991:43 on the role of co-resident kin in facilitating female labour force participation in cities in sub-Saharan Africa). Having said this, a general study of female employment in the Philippines undertaken in the early 1980s by Virginia Miralao in three regions (Cagayan Valley, the Central Visayas and Southern Mindanao) found that the numbers of employed women living in extended households (and those receiving assistance in housework from their children) did not differ substantially from the corresponding figures for non-working wives (Miralao, 1984:379).

these units; on the contrary, extended households have tended to be 'trimmed down' as a means of coping with financial stringency, even where women have employment (see also Chant, forthcoming a). Thus although in other parts of the world, such as Mexico, where recession in the 1980s led to an increased frequency of extended households, the situation in the Visayas seems more akin to that of countries like Zimbabwe, where economic exigency has placed a brake on this particular kind of reciprocity and has converted extended units into something of a luxury (ibid.; see also Kanji, 1994:117–18).

One important issue here is that a possible 're-nuclearisation' of household units in the wake of anticipated continuation of the Philippine debt crisis (with its attendant pressure on prices, public service cutbacks and so on) might be associated with even greater burdens of labour for women in the home: in other words, with households possibly having to curtail their absorption of kin, female wage-earners may lose the support which has been so helpful in facilitating their labour force participation until now. This also points to the fact that even if household composition in the Visayas is perhaps less dependent on whether or not adult women work than is the case in other places, the nature of gender roles and relations is a vital element, insofar as the extent to which labour can be extracted from individual women (and/or their daughters) may well determine the configuration of households in future. Indeed, the fact that so many women in nuclear households work, both among the target occupational groups and in the household populations, bears witness to the fact that the double burden is already highly inscribed within several women's daily lives (see Chapters 3–5).

Setting aside the specific influences of both women's work and recession upon household composition in the Visayas, and turning to the broader question of changes in household structure, the research supports the general argument that Philippine urbanisation and economic development tend to be associated with a greater incidence of household extension (see Chapter 1). The proportions of extended households in our community surveys in Cebu, Lapu-Lapu and Boracay are not only high in absolute terms (see Chapter 3), but also in relation to the former households of women migrants. Among migrants in our semi-structured household interview survey, for example, only 28 per cent of those from rural areas had actually lived in extended households prior to migration. These findings add weight to the notion that extended-to-nuclear trajectories in household form are inappropriate for developing countries in any generalised sense (see Brydon and Chant, 1993:139–45). Even if there is not a noticeably greater proportion of extended households compared with nuclear structures among the 160 migrants in our household questionnaire surveys (46 per cent versus 42 per cent), the fact remains that they are a significant component of the urban population. Also important is that while women-headed households (whether extended, non-extended or single-person) form a relative minority, both in low-income communities and among most occupational groups, fewer migrants belonged to female-headed units in rural areas. In other words, composition and headship alike seem to be undergoing changes in the course of contemporary development, with women's employment appearing to be a core factor, particularly in respect of the latter. Future analyses of household evolution should therefore not only take into account the nature of household organisation and livelihood in rural source areas, but should consider how different forms give rise to variations in gender-selective migration and how these intersect with the character of labour markets and female employment opportunities in different destinations. Indeed, mainstream models of household formation have much to gain from devoting greater analytical weight to female employment and migration, as well as giving women their overdue centrality within this arena (see also Chant, 1991a:9–11).

Having pointed up the ways in which various types of export-oriented employment in the Visayas are associated with fairly distinctive patterns of mobility and household arrangements, and having explored their implications for models of migration and household evolution, it is also important to consider the implications of these phenomena for female status. Recognising that new (and alternative) demographic and domestic circumstances may be linked with certain modifications in the lives of Filipino women, the nature of jobs themselves is also likely to play a role in influencing normative and pragmatic aspects of gender roles and relations. In exploring the outcomes of employment for women, therefore, it is first necessary to give some attention to the bases of female labour demand in different sectors, the relative departure from existing gender stereotypes represented by different jobs, and the resources for change in gender roles and relations they may provide.

GENDER DIMENSIONS OF WOMEN'S WORK: DIFFERENCES BETWEEN OCCUPATIONAL SEGMENTS

Feminisation and gender-stereotyping

As documented in previous chapters, gender-stereotyping of one form or another underpins female recruitment in all sectors. Assuming some consonance with levels of female recruitment and the power of broad and generalised stereotypes about women, it is useful to consider how these interrelate with degrees of 'feminisation' in each domain of activity; sex work is clearly the most feminised, with industrial employment (particularly in the garment industry in the Mactan Export Processing Zone) following close on its heels, and the lowest overall levels applying to tourism employment in Boracay and Cebu.

Sex work's overwhelming recruitment of female labour is undoubtedly due to the fact that prostitution has historically centred upon the purchase of women by men, with notions of women as passive objects of male sexual gratification critical in this phenomenon. While stereotyped notions of the character and purpose of female sexuality may be most apparent in the entertainment sector, however, their influence is also clear within certain segments of conventional tourism employment, especially in frontline/customer relations positions in reception work, sales and restaurants (see Chapter 5). Given the pervasive association between women's sexual attractiveness and their physical attributes, women workers in both the entertainment and conventional tourism industries are usually recruited at an age when they are deemed (by male employers) to be in their 'prime' – further exacerbating the tendency for recruitment, across all sectors, of women who are young and single.

Another important stereotype shaping female recruitment in tourism employment stems from women's cultural assignation to reproductive labour and the assumption that they have a 'natural affinity' for domestic work. This especially applies to posts in laundrywork, bedmaking and cleaning, although women are not always employed in these departments (see Chapter 5). The cultural–domestic association surfaces strongly in the industrial sector, however, particularly in garment production, where women's presumed aptitude for sewing (and other repetitive manual tasks) results in their preponderance on factory assembly lines. Beyond this, export manufacturing draws on related female stereotypes such as docility, capacity for detailed monotonous work and commitment to high productivity. Again, younger workers are often preferred (at the recruitment stage at least) because of their perceived innocence of industrial labour practices, their supposed willingness to accept orders as a result of their junior status and lack of power within patriarchal households, and the presumed absence of conflicting responsibilities brought about by marriage and motherhood.

As well as the attributes and dispositions thought to characterise women workers, we should bear in mind that assumptions about what they *lack* are also important in patterns of feminisation and gender segmentation within and between sectors. One major factor, apparent both in tourism and manufacturing, is the idea that women are unsuited to jobs which demand undue physical exertion. In other words, women's 'weakness' constitutes grounds for their exclusion from jobs identified with strenuous muscular activity – such as maintenance posts in hotels and major machine operations in factories. The inter-related assumption that women are unable to understand and operate technical equipment again excludes them from employment such as kitchen work in hotels with large industrial dishwashers, and from mechanised aspects of factory production (see Chapters 4 and 5). Added to this, and applicable to all sectors (albeit in varying degrees), is the idea that women are not suited to high-level managerial or decision-making positions, with the absence of female representation in the upper echelons of firms' hierarchies undoubtedly contributing not only to the reinforcement of women's self-perceptions as 'secondary workers', but to the exclusion of their interests within recruitment, placement or promotion practices (see also Eviota, 1992:115).

Given that these general stereotypes play, in varying degrees and in varying combinations, a major role in determining women's involvement and status within the sectors under discussion, it is also important to assess the extent to which these are carried through into the daily execution of jobs and act to reinforce particular inequalities and/or specific kinds of self-image.

Gender ideologies at work: internalisation or resistance?

As the group most subject to gendered recruitment and sexualised stereo-types, hospitality workers in many respects have the greatest difficulty in breaking away from a reactionary set of gender ideologies which allot them to their occupations. Operating within a system where women's main task is to gratify men's sexual needs, the way women dress, make themselves up, dance, interact with customers and so on is primarily a response to male fantasies about what women should be (pretty, ornamental, sweet, gentle, unassertive, willing and so on – see also Høigård and Finstad, 1992:55). For those women who actually sleep with men, personal sexual desires are rarely indulged; as we saw in Chapter 6, most direct their thoughts to other matters during the act of intercourse.[18] The fact that women are used to being 'taken' and dominated by men also means that they become accustomed to being objects rather than agents in sexual activity. Daily life proceeds in accordance with the idea that women are sexual commodities for the pleasure of men, with the extremely fundamental and pragmatic participation of women in playing out this ideology meaning that they may find it very hard to divorce themselves from the belief that patriarchy is legitimate and/or acceptable. Indeed, lying as it does at the intersection between (private) sexuality and (public) gender relations, sex work perhaps poses the most serious obstacles to any emancipatory prospects for women.

At the same time, it is important to recognise that within this general framework of gender inequality there are certain features at odds with what we might call 'traditional' behaviour and which in some senses invert dominant stereotypes. One is that sex workers actually take a very proactive role in their initial interaction with men. Unlike other women, for example, 'bar girls' are accustomed to approaching men (at any rate in clubs, and although floor managers may well dictate to whom they go), instigating the process of getting to know them, chatting them up and seducing them into transactions. Moreover (and recognising that any advantage experienced by women in this industry is usually double-edged), while entertainment workers may go some way to shrouding the baseness of exchanging sex for money by giving the impression to clients that there is potential for longer-

---

18 Psychological detachment from physical interaction seems to be fairly standardised practice among women in this occupation elsewhere in the world. With reference to prostitution in Oslo, for example, Høigård and Finstad (1992:63–75) describe this as one of women's defence mechanisms in the sex trade. Along with taking drugs, avoiding use of certain parts of the body (especially the mouth), being nice to customers (in order that the act will take less time), using false names and so on, 'prostitutes have worked out an ingenious, complex system to protect "the real me", the self, the personality from being invaded and destroyed by customers'.

term and more rounded relationships (perhaps even partly convincing themselves of this in the process), the fact remains that this is done primarily to enhance earnings. In other words, sex workers not only succeed in 'duping' men in some fashion, they are effectively able to extract what they want from them: money for their time and labour (see Alexander, 1988:189). Other women, however, cannot make these demands anywhere like as directly and often gain little from partnerships apart from a legal father for their children and the social legitimacy which surrounds marriage and dual parenthood. Having said this, the guilt, shame and general distaste most hospitality workers feel about their jobs often outweigh elements that might be viewed in their favour. Sex workers usually see themselves as 'bad' women and have few opportunities to exorcise their disquiet except in the worlds they inhabit outside work, where parenting gives them an opportunity to fulfil a responsible and socially acceptable role in life, and solidarity with other women (especially friends or co-workers) affords them support and companionship which women in other households rarely derive from husbands. Indeed, somewhat ironically, although inequitable gender ideologies are arguably most apparent within the working lives of hospitality women, their financial gains often provide a route to more liberating domestic environments than are available to most of their counterparts. It is this disjuncture between home and work which makes it necessary to explore the intersection of a broad range of factors in assessing the outcomes of employment for women (see below).

As to the sexualised nature of certain jobs within conventional tourism employment, notably frontline posts in hotels, shops and restaurants, it is again possible to see women conforming with notions of women as objects for the visual (if not the physical) attentions of men. As noted in Chapter 5, pandering to male images of what women should be involve women having to adopt feminine forms of dress, to be charming, sweet-mannered, flattering and often discreetly flirtatious as well. Again, however, the underlying objective is to extract money from customers (not on women's own behalf but that of their employers); moreover, the lack of direct physical engagement with men means that it is probably slightly easier for the women concerned to recognise that this is play-acting rather than real life. Indeed, in Boracay one of our respondents (a waitress), who had just finished a lengthy and embarrassingly coquettish conversation with a group of middle-aged German men, turned to us with a knowing wink and commented: 'These men are all the same!' In other words, there seemed to be considerable awareness on her part that she was subscribing to stereotypical behaviour as part of her job and, while not particularly comfortable with this, it was clear that the customers (rather than her) were the ones being taken in.

The other main stereotype underpinning women's recruitment into tourism employment, and into certain kinds of factory job (the 'cultural–domestic' stereotype), may in some respects be less easy for these workers to disentangle from their home lives insofar as virtually all women are involved in some reproductive labour within their households. Women's allocation to jobs with a strong domestic component – washing, bedmaking, cleaning, sewing and so on – fails to expand their skills and, intermeshed with female exclusion from mechanised or heavy jobs in both sectors, may well be regarded as embedding women further within their traditional gender-assigned activities. Having said this, the fact that these jobs are paid may give women a slightly different perspective on the work they routinely perform in the home. Regardless of how menial the task, this still represents employment and where men can be seen to be engaged in the same activities (as in tourism establishments in Boracay in particular) greater status may be attached to the labour involved. However, other factors do contribute to the continuity of patriarchal ideologies in both spheres, especially in the industrial sector.

As discussed in Chapter 4, for example, women's usual inability to move sideways or vertically out of feminised factory departments tends to reinforce the notion of them as secondary workers beholden to male directives. In addition, the drudgery and monotony involved in routine assembly work are likely to have a nullifying effect on women's personal aspirations: just as in the home where the never-ending cycle of housework and childcare often pushes housewives into a position where they cannot see a way out, few factory workers either in Cebu and Lapu-Lapu have the time or space to think about their lives when the tasks they do are not only exhausting but demand their full and constant attention (see Chapter 4).

While tourism workers, especially those in the formal sector, are also exposed to patriarchal ideologies in the workplace, we have noted that they probably have greater scope to disengage themselves from sexual stereotypes, and may be at an advantage in being in contexts where male workers are not only more numerous but often do the same jobs. This is not to say, however, that women tourism workers are by any means free of gender-typing or occupational discrimination. Moreover, the fact that in Boracay many workers live on the premises of their employers means that individual freedom may be rather constrained by paternalistic, if not patriarchal, work practices (see Chapter 5). Having said this, four factors seem to offer departures from prevailing gender inequalities and stereotypes that other sectors do not so obviously allow. One is the fact that many workers, especially those in frontline posts, have the opportunity to meet people from a wide range of backgrounds and to observe their behaviour at close range (especially in Boracay, where female tourists are almost as numerous as men). As noted earlier in the book, this may open up possibilities for greater reflection on the nature of women' lives and lead them to develop more critical assessments of their own positions. Second, the potential for promotion within tourism establishments (see below) is likely to give women the chance of conceiving their jobs as a step on some kind of career ladder. Third, and related to this, the opportunities provided by informal employment in tourism destinations (again, particularly in Boracay) may give rise to greater possibilities for lucrative self-employment or entrepreneurship than other types of labour do. Fourth, even if most women live in workplace dormitories as a condition of employment, the opportunity to share living quarters with other women (and away from men) may (as is often the case with the households of sex workers) sow seeds of solidarity among women (see Chapter 5).

Comparative perspectives on job satisfaction: the views of women

In conjunction with these observations, it is also critical to bear in mind women's own opinions of their work. Not surprisingly perhaps, the vast majority who do not enjoy their jobs are sex workers, while those who do are in conventional tourism establishments, especially in Boracay. As noted in Chapter 6, the bulk of hospitality employees find their jobs both disagreeable and hazardous, especially those involved in direct sexual transactions. They derive little pride from their work (merely in what the proceeds can do for their children) and are wont to be extremely fatalistic about their futures. Tourism workers, on the other hand, in both the formal and informal sectors, enjoy the contact their work brings with other people and their physical and environmental surroundings (particularly in Boracay), and usually have a more optimistic outlook on their lives. Factory workers lie somewhere in between: on the one hand, gratified that they are in reasonably well-paid jobs; on the other, gaining little pleasure from their routine, and usually exhausting, manual tasks.

These findings are also interesting insofar as the overall degree of contentment apparent within each occupational segment tends to display an inverse relationship with levels of feminisation. In other words, sex workers, whose profession is virtually exclusively female, are those who are most unhappy about their employment, whereas tourism workers seem to be the most satisfied. Although feminisation was not explictly mentioned as a factor in job fulfilment, it is tempting to ask whether this has some subconscious effects, especially in the light of potentially countervailing influences, such as a high incidence of overqualification in the tourism sector. Indeed, although differences in educational achievement are not especially significant among occupational groups, formal tourism workers in Boracay are marked by the fact that all hold a post-high-school qualification of some description, whether vocational or academic. A total of four of the 13 tourism employees in Boracay held college diplomas (mostly in Hotel and Restaurant Management) and a further three were qualified teachers. Given that the majority presently occupy fairly modest positions within hotels, shops and restaurants, it is perhaps surprising that there is so little motivation to move into other professions. One contributory factor might be that possibilities for intra-establishment promotion to positions more commensurate with their education and training may make workers feel their present jobs are worth putting up with, at least in the short term. A second is that people usually have to use foreign language skills in international tourism, which may give some sense of utilising their education (see Chapter 5). As for the question of feminisation per se, however, it is perhaps also the case that those occupations which are least crowded by women are those which are less subject to vulnerability, exploitation and resignation to patriarchal controls. Educated or otherwise, and even where their jobs might reflect and reinforce strong sexual stereotypes, formal tourism workers are therefore at least in the position of having a certain occupational parity with men and, conceivably, of feeling more fully integrated within the labour force than their counterparts in marginalised, low-grade, female-only activities. Indeed, before moving on to look at the outcomes of employment for women, it is interesting to take a brief look at how levels of feminisation per se may affect women's attitudes and long-term commitment to their jobs.

Feminisation: power or vulnerability?

Bearing in mind the difficulties of separating out the vertical from the horizontal dimensions of feminisation (in other words, women's perceptions of feminised jobs may be influenced as much by where these jobs are in the occupational hierarchy as by the sex of fellow workers), the experience of working alongside other women might conceivably provide scope for collective identity and joint action on common interests, with potential for converting feminisation into a source of power among women. The fact that this (admittedly idealised) scenario does not seem to obtain in the Visayas is due to a number of factors. One is that women do not have much time to converse with each other at work (especially in export factories, where there is little flexibility in production schedules and where rest periods are limited). A second is that although women may be found in the same department or occupation, they may well be in competition with one another. For example, the imposition of productivity bonuses in factories means that women may eschew female collegiality in order to improve their own performance targets; while in sex bars women may find themselves competing over male clients. Beyond this, the tendency for women's work to be undervalued relative to men's may mean that the absence of male co-workers in similar ranks might lead to a greater sense of 'ghettoisation' rather than group strength, especially given that their superiors are likely to be overwhelmingly male.

Indeed, apart from the fact that women (and men) in conventional tourism establishments have a vested interest in pulling together (with service charges and gratuities normally shared by all employees in the establishments – see Chapter 5), the greater prevalence of mixed (and less consistently feminised) departments (especially in Boracay) could be conducive to rather more positive feelings about their jobs among women. Even if workforces comprising a more balanced distribution of men and women may not be characterised by greater professionalisation than women-only domains in any objective sense, they may be *perceived* as being so. Moreover, somewhat greater potential for female career mobility does appear to exist in such scenarios.

Feminisation: impacts on long-term employment and occupational mobility

The question of occupational mobility is integral to the issue of how the frequent conjuncture of feminisation with concentration in low-ranking positions may affect women's attitudes to work. To what extent does assignation to 'dead-end' jobs (with few promotion prospects) dissuade women from forming permanent commitments to their employment, especially if their years in particular professions are numbered (as is usually the case in the sex industry)? Our interviews with sex workers indicated strongly that even in the unlikely event of being able to continue working in their present establishments in the longer term, most do not envisage (or want) to stay, although they are often profoundly insecure about the alternatives open to them in later life, and particularly about how they will be able to support their children. With marriage to a foreigner (especially given the openings for overseas migration this offers) tending to be seen as one of the only ways out (see Chapter 6), it is nonetheless important to recognise that women do not plan on being kept by foreign men; rather, they see matrimony as a way of leaving their pasts behind them and/or moving to higher wages in jobs abroad. In other words, sex workers might not be particularly committed to their current occupations, but they have no obvious desire to give up working.

This also tends to apply to factory operatives, although the situation is somewhat different in that greater potential exists for women to stay in their posts (marriage is rarely grounds for dismissal; and unlike sex workers their employment does not depend on physical beauty and so on) and, as noted in Chapter 4, a considerable number actually remain in the sector on a long-term basis (viz. the high proportions of wives and mothers among factory workers in Cebu and Lapu-Lapu). Nonetheless, younger industrial operatives who do not yet have their own families are rather more circumspect about their capacity to endure this work indefinitely. Although voluntary labour turnover is very low in both Cebu and the Mactan Export Processing Zone, most factories have not been open more than a few years, which makes it very difficult to project the likely duration of workers. Moreover, studies of women in export manufacturing firms elsewhere have noted that the rigid and tiring regimes which characterise these operations make it impossible for most workers to maintain sufficient productivity over the long term either to want or to be able to remain in their positions (Fernández-Kelly, 1983b:220; Hossfeld, 1991:16; G.Standing, 1989:1080). For this reason it is perhaps not surprising that younger operatives are often in the process of saving some of their wages to transfer themselves to other career paths (see Chapter 4). Again, however, the influence of low-ranking feminised positions does not seem to have weakened their resolve to stay employed; if anything, it has given rise to hopes of occupational betterment (and some financial means of achieving it).

Workers in the tourism sector, however, are perhaps the only group who seem content to stay where they are: employees in formal parts of the industry tend to like their jobs because they are sociable and relatively undemanding in physical terms, and probably also because there are slightly greater prospects for mobility. As noted earlier (see also note 8 above), the wider range of openings for women and lower incidence of gender-typing within tourism enterprises conceivably lessen the likelihood of arbitrary bars to female promotion. In addition, we have to recognise that tourism comprises a wide spectrum of informal as well as formal types of employment. This is important, in that the ready visibility of related alternatives may offer women broader horizons in respect of earnings or occupational status, especially since many informal enterprises may benefit from the skills (and contacts) women have acquired in formal jobs. Indeed, formal workers often improve their financial position by moving into informal/own-account ventures catering to the tourism market – as in Boracay, where informal operators of *sari-sari* stores and *carinderias* may have started life as formal tourism employees but have found their own businesses more profitable, as well as deriving pleasure from being their own boss (see Chapter 3; also Chant, forthcoming b).

Again, however, workers in other sectors are less privileged. Even if sex workers have the potential to make more money by venturing to operate independently of bars and massage parlours, either as call-girls or as long-term 'girlfriends' of foreign men (see Chapter 6), there is hardly a readily accessible and guaranteed market. As for manufacturing operatives, self-employment in the same domain (which usually means piecework rather than heading independent production units) is generally much less remunerative than factory-based employment (see Chapter 4) – which is not to say that other informal activities spawned by industrial development, such as commerce and real estate (renting out rooms to manufacturing workers, for example) do not provide lucrative alternatives (see Chapter 3). While factory workers may benefit from moving into these activities, however, it is only their wages (or more specifically their savings) that they can usually take with them, not their specialised assembly skills (see also Eviota, 1992:121; Pineda-Ofreneo, 1987:96). Having said this, of all the dimensions of employment which, in a more general sense, may affect women's lives (and their ability to negotiate gender), wages are undoubtedly one of the most critical, as discussed below.

OUTCOMES FOR WOMEN OF EMPLOYMENT

A huge range of influences obviously affect the implications of employment for women. As John Gledhill (1994:200) points out, 'the relationship between changes in the economy and "gender roles" is mediated by a politics of gender relations concerned with power, value and sexuality' and cannot be understood in 'mechanical terms'. Nonetheless, it is clear from the present study that women in the Visayas are affected in various ways by different types of export-oriented employment, not only on account of their jobs per se but also through the migration and household characteristics with which they are associated. Indeed, recognition of the interplay of these factors is essential in understanding the gender implications of employment in general, and of export-oriented work in particular.

In respect of the economic corollaries of employment, for example, it is difficult, if not impossible, to evaluate whether earning an income empowers women or subordinates them further, without reference to overall structures of gender inequality (see Faulkner and Lawson, 1991:40–1; Moghadam,1994:99–102; Safa, 1990,1993; Walby, 1990 for general discussions). As Rae Lesser Blumberg (1989,1991c) suggests, women's employment may give them greater control over their own lives, but this is heavily contingent upon whether they have the liberty to control the income they derive from it.[19] The only group in the

---

19 Blumberg is further concerned to stress that the 'degree of control over *surplus* allocation is held to be more important for relative male/female economic power than the degree of control over resources needed for bare subsistence', concluding that 'for both genders, the more surplus controlled, the greater the leverage' (Blumberg, 1989:63; original emphasis).

Visayas in the position of having major control is effectively sex workers, whose high earnings, social (and often geographical) distance from kin and, most importantly, lack of male partners entitle them to establish households of their own and to manage their own affairs. Yet it is vital also to acknowledge that while high earnings among sex workers might represent a means by which they can loosen the shackles of male domination in the context of home and family, as well as fulfil obligations as single parents, these are rarely deemed of enough value in themselves to rid women of their considerable anxieties about how they actually earn their living, what this means in respect of isolation from kin, how social ostracism and 'deviance' may affect their children, and how they cope with male abuse in the workplace. As Wendy Lee (1991:88) points out, prostitution may give the 'illusion of freedom', but women effectively exchange the domination of fathers, brothers and husbands for that of male managers, pimps and the police. In other words, empowerment through wage-earning is likely to be highly fragmented and incomplete as long as patriarchal ideologies continue to present women with the contradictory situation where demand for their sexual labour is commoditised and legally endorsed, but where engaging in this activity renders them unable to fulfil the requirements for female legitimacy in wider society.

For similar kinds of reasons, wage-earning in a more general sense is often as much a conduit for exploiting as for emancipating women. As noted earlier, women's potential for using their wages for their own ends is often heavily limited. Instead of creating greater personal freedom as a result of moving away from natal kin and into paid work, for example, women usually find themselves called upon to support large numbers of people in their places of origin. Although this in fact is often a prime objective of migration, the fact remains that most women can only break the cycle by transferring themselves into another patri-archal institution – marriage. Once within the context of households headed by male partners, women's employment gives rise to situations where their time and labour may be stretched to a maximum and where scope to use the financial proceeds of their work, even for their children's welfare, is frequently constrained by husbands' personal demands.

This underlines the critical importance of household circumstances (and intra-domestic power relations) in stimulating female labour force participation in the first place. Most women's search for employment in the Visayas, as we have seen, is highly motivated by the needs of their households whether in their places of origin or in their current places of residence. These needs are not just borne out of poverty, but, importantly, are conceptualised by women as their principal rationale for working. In other words, women rarely enter the labour force for themselves but for *others*, even where it is obvious that their earnings will not necessarily enhance household well-being so much as indulge patriarchal privileges (their menfolk's personal expenditures, for example), so acting to undercut the very coherence and viability of the institutions women are trying to sustain. The complicity (albeit unwitting) of women with ideologies which combine to undermine their interests (and which weaken their power to generate change) is one clearly born out of a lack of tangible alternatives, and one which means that gains are likely to be very slow in coming and to be confined to very few arenas, at least in the first instance.

The gains from Filipino women's involvement in export-oriented employment conform very much to this expectation, being decidedly hesitant and limited in scope thus far. Nonetheless, three tendencies of a potentially positive nature should be highlighted. One is that comparatively high wages seem to be providing some women with the power to exercise slightly greater control over their own lives. Even if those already married are in a position where their negotiating power has undergone little change, single women are in a stronger position: not only do they seem able to postpone the eventuality of marriage, but they arguably have greater opportunity to resist proposals from men who are likely to exploit them. Wage-earning also gives women scope to reduce their fertility (and, importantly, to justify it), because they are likely to marry later and because rationalising the number of births is often in the interests of their households as well as of themselves (see also Moghadam, 1994:100–1).

A second, and related, outcome of women's employment in the export sector seems to be some modification in their relationships with housework and childcare. Women work long hours in most export-oriented jobs, which means that they are not on hand to undertake every aspect of reproductive labour in their households. Although this is not to say that women workers escape core domestic responsibilities (and indeed many have extremely heavy dual burdens of waged and unwaged work), most do have to engage help of some description, whether by extending their households and passing on various tasks to female kin, by reassigning a range of responsibilities within nuclear households and/or by having recourse to outside parties. This is important not only in pragmatic terms but ideologically, insofar as if the bulk of women's day is spent in the workplace rather than in the home, and if some of their housework and childcare is delegated to others, the symbolic association of female roles with domestic labour may lessen, even if the employment in which they are involved continues to be highly imbued with patriarchy.

Having said this, scope for reidentification of reproductive labour as a set of activities to be more fully shared among household members and less assigned to one sex only is likely to be limited in the medium term – first, because men appear to have little interest in becoming more involved in household life (indeed, when women work and earn a reasonable income, men may spend even more time away from the family because the resources exist to do so); and second (and partly as a response to this), because working women's tasks are usually passed on to other women (whether kin or daughters), even if sons may be given some responsibility (see also Chant, 1994b). It should also be noted that these findings might not apply everywhere in the country. For example, Virginia Miralao's broad-based study of women's employment in the Philippines in the early 1980s (see note 17 above) found that husbands of working women did not increase their inputs of time to domestic labour, although there did seem to be some real-location of their inputs towards tasks traditionally reserved for females (Miralao, 1984:379). Indeed, Miralao's overall conclusion was that even if the employment of women did not seem to bring about 'dramatic redefinitions of wives' and husbands' roles in household management', it did give rise to 'a greater amount of gender-crossing in the activities of the household' (ibid.:386).

Even if the latter is not particularly evident in male-headed households in the Visayas, there is possibly greater scope for it to emerge in the context of a third main outcome of women's involvement in certain types of export-oriented employment (especially sex work), namely the ability to establish female-headed or female-only living arrange-ments (see also note 10 above). Although, as discussed earlier, these units often arise through default rather than design, they do provide environments where immediate encounters with men and with patri-archal ideologies are excluded from a very personal arena of women's lives. Although we cannot project the likely longer-term consequences, such structures possibly constitute a critical first step for women in the fragmentation of a set of gender ideologies which have customarily placed them under the direct control of men. In turn, the fact that female-headed households provide a space for mothers to be the sole parents of sons and daughters, and, importantly, to have the opportunity to exert authority over males (even if these are only children), may be crucial in shaping future attitudes and behaviour and in forging further paths for change. Although Henrietta Moore (1988:111) points out that the question of 'the relationships between employment and increased social and economic autonomy for women is a vexed one', she also notes that 'many women themselves feel there is a connection'. In this light, it is conceivable that women workers in the Visayas may come to realise (and accept) their earnings as a source of personal power and use this to create spaces, however small, where they (and their children) are free from immediate male domination. Indeed, as Helen Safa (1992:78–9) notes of Puerto Rico and the Dominican Republic, the greatest changes arising for women workers in export manufacturing almost invariably occur within the home (rather than in the workplace or in politics). Despite the desirability of effecting changes in male-female relations at wider levels (see below), the frequent identification of household organisation with primary structures of gender subordination (see Chapter 1) suggests that shifts in the domestic arena are an essential component of any move in the direction of greater equality.

Yet momentum for equality will also have to come from men, and at present it is not clear that women's new positions in the labour force are engendering major increases in male contributions to household life or fostering more positive relationships between husbands and wives. Indeed, the continued absorption of female workers into mainstream export activity could conceivably lead to greater polarisation (and alienation) between the sexes. In her research on Puerto Rico and the Dominican Republic, for example, Safa (1992:78) notes that women's privileged access to employment, together with their stronger and more independent roles within the home, may result in considerable demoralisation among men. Studies in places where similar situations prevail, such as Guanacaste, Costa Rica (Chaverría et al., 1987), and Puerto Vallarta, Mexico (Chant, 1991a:168; COCODERA, 1980:518–19), have also noted that men may resort to 'backlashes' in the form of withdrawing economic support from wives or indulging in greater levels of drinking and gambling (see also Chant, forthcoming a), thereby underlining a more general observation that 'patriarchy may reassert itself even in contexts where women are asserting themselves' (Gledhill, 1994:200). On the other hand, a more optimistic scenario is that men may come to realise that women are in a position where they will not necessarily adopt the inequities of patriarchy in the home, and that it will be necessary to prove themselves as worthier candidates for marriage and parenthood than has been the case in the past. In addition, fathers, who have traditionally played a strong role in determining the lives of their daughters, may also find themselves unable to wield as much influence as previously, notwithstanding the fact that changes at a wider societal level are necessary before there can be any gener-alised diminution of gender inequalities.

Indeed, even if some women make gains within the domestic sphere as a result of particular aspects of their jobs (earnings, the need for certain kinds of domestic arrangement and so on), it is clear that this rarely translates into major changes in gender roles and relations beyond the confines of the household. In fact sex workers in particular may face further discrimination, not least from other women, as a result of their alternative lifestyles or 'otherness' (see Chapter 6). In some respects, therefore, an indirect effect of personal empowerment and/or the creation of emancipatory domestic spaces among one particular group of women may be the erection of barriers to the solidarity so necessary for any generalised improvement in women's situation (see Chapter 1). Thus at one extreme, divisions among women, arising from employment and its corollaries, could provoke grounds for even greater fragmentation of women's interests, let alone those of men and women.

CONCLUSION

On balance, the overall framework of gender inequality in which women's work takes place in the Philippine Visayas means that labour force participation is often a double-edged sword. As a result of the demographic and domestic circumstances with which different types of employment are associated, the outcomes of women's work are frequently highly ambiguous, with gains in one domain often con-tradicted, if not cancelled, in others (viz. the possibilities for autonomy opened up in the domestic sphere for sex workers counterposed against a profession strongly laced with patriarchal ideology and practice, and a social context in which scope for contact, let alone cooperation, with other women is negligible). It must also be recognised that women's involvement in export-oriented development does not mean major transformations in their positions vis-à-vis men in the same sectors. Men are not only women's overall employers (and often customers as well), but as workers they are usually in higher-status occupations within the enterprises concerned. These findings tend to underline the arguments of Alison McEwen Scott (1986) and Faulkner and Lawson (1991) (see also Chapter 1) that the *incorporation* of women into employment may well be as exploitative as the exclusion traditionally emphasised by advocates of the female marginalisation thesis. Moreover, women may form the numerical majority in the mainstream (rather than the margins) of export-oriented activity, but this does not mean any substantial improvement in their societal position. Although this might have much to do with feminisation and gender-segregation, it perhaps has less to do with economic inequality (Chapter 1) in that women in the Visayas do not necessarily receive lower wages or fewer fringe benefits than their male counterparts. Yet even where women earn more than men (if not in the same sectors of employment, then at least compared with others), their ability to capitalise on this in any major way is usually held in check by gender inequalities in the sphere of their households, kinship and wider society (see also Chant and McIlwaine, 1994; Eviota, 1992:123). Indeed, the frequently contradictory influences of home and workplace indicate that broader changes are necessary if women workers in the export sector are to see any gains from their endeavours. It is to this and related issues which our final chapter is addressed.

8 CONCLUSION: POLICY IMPLICATIONS AND DIRECTIONS FOR FUTURE RESEARCH

We have now provided a synthesis not only of the interrelationships between migration, household formation and export-oriented employment, but also of the possible outcomes and implications for women of outward-looking development strategies. This chapter takes one step further and asks where we go from here. Given the often contradictory consequences of women's incorporation into different economic sectors in the Visayas, what actions might be taken to lessen those that seem to be negative, and/or to enhance those that contain seeds from which greater equalities between the sexes might grow? With this in mind, our discussion considers the various arenas in which initiatives to minimise women's disadvantage might be formulated and/or strengthened. Since detailed research is essential in understanding women's position within society and economy, the first section highlights some core factors, particularly of a methodological nature, which future country-specific and comparative research might usefully embrace. Following this, we explore some of the policy implications raised by the study, at both a national and a global level. Given the difficulties inherent in the implementation and monitoring of policy, alternative routes for action are also addressed, focusing on international pressure groups on the one hand, and on the other, on grassroots organisations concerned with initiating change from the bottom up .

SUGGESTIONS FOR FUTURE RESEARCH

While this book has examined a wide range of demographic, social and economic implications of women's involvement in export manufacturing, international tourism and sex work, these are by no means

304

exhaustive, nor necessarily indicative of what might be occurring in other parts of the Philippines or elsewhere in the world. Indeed, if anything, the research raises more questions than it answers, which is not to say that this does not provide us with some productive starting points for further exploration. The most significant conceptual implications were summarised in the previous chapter, notably the need for holistic analyses of female labour force participation (i.e. those which take into account the demographic and social, as well as the economic, corollaries of women's employment), the need to recognise differences according to occupational segments (both individually and in combination with one another) and the need for theories (of migration, of household evolution, of the impacts of development on women's status and so on) to be broad, to be open to notions of multiple causality and to be sensitive to the contradictions so often apparent in the various domains which mediate female economic activity.

In order to extend these, in terms both of future research on the Philippines and of international comparative enquiry, it is desirable, where possible, for future studies to be based on larger samples of informants than those selected for the present one. While we have been able to paint a broad picture of women's experiences in the home and the workplace from their own perspectives, as well as those of other parties involved, we have been somewhat constrained by small numbers of respondents, particularly in regard to interviews with workers and employers in specific sectors and places.[1] Thus, although future research would benefit from drawing upon interviews with a similarly broad-ranging cross-section of people, larger numbers would be helpful in order to provide greater representativeness and to allow clearer derivation of patterns and linkages.

---

1 For example, ideally we should have interviewed greater numbers of hotel employees in Cebu, greater numbers of garment workers in Lapu-Lapu, greater numbers of shopworkers in Boracay and so on. At the very least it would have been helpful to have had equal sample sizes in each of the interview categories. We make no excuses for these omissions, since the necessary use of 'snowballing' techniques in contacting certain workers or employers often restricted the range of people with whom we could talk. Moreover, the sheer scale of the overall research project, our concern to base the study on information from a broad range of sources and our desire to be involved personally in the interviews meant that increasing the numbers was physically impossible within the funded core fieldwork period of eight months. This has obvious time and resource implications for research of a similar nature in the future.

Apart from increased sample sizes, longitudinal research is also crucial, especially when attempting to assess the outcomes of export-oriented employment for women over time. The key sectors examined in the Visayas are relatively new within the localities concerned, and for this reason it is difficult to project longer-term consequences. Integral to this objective is follow-up research with the same households and workers at subsequent stages in order to assess whether shifts in such factors as domestic organisation and intra-household decision-making patterns have become permanently incorporated into the lives of women in particular occupational groups, and how these may influence changes among the population in general. It would also be desirable to try to interview new households of a similar nature (e.g. in terms of stages in the life-cycle, composition, headship, employment) to those in previous periods in order to maintain comparability and to avoid the problems of interpretation which arise when trying to distinguish the issue of the ageing of interview samples from other factors responsible for change (see, for example, Chant, 1994b). In addition, the incorporation of inter-generational perspectives would be helpful: the effects of increased employment and new jobs for women may clearly take a generation or two to filter through to society in any generalised sense; moreover, it is important to explore the effects of women's employment and household and migratory corollaries on sons and daughters.

EXPORT-ORIENTED EMPLOYMENT: THE DILEMMAS FACING WOMEN AND THE ROLE OF POLICY

Although further enquiry into a number of aspects relating to export-oriented employment and women's status is necessary, the present study has been able to reveal that the various outcomes and implications for women of this type of development strategy are by no means straightforward, with benefits in one sphere often undermined in another (see Chapter 7). Moreover, it is possible to see that female labour demand in all sectors is predicated on gender inequalities of one form or another which tend to remain and/or reconstitute themselves, if not in the workplace, then in other dimensions of women's lives.

Given these problems, it is important to ask whether there are policy interventions which could help to soften the worst inequities of export-oriented development, bearing in mind that these themselves are likely to face obstacles. One major constraint to gender-aware policy formulation and implementation, for example, is that in any society the state is not a neutral or altruistic entity: instead it represents particular interests and almost invariably acts to reinforce male hegemony (see Alvarez, 1990; Chant, 1992b:205; Charlton et al., 1989:2–12; Moghadam, 1994:109). Moreover, not only is legislation likely to reflect the needs and desires of those in closest league with the state itself, but policy may not necessarily be accompanied by effective execution and monitoring.[2] In addition, while recognising that specific policies are necessary for particular aspects of social and economic organisation, those adopted without due regard for their ramifications in other spheres may well create more problems than they solve. For example, even if strategies to attract foreign investment are designed with the idea of using female labour, whether explicitly or implicitly, this may not be feasible if women continue to face barriers to their involvement in the workforce on grounds relating to specific factors such as family legislation and fertility control, quite apart from social attitudes circumscribing female roles.[3] Attempts to improve the status of women in export-oriented employment must therefore embrace all facets of their lives, not just those relating to the workplace. This also highlights the need not only to address the pragmatic and/or material circumstances of women in terms of pay, working conditions and so on, but

---

2 A number of issues are relevant here. One relates to the means ensuring that policy recommendations and/or legislative measures are actually adhered to by the parties involved (here it may be necessary to institute 'watchdog committees', similar to the Law Promoting the Social Equality for Women in Costa Rica – see, for example, Chant, 1991b; McIlwaine, 1993: Chapter 3). Additionally, it is necessary to ensure that policy initiatives do not end up damaging those they aim to help. Here the issue of protective legislation for working women has been seen as particularly open to abuse. For instance, legislative clauses precluding female workers from participation in night shifts, exposure to 'dangerous' conditions and the like, often militate against women's full incorporation into the workforce and may also result in their replacement by male labour in an attempt to circumvent regulations (see Anker and Hein, 1986:16–19; Brydon and Chant, 1993:185; Rohini, 1991:269; Tidalgo, 1985:365).

3 Jean Pyle (1990:157–8), for example, points out in relation to Ireland that although employment policies based on export-led development between 1961 and 1981 ostensibly encouraged women to enter the labour force, participation rates remained low. This is partly because family law continued to identify women's main obligations within the household as those of wife and mother, and partly because contraception and abortion remained unattainable, with the result that women's high fertility persisted and most had to continue to devote the vast majority of their time to childcare.

to deal with the ideological underpinnings of gender inequalities which allot them to these positions in the first place (see below; also Moghadam, 1994:109–10). Specific changes such as relaxing restrictions on divorce, granting women full reproductive rights and control over their fertility,[4] and ensuring that the sectors in which women are employed are fully entitled to unionisation (see Reyes, 1992:47–8; also Chapter 1), would obviously represent critical first steps in this direction.

We saw in Chapter 1, of course, that gender has increasingly been taken into consideration by the Philippine state since the late 1980s, with the revision of the Family Code, the inauguration of the Philippine Development Plan for Women, the outlawing of the mail-order bride business and recommendations for the provision of community-based childcare facilities (see also Reyes, 1992:45–6). However, we also noted that while these initiatives may have brought gender issues more squarely into the public arena, they are still regarded as overly piecemeal, compartmentalised and subordinate to overall policies operating in a gender-blind, not to mention gender-unequal, decision-making environment (Eviota, 1992:155; Reyes, 1992:47–8). Despite attempts to counter this tendency, particularly through lobbying on the part of such coalitions as the Ad Hoc Committee on a Women's Legislative Agenda,[5] the full integration of gender into public policy formulation remains a long way off (see Reyes, 1992:58).

One major, and probably inevitable, obstacle to achieving this goal is that 'women's interests' are often highly diverse, not least within the Philippines, where more radical elements of the women's movement have historically distanced themselves from working within the state

---

4 Women's reproductive rights and control over fertility management are currently characterised by extreme contradictions. On the one hand, abortion is prohibited (see Chapter 1), yet on the other, government incentives such as tax exemptions, discounts on hospital fees, exemption from application expenses for local and foreign jobs and cash rewards for those submitting themselves to sterilisation (or vasectomy) are provided for couples who have limited their number of children to two or less (see Reyes, 1992:47). Given the strength of the Roman Catholic Church and its opposition to abortion, these contradictions are likely to continue in the future.

5 The Ad Hoc Committee on a Women's Legislative Agenda (later named Samasamang Inisyatiba ng Kababaihan para sa Pagbabago ng Batas at Lipunan/SIBOL) highlights six major components to be prioritised and around which strategies must be developed to lobby Congress for legislative action. These include women in agriculture; violence against women; marriage and the family; health and reproduction; work/labour; and education, culture and political participation (see Reyes, 1992:48).

apparatus and have instead preferred to put pressure on the government from the outside (see, for example, Israel-Sobritchea, 1994). Apart from the danger of 'appropriation and reinterpretation of the feminist agenda by conservative elements' (ibid.), therefore, there is also the difficulty that more progressive initiatives might be curbed by lack of unity among different feminist factions.

Moreover, while policies regarding gender might be devised and introduced, as with other policies, they are based on a so-called indicative system (Tidalgo, 1985:355) whereby the government compiles a formal document outlining national goals which it then tries to convince the private sector to adopt. Thus the likelihood of private capitalists adopting the Philippine Development Plan for Women is obviously a long shot unless doing this serves the interests of such groups. Indeed, government policy in general tends to be prognostic, providing only recommendations rather than concrete legislative initiatives, with very little in the way of follow up (viz. the widespread disregard of minimum wage laws; see Chapters 4–6). One of the most striking examples of the kind of contradictions arising from lack of policy enforcement (and integration) is the Philippines 2000 Development Plan, whereby the interests of foreign investors and Filipino businessmen have been served by strategies to liberalise the economy and encourage the continued pursuit of export-led development; at the same time women are expected to power these operations in the workplace as well as picking up the tab (in their roles as reproductive labour) of rising prices and reduced real incomes within the home (Taganahan, 1993; WRCC, 1993b; see also Moghadam, 1994:108). In fact, one major current debate among women's groups in the country revolves around whether the Philippines should adopt inward-looking, agriculturally-based development strategies in order to avoid outright exploitation of the female population (Taganahan, 1993; WRCC, 1993b; see also Israel-Sobritchea, 1994).

Yet, although it is clear that significant profits accrue from reliance on female labour, in both productive and reproductive domains, there should perhaps be slightly greater acknowledgement, as indicated in this book, that some benefits might be reaped by women from their involvement in export-oriented employment. It is also important to recognise that alternative development strategies might not be much less exploitative (indeed agriculture, whether cash crop or subsistence, is probably even more dominated by men than urban-based activities are). In addition, the complete withdrawal of foreign investment may not be in the interests of either male or female Filipinos; first, because of the sheer numbers of jobs that would be lost in the formal sector; and second, because of the knock-on effect in informal activities integrally linked with export-manufacturing and tourism (see Chapters 5 and 7).

Debt relief

The debate on the Philippines 2000 policy also raises the more general issue of how international, as well as national, factors need to be taken into consideration, especially since so many foreign interests are served in the process of export-led growth (multilateral financial institutions, investors, industrialists, tourists, consumers of sexual services and so on). One important area of policy potentially linking national and inter-national initiatives is that relating to the country's immense debt burden. As noted in Chapter 2, organisations such as the Freedom from Debt Coalition are keen to achieve reductions in debt service payments, to write off the loans diverted to personal projects under the Marcos regime and to persuade creditors to accept tougher terms from the Philippine government (see also FFDC, 1992:110). Although the United Nations, among others, has taken a series of small steps to address the problems of the debt crisis, developing countries have so far had little international support for their crippling economic difficulties (see, for example, Espiritu, 1992). This highlights a gap which global col-laboration could go some way to fill.

International migration

Another, more specific, area meriting bilateral and multilateral action, and one which is heavily linked to Philippine debt, is overseas migration. As discussed in Chapter 1, approximately half of all overseas contract workers from the Philippines are women, and whether they migrate abroad as domestic servants, nurses or entertainment workers, gender inequalities permeate every aspect of their movement. Not only is women's international migration per se motivated by poverty within the Philippines and by gender differentials in responsibilities for natal kin or their own dependents, but the women often end up in jobs which are of considerably lower status than their educational attain-ments suggest they could achieve, and frequently have to put up with extremely poor working and living conditions (see, for instance, CIIR, 1987a; Tacoli, 1994). Women are also often at the mercy of private, and often illegal, recruiters who charge exorbitant placement fees and may send workers to jobs which differ from those they applied for, such as prostitution (see Chapter 1; also Alexander, 1988:200; CIIR, 1987a:26–8). Here the Philippine government could clearly play a more active role not only in ensuring that existing legislation regarding overseas migration is adhered to, but in monitoring what women end up doing and in helping them gain redress for grievances. At present, abuses relating to overseas workers are the responsibility of labour attachés of understaffed consulates who may not have the requisite expertise or jurisdiction to contest the laws of host countries (see Santos and Lee, 1992:66).

Positive action by receiving countries in their treatment of immigrant workers is also essential,[6] not to mention the role of international agencies and pressure groups. In order to raise awareness of the violence and abuses faced by Filipino workers overseas, for example, in 1994 Babaylan (Philippine Women's Network in Europe) launched a year-long campaign entitled 'Violence No More!', where efforts were made to stimulate consciousness of violence among women; to feed information to the European Women's Lobby and the Women's Committee of the Migrant Women Forum in an attempt to ensure that European Union policies on migrants address the issue of violence; and to lobby the United Nations (see also note 6 above).

Employment interventions

Indeed, the UN might be expected to play a particularly important part in this, given its comparatively prominent concern with women's rights, evidenced in the Decade for Women (1975–85) and its

6 One example of initiatives being taken in developed countries is the Early Day Motion in the British House of Commons. This calls for overseas domestic workers (of whom the majority are Filipinas) to be granted immigrant status; it was signed by 160 MPs in April 1994 after pressure from KALAYAAN (the campaign for justice for overseas workers). As the law stands at present, wealthy foreign nationals and expatriates are permitted to bring domestic servants to Britain on tourist visas, effectively denying them any rights to leave their employers and laying them open to abuse and deportation if they try to infringe their contracts. The European Parliament Civil Liberties Committee is also expected to intervene to step up the pressure on the British government to change existing legislation (article in *Philippines Information Exchange*, no.2, April 1994, p.2).

Convention on the Elimination of all Forms of Discrimination against Women (1979). In addition, the United Nations' concern for prostituted women, illustrated by its 1949 Convention for the Suppression of Traffic in Persons and the Exploitation of the Prostitution of Others (to which 59 countries had subscribed by 1988), could be extremely helpful in putting pressure on unscrupulous operators in the international sex trade and in encouraging state action (Pietilä and Vickers, 1990:117–8). Although relatively few countries have ratified the 1949 Convention and prostitution continues to persist with equal, if not more, vigour today than half a century ago, such measures are important, with Pietilä and Vickers (1990:118) pointing out that the Convention

gives international justification to attempts to spotlight these and other related problems (such as the sexual harassment and exploitation of women workers in transnational corporations in developing countries), and like all other intergovernmental conventions provides a strong, legitimate basis for people to put pressure on governments to take adequate remedial measures.[7]

The actions of bodies such as the International Labour Office are also important in terms of putting pressure on employers to comply with minimum norms for working hours, wages and so on. Of particular relevance to the present study is the ILO's Convention on Equal Remuneration for Men and Women Workers for Work of Equal Value. Although this was adopted in 1951, and by 1988 had still not been signed by several countries with export processing zones (Korea, Malaysia, Singapore, Sri Lanka, Thailand, for example – see G.Standing, 1989:1082), the fact remains that pressure of this nature is an essential component of women's struggle for justice on a global scale.

ALTERNATIVE POLICIES: INTERNATIONAL PRESSURE AND GRASSROOTS ORGANISATIONS

In view of the constraints encountered through institutionalised ways of bringing about change in society, there is obviously also a need to look elsewhere for ways in which to address problems. Perhaps in

---

7 It should also be noted, however, that without effective international monitoring (in the form of an international inspectorate with powers to override national governments, for example) little may be achieved (see Kent, 1991:80–1 on child prostitution and the UN Convention on the Rights of the Child).

particular need of attention from alternative initiatives is sex work, where problems in the industry are largely ignored by national governments.

The sex trade and international tourism

One of the major international actors in this domain is the Ecumenical Coalition on Third World Tourism, which is widely involved in fighting campaigns against the more exploitative aspects of the sex industry at an international level. Operating in conjunction with other religious and human rights groups, the ECTWT has succeeded in putting significant pressure on various countries in the developed world to modify their treatment of sex trade migrants. For example, the Coalition petitioned the Swiss government to recognise the quasi-slavery conditions of Asian 'go-go' girls brought into the country and managed to have legislation passed to abolish its most extreme forms (see Holden et al., 1983: 106; also De Stoop, 1994 on Belgium). Other groups which have been successful in reducing the extent, if not the overall operation, of international sex work within the Third World (and specifically the Philippines) include the Asian Women's Association, which campaigned to ban Japanese sex tours to the country during Prime Minister Suzuki's visit to the Philippines in 1981 (see Matsui, 1991b:102; also Chapter 2, this volume). Moreover, while the voices of prostitutes themselves have increasingly been heard on the international scene during the 1980s and 1990s, largely through the International Committee for Prostitutes Rights and the statements and charters arising from two world congresses (International Committee for Prostitutes Rights, 1988; Sturdevant and Stoltzfus, 1992c),[8] only scant attention has been paid to the plight of sex workers in developing countries, where arguably some of the most degrading aspects of prostitution occur (Sturdevant and Stoltzfus, 1992c:300–2). In view of this, the demands of Philippine women's organisations such as GABRIELA that the needs of prostitutes here and in other developing nations should

---

8 The two congresses in question (the World Whores' Congresses), which took place in 1985 and 1986, were concerned with issues of decriminalisation, regulating third parties involved in prostitution (pimps, for example), human rights, working conditions, health screening, housing and counselling services, taxation, educational programmes for the population at large, and, more broadly, how women's movements have only dealt with the sex industry and prostitutes in a marginal sense (Alexander, 1988:305–7).

be recognised as different, and as requiring alternative action sensitive to the socio-economic and cultural background to sex work (ibid.; Raquisa, 1987:222–4; also Skrobanek, 1987:212–13), are obviously vital. Again, the alleviation of poverty and uneven development is a crucial component of strategies able to forge any kind of substantial change. As Wendy Lee (1991:100) points out: 'the long-term solution to prostitution in South-East Asia involves not only a complete change in the distribution of resources between rural and urban people, but also between rich and poor nations'.

While various shifts might be initiated through formalised action, however, it is also important to recognise the valuable achievements that might be attained by changes of a personal nature among the individuals who, wittingly or otherwise, perpetrate exploitative economic and social practices. In the sphere of international tourism, for example, much might be gained from individuals adopting initiatives introduced by the ECTWT, such as the Code of Ethics for Tourists, which encourages respect and sensitivity for other cultures (see Holden et al.,1983:117–19). Still more benefits might arise from genuine change on the part of men as to how they view women and how they interact with them on a sexual basis, as well as recognising their frequent complicity with criminal activities in Third World countries (see Maurer, 1991:97).

HIV/AIDS

Related to sex tourism, although certainly not confined to this sector, is the spread of HIV/AIDS, which requires urgent and effective policy intervention at both national and global levels. While the threat of HIV/AIDS has now been recognised by the Philippine government, perceptions of the transmission of the disease (and its control) are marred by sensationalising on the part of the media and the focus on the sex industry as the major high-risk sector (see Nichter and Abellanosa, 1994). Although existing monitoring procedures and preventive education programmes provided by Social Hygiene Clinics in the country are a step in the right direction, these measures often have limited efficacy and undoubtedly need to be widened to encompass both the clients of prostitutes and the population at large (see Chapter 6; also Klouda, 1994; Nichter and Abellanosa, 1994). As it stands at present, targeted intervention effectively scapegoats sex workers and fails to cover those primarily responsible for the spread of the disease (see Maurer, 1991:97; also Chapter 6, this volume). One important starting point in altering attitudes and behaviour at an international level is to change the commonly used terminology of 'high-risk groups' to 'high risk-behaviour' (Maurer, 1991:97; see also Panos Institute, 1990:81–4). In addition, the disease is likely to continue to spread unless programmes are directed to other parties such as male tourists, not to mention the wider population (see Klouda, 1994:5–6). Policy interventions in and for specific countries like the Philippines should also be formulated in ways that are sensitive to the prevailing culture and mores, rather than replicating initiatives created for the developed world (see Klouda, 1994).

It is also important to remember that tourism in the Philippines might bear the scars and on-going problems associated with a longstanding sex trade, yet the industry is much bigger than this and the initiatives of local (and national) organisations in places like Boracay to promote a resort that is not only free of sex work but is one where development is environmentally sensitive and sustainable, should undoubtedly be encouraged and supported by international organisations (see, for example, Bramwell and Lane, 1993; McKercher, 1993; Republic of the Philippines with UNDP and WTO, 1991 for wider discussions).

Actors in export-oriented development

While it may be a relatively straightforward task to persuade international agencies to recognise gender inequalities, however, and even to convince national governments at least to pay lip service to women's exploitation, the biggest sticking point is likely to be foreign investors and employers whose actions are invariably driven by the pursuit of profit, and who frequently exploit and intensify existing inequities. While it may not be necessary to halt the recruitment of female labour in export sector activity, women workers should at least be granted equal entitlement to the pay, conditions and promotion prospects that accrue to their male counterparts.

It is also important to recognise that export-oriented activities do not necessarily need to be large-scale and dominated by multinational capital. As noted earlier in the book, women in international tourism resorts often build up profitable businesses under their own steam and with state assistance could probably do even more see (Chapter 5). Indeed, one interesting example of state- and NGO-backed initiatives of this description is the income-generating projects which have taken place in the former base areas of Olongapo and Angeles with the aim of providing alternative livelihoods for women who have depended on the sex trade (see WEDPRO 1990a, 1990b). These schemes are important insofar as they have attempted to integrate small-scale projects with larger economic, environmental and feminist goals, to tap previously under-utilised resources and to incorporate women's own views into the programmes (see also Chen, 1989 on the value of linking women's projects with larger sectoral objectives). Specific 'bottom-up' initiatives have included the cultivation and processing of mushrooms (an activity designed to reduce dependence on expensive canned imports), and the production of handmade paper out of rice straw (less ecologically destructive than timber-based manufacture). Another project, the design and production of educational and non-sex-typed toys, games and materials for children, deals more specifically with 'strategic' as well as 'practical' gender needs (see Molyneux, 1986:284; Moser, 1993a:38–41 for discussions and references about gender needs): not only does this initiative attempt to reduce gender inequalities, it also tries to instigate change on an intergenerational basis. Again, by taking women's own ideas into consideration, it assists in furthering their empowerment.

Empowerment for women?

The 'empowerment approach' to development for women is discussed at length by Moser (1993a) as one in which change is initiated by women themselves with a minimum of outside intervention (at least of a proactive, top-down nature), and where power accrues through self-reliance and internal strength (ibid.:74-5). More specifically, 'Women's subordination is seen not only as the problem of men but also of colonial and neo-colonial oppression. It recognises women's triple role, and seeks to meet strategic gender needs indirectly through bottom-up mobi-lization around practical gender needs' (ibid.:74).

What must also be taken into consideration, therefore, is the role men play in this scenario, in that any major change can only come about through their involvement. If men are also integrated into the same development initiatives, then there may be scope for greater col-laboration. If, on the other hand, men are excluded (as they often are from employment opportunities in the large-scale export sector, for example), then, as noted in Chapter 7, greater polarisation between the sexes might develop (see also Safilios-Rothschild, 1990:227). Indeed, while recruitment into export-oriented activities per se is usually predicated on gender inequalities, it often has the effect of diminishing the divide between male and female roles, yet a counter-implication is frequently greater alienation in terms of men's and women's relations with one another, in the home as well as in the workplace. For this reason, gender-aware development that empowers women will also need to address the issue of male employment opportunities, with the actions of the state and investors likely to be vital in this regard.

At the end of the day, however, women themselves need to decide what is right for them; indeed, despite their traditional lack of formal representation in institutions of the state and global governance, they have done remarkably well in acting on their own behalf thus far. As Valentine Moghadam (1994:110) points out: 'the women's rights movement around the world has highlighted gender oppression, encouraged activists, brought pressure to bear on elites and governments, led to important changes in legislation and social policy, and in many countries, created a significant new constituency – women'.

Moghadam adds that women's increasing role in economic activity is also making their presence felt (ibid.:111). This is hardly surprising, since women are clearly contributing to accumulation at a global scale, not just in the Philippines. For this growth to be converted to development in a fuller, more humane sense, the Philippine state (and others in similar positions) should ensure that multinational investment comes with firm guarantees of how long it will stay in the country, whether it will be involved in sustainable activities, if the degree of transfer of skills and technology is substantial, and whether multiplier effects are likely. Moreover, it is vital to explore whether such investment will have positive or negative effects on gender inequalities, and in the event of the latter, what might be done to ensure that these do not end up seriously weakening women's positions in society. For this, of course, it is necessary for gender awareness and concern to permeate the hearts and minds not only of government agencies and hegemonic groups within the Philippines, but those of men, women and the economies and institutions they support at an international level. Until such time, the true worth of female labour in the Visayas will remain obscured and undervalued, the 'lesser cost' for those who utilise it achieved at the greater expense of the personal and working lives of the women involved.

APPENDIX: METHODOLOGY

The bulk of the material on which this book is based comes from a series of surveys conducted by the authors with individuals and/or groups in Cebu, Lapu-Lapu and Boracay during 1993. The surveys fall into five main categories, brief details of which are given below. Further information, together with copies of the household and employer questionnaires and topic guides for semi-structured interviews, is available from Sylvia Chant at the London School of Economics on request.

1. HOUSEHOLD SURVEY

The household survey elicited information on socio-economic and demographic characteristics of low-income groups in the three study centres. It comprised two parts: a structured questionnaire survey applied to a total of 240 households, and a sub-sample of in-depth interviews with respondents in 30 of these. The chief purpose of these interviews was to generate an overview of household survival and gender roles and relations among the poor which would act as a basis of comparison with the migration and household characteristics of workers in specific occupational groups (export manufacturing, tourism and sex work – see below). The data from the questionnaire interviews were computer-coded and analysed. The semi-structured household interviews, on the other hand, gathered information of a more qualitative nature, with particular attention paid to reconstructing women's life-histories in a manner that allowed the interrelations between their demographic, household and employment circumstances to be examined over time and across space. The findings of the household survey are introduced in Chapter 3 and are referred to at various points in the text thereafter.

Household definition

A household was defined as a group of people living under the same roof and sharing basic tasks of consumption and reproduction, accepting that constituent individuals' participation in these activities might not always be equal (see Brydon and Chant, 1993:8–10; Chapter 1). Households usually comprised people related by blood or marriage, but sometimes consisted of unrelated members such as friends or co-workers. The typology of household structure utilised embraces varying combinations of both headship and composition; it is based on a classification originally presented by Brydon and Chant (1993: 134–9), and further developed by Chant (1991a:234–5) with regard to work on low-income households in Mexico and subsequently in Costa Rica (Chant, 1991b:64–6).

Typology of household structure

- Nuclear (male-headed unit consisting of a couple and their children)
- Male extended (nuclear core unit with additional relatives)
- Female-headed one-parent (woman living alone with her children; sometimes referred to in text as single-parent, solo-parent or lone-parent)
- Female extended (one-parent unit with additional relatives)
- Couple (male–female union without children)
- Grandmother-headed (female head living alone with grandchildren and no intermediate generation)
- Grandfather-headed (couple living alone with grandchildren and no intermediate generation)
- Single-person (male or female living alone)
- Single-sex (members of the same sex, usually unrelated, living without children)
- Brother/sister (male/female siblings living without children)
- Semi-family (core nuclear, one-parent or extended unit also incorporating unrelated members, such as lodgers, work colleagues or apprentices)

2. WORKER SURVEY

The worker survey was carried out among a total of 77 employees in the three key sectors in the Visayan study centres: export manufacturing, international tourism and sex work (see Tables A2.1–3). The aim of the survey was to explore the household circumstances, migration characteristics and employment conditions of different occupational groups (much along the lines of the household survey) and to see how these compared with the population in general (especially women).

Drawing respondents from the workplace, rather than the household, allowed the inclusion of certain groups such as sex workers, hotel and restaurant staff residing in their places of employment as live-ins and/or factory operatives in boarding house lodgings, who might otherwise have proved difficult to trace. The worker interviews (which are utilised mainly in Chapters 4 to 6) also provide a counterpoint to the information given by managers and personnel officers in the employer survey (see below).

Table A2.1: Worker sample in export manufacturing firms, Cebu and Lapu-Lapu

Locality	Firm type	No. of respondents and job types	
		Female	Male
Cebu	Fashion accessories	5 (assemblers, packers)	–
	Rattan furniture and handicrafts	3 (cutters, finishers)	4 (sanders, dyers, framers)
Lapu-Lapu (MEPZ)	Electronics	3 (assemblers, recorders)	–
	Garments	2 (sewers)	4 (sewers, cutters, stockman)
	Wood products	3 (splicers)	–

Table A2.2: Worker sample in tourism establishments, Boracay and Cebu

Locality	Establishment/activity	No. of respondents and job types Female	Male
FORMAL			
Boracay	Hotels	6 (chambermaids, waitresses)	2 (cook, room boy)
	Restaurants	3 (waitresses, cashiers)	1 (waiter)
	Shops	4 (sales assistants)	–
Cebu	Hotels, restaurants	5 (chambermaids, cashiers, sales assistants)	2 (waiter, bartender)
INFORMAL			
Boracay	Beach-vending	11 (manicurists, masseuses, handicraft vendors, T-shirt vendors)	3 (ice-cream vendor, newspaper vendor, handicraft vendor)

Table A2.3: Worker sample in entertainment establishments, Cebu City

Establishment	Job	Female	Male
Girlie bar	Dancers	6	–
	Hostess	1	–
	Waitress/bartender	1	1
Karaoke bar	Guest-relations lady	1	–
	Mamasan	1	–
Cultural cabaret	Dancers	2	–
	Waitress	1	–
	Choreographer		1
Massage parlour	Masseuse	1	–

3.   EMPLOYER SURVEY

The employer survey was conducted among 38 owners or personnel managers in Cebu, Lapu-Lapu and Boracay (22 in export-oriented manufacturing firms and 16 in tourism establishments). The aim of the survey was to generate information on the nature of labour demand within key sectors of employment, incorporating details on company structure, recruitment policies, labour practices and workforce composition, especially with regard to gender segregation, segmentation and occupational mobility. This information forms a major part of our substantive sections on employment in Chapters 4 and 5.

Entertainment establishments were excluded from the employer survey, following advice from Filipino colleagues who pointed to a range of difficulties, if not dangers, associated with openly interviewing the industry's operators. To compensate for this omission, discussions were held with floor managers in Cebu-based establishments, alongside interviews here and in Boracay with actual and potential consumers of sexual services (i.e. male tourists, businessmen, visitors and expatriates). The latter gave an idea of the nature of demand for female labour insofar as their preferences and predilections undoubtedly play a role in influencing establishments' recruiting policies.

4.   INTERVIEWS WITH TARGET AUXILIARIES

While the household, worker and employer surveys form the bulk of the data gathered in the three study localities, additional interviews were held with what we collectively termed 'target auxiliary' organisations or personnel, using an informal, open-ended format. Seven main groups of auxiliaries were involved in this aspect of the research, and these inteviews are drawn upon at various junctures in Chapters 3 to 6. The groups included: consumers of sexual services/male tourists (see Tables 6.1 and 6.2); tour operators; business associations; trade union officials; boarding house owners; women's groups/non-governmental organisations; and government bodies related to the hospitality sector (for instance, the Social Hygiene Clinic in Cebu).

5. INTERVIEWS IN MIGRANT SOURCE AREAS

Given the tendency for rural–urban migration in the Philippines to be female-dominated (see Chapter 1), we conducted a survey of 20 households in two rural communities in the Visayas to assess the impacts of female out-migration on migrant source areas. The survey's particular concerns were to discover how household organisation and welfare were affected by the departure of larger numbers of female than male migrants, and how men who remained behind reacted to the resultant imbalance. The results appear in our review of migration in Chapter 3.

BIBLIOGRAPHY

Abbott, Gary and Panos (1992), Along for the Ride: HIV and Sex Tourism. In *WorldAIDS*, 20, 5–8.

Abbu, Gloricris (1991), Factors Affecting Utilisation of Maternal and Child Health Care Services in Selected Urban Poor Communities: Analysis from Household Survey Data. Thesis submitted for partial fulfilment of MA degree in economics, University of the Philippines: Quezon City.

Abenoja, Macrina (1982), Tables of Working Life for Filipino Males and Females in 1980: Regional Estimates. In *Philippine Quarterly of Culture and Society*, 10: 1 and 2, 45–97.

Addison, Tony and Demery, Lionel (1988), Wages and Labour Conditions in East Asia: A Review of Case Study Evidence. In *Development Policy Review*, 6, 371–93.

Adkins, Lisa (1993), Hors d'Oeuvres. In *Tourism in Focus*, 10 (special issue on Women and Tourism Development), 6–7.

Aguado, Rex (1988), Division of Labour. In *Midweek*, 4 May, 9–11.

Aguilar, Delia (1988), *The Feminist Challenge: Initial Working Principles towards Reconceptualising the Feminist Movement in the Philippines*, Asian Social Institute in cooperation with the World Association for Christian Communication: Manila.

Aguilar, Delia (1991), *Filipino Housewives Speak*, Rainfree Trading and Publishing: Manila.

Alcid, Mary Lou (1989), The Recruitment Process of Filipina Domestic Helpers in Hong Kong, Singapore and Saudi Arabia. In Asian and Pacific Development Centre (ed.), *The Trade in Domestic Helpers: Causes, Mechanisms and Consequences*, APDC: Kuala Lumpur, 255–71.

Aldana, Cornelia A. (1989), *A Contract for Underdevelopment: Subcontracting for Multinationals in the Philippine Semiconductor and Garment Industries*, IBON Databank Phil: Manila.

Aleta, Isabel; Silva, Teresita; and Eleazar, Christine (1977), *A Profile of Filipino Women*, Capitol Publishing: Quezon City.

Alexander, Priscilla (1988), Prostitution: A Difficult Issue for Feminists. In Frédérique Delacoste and Priscilla Alexander (eds), *Sex Work: Writings by Women in the Sex Industry*, Virago: London, 184–214.

Alvarez, Sonia (1990), *Engendering Democracy in Brazil: Women's Movements in Transition Politics*, Princeton University Press: Princeton, NJ.

Amnesty International (1991), *Philippines: Human Rights Violations and the Labour Movement*, International Secretariat, Amnesty International: London.

Angeles, Leonora (1990), Women's Roles and Status in the Philippines: A Historical Perspective. In Margorie Evasco, Aurora Javate de Dios and Flor Caagusan (eds), *Women's Springbook: Readings on Women and Society*, Fresam Press: Quezon City, 15–24.

Anker, Richard and Hein, Catherine (1986), Introduction and Overview. In Richard Anker and Catherine Hein (eds), *Sex Inequalities in Urban Employment in the Third World*, Macmillan: Basingstoke, 1–56.

Anti-Slavery Society (1983), *The Philippines: Authoritarian Government, Multinationals and Ancestral Lands*, Indigenous Peoples and Development Series, Anti-Slavery Society: London.

Appleton, Simon (1991), Gender Dimensions of Structural Adjustment: The Role of Economic Theory and Quantitative Analysis. In *IDS Bulletin* (Sussex), 22:1, 17–22.

Armstrong, Warwick and McGee T.G. (1985), *Theatres of Accumulation: Studies in Asian and Latin American Urbanisation*, Methuen: London.

Asia Partnership for Human Development [APHD] (1985), *Awake: Asian Women and their Struggle for Justice*, APHD: Sydney.

Asian Development Bank [ADB] (1993), *Asian Development Outlook 1993*, Oxford University Press: Oxford.

Azarcon de la Cruz, Pennie (1985), *Filipinas for Sale: An Alternative Philippine Report on Women and Tourism*, Philippine Women's Research Collective: Quezon City.

Badger, Anne (1993), Why Not Acknowledge Women? In *Tourism in Focus*, 10 (special issue on Women and Tourism Development), 2–3 and 5.

Bagasao, Teresita Marie (1992), Streetchildren for Sale in the Philippines. In *WorldAIDS*, 20, 7.

Ballescas, Ma Rosario Piquero (1993), Reconciling Growth and Development: The Labor Situation in Cebu. In *Data Links* (Cebu Data Bank, University of the Philippines Cebu College), 2:2, 1–8.

Banzon-Bautista, Ma Cynthia Rose (1989), Studies of Women in terms of Socio-cultural Dimensions. In Amaryllis Torres (ed.), *The Filipino Woman in Focus: A Handbook of Reading*, UNESCO: Bangkok.

Barbieri, Teresita and de Oliveira, Orlandina (1989), Reproducción de la Fuerza de Trabajo en América Latina: Algunas Hipótesis. In Martha Schteingart (ed.), *Las Ciudades Latinoamericanos en la Crisis*, Editorial Trillas: Mexico DF, 19–29.

Bello, Walden (1993), The Philippine Government Plan in the Context of Asian Experience. Paper presented at joint CIIR/LSE forum 'The Philippines: A NIC by the Year 2000?', London School of Economics, 30 November 1993.

Benería, Lourdes and Roldan, Martha (1987), *The Crossroads of Class and Gender: Industrial Homework, Subcontracting and Household Dynamics in Mexico City*, University of Chicago Press, Chicago.

Birindelli, Anna Maria (1988), La Presenza a Roma degli Stranieri Proveniente de alcune aree dell'Africa e dell'Asia: Risultati Preliminari dell'Indagine. In *Studi Emigrazione*, xxv:91–2, 389–99.

Blanc-Szanton, Cristina (1990), Collision of Cultures: Historical Reformulations of Gender in the Lowland Visayas. In Jane A. Atkinson and Sherry Errinston (eds), *Power and Difference*, Stanford University Press: Stanford, CA, 345–83.

Blumberg, Rae Lesser (1978), The Political Economy of the Mother–Child Family Revisited. In André Marks and René Römer (eds), *Family and Kinship in Middle America and the Caribbean*, University of the Netherlands Antilles and Department of Caribbean Studies, Royal Institute of Linguistics and Anthropology: Leiden, 526–75.

Blumberg, Rae Lesser (1989), Towards a Feminist Theory of Development. In Ruth Wallace (ed.), *Feminism and Sociological Theory*, Sage: Newbury Park, 161–99.

Blumberg, Rae Lesser (ed.), (1991a), *Gender, Family and Economy: The Triple Overlap*, Sage: Newbury Park.

Blumberg, Rae Lesser (1991b), Introduction. The 'Triple Overlap' of Gender Stratification, Economy and the Family. In Rae Lesser Blumberg (ed.), *Gender, Family and Economy: The Triple Overlap*, Sage: Newbury Park, 7–32.

Blumberg, Rae Lesser (1991c), Income under Female Versus Male Control: Hypotheses from a Theory of Gender Stratification and Data from the Third World. In Rae Lesser Blumberg (ed.), *Gender, Family and Economy: The Triple Overlap*, Sage: Newbury Park, 97–127.

Blumberg, Rae Lesser with García, María Pilar (1977), The Political Economy of the Mother–Child Family: A Cross-Societal View. In Luis Leñero-Otero (ed.), *Beyond the Nuclear Family Model*, Sage: London, 99–163.

Board of Investments [BOI]/Private Investment and Trade Opportunities–Philippines [PITO–P] (1991), *Primer: Foreign Investments Act 1991*, BOI/PITO-P: Manila.

Boyd, Monica (1989), Family and Personal Networks in International Migration: Recent Developments and New Agendas. In *International Migration Review*, xxiii:3, 638–79.

Bradshaw, Sarah (1994), Female-headed Households in Honduras: Formation, Survival and Self-Perception in Rural and Urban Areas. PhD thesis in preparation, Department of Geography, London School of Economics.

Bradshaw, Sarah (forthcoming), Women's Access to Employment and the Formation of Female-headed Households in Rural and Urban Honduras. In *Bulletin of Latin American Research*, 13.

Bramwell, Bill and Lane, Bernard (1993), Sustainable Tourism: An Evolving Global Approach. In *Journal of Sustainable Tourism*, 1:1, 1–5.

Bruce, Judith and Lloyd, Cynthia (1992), *Finding the Ties that Bind: Beyond Headship and the Household*, International Center for Research on Women: Washington DC.

Bruegel, Irene (1979), Women as a Reserve Army of Labour: A Note on Recent British Experience. In *Feminist Review*, 3, 12–23.

Brydon, Lynne (1987), Who Moves? Women and Migration in West Africa in the 1980s. In Jeremy Eades (ed.), *Migrants, Workers and the Social Order*, Association of Social Anthropologists Monograph no.26, Tavistock: London, 165–80.

Brydon, Lynne and Chant, Sylvia (1993), *Women in the Third World: Gender Issues in Rural and Urban Areas*, (reprinted ed.; first publ. 1989), Edward Elgar: Aldershot.

Buang, Amriah (1993), Development and Factory Women: Negative Perceptions from a Malaysian Source Area. In Janet Momsen and Vivian Kinnaird (eds), *Different Places, Different Voices: Gender and Development in Africa, Asia and Latin America*, Routledge: London, 197–210.

Bucoy, Rhodora (1992), Some Notes on the Status of Women in Cebu. In *Review of Women's Studies* (University of the Philippines, Quezon City), 3:1, 33–50.

Bucoy, Rhodora (1993), Some Insights into Labor Unionism in Cebu. In *Data Links* (Cebu Data Bank, University of the Philippines Cebu College), 2:2, 9–12.

Buenaventura-Ojeda, Amparo (1973), Barrio Luz: The Impact of Urbanisation on the Socioeconomic Structure and its Implications for Institutional Development. Thesis submitted in partial fulfilment of a PhD degree in Anthropology, Graduate School, University of San Carlos, Cebu City.

Bureau of Women and Minors [BWM] (1985), *Exploratory Survey on the Skills Training Needs of Rural Women in a Selected Area*, BWM, Ministry of Labor and Employment: Manila.

Bureau of Women and Young Workers [BWYW] (1986), *A Study of Working Women's Participation in Industrial Relations*, BWYW, Ministry of Labor and Employment: Manila.

Bureau of Women and Young Workers [BWYW] (1988), *Working and Living Conditions of Domestic Helpers in Metro Manila*, BWYW, Department of Labor and Employment: Manila.

Bureau of Women and Young Workers [BWYW] (1990), *Comparative Study of Local and International Labour Standards Affecting Women and Young Workers*, BWYW, Department of Labor and Employment: Manila.

Buvinić, Mayra and Gupta, Geeta Rao (1993), Responding to Insecurity in the 1990s: Targeting Woman-headed Households and Woman-maintained Families in Developing Countries. Paper presented at the international workshop 'Insecurity in the 1990s: Gender and Social Policy in an International Perspective', London School of Economics and European Association of Development Institute, London, 5–6 April 1993.

Buvinić, Mayra; Valenzuela, Juan Pablo; Molina, Temistocles; and González, Electra (1992), The Fortunes of Adolescent Mothers and their Children: The Transmission of Poverty in Santiago, Chile. In *Population and Development Review*, 18:2, 269–97.

Cammack, Paul; Pool, David; and Tordoff, William (1993), *Third World Politics: A Comparative Introduction* (2nd edn.), Macmillan: Basingstoke.

Canlas, Mamerto (1988), The Political Context. In Mamerto Canlas, Mariano Miranda and James Putzel, *Land, Poverty and Politics in the Philippines*, Catholic Institute for International Relations: London, 71–87.

Canlas, Mamerto; Miranda, Mariano; and Putzel, James (1988), *Land, Poverty and Politics in the Philippines*, Catholic Institute for International Relations: London.

Carney, Larry and O'Kelly, Charlotte (1990), Women's Work and Women's Place in the Japanese Economic Miracle. In Kathryn Ward (ed.), *Women Workers and Global Restructuring*, ILR Press, Cornell University: Ithaca, NY, 113–45.

Casinader, Rex; Fernando, Sepalika; and Gamage, Karuna (1987), Women's Issues and Men's Roles: Sri Lankan Village Experience. In Janet Momsen and Janet Townsend (eds), *Geography of Gender in the Third World*, Hutchinson: London, 309–22.

Castillo, Gelia (1991), Family and Household: The Microworld of the Filipino. In Department of Sociology-Anthropology (eds), *SA 21: Selected Readings*, Office of Research and Publications, Ateneo de Manila University: Quezon City, 244–50.

Catholic Institute for International Relations [CIIR] (1987a), *The Labour Trade: Filipino Migrant Workers around the World*, CIIR: London.

Catholic Institute for International Relations [CIIR] (1987b), *European Companies in the Philippines*, CIIR: London.

Cebu Chamber of Commerce and Industry [CCCI] (1992), *Cebu Business Directory*, CCCI: Cebu City.

Cebu Chamber of Commerce and Industry [CCCI] (1993), Philippine Trade and Industrial Policy: Latin American Mode. In *Cebu Business*, 4:3, 3 (report condensed from Paul Krugman et al., 'Transforming the Philippine Economy', produced by the Philippines Exporters Confederation: Manila).

Center for Social Policy and Public Affairs [CSPPA] (1989), *The Implications of a Minimum Wage and Regional Wage Fixing*, CSPPA, Ateneo de Manila University: Quezon City.

Central Book Supply, Inc. [CBSI] (1990), *The Revised Penal Code: Act no. 3815 as Amended* (18th edn.), CBSI: Manila.

de la Cerna, Madrileña (1992), Women Empowering Women: The Cebu Experience. In *Review of Women's Studies* (University of the Philippines, Quezon City), 3:1, 51–66.

Chant, Sylvia (1985), Single-parent Families: Choice or Constraint? The Formation of Female-headed Households in Mexican Shanty Towns. In *Development and Change*, 16:4, 635–56.

Chant, Sylvia (1991a), *Women and Survival in Mexican Cities: Perspectives on Gender, Labour Markets and Low-Income Households*, Manchester University Press: Manchester.

Chant, Sylvia (1991b), Gender, Households and Seasonal Migration in Guanacaste, Costa Rica. In *European Review of Latin American and Caribbean Studies*, 50, 51–85.

Chant, Sylvia (1992a), Migration at the Margins: Gender, Poverty and Population Movement on the Costa Rican Periphery. In Sylvia Chant (ed.), *Gender and Migration in Developing Countries*, Belhaven: London, 109–38.

Chant, Sylvia (1992b), Conclusion: Towards a Framework for the Analysis of Gender-Selective Migration. In Sylvia Chant (ed.), *Gender and Migration in Developing Countries*, Belhaven: London, 197–206.

Chant, Sylvia (1992c), Tourism in Latin America: Perspectives from Mexico and Costa Rica. In David Harrison (ed.), *Tourism and the Less Developed Countries*, Belhaven: London, 85–101.

Chant, Sylvia (1993a), Women's Work and Household Change in the 1980s. In Neil Harvey (ed.), *Mexico: Dilemmas of Transition*, Institute of Latin American Studies, University of London/British Academic Press: London, 318–54.

Chant, Sylvia (1993b), Working Women in Boracay. In *Tourism in Focus*, 10 (special issue on Women and Tourism Development), 8–9 and 17.

Chant, Sylvia (1994a), Women and Poverty in Urban Latin America: Mexican and Costa Rican Experiences. In Fatima Meer (ed.), *Poverty in the 1990s: The Responses of Urban Women*, UNESCO/International Social Science Council: Paris, 87–115.

Chant, Sylvia (1994b), Women, Work and Household Survival Strategies in Mexico, 1982–1992: Past Trends, Current Tendencies and Future Research. In *Bulletin of Latin American Research*, 13:2, 203–33.

Chant, Sylvia (forthcoming a), Women's Roles in Recession and Economic Restructuring in Mexico and the Philippines. In Alan Gilbert (ed.), *Poverty and Global Adjustment: The Urban Experience*, Blackwell: Oxford.

Chant, Sylvia (forthcoming b), Gender and Tourism Employment in Mexico and the Philippines. In M. Thea Sinclair (ed.), *Gender and Tourism: Cross-Country Comparisons*, Routledge: London.

Chant, Sylvia and McIlwaine, Cathy (1994), Gender and Export Manufacturing in the Philippines: Continuity or Change in Female Employment? The Case of Mactan Export Processing Zone. Paper delivered at the panel 'Negotiating Gender in the Philippines', European Conference on Philippine Studies, School of Oriental and African Studies, University of London, 13–15 April 1994.

Chant, Sylvia and Radcliffe, Sarah (1992), Introduction. Migration: The Importance of Gender. In Sylvia Chant (ed.), *Gender and Migration in Developing Countries*, Belhaven: London, 1–39.

Charlton, Sue Ellen; Everett, Jana; and Staudt, Kathleen (1989), Women, the State and Development. In Sue Ellen Charlton, Jana Everett and Kathleen Staudt (eds), *Women, the State and Development*, State University of New York Press: Albany, NY, 1–19.

Chaverría, Carmen; Elizondo, María Elena; García, Carmen; and Martínez, María del Rosario (1987), Algunas Consideraciones Sobre la Familia de Mujeres Guanacastecas Organizadas: Análisis de Tres Grupos Femininos Productivos. Thesis for Licenciado en Trabajo Social, Universidad de Costa Rica, Centro Universitario de Guanacaste: Liberia.

Chen, Marty (1989), A Sectoral Approach to Promoting Women's Work: Lessons from India. In *World Development*, 17:7, 1,007–16.

Church, A. Timothy (1986), *Filipino Personality: A Review of Research and Writings*, Monograph Series, no.6, De La Salle University Press: Manila.

Clarke, Noel (1981), A Study on Perceived Mobility: Life Experiences of Selected Families in a Cebu Squatter Community. MA thesis presented to the Faculty of the Graduate School, University of San Carlos, Cebu City.

Cleves Mosse, Julia (1993), *Half the World, Half a Chance: An Introduction to Gender and Development*, Oxfam: Oxford.

Collas-Monsod, Solita (1991), The IMF Stabilisation Programme: Implications for the Philippines. mimeo, Philippine Resource Centre: London.

Collins, Joseph (1989), *The Philippines: Fire on the Rim*, Institute for Food and Development Policy: San Francisco.

Committee for Asian Women [CAW] (ed.), (1991), *Many Paths, One Goal*, CAW: Hong Kong.

Comisión Co-ordinadora del Desarrollo de la Desembocadura del Río Ameca [COCODERA], (1980), *Programa de Ordenación de la Zona Conurbada de la Desembocadura del Río Ameca*, COCODERA: Puerto Vallarta.

Connell, John (1984), Status or Subjugation? Women, Migration and Development in the South Pacific. In *International Migration Review*, xviii:4, 964–83.

Costello, Michael; Leinbach, Thomas; and Ulack, Richard (1987), *Mobility and Employment in Urban Southeast Asia: Examples from Indonesia and the Philippines*, Westview: Boulder, CO.

Cruz, Romeo V. (1991), The Filipino at the Time of the Fil-American Revolution. In Sister Mary John Mananzan (ed.), *Essays on Women*, Institute of Women's Studies, St Scholastica's College, Manila (revised edn.), 52–56.

Cruz, Wilfrido and Repetto, Robert (1992), *The Environmental Effects of Stabilisation and Structural Adjustment Programs: The Philippines Case*, World Resources Institute: Washington DC.

Daño, Neth (1990), A Historical Look at Filipino Sexuality and the Rise of Prostitution. In *Flights*, 4:2, 7–8.

Day, Sophie (1988), Prostitute Women and AIDS: Anthropology. In *AIDS*, 2, 421–8.

De Stoop, Chris (1994), *They Are so Sweet, Sir: The Cruel World of Traffickers in Filipinas and other Women*, Limitless Asia: Belgium.

Department of Health [DOH] (1990), *The Philippine Family Planning Program (1990–1994)*, DOH: Manila.

Department of Social Welfare and Development [DSWD], National Council of Social Development Foundation of the Philippines [NSCD] and UNICEF (1988), *The Situation of Street Children in Ten Cities*, DSWD/NSCD/UNICEF: Manila.

Department of Tourism [DOT] (1991a), *Boracay Island Tourism Development Project: Environmental Impact Statement*, DOT, Office of Tourism Development Planning: Manila.

Department of Tourism [DOT] (1991b), *Summary of Accomodation Establishments in Boracay*, DOT: Manila.

Department of Tourism [DOT] (1991c), *Tourism Situation Report*, Region VII, DOT: Manila.

Department of Tourism [DOT] (1991d), *Boracay Beat: Community Bulletin*, 1:1, DOT: Boracay.

Department of Tourism [DOT] (1992a), *Boracay Island Master Development Plan: Final Report*, Boracay Inter-Agency Development Project Team, DOT: Manila.

Department of Tourism [DOT] (1992b), *Summary of Tourist Arrivals to Boracay 1991*, DOT: Manila.

Department of Trade and Industry [DTI] (1992a), *Foreign Investments Act of 1991, R.A 7042: Implementing Rules and Regulations*, DTI: Manila.

Department of Trade and Industry [DTI] (1992b), *Updates on Investment Law in the Philippines*, DTI: Manila.

Department of Trade and Industry [DTI] (1993), *Medium-term Philippine Export Development Plan*, DTI: Manila.

Department of Trade and Industry [DTI] Region VII (1991), *Cebu: Asia's Investment Destination*, DTI Region VII Office: Cebu City.

Department of Trade and Industry [DTI] Region VII (1992), *Make it Cebu*, DTI: Cebu City.

Department of Trade and Industry International Trade Group [DTIITG] (1993), *Philippines Export Development Plan and How to Achieve it*, DTI: Cebu City.

Dicken, Peter (1990), Mining and Manufacturing. In Denis Dwyer (ed.), *South East Asian Development*, Longman: Harlow, 193–224.

Dierckxsens, Wim (1992), Impacto del Ajuste Estructural sobre la Mujer Trabajadora en Costa Rica. In Marvin Acuña Ortega (ed.), *Cuadernos de Política Económica*, Universidad Nacional de Costa Rica: Heredia, 2–59.

Dioneda, Ma Lisa C. (1993), The Debt Crisis: Why Women Suffer More. In *Bakud* (Women's Resource Center of Cebu), 3:1, 6–7 and 11.

de Dios, Emmanuel (1992), The Aquino-Estanislao Recession. In Emmanuel de Dios and Joel Rocamora (eds), *Of Bonds and Bondage: A Reader on Philippine Debt*, Transnational Institute/Philippine Center for Policy Studies/Freedom from Debt Coalition: Manila, 97–105.

Donald, Alice (1991), The Philippines. In Women Working Worldwide (ed.), *Common Interests: Women Organising in Global Electronics*, Women Working Worldwide: London, 173–193.

Drakakis-Smith, David (1987), *The Third World City*, Methuen: London.

Drakakis-Smith, David (1992), *Pacific Asia*, Routledge: London.

Dwyer, Daisy and Bruce, Judith (eds), (1988), *A Home Divided: Women and Income in the Third World*, Stanford University Press: Stanford, CA.

Economist Intelligence Unit [EIU] (1991), *Country Profile: Philippines, 1991–92*, EIU: London.

Economist Intelligence Unit [EIU] (1992), *Philippines Country Report no.4 1992*, EIU: London.

Economist Intelligence Unit [EIU] (1993a), *Philippines Country Report no.1 1993*, EIU: London.

Economist Intelligence Unit [EIU] (1993b), *Philippines Country Report, 2nd quarter 1993*, EIU: London.

Economist Intelligence Unit [EIU] (1993c), *Philippines Country Report, 4th quarter 1993*, EIU: London.

Eden, J.A. (1990), Race and Reproduction of Factory Labor in Malaysia. In *Environment and Planning D: Society and Space*, 8, 175–90.

Elson, Diane (1983), Nimble Fingers and Other Fables. In Wendy Chapkis and Cynthia Enloe (eds), *Of Common Cloth: Women in the Global Textile Industry*, Transnational Institute: Amsterdam, 5–13.

Elson, Diane (1991), Structural Adjustment: Its Effect on Women. In Tina Wallace with Candida March (eds), *Changing Perceptions: Writings on Gender and Development*, Oxfam: Oxford, 39–53.

Elson, Diane and Pearson, Ruth (1981), 'Nimble Fingers Make Light Work': An Analysis of Women's Employment in Third World Export Manufacturing. In *Feminist Review*, 7, 87–107.

Elson, Diane and Wright, Caroline (1993), *Gender Issues in Contemporary Industrialisation: An Annotated Bibliography of the Research of Two Decades on Women in the Changing International Division of Labour*, University of Manchester, Graduate School: Manchester.

Enario, Ruby (1992), Bag-ong Tubo. In *Review of Women's Studies* (University of the Philippines, Quezon City), 3:1, 80.

Engracia, Luisa T. and Herrin, Alejandro N. (1984), Employment Structure of Female Migrants to the Cities in the Philippines. In Gavin Jones (ed.), *Women in the Urban Industrial Workforce: Southeast Asia and East Asia*, Australian National University: Canberra, 293–303.

Enrile, Carmen and Illo, Jeanne Frances (1991), Working for and with Women: The Women-in-Development Experience in the Philippines. In Jeanne Frances Illo (ed.), *Gender Analysis and Planning: The 1990 IPC-CIDA Workshops*, Institute of Philippine Culture, Ateneo de Manila University: Quezon City, 29–38.

Enriquez, Virgilio G. (1991), Kapwa: A Core Concept in Filipino Social Psychology. In Department of Sociology-Anthropology (ed.), *SA 21: Selected Readings*, Office of Research and Publications, Ateneo de Manila University: Quezon City, 98–105.

Espinosa, Estrella (1993), Women in Governance: Fact or Myth? In *Bakud* (WRRC), 3:1, 8–11.

Espiritu, Augusto Caesar (1992), Some Legal Aspects. In Emmanuel de Dios and Joel Rocamora (eds), *Of Bonds and Bondage: A Reader on Philippine Debt*, Transnational Institute/Philippine Center for Policy Studies/Freedom from Debt Coalition: Manila, 153–69.

Espiritu, Bayani (1988), The Transfer of Technology in Light Industries and the Requisites of Genuine Industrialisation. In SIBAT–Women, Development and Technology (eds), *Labor in Women, Women in Labor: What's in Store?*, SIBAT: Quezon City, 5–9.

Estanislao, Jesus (1986), Economic Relations. In John Bresnan (ed.), *Crisis in the Philippines: The Marcos Era and Beyond*, Princeton University Press: Princeton, NJ, 200–27.

Etienne, Mona (1983), Gender Relations and Conjugality among the Baule. In Christine Oppong (ed.), *Female and Male in West Africa*, Allen and Unwin: London, 32–53.

Eviota, Elizabeth (1986), The Articulation of Gender and Class in the Philippines. In Eleanor Leacock and Helen Safa (eds), *Women's Work*, Bergin and Garvey: Massachusetts, 194–206.

Eviota, Elizabeth (1988), Relations between Women and Men. In SIBAT/CWR (eds), *A Development Framework for Women Socio-economic Projects*, SIBAT: Quezon City, 46–8.

Eviota, Elizabeth (1991), Sex as a Differentiating Variable in Work and Power Relations. In Department of Sociology-Anthropology (eds), *SA 21:*

Selected Readings, Office of Research and Publications, Ateneo de Manila University: Quezon City, 157–69.

Eviota, Elizabeth (1992), *The Political Economy of Gender: Women and the Sexual Division of Labour in the Philippines*, Zed: London.

Eviota, Elizabeth and Smith, Peter C. (1984), The Migration of Women in the Philippines. In James Fawcett, Siew-Ann Khoo and Peter C. Smith (eds), *Women in the Cities of Asia: Migration and Urban Adaptation*, Westview: Boulder, CO., 165–90.

Export Processing Zone Authority [EPZA] (1991), *Briefing Materials, January 1991*, Corporate Planning and Management Office, EPZA: Manila.

Export Processing Zone Authority [EPZA] (1992), *Economic Performance: Accomplishments versus Targets*, EPZA: Manila.

Export Processing Zone Authority [EPZA] (1993), *EPZA Economic Performance Accomplishments versus Targets*, EPZA: Manila.

Faulkner, Anne and Lawson, Victoria (1991), Employment versus Empowerment: A Case Study of the Nature of Women's Work in Ecuador. In *Journal of Development Studies*, 27:4, 16–47.

Fernandes, Kenneth (1991), An Exploratory Study of Women in the Survival Economy: Fifteen Lifestories of Women in the Reclamation Area, Manila. A thesis in partial fulfillment of an MSc degree in economics, Asian Social Institute, Islamabad.

Fernández-Kelly, María Patricia (1983a), *For We Are Sold, I and My People: Women and Industry in Mexico's Frontier*, State University of New York Press: Albany, NJ.

Fernández-Kelly, María Patricia (1983b), Mexican Border Industrialisation, Female Labour Force Participation and Migration. In June Nash and María Patricia Fernández-Kelly (eds), *Women, Men and the International Division of Labor*, State University of New York Press: Albany, NJ, 205–23.

Fernandez-Magno, Susan (1991), Child Prostitution: Image of a Decadent Society. In Sister Mary John Mananzan (ed.), *Essays on Women*, Institute of Women's Studies, St Scholastica's College: Manila (revised edn.), 129–43.

Findley, Sally (1987), *Rural Development and Migration: A Study of Family Choices in the Philippines*, Brown University Studies in Population and Development, Westview: Boulder, CO.

Fonseca, Claudia (1991), Spouses, Siblings and Sex-linked Bonding: A Look at Kinship Organisation in a Brazilian Slum. In Elizabeth Jelin (ed.), *Family, Household and Gender Relations in Latin America*, Kegan Paul International: London/UNESCO: Paris, 133–64.

Foo, Gillian and Lim, Linda (1989), Poverty, Ideology and Women Export Factory Workers in South-East Asia. In Haleh Afshar and Bina Agarwal (eds), *Women, Poverty and Ideology in Asia*, Macmillan: Basingstoke, 212–33.

Francisco, Josefa (1989), Domestic Helpers in the Middle East. In Asian and Pacific Development Centre (ed.), *The Trade in Domestic Helpers: Causes, Mechanisms and Consequences*, APDC: Kuala Lumpur, 162–9.

Francisco, Josefa (1990), Studies on Women Working and Living in Poverty. In Marjorie Evasco, Aurora Javate de Dios and Flor Caagusan (eds), *Women's Springbook: Readings on Women and Society*, Fresam Press: Quezon City, 25–33.

Francisco, Josefa and Carlos, Celia (1988), Women in Economic Crisis: A Study of Women's Conditions and Work in Households of Selected Poverty Groups, mimeo, Women's Research and Resource Center, Maryknoll College Foundation: Quezon City.

Frankel, Mark with Clifton, Tony and Vitug, Marites (1993), Asia: A Make or Break Year. In *Newsweek*, 8 February 1993, 22–4.

Freedom from Debt Coalition [FFDC] (1989), *The Philippine Debt Crisis*, FFDC: Quezon City.

Freedom from Debt Coalition [FFDC] (1992), What Can Be done? In Emmanuel de Dios and Joel Rocamora (eds), *Of Bonds and Bondage: A Reader on Philippine Debt*, Transnational Institute/Philippine Center for Policy Studies/Freedom from Debt Coalition: Manila, 109–13.

Fuentes, Annette and Ehrenreich, Barbara (1983), *Women in the Global Factory*, South End Press: Boston, MA.

Gallin, Rita (1990), Women in the Export Industry in Taiwan: The Muting of Class Consciousness. In Kathryn Ward (ed.), *Women Workers and Global Restructuring*, ILR Press, Cornell University: Ithaca, NY, 179–92.

García, Brígida; Muñoz, Humberto and de Oliveira, Orlandina (1983), *Familia y Mercado de Trabajo: Un Estudio de Dos Ciudades Brasileñas*, El Colegio de México/ UNAM: México DF.

García-Moreno, Claudia (1991), AIDS: Women Are not just Transmittors. In Tina Wallace with Candida March (eds), *Changing Perceptions: Writings on Gender and Development*, Oxfam: Oxford, 91–102.

Gledhill, John (1994), *Power and its Disguises: Anthropological Perspectives on Politics*, Pluto: London.

González de la Rocha, Mercedes (1988), Economic Crisis, Domestic Reorganisation and Women's Work in Guadalajara, Mexico. In *Bulletin of Latin American Research*, 7:2, 207–23.

Goodno, James B. (1991), *The Philippines: Land of Broken Promises*, Zed: London.

Gordon, Elizabeth (1981), An Analysis of the Impact of Labour Migration on the Lives of Women in Lesotho. In *Journal of Development Studies*, 17:3, 59–76.

Gothoskar, Sujata (1991), Women's Struggles in the Pharmaceutical Industry. In Committee for Asian Women (ed.), *Many Paths, One Goal*, CAW: Hong Kong, 100–11.

Graburn, Nelson H.H. (1983), Tourism and Prostitution. In *Annals of Tourism Research*, 10, 437–43.

Grown, Caren and Sebstad, Jennefer (1989), Introduction: Towards a Wider Perspective on Women's Employment. In *World Development*, 17:7, 937–52.

Gulati, Leela (1993), *In the Absence of Their Men: The Impact on Women of Male Migration*, Sage: London.

Harris, Olivia (ed.), (1982), *Latin American Women*, Minority Rights Group: London.

Harrison, David (1992), International Tourism and the Less Developed Countries: The Background. In David Harrison (ed.), *Tourism and the Less Developed Countries*, Belhaven: London, 1–18.

Hart, Donn (1971), Philippine Rural–Urban Migration: A View from Caticugan, a Bisayan Village. In *Behaviour Science Notes*, 6:2, 103–37.

Health Action Information Network [HAIN] (1987), *Pom Pom: Child and Youth Prostitution in the Philippines*, Health Action Information Network: Quezon City.

Hein, Catherine (1986), The Feminisation of Industrial Employment in Mauritius: A Case of Sex Segregation. In Richard Anker and Catherine Hein (eds), *Sex Inequalities in Urban Employment in the Third World*, Macmillan: Basingstoke, 277–311.

Heng Leng, Chee and Ng Choon Sim, Cecilia (1993), Economic Restructuring in a NIC: Implications for Women Workers. Paper presented at Conference on Insecurity in the 1990s: Gender and Social Policy in an International Perspective, London School of Economics, 5–6 April 1993.

Hetler, Carol (1990), Survival Strategies, Migration and Household Headship. In Leela Dube and Rajni Palriwala (eds), *Structures and Strategies: Women, Work and Family*, Sage: New Delhi, 175–99.

Heyzer, Noeleen (1986), *Working Women in South-East Asia: Development, Subordination and Emancipation*, Open University Press: Milton Keynes.

Hodder, Rupert (1992), *The West Pacific Rim: An Introduction*, Belhaven: London.

Hoddinott, John and Haddad, Lawrence (1991), *Household Expenditures, Child Anthropomorphic Status and the Intra-Household Division of Income: Evidence from the Côte d'Ivoire*, Unit for the Study of African Economics, University of Oxford: Oxford.

Høigård, Cecilie and Finstad, Liv (1992), *Backstreets: Prostitution, Money and Love*: Polity Press: Cambridge.

Holden, Peter; Pfäfflin, Jürgen; and Georg, Friedrich (eds) (1983), *Tourism Prostitution Development*, Ecumenical Coalition on Third World Tourism: Bangkok.

Hollnsteiner, Mary (1991a), The Wife. In Department of Sociology-Anthropology (eds), *SA 21: Selected Readings*, Office of Research and Publications, Ateneo de Manila University, Quezon City, 251–75.

Hollnsteiner, Mary (1991b), The Husband. In Department of Sociology-Anthropology (eds), *SA 21: Selected Readings*, Office of Research and Publications, Ateneo de Manila University, Quezon City, 276–84.

Hossfeld, Karen (1991), Introduction. In Women Working Worldwide (ed.), *Common Interests: Women Organising in Global Electronics*, WWW: London, 13–17.

Humphrey, John (1985), Gender, Pay and Skill: Manual Workers in Brazilian Industry. In Haleh Afshar (ed.), *Women, Work and Ideology in the Third World*, Tavistock: London, 214–31.

IBON (1990), *The Semiconductor Industry*, IBON Databank Phil: Manila.

IBON (1991a), *Facts and Figures, vol.14, no.22 'The Philippine Population'*, IBON Databank Phil: Manila.

IBON (1991b), *Facts and Figures, vol.14, no.23 'The Philippine Peso'*, IBON Databank Phil: Manila.

IBON (1992a), *Facts and Figures, vol. 15, no.10 'Jobs'*, IBON Databank Phil: Manila.

IBON (1992b), *Facts and Figures, vol. 15, no.18 'Bases Conversion'*, IBON Databank Phil: Manila.

IBON (1992c), *Facts and Figures, vol. 15, no.21 'The Ramos Administration'*, IBON Databank Phil: Manila.

IBON (1992d), *Facts and Figures, vol. 15, no.22 'GSIS and SSS'*, IBON Databank Phil: Manila.

Illo, Jeanne Frances (1988), Putting Gender up Front: Data, Issues and Prospects. In Jeanne Frances Illo (ed.), *Gender Issues in Rural Development: A Workshop Report*, Institute of Philippine Culture, Ateneo de Manila University: Quezon City, 9–20.

Illo, Jeanne Frances (1989), Who Heads the Household? Women in Households in the Philippines. In Amaryllis Torres (ed.), *The Filipino Woman in Focus: A Handbook of Reading*, UNESCO: Bangkok, 245–266.

Illo, Jeanne Frances (1991), Putting Gender up Front: Data, Issues and Prospects. In Jeanne Frances Illo (ed.), *Gender Analysis and Planning*, Institute of Philippine Culture, Ateneo de Manila University: Quezon City, 39–58.

Illo, Jeanne Frances and Lee, Rona C. (1991), Women and Men in a Rainfed Farming Systems Project: The Cahabaan Case. In Jeanne Frances Illo (ed.), *Gender and Analysis and Planning*, Institute of Philippine Culture, Ateneo de Manila University: Quezon City, 65–74.

Illo, Jeanne Frances and Pineda-Ofreneo, Rosalinda (1989), Producers, Traders, Workers: Philippine Women in Agriculture. Paper presented at Food and Agriculture Organisation (FAO), Southeast Asian seminar on Women in Agriculture, Bangkok, 7–11 August, 1989.

Illo, Jeanne Frances and Polo, Jaime B. (1990), *Fishers, Traders, Farmers, Wives*, Institute of Philippine Culture, Ateneo de Manila University: Quezon City.

Illo, Jeanne Frances and Veneracion, Cynthia (1988), *Women and Men in Rainfed Farming Systems: Case Studies of Households in the Bicol Region*, Institute of Philippine Culture, Ateneo de Manila University: Quezon City.

Industan, Edmund Melig (1992), The Family among the Ata Manobo of Davao del Norte. In *Philippine Quarterly of Culture and Society* (University of San Carlos, Cebu), 20:1, 3–13.

Institute of Labor and Manpower Studies [ILMS] (1984), *Women in TNCs: The Philippine Case (Are Women in TNCs Exploited?)*, DOLE: Manila.

Institute for Social Studies and Action [ISSA] (1991), *Women's Health: Facts and Figures*, ISSA: Manila.

Institute for Social Studies and Action [ISSA] and Women's Health Care Foundation [WHCF] (1990), *Taking Care of Our Health and Lives as Women*, ISSA/WHCF: Manila.

Inter-Agency Committee on Domestic Violence, Cebu [IACDVC] (1992), *Initial Results of the Study on Incidence of Domestic Violence in Cebu City*, IACDVC: Cebu City.

International Committee for Prostitutes' Rights (1988), International Committee for Prostitutes' Rights World Charter and World Whores' Congress Statements. In Frédérique Delacoste and Priscilla Alexander (eds), *Sex Work: Writings by Women in the Sex Industry*, Virago: London, 305–21.

International Labour Office [ILO] (1991), *Migrant Women in Domestic Work in Italy*, World Employment Programme working paper, ILO: Geneva.

International Labour Office [ILO] (1992), *Yearbook of Labour Statistics 1992*, ILO: Geneva.

Israel-Sobritchea, Carolyn (1991), Gender Ideology and the Status of Women in a Philipine Rural Community. In Sister Mary John Mananzan (ed.), *Essays on Women*, Institute of Women's Studies, St Scholastica's College: Manila (revised edn.), 90–103.

Israel-Sobritchea, Carolyn (1994), 'Getting the Right Mix of Feminism and Nationalism': Some Reflections on Recent Developments in the Women's Movement in the Philippines. Paper delivered at the panel 'Negotiating Gender in the Philippines', European Conference on Philippine Studies, School of Oriental and African Studies, University of London, 13–15 April 1994.

Izzard, Wendy (1985), Migrants and Mothers: Case Studies from Botswana. In *Journal of Southern African Studies*, 11:2, 258–80.

Jackson, Peter (1994), Over the Seas or to the Hills: Population Growth and Impact in the Philippines. In *Geography*, 79:1, 78–83.

Javate de Dios, Aurora (1989), Filipinas as Commodities: The Plight of the Japayukisan. In Asian and Pacific Development Centre (ed.), *The Trade in Domestic Helpers: Causes, Mechanisms and Consequences*, APDC: Kuala Lumpur, 153–61.

Javate de Dios, Aurora (1990), The Case of the Japayuki-san and the Hananyome-san: A Preliminary Inquiry into the Culture of Subordination. In Marjorie Evasco, Aurora Javate de Dios and Flor Caagusan (eds), *Women's Springbook: Readings on Women and Society*, Fresam Press: Quezon City, 35–41.

Javier, Casino (1991), The Queen of the South. In *Cebu* (DOT Regional Office, Cebu City), 1:43, 1–4.

Joekes, Susan (1985), Working for Lipstick? Male and Female Labour in the Clothing Industry in Morocco. In Haleh Afshar (ed.), *Women, Work and Ideology in the Third World*, Tavistock: London, 183–213.

Joekes, Susan (1987), *Women in the World Economy: An INSTRAW Study*, Oxford University Press: New York and Oxford.

Johnson, Mark (1994), Cross-Gender Men and Homosexuality in the Southern Philippines: Ethnicity, Political Violence and the Protocols of Engendered Sexualities amongst the Muslim Tausug and Sama. Paper delivered at the panel 'Negotiating Gender in the Philippines', European Conference on Philippine Studies, School of Oriental and African Studies, University of London, 13–15 April 1994.

Kabeer, Naila and Joekes, Susan (1991), Editorial. Special issue of *IDS Bulletin* (Sussex), 'Researching the Household: Methodological and Empirical Issues', 22:1, 1–4.

Kanji, Nazneen (1994), Gender and Structural Adjustment: A Case Study of Harare, Zimbabwe. Unpublished PhD dissertation, Department of Geography, London School of Economics.

Katz, Cindi and Monk, Janice (eds), (1993), *Full Circles: Geographies of Women over the Life Course*, Routledge: London.

Kenney, Martin and Florida, Richard (1994), Japanese Maquiladoras: Production Organisation and Global Commodity Chains. In *World Development*, 22:1, 27–44.

Kent, George (1991), Our Children, Our Future. In Koson Srisang (ed.), *Caught in Modern Slavery: Tourism and Child Prostitution in Asia*, Ecumenical Coalition on Third World Tourism: Bangkok, 71–82.

Kerkvliet, Benedict and Mojares, Resil (1991), Themes in the Transition form Marcos to Aquino: An Introduction. In Benedict Kerkvliet and Resil Mojares (eds), *From Marcos to Aquino: Local Perspectives on Political Transition in the Philippines*, Ateneo de Manila University Press: Quezon City, 1–12.

King, Elizabeth M. and Domingo, Lita J. (1986), The Changing Status of Filipino Women across Family Generations. In *Philippine Population Journal*, 2:1–4, 1–31.

Klouda, Anthony (1994), Investing in the Future: A Summary of the Review of Global Policies for the Prevention and Control of HIV. Paper prepared for the HIV/STD Advisory Centre (ACT-HIV), for ODA, London.

KMU Visayas (1992), *Cebu's Labor Situation*, KMU Visayas: Cebu City.

Koussoudji, Sherrie and Mueller, Eva (1983), The Economic and Demographic Status of Female–headed Households in Rural Botswana. In *Economic Development and Cultural Change* 21, 831–59.

Krinks, Peter (1987), The Economic Context. In Peter Krinks (ed.), *The Philippines under Aquino*, Australian Development Studies Network, Australian National University: Canberra, 35–47.

Kuzesnof, Elizabeth (1989), The Family in Latin America: A Critique of Recent Work. In *Latin American Research Review* 24:2, 168–86.

Lande, Carl H. (1986), The Political Crisis. In John Bresnan (ed.), *Crisis in the Philippines*, Princeton University Press: Princeton, NJ, 114–44.

Lanot, Marra P.L. (1991), The Filipinas Have Come and They're Still Coming. In Sister Mary John Mananzan (ed.), *Essays on Women*, Institute of Women's Studies, St Scholastica's College: Manila (revised edn.), 66–79.

Lauby, Jennifer Lynn (1987), The Migration of a Daughter as a Family Strategy: Effects on the Occupations and Marital Experience on Women in the Philippines. Unpublished PhD thesis, Harvard University, Cambridge, MA.

Le Guen, Haude (1994), An Analysis of Some Tausug Myths. Paper delivered at the panel 'Religion, Ritual and Identity', European Conference on Philippine Studies, School of Oriental and African Studies, University of London, 13–15 April 1994.

Lee, Pat (1981), Hotel and Restaurant Workers in the Philippines. mimeo, Philippine Resource Centre: London.

Lee, Robyn (1987), The Heir Apparent: *Kilusang Mayo Uno* and the Radical Tradition in Philippine Labour. In Peter Krinks (ed.), *The Philippines under Aquino*, Australian Development Studies Network, Australian National University: Canberra, 103–13.

Lee, Sun-Hee (1985), *Why People Intend to Move: Individual and Community-Level Factors of Out-Migration in the Philippines*, Westview: Boulder CO.

Lee, Wendy (1991), Prostitution and Tourism in South-East Asia. In Nanneke Redclift and M. Thea Sinclair (eds), *Working Women: International Perspectives on Labour and Gender Ideology*, Routledge: London and New York, 79–103.

de Leon, Adul (1991), Economic, Political, Legal, Cultural and Psychological Aspects: A Philippine Perspective. In Koron Srisang (ed.), *Caught in Modern Slavery: Tourism and Child Prostitution in Asia*, Ecumenical Coalition on Third World Tourism: Bangkok, 87–8.

Levy, Diane and Lerch, Patricia (1991), Tourism as a Factor in Development: Implications for Gender and Work in Barbados. In *Gender and Society*, 5:1, 67–85.

Licuanan, Patricia (1991), A Situation Analysis of Women in the Philippines. In Jeanne Frances Illo (ed.), *Gender Analysis and Planning: The 1990 IPC–CIDA Workshop*, Institute of Philippine Culture, Ateneo de Manila University: Quezon City, 15–28.

Lim, Linda (1983), Capitalism, Imperialism and Patriarchy: The Dilemma of Third World Women Workers in Multinational Factories. In June Nash and María Patricia Fernández Kelly (eds), *Women, Men and the International Division of Labor*, State University of New York Press: Albany, NJ, 70–91.

Little, Kenneth (1973), *African Women in Towns* Cambridge University Press: Cambridge.

Loyré, Ghislaine (1994), Foreign Influences on Traditional Rituals. Paper delivered at the panel 'Religion, Ritual and Identity', European Conference on Philippine Studies, School of Oriental and African Studies, University of London, 13–15 April 1994.

Mackie, Vera (1992), Japan and South-East Asia: The International Division of Labour and Leisure. In David Harrison (ed.), *Tourism and Less Developed Countries*, Belhaven: London, 75–84.

Mactan Export Processing Zone Authority [MEPZA] (1993), *Mactan Export Processing Zone: List of Employers*, MEPZA: Lapu-Lapu.

Mananzan, Sister Mary John (1991a), Women in Philippine History. In Sister Mary John Mananzan (ed.), *Essays on Women*, Institute of Women's Studies, St Scholastica's College: Manila (revised edn.), 6–35.

Mananzan, Sister Mary John (1991b), Sexual Exploitation of Women in a Third World Setting. In Sister Mary John Mananzan (ed.), *Essays on Women*, Institute of Women's Studies, St Scholastica's College: Manila (revised edn.), 104–112.

Mangahas, Fe and Pasalo, Virginia (1994), Devising an Empowerment Paradigm for Women in the Philippines: The Importance of the Family in Micro-Urban Enterprises. In Fatima Meer (ed.), *Poverty in the 1990s: The Responses of Urban Women*, UNESCO/International Social Science Council: Paris, 243–68.

Marcelo, Alexandrina (1991), Advocacy for Women's Health and Reproductive Rights: A Philippine NGO Experience. Paper presented at the 1991 AWID International Forum 'Panel on Advocacy for Women's Health', Washington DC, 20–24 November 1991.

Mather, Celia (1988), Subordination of Women and Lack of Industrial Strife in West Java. In John Taylor and Andrew Turton (eds), *Sociology of 'Developing Societies': Southeast Asia*, Macmillan: Basingstoke, 147–57.

Matsui, Yayori (1991a), *Women's Asia* (second impression; first publ. 1989), Zed: London.

Matsui, Yayori (1991b), Asian Migrant Women Working at Sex Industry in Japan Victimized by International Trafficking. In Koron Srisang (ed.), *Caught in Modern Slavery: Tourism and Child Prostitution in Asia*, Ecumenical Coalition on Third World Tourism: Bangkok, 100–102.

Matthaei, Julie and Amott, Teresa (1990), Race, Gender, Work: The History of Asian and Asian Women. In *Race and Class*, 31:3, 61–79.

Maurer, Mechtild (1991), Tourism, Prostitution and AIDS. In Koron Srisang (ed.), *Caught in Modern Slavery: Tourism and Child Prostitution in Asia*, Ecumenical Coalition on Third World Tourism: Bangkok, 96–99.

McCoy, Alfred (1987), After the Yellow Revolution: Filipino Elite Factions and the Struggle for Power. In Peter Krinks (ed.), *The Philippines under Aquino*, Australian Development Studies Network, Australian National University: Canberra, 9–33.

McIlwaine, Cathy (1993), Gender, Ethnicity and the Local Labour Market in Limón, Costa Rica. Unpublished PhD dissertation, Department of Geography, London School of Economics.

McIlwaine, Cathy (1994a), 'People in Glass Boxes': Gender and Ethnic Constraints on Labour Mobility in Limón, Costa Rica. Paper delivered at the symposium 'Gender in Latin America', annual conference of the Society of Latin American Studies, University of Liverpool, 25–7 March 1994.

McIlwaine, Cathy (1994b), Gender and Ethnicity in the Labour Market: Perspectives on Employment Divisions in Limón, Costa Rica. In *Geographical Discussion Papers New Series*, 27 (London School of Economics), 52–80.

McKercher, Bob (1993), Some Fundamental Truths about Tourism: Understanding Tourism's Social and Environmental Impacts. In *Journal of Sustainable Tourism*, 1:1, 6–16.

Medel-Añonuevo, Carol (1992), Feminist Reflections on the International Migration of Women. In *Lila: Asia Pacific Women's Studies Journal*, 1, 42–9.

Medel-Añonuevo, Carol (1993a), Doing Development Work in the Name of Women: Opportunities and Limitations for Change. Paper presented at the conference 'Women and Aid in the Philippines: Management or Empowerment?' Catholic Institute for International Relations, London, 15 June 1993.

Medel-Añonuevo, Carol (1993b), Urban Poor Women and Structural Adjustment in Philippines. Seminar paper presented at the Catholic Institute for International Relations, London, 18 June 1993.

Medel-Añonuevo, Carolyn; Abad-Sarmiento, La Rainne; and Oliveros-Vistro, Teresita (1989), Filipina Domestic Helpers in Hong Kong and Singapore. In Asian and Pacific Development Centre (ed.), *The Trade in Domestic Helpers: Causes, Mechanisms and Consequences*, APDC: Kuala Lumpur, 162–9.

Medina, Belen T.G. (1991), *The Filipino Family: A Text with Selected Readings*, University of the Philippines Press: Quezon City.

Mercado, Arni (1991), There is Hope. In Aida Santos (ed.), *Pangarap at Hinagpis: Mga Awit ng Kababaihang Maralita (Dreams and Woes: Songs of Poor Women)*, GABRIELA/Institute of Women's Studies, St Scholastica's College: Manila, 5–6.

Metro Cebu Development Council [MCDC] (1991), *Proposal for Restructural Program for the Urban Poor of Cebu City*, MCDC: Cebu City.

Milkman, Ruth (1979), Women's Work and Economic Crisis: Some Lessons of the Great Depression. In *Review of Radical Political Economy*, 8:1, 73–97.

Miralao, Virginia (1984), The Impact of Female Employment on Household Management. In Gavin Jones (ed.), *Women in the Urban and Industrial Workforce: Southeast and East Asia*, Development Studies Centre Monograph no.33, Australian National University: Canberra, 369–86.

Miralao, Virginia (1989), *State Policies and Women's Health and Reproductive Rights*, Women and Health Booklet Series no.1, ISSA: Manila.

Miralao, Virginia; Carlos, Celia; and Santos Fulleros, Aida (1990), *Women Entertainers in Angeles and Olongapo: A Survey Report*, WEDPRO/ KALAYAAN: Manila.

Miranda, Mariano (1988), The Economics of Poverty and the Poverty of Economics: The Philippine Experience. In Mamerto Canlas, Mariano Miranda and James Putzel *Land, Poverty and Politics in the Philippines*, Catholic Institute for International Relations: London, 11–46.

Mitter, Swasti and van Luijken, Anneke (1983), A Woman's Home is her Factory. In Wendy Chapkis and Cynthia Enloe (eds), *Of Common Cloth: Women in the Global Textile Industry*, Transnational Institute: Amsterdam, 61–7.

Moghadam, Valentine (1993a), *Social Protection and Women Workers in Asia*, Working Paper no.110, United Nations University/World Institute for Development Economics Research: Helsinki.

Moghadam, Valentine (1993b), *Gender and the Development Process in a Changing Global Environment*, United Nations University/World Institute for Development Economics Research: Helsinki.

Moghadam, Valentine (1994), Women in Societies. In *International Social Science Journal*, 139, 95–115.

Molyneux, Maxine (1986), Mobilisation without Emancipation? Women's Interests, State and Revolution in Nicaragua. In Richard Fagan, Carmen Diana Deere and José Luis Coraggio (eds), *Transition and Development: Problems of Third World Socialism*, Monthly Review Press: New York, 280–302.

Montes, Manuel (1992a), The Effects of External Adjustment on the Population. In Emmanuel de Dios and Joel Rocamora (eds), *Of Bonds and Bondage: A Reader on Philippine Debt*, Transnational Institute/Philippine Center for Policy Studies/Freedom from Debt Coalition: Manila, 48–58.

Montes, Manuel (1992b), The World Debt Crisis: Consequences for the Philippines and her People. In Emmanuel de Dios and Joel Rocamora (eds), *Of Bonds and Bondage: A Reader on Philippine Debt*, Transnational Institute/Philippine Center for Policy Studies/Freedom from Debt Coalition: Manila, 69–77.

Moore, Henrietta (1988), *Feminism and Anthropology*, Polity Press: Cambridge.

Moore, Henrietta (1994), The Cultural Constitution of Gender. In *The Polity Reader in Gender Studies*, Polity Press: Cambridge, 14–21.

Moselina, Leopoldo (1981), Olongapo's R and R Industry: A Sociological Analysis of Institutionalised Prostitution. In *Ang Makatao* (Asian Social Institute), 1:1, 5–42.

Moser, Caroline (1989), The Impact of Recession and Structural Adjustment Policies at the Micro-Level: Low-income Women and their Households in Guayaquil, Ecuador. In UNICEF (ed.), *Invisible Adjustment* vol.2, UNICEF Americas and Caribbean Regional Office: New York, 137–62.

Moser, Caroline (1993a), *Gender Planning and Development: Theory, Practice and Training*, Routledge: London and New York.

Moser, Caroline (1993b), Women, Gender and Urban Development: Challenges for the 1990s. Paper prepared for final workshop of Ford Foundation Research Project on Urban Research in the Developing World: Towards an Agenda for the 1990s, Cairo, 14–18 February 1993.

Mulder, Niels (1994), Filipino Culture and Social Analysis. Paper delivered at the panel 'Religion, Ritual and Identity', European Conference on Philippine Studies, School of Oriental and African Studies, University of London, 13–15 April 1994.

Murray, Colin (1981), *Families Divided: The Impact of Migrant Labour in Lesotho*, Cambridge University Press: Cambridge.

Nagot, Ma Cristina D. (1991), Preliminary Investigation on Domestic Violence against Women. In Sister Mary John Mananzan (ed.), *Essays on Women*, Institute of Women's Studies, St Scholastica's College: Manila (revised edn.), 113–128.

National Commission on the Role of Filipino Women [NCRFW] (1989), *Philippine Development Plan for Women, 1989–1992*, NCRFW: Manila.

National Commission on the Role of Filipino Women [NCRFW] (1991), *Updates of the Philippine Development Plan for Women, 1991–1992*, NCRFW: Manila.

National Economic Development Authority [NEDA] (1990), *Updates on the Medium-term Philippine Development Plan 1990–1992*, NEDA: Manila.

National Economic Development Authority [NEDA] (1991), *1990 Philippine Development Report*, NEDA: Manila.

National Economic Development Authority [NEDA] Region VI (1992), *Boracay Services Infrastructure Project*, NEDA Regional Office no.VI: Iloilo City.

National Economic Development Authority [NEDA] Region VI (1993), *The Western Visayas Region Development Plan 1993–1998: Executive Summary*, Regional Development Council, Region VI/NEDA Region VI: Iloilo City.

National Economic Development Authority [NEDA] Region VII (1992a), *Profile of Central Visayas*, NEDA Regional Office no.VII: Cebu City.

National Economic Development Authority [NEDA] Region VII (1992b), *Major Development Programs and Projects 1986–1992: Province of Cebu*, NEDA Regional Office no.VII: Cebu City.

National Economic Development Authority [NEDA] Region VII (1992c), *Major Development Programs and Projects 1986–1992: Cebu City*, NEDA Regional Office no.VII: Cebu City.

National Economic Development Authority [NEDA] Region VII (1993a), *Region VII: An Executive Summary of the Regional Development Plan*, NEDA Regional Office no.VII: Cebu City.

National Economic Development Authority [NEDA] Region VII (1993b), *Brief Report on the Performance of the Economy of the Central Visayas Region in 1992*, NEDA Regional Office no.VII: Cebu City.

National Economic Protectionism Association [NEPA] (1992), From Crisis to Crisis. In Emmanuel de Dios and Joel Rocamora (eds), *Of Bonds and Bondage: A Reader on Philippine Debt*, Transnational Institute/Philippine Center for Policy Studies/Freedom from Debt Coalition: Manila, 201–8.

National Statistical Coordination Board [NSCB] (1991), *1991 Philippine Statistical Yearbook*, NSCB: Manila.

National Statistics Office [NSO] (1992a), *1990 Census of Population and Housing, Report no.3: Socio-Economic and Demographic Characteristics*, NSO: Manila.

National Statistics Office [NSO] (1992b), *1990 Census of Population and Housing, Report no.3–29G: Socio-Economic and Demographic Characteristics, Cebu*, NSO: Manila.

National Statistics Office [NSO] (1992c), *NSO Monthly Bulletin of Statistics: Special Feature: The Electronics Industry*, NSO: Manila.

National Statistics Office [NSO] (1992d), *Labor Force Survey*, NSO: Manila.

Nelson, Nici (1992), The Women Who Have Left and Those Who Have Stayed Behind: Rural–Urban Migration in Central and Western Kenya. In Sylvia Chant (ed.), *Gender and Migration in Developing Countries*, Belhaven: London, 109–38.

Nichter, Mark and Abellanosa, Ilya (1994), STD/AIDS Prevention and Prophylaxis in Cebu: Popular Beliefs and Practices among Youth and Commercial Sex Workers. Research proposal, Department of Anthropology, University of Arizona, Tucson.

Nolasco, Cynthia (1991), The Woman Problem: Gender, Class and State Oppression. In Sister Mary John Mananzan (ed.), *Essays on Women*, Institute of Women's Studies, St Scholastica's College: Manila (revised edn.), 80–89.

Nolledo, Jose (1992), *The Labor Code of the Philippines with Implementing Regulations, Related Laws and Other Issuances*, National Book Store: Manila.

Obbo, Christine (1980), *African Women: Their Struggle for Independence* Zed: London.

O'Brien, Thomas (1990), *Crisis and Instability: The Philippines Enters the Nineties*, Philippine International Forum: Davao City.

O'Connor, David C. (1987), Women Workers and the Changing International Division of Labor in Microelectronics. In Lourdes Benería and Catherine Stimpson (eds), *Women, Households, and the Economy*, Rutgers University Press: New Brunswick, NJ, 243–67.

O'Grady, Ron (1983), Prostitution Tourism. In Peter Holden, et al. (eds), *Tourism Prostitution Development*, Ecumenical Coalition on Third World Tourism: Bangkok, 11–13.

Olofson, Harold and Crisostomo, Lorelie (1989), *Outsiders and Insiders: A Comparative Study of Socioeconomic Benefits to Locals from Two Types of Beach Resort Developments in Cebu*, Area Research Training Center, University of San Carlos: Cebu City.

Ong, Aihwa (1987), *Spirits of Resistance and Capitalist Discipline: Factory Women in Malaysia*, State University of New York Press: Albany, NY.

Palriwala, Rajni (1990), Introduction. In Leela Dube and Rajni Palriwala (eds), *Structures and Strategies: Women, Work and Family*, Sage: New Delhi, 15–55.

Panos Institute (1990), *Triple Jeopardy: Women and AIDS*, Panos Institute: London.

Pavia-Ticzon, Lucia (1990), A Feminist Reflection on Organisation Development. In Marjorie Evasco, Aurora Javate de Dios and Flor Caagusan (eds), *Women's Springbook: Readings on Women and Society*, Fresam Press: Quezon City, 115–20.

Pearson, Ruth (1986), Latin American Women and the New International Division of Labour: A Reassessment. In *Bulletin of Latin American Research*, 5:2, 67–79.

Perez, Aurora (1992), The Economic Integration of Female Migrants in Urban Labor Markets: The Philippine Case. Paper presented to the pre-conference seminar for the Fourth Asian and Pacific Population Conference, 21–5 January, Seoul, South Korea.

Perpiñan, Sister Mary Soledad (1983), Philippine Women in the Service and Entertainment Sector. mimeo, Philippine Resource Centre: London.

Pertierra, Raul (1991), Viscera Suckers and Female Sociality: The Philippine Asuang. In Department of Sociology-Anthropology (eds), *SA 21: Selected Readings*, Office of Research Publications, Ateneo de Manila University: Quezon City, 184–201.

Peterson, Jean Treloggen (1993), Generalised Extended Family Exchange: A Case from the Philippines. In *Journal of Marriage and the Family*, 55, 570–84.

Phillips, Anne (1983), *Hidden Hands: Women and Economic Policies*, Pluto: London.

Phongpaichit, Pasuk (1984), The Bangkok Masseuses: Origins, Status and Prospects. In Gavin Jones (ed.), *Women in the Urban and Industrial Workforce: Southeast Asia and East Asia*, Development Studies Center Monograph no.33, Australian National University: Canberra, 251–77.

Pietilä, Hilkka and Vickers, Jeanne (1990), *Making Women Matter: The Role of the United Nations* Zed: London.

Pineda, Ernesto L. (1991), *The Family Code of the Philippines Annotated* (2nd edn.), Central Lawbook Publishing Co.: Quezon City.

Pineda Deang, Lionel (1992), Living Arrangements of Mothers Following Childbirth: Do they Affect Subsequent Fertility? Unpublished PhD dissertation, Department of Sociology, University of North Carolina at Chapel Hill.

Pineda-Ofreneo, Rosalinda (1985), *Women of the Soil: An Alternative Philippine Report on Rural Women*, Philippine Women's Research Collective: Manila.

Pineda-Ofreneo, Rosalinda (1987), Women in the Electronics Industry in the Philippines. In Cecilia Ng (ed.), *Technology and Gender: Women's Work in Asia*, Women's Studies Unit, University of the Philippines, Quezon City and Malaysian Social Science Association: Kuala Lumpur, 92–106.

Pineda-Ofreneo, Rosalinda (1988), Philippine Domestic Outwork: Subcontracting for Export-oriented Industries. In John G. Taylor and Andrew Turton (eds), *Sociology of 'Developing Societies': Southeast Asia*, Macmillan: Basingstoke, 158–64.

Pineda-Ofreneo, Rosalinda (1991), *The Philippines: Debt and Poverty*, Oxfam: Oxford.

Ploteña, Mark Anthony (1987), Batang Plaza. In Health Action Information Network (ed.), *Pom Pom: Child Prostitution in the Philippines*, HAIN: Quezon City, 31–7.

Porpora, Douglas; Lim, Mah Hui; and Prommas, Usanee (1989), The Role of Women in the International Division of Labour: The Case of Thailand. In *Development and Change*, 20, 269–94.

Prates, Susana (1990), Participación Laboral Femenina en un Proceso de Crisis. In DAWN/MUDAR (eds), *Mujer y Crisis: Respuestas Ante la Recesión*, Editorial Nueva Sociedad: Carácas, 75–92.

PROCESS (1993), *Gender Needs Assessment in PROCESS-supported Areas in Panay, Bohol and Northern Luzon*, PROCESS: Iloilo City.

Putzel, James (1988), Prospects for Agrarian Reform under the Aquino Government. In Mamerto Canlas, Miranda Mariano and James Putzel, *Land, Poverty and Politics in the Philippines*, Catholic Institute for International Relations: London, 47–70.

Putzel, James (1992), *A Captive Land: The Politics of Agrarian Reform in the Philippines*, Catholic Institute for International Relations: London/Monthly Review Press: New York.

Putzel, James (1994), Managing the 'Motive Force': The Communist Party and the Peasantry. Paper delivered at the panel 'On State-Society Contests', European Conference on Philippine Studies, School of Oriental and African Studies, University of London, 13–15 April 1994.

Pyle, Jean (1990), Female Employment and Export-led Development in Ireland: Labour Market Impact of State-reinforced Gender Inequality in the Household. In Sharon Stichter and Jane Parpart (eds), *Women, Employment and the Family in the International Division of Labour*, Macmillan: Basingstoke, 137–60.

Quisumbing, Purificacion (1990), Taming the Law. In Marjorie Evasco, Aurora Javate de Dios and Flor Caagusan (eds), *Women's Springbook: Readings on Women and Society*, Fresam Press: Quezon City, 43–54.

Radcliffe, Sarah (1986), Gender Relations, Peasant Livelihood Strategies and Migration: A Case Study from Cuzco, Peru. In *Bulletin of Latin American Research* 5:2, 29–47.

Radcliffe, Sarah (1991), The Role of Gender in Peasant Migration: Conceptual issues from the Peruvian Andes. In *Review of Radical Political Economy*, 23:3–4, 148–73.

Rahat, Naveed-I (1986), Meharabad, a Punjabi Village: Male Out-migration and Women's Changing Roles. In Frits Selier and Mehtab S. Karim (eds), *Migration in Pakistan: Themes and Facts*, Vanguard: Lahore, 139–60.

Rakodi, Carole (1991), Women's Work or Household Strategies? In *Environment and Urbanisation*, 3:2, 39–45.

Rao, Rukmini and Husain, Sahba (1987), Invisible Hands: Women in Home-based Production in the Garment Export Industry in Delhi. In Andrea Menefee Singh and Anita Kelles-Viitanen (eds), *Invisible Hands: Women in Home-Based Production*, Sage: Newbury Park and London, 51–67.

Ramirez, Mina (1984), *Understanding Philippine Social Realities through the Filipino Family: A Phenomenological Approach*, Asian Social Institute Communication Center: Manila.

Ramos, Elias T. (1987), Labor Conflict and Recent Trends in Philippine Industrial Relations. In *Philippine Quarterly of Culture and Society*, 15, 173–97.

Ramos-Jimenez, Pilar; Chiong-Javier, Ma Elena; and Sevilla, Judy Carol (1986), *Philippine Urban Situation Analysis*, UNICEF: Manila.

Raquisa, Tonette (1987), Prostitution: A Philippine Experience. In Miranda Davies (ed.), *Third World, Second Sex 2*, Zed: London, 218–24.

Reardon, Geraldine (1991a), South Korea. In Women Working Worldwide (ed.), *Common Interests: Women Organising in Global Electronics*, WWW: London, 19–26.

Reardon, Geraldine (1991b), India. In Women Working Worldwide (ed.), *Common Interests: Women Organising in Global Electronics*, WWW: London, 151–6.

Reardon, Geraldine and Rivers, Yvonne (1991), Thailand. In Women Working Worldwide (ed.), *Common Interests: Women Organising in Global Electronics*, WWW: London, 99–104.

Redclift, Nanneke and Sinclair, M. Thea (eds), (1991), *Working Women: International Perspectives on Labour and Gender Ideology*, Routledge: London and New York.

Republic of the Philippines (1986), *Medium-Term Western Visayas Region Development Plan*, Regional Development Council Western Visayas: Iloilo City.

Republic of the Philippines (1990), *Updated Central Visayas Regional Development Plan 1990–1992*, Regional Development Council Central Visayas: Cebu City.

Republic of the Philippines (1993), *Investment Priorities Plan 1993*, Office of the President: Manila.

Republic of the Philippines and the United Nations Children Fund [UNICEF] (1990), *Situation of Children and Women in the Philippines*, RP and UNICEF: Manila.

Republic of the Philippines with United Nations Development Programme [UNDP] and World Tourism Organisation [WTO] (1991), *Tourism Master Plan for the Philippines*, UNDP/WTO: Madrid.

Resurrecion-Elviña, Lutgarda (1990), Women and the Popular Media. In Marjorie Evasco, Aurora Javate de Dios and Flor Caagusan (eds), *Women's Springbook: Readings on Women and Society*, Fresam Press: Quezon City, 85–9.

Reyes, Socorro (1992), Legislative Agenda on Women's issues for the New Congress. In *Lila: Asia Pacific Women's Studies Journal* (Institute of Women's Studies, St Scholasticas College, Manila), 2, 45–64.

Reyes Churchill, Paul (1993), Cebu: Aberration or Model for Growth? In *Philippine Quarterly of Culture and Society*, 21, 3–16.

Rigg, Jonathan (1991), *Southeast Asia: A Region in Transition*, Unwin Hyman: London.

Roberts, Pepe (1991), Anthropological Perspectives on the Household. In *IDS Bulletin* (Sussex), 22:1, 60–4.

Rohini, P.H. (1991), Women Workers in Manufacturing Industry in India: Problems and Possibilities. In Haleh Afshar (ed.), *Women, Development and Survival in the Third World*, Longman: Harlow, 260–87.

de la Rosa, R.J. (1993), *Beyond Social Conscience: The Case of Del Monte Pineapples*. Philippines Development Briefing 6, Catholic Institute for International Relations: London.

Rosario, Rosario del (1985), *Life on the Assembly Line: An Alternative Philippine Report on Women Industrial Workers*, Philippine Women's Collective: Quezon City.

Ruiz, Angeles (1993), Cebu City's Informal Sector: A Profile. In *Data Links* (University of Philippines Cebu College), 2:4, 1–7.

Rutten, Rosanne (1990), *Artisans and Entrepreneurs in the Rural Philippines: Making a Living and Gaining Wealth in Two Commercialised Crafts*, VU University Press: Amsterdam.

Safa, Helen (1980), Class Consciousness among Working Class Women in Latin America: Puerto Rico. In June Nash and Helen Safa (eds), *Sex and Class in Latin America*, Bergin: New York, 69–85.

Safa, Helen (1981), Runaway Shops and Female Employment: The Search for Cheap Labour. In *Signs: Journal of Women in Culture and Society*, 7:2, 418–33.

Safa, Helen (1990), Women and Industrialisation in the Caribbean. In Sharon Stichter and Jane Parpart (eds), *Women, Employment and the Family in the International Division of Labour*, Macmillan: Basingstoke, 72–97.

Safa, Helen (1992), Development and Changing Gender Roles in Latin America and the Caribbean. In Hilda Kahne and Janet Giele (eds), *Women's Work and Women's Lives: The Continuing Struggle Worldwide*, Westview Press: Boulder, CO, 69–86.

Safa, Helen (1993), The New Women Workers: Does Money Equal Power? In *NACLA Report on the Americas*, XXVII:1, 24–9.

Safilios-Rothschild, Constantina (1990), Socio-economic Determinants of the Outcomes of Women's Income-Generation in Developing Countries. In Sharon Stichter and Jane Parpart (eds), *Women, Employment and the Family in the International Division of Labour*, Macmillan: Basingstoke, 221–8.

St Hilaire, Colette (1992), *Canadian Aid, Women and Development: Re-baptizing the Filipina*, Philippine Development Briefing 3, Catholic Institute for International Relations: London.

Sala-Boza, Astrid (1982), The Sitio Sta Ana Cebuana: A Sociocultural Study. MA thesis presented to the Faculty of the Graduate School, University of San Carlos, Cebu City.

Salaff, Janet (1990), Women, Family and the State: Hong Kong, Taiwan, Singapore – Newly Industrialised Countries in Asia. In Sharon Stichter and Jane Parpart (eds), *Women, Employment and the Family in the International Division of Labour*, Macmillan: Basingstoke, 98–136.

Santa Maria, Felice (1991), The Ballad of Boracay. In *Mabuhay*, April 1991.

Santos, Aida F. (1991), Do Women Really Hold up Half the Sky? Notes on the Women's Movement in the Philippines. In Sister Mary John Mananzan (ed.), *Essays on Women*, Institute of Women's Studies, St Scholastica's College: Manila (revised edn.), 36–51.

Santos, Aida (1992), Gathering the Dust: The Bases Issue in the Philippines. In Saundra Pollock Sturdevant and Brenda Stoltzfus (eds), *Let the Good Times Roll: Prostitution and the U.S. Military in Asia*, New Press: New York, 32–44.

Santos, Aida and Lee, Lynn (1989), *The Debt Crisis: A Treadmill of Poverty for Filipino Women*, KALAYAAN: Quezon City.

Santos, Aida and Lee, Lynn (1992), A Treadmill of Poverty for Filipino Women. In Emmanuel de Dios and Joel Rocamora (eds), *Of Bonds and Bondage: A Reader on Philippine Debt*, Transnational Institute/Philippine Center for Policy Studies/Freedom from Debt Coalition: Manila, 59–66.

Santos, Marichu (1988), The Relationship between High Production Quotas and the Incidences of Women Getting Sick. In SIBAT–Women, Development and Technology (eds), *Labor in Women, Women in Labor: What's in Store?*, SIBAT: Quezon City, 15–18.

Sassen-Koob, Saskia (1984), From Household to Workplace: Theories and Survey Research on Migrant Women in the Labour Market. Notes on the Incorporation of Women through Immigration and Offshore Production. In *International Migration Review*, xviii:4, 1,144–67.

Schneider, Helmut (1994), Ethnicity and Migration to Secondary Cities – A Comparison of Baguio City and Zamboanga City, Philippines. Paper delivered at the panel 'Urbanising the Countryside and Populating the Cities', European Conference on Philippine Studies, School of Oriental and African Studies, University of London, 13–15 April 1994.

Scott A.J. (1987), The Semiconductor Industry in South-East Asia: Organisation, Location and the International Division of Labour. In *Regional Studies*, 21:2, 143–60.

Scott, Alison MacEwen (1986), Women and Industrialisation: Examining the 'Female Marginalisation' Thesis. In *Journal of Development Studies*, 22:4, 649–80.

Sempio-Diy, Alicia V. (1988), *Handbook on the Family Code in the Philippines*, Joer Printing Services: Quezon City.

Sen, Amartya K. (1987), *Gender and Cooperative Conflicts*. Working Paper no.18, World Institute for Development Economics Research [WIDER]: Helsinki.

Sen, Amartya K. (1990), Gender and Cooperative Conflicts. In Irene Tinker (ed.), *Persistent Inequalities: Women and World Development*, Oxford University Press: New York, 123–49.

Sen, Gita and Grown, Caren (1987), *Development, Crises and Alternative Visions*, New Feminist Library: New York.

Sevilla, Judy Carol (1989), The Filipino Woman and the Family. In Amaryllis Torres (ed.), *The Filipino Woman in Focus: A Handbook of Reading*, UNESCO: Bangkok.

SGV and Co/Private Investment and Trade Opportunities Philippines [PITO-P] (1992), *Doing Business in the Philippines*, PITO-P: Manila.

Shibusawa, Masahide; Ahmad, Zakaria Haji; and Bridges, Brian (1992), *Pacific Asia in the 1990s*, Routledge: London.

Shimuzu, Hiromu (1991), Filipino Children in the Family and Society: Growing up in a Many-People Environment. In Department of Sociology-

Anthropology (ed.), *SA 21: Selected Readings*, Office of Research and Publications, Ateneo de Manila University: Quezon City, 106–25.

Shivanath, Suhith (1982), Repression and Resistance in Bataan Export Processing Zone in the Philippines, mimeo, Philippine Resource Centre: London.

Shoesmith, Dennis (1986), *Export Processing Zones in Five Countries: The Economic and Human Consequences*, Asia Partnership for Development: Hong Kong.

Sinclair, M. Thea (1991), Women, Work and Skill: Economic Theories and Feminist Perspectives. In Nanneke Redclift and M. Thea Sinclair (eds), *Working Women: International Perspectives on Labour and Gender Ideology*, Routledge: London and New York, 1–24.

Singh, Andrea and Kelles-Viitanen, Anita (eds), (1987), *Invisible Hands: Women in Home-based Production*, Sage: Newbury Park and London, 13–26.

Singhanetra-Renard, Anchalee and Prabhudhanitisarn, Nitaya (1992), Changing Socio-economic Roles of Thai Women and their Migration. In Sylvia Chant (ed.), *Gender and Migration in Developing Countries*, Belhaven: London, 154–73.

Sison, Jose Maria (1988), Continuing Struggle in the Philippines. mimeo, Philippine Resource Centre: London.

Sklair, Leslie (1990), Regional Consequences of Open-door Development Strategies: Export Zones in Mexico and China. In David Simon (ed.), *Third World Regional Development*, Paul Chapman: London, 109–26.

Sklair, Leslie (1991), *Sociology of the Global System*, Harvester Wheatsheaf: Hemel Hempstead.

Skrobanek, Siriporn (1987), Strategies against Prostitution in Thailand. In Miranda Davies (ed.), *Third World – Second Sex 2*, Zed: London, 211–17.

Smith, Joan and Wallerstein, Immanuel (eds), (1992), *Creating and Transforming Households: The Constraints of the World Economy*, Cambridge University Press: Cambridge.

Spindel, Cheywa (1990), Mujer y Crisis en los Años Ochenta. In DAWN/MUDAR (eds), *Mujer y Crisis: Respuestas Ante la Recesión*, Editorial Nueva Sociedad: Carácas, 105–30.

Srisang, Koron (1991), Introduction: The Child: The Greatest Who Suffers Most. In Koron Srisang (ed.), *Caught in Modern Slavery: Tourism and Child Prostitution in Asia*, Ecumenical Coalition on Third World Tourism: Bangkok, 4–8.

Standing, Guy (1989), Global Feminisation through Flexible Labor. In *World Development*, 17:7, 1,077–95.

Standing, Hilary (1985), Resources, Wages and Power: The Impact of Women's Employment on the Urban Bengali Household. In Haleh Afshar (ed.), *Women, Work and Ideology in the Third World*, Tavistock: London, 232–57.

Stanyukovich, Maria (1994), Ideology of Gender in an Ifugao Setting. Women's Epic and Male Ritual Performances. Paper delivered at the panel 'Religion, Ritual and Identity', European Conference on Philippine Studies, School of Oriental and African Studies, University of London, 13–15 April 1994.

Steinberg, David (1986), Tradition and Response. In John Bresnan (ed.), *Crisis in the Philippines*, Princeton University Press: Princeton, NJ, 30–54.

Stewart, Frances (1992), Can Adjustment Programmes Incorporate the Interests of Women? In Haleh Afshar and Carolyne Dennis (eds), *Women and Adjustment Policies in the Third World*, Macmillan: Basingstoke, 13–45.

Stichter, Sharon (1990), Women, Employment and the Family: Current Debates. In Sharon Stichter and Jane Parpart (eds), *Women, Employment and the Family in the International Division of Labour*, Macmillan: Basingstoke, 221–8.

Stolcke, Verena (1991), The Exploitation of Family Morality: Labour Systems and Family Structure on São Paulo Coffee Plantations, 1850–1979. In Elizabeth Jelin (ed.), *Family, Household and Gender Relations in Latin America*, Kegan Paul International/UNESCO: London/Paris, 69–100.

Sturdevant, Saundra Pollock and Stoltzfus, Brenda (eds), (1992a), *Let the Good Times Roll: Prostitution and the U.S. Military in Asia*, New Press: New York.

Sturdevant, Saundra Pollock and Stoltzfus, Brenda (1992b), Olongapo: The Bar System. In Saundra Pollock Sturdevant and Brenda Stoltzfus (eds), *Let the Good Times Roll: Prostitution and the U.S. Military in Asia*, New Press: New York, 45–7.

Sturdevant, Saundra Pollock and Stoltzfus, Brenda (1992c), Disparate Threads of the Whole: An Interpretative Essay. In Saundra Pollock Sturdevant and Brenda Pollock (eds), *Let the Good Times Roll: Prostitution and the U.S. Military in Asia*, New Press: New York, 300–34.

Sudarkasa, Niara (1977), Women and Migration in Contemporary West Africa. In Wellesley Editorial Committee (ed.), *Women and National Development: The Complexities of Change* University of Chicago Press: Chicago, 178–89.

Tacoli, Cecilia (1994), Gender and International Survival Strategies: Filipino Labour Migrants in Rome. PhD thesis in preparation, Department of Geography, London School of Economics.

Taganahan, Nancy (1993), Forum on Philippines 2000 Held. In *Bakud* (WRRC), 3:3, 3.

Taguiwalo, Judy (1993), Rural Women, Debt and Structural Adjustment. In Lita Mariano, Teresita Oliveros and Adora Faye E. de Vera (eds), *Nurture and Seeds of Unity, Take Root and Reclaim our Lives! Papers on the Asian Peasant Women Dialogue on GATT and SAPs*, AMIHAN: Manila, 40–52.

Tan, Michael; de Leon, Adul; Stoltzfus, Brenda; and O'Donnell, Cindy (1989), AIDS as a Political Issue: Working with the Sexually Prostituted in the Philippines. In *Community Development Journal*, 24:3, 186–94.

Tanchoo-Subido, Chita (1979), *Employment Effects of Multinational Enterprises in the Philippines*, Working Paper no.11, ILO: Geneva.

Taylor, John and Turton, Andrew (1988), Production and Gender Relations: Introduction. In John Taylor and Andrew Turton (eds), *Sociology of 'Developing Societies': Southeast Asia*, Macmillan, Basingstoke, 145–6.

Tharan, Caridad (1989), Filipina Maids in Malaysia. In Asian and Pacific Development Centre (ed.), *The Trade in Domestic Helpers: Causes, Mechanisms and Consequences*, APDC: Kuala Lumpur, 272–86.

Tiano, Susan (1990), Maquiladora Women: A New Category of Workers. In Kathryn Ward (ed.), *Women Workers and Global Restructuring*, ILR Press, Cornell University: Ithaca, NY, 192–223.

Tidalgo, Rosa Linda (1985), The Integration of Women in Development and Philippine Development Planning. In Noeleen Heyzer (ed.), *Missing Women: Development Planning in Asia and the Pacific*, Asian and Pacific Development Centre: Kuala Lumpur, 355–405.

Thirkell, Allyson (1994), The Informal Land Market in Cebu City, the Philippines: Accessibility, Settlement Development and Residential Segregation. PhD thesis in preparation, Department of Geography, London School of Economics.

Tiglao-Torres, Amaryllis (1990), Directions for Third World Feminism: In the Philippine Locale. In *Sarilakas Grassroots Development* (Manila), IV, 3/4, 13–18.

Tiukinhoy, Araceli and Remedio, Elizabeth (1992), *Employment and Industrial Relations Conditions in the Mactan Export Processing Zone*, Institute for Labor Studies, Department of Labor and Employment, University of San Carlos: Cebu City.

Tornea, Vivian and Habana, Esther (1989), Women in International Labour Migration: The Philippine Experience. In Asian and Pacific Development Centre (ed.), *The Trade in Domestic Helpers: Causes, Mechanisms and Consequences*, APDC: Kuala Lumpur, 255–71.

Townsend, Janet and Momsen, Janet (1987), Towards a Geography of Gender in the Third World. In Janet Momsen and Janet Townsend (eds), *Geography of Gender in the Third World*, Hutchinson: London, 27–81.

Trager, Lillian (1984), Family Strategies and the Migration of Women: Migrants to Dagupan City, Philippines. In *International Migration Review*, xviii:4, 1,264–77.

Trager, Lillian (1988), *The City Connection: Migration and Family Interdependence in the Philippines*, Ann Arbor, MI.

Truong, Thanh-Dam (1990), *Sex, Money and Morality: Prostitution and Tourism in Southeast Asia*, Zed: London.

Tuazon, Romulo (1991), Under the Philippine Volcano. In *WorldAIDS*, 18, 9.

Unas, Rowena (1992), Violence against Women in the Philippines. In *Lila: Asia Pacific Women's Studies Journal*, 1, 5–11.

UNICEF, Manila (1988), Redirecting Adjustment Programmes towards Growth and the Protection of the Poor. In Giovanni Andrea Cornea, Richard Jolly and Frances Stewart (eds), *Adjustment with a Human Face*, vol.II: *Country Case Studies*, Clarendon: Oxford, 184–217.

United Nations [UN] (1990), *Demographic Yearbook 1988*, UN: New York.

United Nations Development Programme [UNDP] (1992), *Human Development Report 1992*, Oxford University Press: New York.

University of the Philippines Asian Institute of Tourism [UP AIT] (1990), *Study on Regional Travel in the Philippines 1990*, vol.III, DOT: Manila.

Urban Poor Development Center [UPDC] (1992), *Primer on the Metro Cebu Development and Investment Plans*, UPDC: Cebu City.

Varley, Ann (1993), Gender, Household Structure and Accommodation for Young Adults in Urban Mexico. In Hemalata Dandekar (ed.), *Shelter, Women and Development: First and Third World Perspectives*, George Wahr: Ann Arbor MI, 304–19.

Veneracion, Jaime (1992), From *Babaylan* to *Beata*: A Study on the Religiosity of Filipino Women. In *Review of Women's Studies* (University of the Philippines, Quezon City), 3:1, 1–15.

Vera-Sanso, Penny (1994), What the Neighbours Say: Gender and Power in Two Low-income Settlements of Madras. PhD thesis in preparation, Department of Anthropology, Goldsmiths College, London.

Vickers, Jean (1991), *Women and the World Economic Crisis*, Zed: London.

Villariba, Mariya (1993), *Canvasses of Women in the Philippines*, International Reports: Women and Society no.7, Change: London.

Villegas, Bernardo (1986), The Economic Crisis. In John Bresnan (ed.), *Crisis in the Philippines*, Princeton University Press: Princeton, NJ, 145–75.

Villegas, Edberto (1988), *The Political Economy of Philippine Labor Laws*, Foundation for Nationalist Studies: Quezon City.

Visayas Labor Development Center [VLDC] (1993), *Evaluation Report of Union Activities in Mactan EPZ 1990*, VLDC: Cebu City.

Vitug, Marites (1993), A Little Something from Cebu. In *Newsweek*, 8 February 1993, p.24.

Walby, Sylvia (1990), *Theorising Patriarchy*, Basil Blackwell: Oxford.

Walby, Sylvia (1992), Post-Post Modernism? Theorising Social Complexity. In Michèle Barrett and Anne Phillips (eds), *Destabilising Theory: Contemporary Feminist Debates*, Polity Press: Cambridge, 31–52.

Ward, Kathryn (1990), Introduction and Overview. In Kathryn Ward (ed.), *Women Workers and Global Restructuring*, ILR Press, Cornell University: Ithaca, NY, 1–24.

Warren, Carol (1988), *Gender Issues in Field Research* Qualitative Research Methods Series 9, Sage: Newbury Park.

Whitam, Frederick *et al* (1985), *Male Homosexuality in Four Societies: Brazil, Guatemala, the Philippines and the US*, Praeger: New York.

White, Sarah (1992), *Arguing with the Crocodile: Gender and Class in Bangladesh*, Zed: London.

Wilke, Renate (1983), Gentle Women for Hard Currency. In Peter Holden *et al* (eds), *Prostitution Tourism Development*, Ecumenical Coalition on Third World Tourism: Bangkok, 14–16.

Wilson, Fiona (1991), *Sweaters: Gender, Class and Workshop-based Industry in Mexico*, Macmillan: Basingstoke.

Wilson, Patricia (1992), *Exports and Local Development: Mexico's New Maquiladoras*, University of Texas Press: Austin.

Wolf, Diane (1990a), Daughters, Decisions and Domination: An Empirical and Conceptual Critique of Household Strategies. In *Development and Change*, 21, 43–74.

Wolf, Diane (1990b), Linking Women's Labor with the Global Economy: Factory Workers and their Families in Rural Java. In Kathryn Ward (ed.), *Women Workers and Global Restructuring*, ILR Press, Cornell University: Ithaca, NY, 25–47.

Wolf, Diane (1991), Female Autonomy, the Family and Industrialisation in Java. In Rae Lesser Blumberg (ed.), *Gender, Family and the Economy: The Triple Overlap*, Sage: Newbury Park, 128–48.

Women's Education Development, Productivity and Research Organisation [WEDPRO] (1990a), *Alternative Employment, Economic Livelihood and Human Resource Development for Women in the Entertainment Sector, Subic*. Final Report, Legislative Executive Bases Council/WEDPRO: Manila.

Women's Education Development, Productivity and Research Organisation [WEDPRO] (1990b), *Alternative Employment, Economic Livelihood and Human Resource Development for Women in the Entertainment Sector, Clark*. Final Report, Legislative Executive Bases Council/WEDPRO: Manila.

Women's Resource and Research Center [WRRC] and the Philippines Steering Committee [PSC] (1990), Towards a Preliminary Viewing of Child Prostitution and Tourism. In *Flights*, 4:2, 4–6.

Women's Resource Center of Cebu [WRCC] Research Collective (1992), The Women of Cebu: Braving the Odds. In *Bakud*, 2:3, 5 and 10.

Women's Resource Center of Cebu [WRCC] (1993a), Editorial: When Power Breeds Powerlessness. In *Bakud*, 3:1, 3.

Women's Resource Center of Cebu [WRCC] (1993b), Editorial: Ramos' Philippines 2000: A Bane to Women. In *Bakud*, 3:3, 2.

Women Working Worldwide [WWW] (ed.), (1991), *Common Interests: Women Organising in Global Electronics*, WWW: London.

World Bank (1992a), *World Development Report 1992*, Oxford University Press: Oxford.

World Bank (1992b), *The World Bank Annual Report 1992*, World Bank: Washington.

World Bank (1993a), *World Development Report 1993*, Oxford University Press: Oxford.

World Bank (1993b), *The World Bank Annual Report 1993*, World Bank: Washington.

World Bank (1993c), *The East Asian Miracle: Economic Growth and Public Policy*, Oxford University Press: Oxford.

World Tourism Organisation [WTO] (1992a), *Yearbook of Tourism Statistics*, vol.1, WTO: Madrid.

World Tourism Organisation [WTO] (1992b), *Yearbook of Tourism Statistics*, vol. 2, WTO: Madrid.

Yap, Virginia (1989), Trade Union Participation of Workers in the Female Populated Garments Corporations. In SIBOL (ed.), *Women, Development and Technology, 2*, Women, Development and Technology Desk: Quezon City, 52–4.

Young, Kate (1992), Household Resource Management. In Lise Østergaard (ed), *Gender and Development: A Practical Guide*, Routledge: London, 135–64.

Youssef, Nadia and Hetler, Carol (1983), Establishing the Economic Condition of Women-headed Households in the Third World: A New Approach. In Mayra Buvinić, Margaret Lycette and William McGreevy (eds), *Women and Poverty in the Third World*, Johns Hopkins University Press: Baltimore, MD, 216–43.

Yu, Elena and Liu, William T. (1980), *Fertility and Kinship in the Philippines*, University of Notre Dame Press: Paris.

Yun, Hing Ai (1988), Wage Labour in West Malaysia: A Study of Five Factories. In John Taylor and Andrew Turton (eds), *Sociology of 'Developing Societies': Southeast Asia*, Macmillan: Basingstoke, 97–106.

Zarate, Jovita (1990), *Health and Safety of Women Workers: A Fundamental Right*, Women, Development and Technology Institute: Quezon City.

Zosa-Feranil, Imelda (1984), Female Employment and the Family: A Case Study of the Bataan Export Processing Zone. In Gavin Jones (ed.), *Women in the Urban and Industrial Workforce: Southeast and East Asia*, Development Studies Centre Monograph no.33, Australian National University: Canberra, 387–403.

Zosa-Feranil, Imelda (1991), Urban Labour Market Adaptation of Women: A Comparison of Migrants and Non-migrants in a Medium-Sized Rapidly Growing Metropolitan Area. Mimeo, Population Institute, University of the Philippines: Quezon City.

INDEX

abortion, 16, 40–1
absence (of men), *see* households, out-migration
absenteeism, 174, 176–7; *see also* employers
abuse (physical, against women), 13, 14, 26, 126–7, 212n, 233, 236, 250–1, 255, 270, 283n, 298, 311; *see also* child abuse; violence
accounting departments, 142, 178–9, 184; *see also* employment; managers
Ad Hoc Committee on a Women's Legislative Agenda, 308
administration, 140, 142, 145, 178–9, 184; *see also* clerical work; employment; managers
advertising, 139, 144, 177, 210
of job vacancies, 139, 144, 177
adultery, *see* fidelity
Africa, 280, 284n
age, 23–4, 32, 36, 96, 100, 103, 122, 160, 161n, 162, 165, 174, 203–6, 222, 223–4, 228, 230, 242, 246, 266, 271, 295
as criteria in recruitment into employment, 24–5, 35, 136–7, 143, 150, 176, 180, 182–4, 188, 191, 221
and female labour force participation, 20, 23–5, 27–8, 82, 109, 111–12, 114, 170, 189, 191, 200, 202
and migration, 32–3, 85, 109, 117, 119, 120–1, 128, 155–7, 191–2, 196, 198, 199, 238, 264

see also employers; employment; life cycle
agrarian reform, 53, 54; *see also* CARP
agricultural development, 31, 46n, 48, 309
agriculture, 31, 116–17, 123
cash crop, 116, 309
export-oriented, 48, 50, 309
subsistence, 116, 156, 309
agro-industry, 50, 54, 309
AIDS/HIV, 40, 80, 224, 233–7, 255, 314–15
prevention, 234–7
see also antibiotics; condoms; disease; Social Hygiene Clinic
Aklan, 72, 79, 93, 95n, 120, 194, 195, 197
alcohol, 123, 125–7, 145, 147, 236, 255
AMIHAN, 42
Angeles, 48n, 238, 239, 240, 250, 251, 259, 316
antibiotics, 233
apprenticeship, 151–2
Aquino, Benigno, 52
Aquino, Cory, 37, 38, 45, 52–5, 67
Antique, 72, 93, 194, 195
ASEAN, 46
asuang ('vampire'), 12
assembly plants, *see* export-manufacturing; export processing zones
Asia, 28, 130, 133n; *see also* Southeast Asia
Asian Development Bank, 55
Associated Labour Union (ALU), 174n

aunts, 195, 203; *see also* household
structure
Australasia, 64
Australia, 80, 228
Australians, 80, 228, 229

Babaylan (Philippine Women's
Network in Europe), 311
Baguio, 47, 60
balance of payments, 48
Bangkok, 45n, 65, 261n
barangay, 40, 81, 84n, 93
barkada (male gang/drinking group),
13, 125, 158, 161, 268
Bataan, 25, 27, 60, 152, 162, 164
beach vending, 113, 189–91, 192,
197, 258–9, 284
Belgium, 313
Bicol, 12, 89, 198
birth rates, 66–7, 164–6
Bohol, 72, 90, 155, 157, 194, 198
Board of Investments (BOI) 75
boarding houses, 102, 104, 160, 161,
161n, 163, 200, 242, 320, 322
Boracay, 2, 29, 35, 36, 43, 45, 64, 71,
73, 79–81, 93–5, 103–6, 112–15,
172–210, 227–30; *see also*
tourism
Brazil, 21, 267n
breadwinners, 6, 9, 95, 111, 114, 159,
163, 202, 209; *see also*
employment; household head;
household structure
brides, *see* mail order brides, marriage
Britain, 23, 53, 78, 130, 222
brothels, 41, 213; *see also* sex work
brothers, 104, 156, 203
Brunei, 46n
Bureau of Investigation, 138

Cagayan de Oro, 35, 155, 158
Canada, 34, 64, 122, 222, 226
Canadian International Development
Agency, 42
carrageenan, 130, 135n, 143n
Capiz, 72
cash crops, *see* agriculture

cashiers, 181
catering, *see* food, hotels, restaurants
carinderias, 104, 107, 110, 113, 191,
192, 296
Catholic Church, 16n, 24, 52, 67,
308n
Catholicism, 13, 16n, 66
Caticlan, 112, 189, 195, 198
Cavite, 60, 198
Cebu, 2, 29, 32, 35, 36, 43, 45, 56,
64, 65, 71, 72, 73–7, 80, 82–7,
95–100, 106–10, 143–8,
171–210, 212–27, 230–7
census, 4n, 16n, 35
chambermaids, *see* cleaning
child abuse, 250
childbearing, *see* childbirth, pregnancy
childbirth, 20, 26, 164–6, 168, 170,
271; *see also* childcare; children;
female labour force
participation
childcare, 6, 8, 103, 109, 112, 118–19,
124, 152, 161–6, 191, 200, 202,
203–7, 238–9, 246–8, 268,
299–300, 308
children, 7, 8, 15, 16, 39, 96, 98, 100,
109, 123, 124, 137, 150, 156,
161–6, 198, 200, 201, 203–7,
246–8, 283
as prostitutes, 24, 64n
see also daughters, sex work, sons
China, 46
Church, 96, 248, 272n, *see also*
Catholic Church
Civil Code, 38
Clark Air Base, 48n, 212, 238, 239,
240
cleaning,
as occupation, 179, 180, 184, 188
see also employment; hotels
clerical work, 107, 109
cock-fighting, 106, 125–6
coconuts, 48, 116, 180
commerce, 107, 110, 172
formal, 107, 113, 173, 184
small-scale/petty, 106, 107, 109,
110–13, 189–93

see also beach vending; employment; informal sector; self-employment; tourism

Commonwealth Act 186 (1936), 68

community, 82, 122, 123

commuting, 121

Comprehensive Agrarian Reform Programme (CARP), 54

concubine, 14n; *see also* sex work

condoms, 213, 234, 235, 236, 237; *see also* AIDS; family planning

conflict (intra-household), 10–11, 125–7

consensual union, 16, 95, 100; *see also* marriage

Constitution, 38, 69

construction, 99, 110, 112, 158

consumption (household), 4, 115

contraception, 16, 38, 66; *see also* family planning

contract worker, *see* labour, migration

Convention on the Elimination of All Forms of Discrimination Against Women (CEDAW), 312

Convention on Equal Remuneration for Men and Women Workers for Work of Equal Value, 312

Convention for the Suppression of Traffic in Persons and the Exploitation of the Prostitution of Others, 312

cooking, 181, 182

cooks, 181, 182; *see also* hotels; restaurants

copper-smelting, 56

corruption, 49, 50, 138, 144

cost of living, 115
  rises in, 115

Cost of Living Allowance (COLA), 150–1, 153

Costa Rica, 261n, 301, 307n, 319

crafts/craft production, 107, 113, 173, 191, 192; *see also* informal sector; furniture industry

credit, 39

Dagupan, 32

Danao, 74

daughters, 7, 16, 33, 109, 149, 163, 243, 270, 271
  obligations to parents, 20, 33, 109, 156, 157

decision-making (household), 6–11, 124–7, 168, 170, 270–1, 282–3

debt (external), 19, 22–33, 47–9, 50, 51, 53, 54–5, 57–9, 69, 285, 310

democracy, 37, 55, 135n

demography/demographic change *see* population

Department of Labor and Employment (DOLE), 135n, 138

Department of Tourism (DOT), 63–5, 76, 80–1, 190n

desertion (of women by men), 14, 127; *see also* household head; household structure

development, *see* economic development; industrialisation; urbanisation

Development Initiatives for Women and Transformative Action (DIWATA), 41, 42

development planning, 38, 39, 42, 306–10
  see also Medium Term Philippine Development Plan; Philippine Development Plan for Women; Philippine Export Development Plan; Philippines 2000

development policy, 39, 42, 306–10
  gender-aware, 39, 42, 306–10, 315–16, 316–17

development projects, 38, 42, 315–16

disaster (natural), 47, 63

discothèques, 214, 227n; *see also* sex work

disease, 68, 228
  sexually transmitted/venereal, 40, 80, 213, 233, 234–7
  see also AIDS; health; health care

division of labour, 6–7, 124–7, 163, 287–92
  household, 5–11, 124–7, 163, 267–8, 269–71, 276, 279, 282–3, 284, 299–300, 302

international, 25, 28
sexual/along lines of gender, 6–7,
124–7, 279, 287–92
see also daughters; employment;
gender; household
divorce, 12, 14, 15, 95, 100n, *see also*
separation
doctors, 138; *see also* health care; Social
Hygiene Clinic
domestic labour, 8–13, 109, 112,
124–5, 161, 163, 164, 185, 268,
269–70, 287–8, 299–300, 302
domestic service, 104, 220n, 259; *see
also* informal sector
domestic violence, 41, 124–7
Dominican Republic, 28, 138, 277,
301
drugs, 119, 123, 232
Dumaguete, 158

Early Day Motion, 311n
earnings, 107, 111, 113–14, 262, 298,
301
in export-manufacturing, 133–4,
137, 150–5
gender differences in, 107, 111,
113–14, 151, 207
men's, 107, 111, 113–14, 151
in sex work, 230–2
in tourism, 113–14, 186–8, 192–3
women's, 107, 111, 113–14, 151,
301
see also wage
economic crisis, *see* debt; household;
recession; structural adjustment
economic development, 18, 36,
45–81, 285
in Boracay, 79–81
in Cebu, 73–7
export-oriented, 59–81
in Lapu-Lapu, 77–9
in Visayas, 72–81
see also export manufacturing;
tourism
economy, 33, 45–81
local, 156, 260
Ecuador, 22

Ecumenical Coalition on Third World
Tourism (ECTWT), 313, 314
education, 69, 85, 91–2, 95n, 109, 115,
168, 194, 195, 248, 268, 293
college, 85, 164, 167, 293
and female employment, 26
men's, 85, 91–2, 95
primary (elementary), 85
as qualification for work, 133, 136,
137, 139, 142, 164, 167n, 175,
176, 188–9, 221, 293
secondary (high school), 85
vocational, 85n–88n, 92, 95n, 164,
248, 293
women's, 85, 91–2, 95, 164
see also training; university
Electric Power Crisis Act (1993), 56–7
electricity, 56–7, 60, 61, 115
electronics industry, 24, 27, 53, 56,
59, 61, 130–42; *see also* export-
manufacturing
Employer Survey, 321–2
employers, 9, 134–5, 141, 166–71
assumptions about gender, 148–50,
166–71, 175–85, 287–92, 299
rationale for employing women,
139–42, 144–8, 166–71, 175–85,
287–92, 299
recruitment policies and practices,
79, 102, 136–9, 143–4, 166–71,
175–85, 220–1, 287–92
relations with workers, 79, 135,
174, 188, 288
see also employment; gender;
managers
employment, 19–29, 69–70, 106–15,
266–72
in Boracay, 79–81, 112–15,
172–210
in Cebu, 74–5, 85, 106–10,
129–36, 143–50, 172–210
in Lapu Lapu, 77–9, 110–12, 129–55
in export-manufacturing, 20, 74–5,
77–9, 110–12, 129–55
gender differences in, 19–23,
129–55, 141–2, 144–8, 166–71,
177–85

gender segregation in, 22, 23,
    139–43, 144–8, 166–71,
    177–85
men's, 85, 90, 141–2, 145–8,
    177–85
in sex work, 76–7
in tourism, 76–7, 79–81, 112–15,
    171–210
trajectories, 23, 29
women's, 19–29, 90, 139–43,
    144–8, 166–71, 177–85
see also employers; female labour
    force participation; migration;
    mobility
empowerment, 294, 316–17; *see also*
    power
entertainment establishments, 25, 26,
    36, 65, 77, 80, 81, 211, 214–19,
    220–7, 237, 241, 322
visitors to, 215–19, 220, 221–7,
    322
see also brothels; employment; girlie
    bars; karaoke bars; massage
    parlours; men; sex work
Ermita, 65n
ethnicity, 80, 226, 251; *see also* racism
Europe, 34, 55, 80, 171n
Eastern, 171n
Europeans (people)
as clients of sex workers, 222–3
expenditure (household), 7–10, 125,
    170, 269
Export Incentives Act (1970), 60
exports, 2, 56, 59–63, 129
export-manufacturing, 1, 20, 24,
    25–9, 59–63, 110–12, 129–55
in Cebu, 74–5, 129–36, 143–50
in Mactan/Lapu-Lapu, 77–9,
    129–55
occupational hazards in, 27, 153,
    169, 263
see also electronics industry; fashion
    accessories industry; furniture
    industry; garment industry
export processing zone, 8, 24–5, 27,
    50, 56, 60–2, 78–9, 88–9,
    130–42,

see also electronics industry; export-
    manufacturing; garment industry;
    Mactan
Export Processing Zone Authority
    (EPZA), 60, 75, 78
extended family, *see* household
    structure, kin, kinship

factory, 24, 26–9, 36, 39, 78, 106–8,
    110–12, 121, 129–71, 259, 287;
    see also electronics industry;
    export-manufacturing; fashion
    accessories industry; furniture
    industry; garment industry
family, 5, 150; *see also* culture;
    household; ideology
Family Code, 38–9, 308
family planning, 38, 66–7, 307; *see also*
    condoms; contraception
family structure, *see* family; household
    structure; kin; kinship
farming, 116, 124, 156, 194; *see also*
    agriculture
fashion accessories industry, 56, 75,
    107, 130–4, 143, 144–5, 147–8,
    163
fathers, 149, 165, 167
female-headed households, *see*
    household head; household
    structure
female labour force participation, 2,
    19–29, 69–70, 106–16, 266–72
and fertility, 164–6, 203–7, 245–8,
    272, 299, 307
and household structure, 19–21,
    266–72
implications for women's lives and
    status, 19–29, 166–71, 207–10,
    251–5
and migration, 32–7, 257–65
see also culture; employers;
    employment; kin; mobility
'Female Marginalisation' Thesis, 21–2,
    303
fertility, 14–16, 38, 96, 164–6, 203–7,
    245–8, 272, 299, 307; *see*
    childbirth; children; family

planning; female labour force participation; population

fidelity (marital), 13, 14, 39, 125–7; *see also* infidelity; marriage; sexuality

fish
  in diet, 58, 115
  selling, 111, 113–14, 190
  see also informal sector; tourism

fishing, 113, 189

food, 58, 68–9, 115
  consumption, 58, 115
  selling, 104, 107, 113, 116

foreign exchange, 1, 56, 60
  and international tourism, 63–5
  see also debt; export-manufacturing; sex work

Foreign Investments Act (1991), 62, 218

formal sector (of urban economy), 70, 109, 115, 172–88
  see also civil service; employment; export-manufacturing; tourism; sex work

fostering, 36, 98, 100, 118–19, 120, 203, 238, 239, 241, 243

France, 78, 222

Free Trade Zone, *see* export processing zone

Freedom From Debt Coalition (FFDC), 59, 310

French, 132, 147, 228, 229

fringe benefits
  in export-manufacturing employment, 112, 152–4, 169
  in sex work, 232–3
  in tourism employment, 174, 187, 192

furniture industry, 56, 75, 107, 130–2, 143, 145–7, 154–5, 158, 162

galang (respect), 15

gambling, 10, 106, 125, 147, 268, 302

Gang of Four, 46

Garcia, Carlos, 48

garment industry, 24, 53, 56, 59, 61–2, 103, 130–42

gender
  discrimination, 149–50, 317
  equality, 7–8, 11, 39, 301
  and household, 4–19
  identity, 11–12
  inequality, 28, 124, 170, 186, 207–10, 217, 251–5, 270, 289, 297, 308, 317
  relations, 5, 124–7, 166–71, 207–10, 251–5, 274, 279, 284, 287–302
  roles, 5, 27–9, 124–7, 166–71, 207–10, 251–5, 274, 279, 285, 287–302
  stereotypes, 11–12, 141–2, 148–50, 166–71, 179–80, 184, 207–10, 251–5, 287–302
  subordination, 5, 8, 28, 270, 280
  see also division of labour; economic development; employers; employment; husbands; ideology; patriarchy; sexual harrassment

General Assembly Binding Women for Reforms, Integrity, Liberty and Action (GABRIELA), 38, 42, 313

Germany, 78

'girlie bars', 80, 211, 214, 216, 221, 241; *see also* sex work

godparent *see* kin, kinship

gossip, 100n, 245, 253, 263

government, 50, 53, 314; *see also* politics; state

grandmothers, 98, 123

Green Revolution, 50

Gross Domestic Product (GDP), 46, 46n, 47, 50, 57, 66

Gross National Product (GNP), 45, 48, 56, 57

Guimaras, 72, 73

Gulf War, 46, 63

hairdressing, 107

health, 68–9, 136, 153; *see also* AIDS; disease; health care; Social Hygiene Clinic

health care, 57, 69
health certificate, 80, 138, 144, 190n, 213, 235, 236; *see also* Social Hygiene Clinic
height (as specification for employment), 139, 142, 175, 176n
hiya (shame/propriety), 15n, 240
Honduras, 281n
Hong Kong, 46, 64, 76, 131n, 168n, 197, 222, 229
'hospitality industry', 2n, 64, 80, 197, 211–55; *see also* sex work
Hotel, Restaurant and Resort Association (HRRA), 64, 75
hotels, 93n, 112, 113, 114, 172–88, 214, 320, 321
household, 4–19, 95–106, 122–4, 160–6, 200–3, 242–5, 266–72, 280–6
    allocation of resources in, 5–10, 170
    composition, 17–19, 266–72
    definition of, 4–5, 84, 319
    formation, 36, 280–6
    theories of, 4–10, 280–6
    size, 84, 96–106, 122, 202
    survival strategies, 30–1, 108, 267–8, 279–80, 282
    see also decision-making; division of labour; economy; family; gender; household head; household structure; income; recession
household head, 10, 18–19, 95–106, 266–72
    definitions, 18, 319
    female, 13–14, 18–19, 99–100, 114, 243, 267, 268, 280–6, 300–1
    male, 18–19, 96, 114, 268, 277, 300
    sex of, 18–19, 266–72
    see also breadwinners; household; household structure
household structure, 17–19, 84, 95–106, 202, 242–5, 266–72, 280–6
    couples (no children/no resident children), 102

definitions, 84n, 98n, 319
    extended, 17–18, 27, 96–106, 161–3, 201, 285–6
    among manufacturing workers, 160–4
    nuclear, 17, 84, 96–106, 161–3, 202, 242, 285
    among sex workers, 242–5
    single person, 102
    among tourism workers, 200–3
    women-headed, 13, 14, 18–19, 77, 79, 81, 99–100, 163, 165, 200, 202, 242, 243, 245, 267, 268, 280–6, 300–1
    extended, 201, 244, 284
    female dominant, 244, 245, 252, 253, 267–8, 301
    male absent, 280–6
    one parent, 102, 165, 243, 276, 280, 281–6
    see also economic development; economy; female labour force participation; household head; kin; urbanisation
Household Survey, 82, 197n, 258n, 284, 285, 318–19, 320
housemaid *see* domestic service
houseperson ('housewife'), 90, 114, 194; *see also* domestic labour
housework *see* domestic labour
housing, 58, 67, 84, 89, 93
husbands, 7–16, 39, 106, 162, 163, 165, 167, 170, 197, 198, 200, 203, 251

illness *see* disease; health
Iloilo, 72, 93, 194, 195
import substitution industrialisation (ISI) *see* industrialisation
International Labour Office (ILO), 312
income, 69–70
    distribution (national), 54, 57
    household (control of), 6–10
    see also employment; expenditure; female labour force participation; informal sector

Independence (of Philippines), 45
India, 100n, 131n, 148, 162, 167,
    281n
Indonesia, 28, 33, 35, 46, 75, 100n,
    171n
industrialisation, 56, 74–5, 129–36
    import substitution, 48, 49
    see also export-manufacturing
infidelity, 14, 39, 125–6; *see also*
    fidelity
informal sector, 58, 70, 172–3, 188–93
International Monetary Fund (IMF),
    47, 49, 51, 54, 57, 59n
investment, 47, 49, 50, 53, 56, 60–3,
    171
    foreign, 47, 50, 53, 56, 60–3
    multinational, 60–3, 171n
Investment Incentives Act (1967), 49,
    60
Investment Priorities Plan (1993), 63
Ireland, 307n
Italians, 130
    as clients of sex workers, 222–3, 244n
    as investors in Philippines, 130

Japan, 34, 53, 55, 64, 73, 76, 98, 102,
    131n, 133n, 214, 240, 244n
Japanese, 47, 53n, 65n, 76, 78, 130,
    131, 133, 134, 140, 212, 217,
    221, 312
    as clients of sex workers, 231
    as employers, 130–4, 140
Java, 26
jeepney, 98, 98n
    driving, 107
jewellery, 75, 130–2, 134, 139, 144,
    145, 147–8, 153–4; *see also*
    commerce; fashion accessories
    industry

Kalayaan, 13, 42, 311n
Kalibo, 95n, 194, 195, 202
karaoke bars, 211, 214, 215
Kilusang Magbubukid ng Pilipinas
    (KMP), 52n
Kilusang Mayo Uno (KMU), 51–2
    KMU Visayas, 79

kin, 15, 17, 96, 98, 99, 102, 105, 121,
    122, 269, 273–4, 298
    as factor influencing migration, 98,
        199, 202, 263, 264, 279
    female, 202, 245, 247, 268–9, 274,
        283, 285, 300
    incorporation in extended
        households, 98, 102, 105, 244,
        285
    links with, 98, 99, 100, 105,
        121–2, 199
    see also childcare; kinship; links
kinship, 5, 98, 99, 102, 105, 273–4,
    279
    networks, 15, 19, 99, 102, 105,
        273–4, 279
Kuwait, 102, 195

labour, 20
    feminisation of, 1, 26, 27, 207,
        287–92, 293–7, 303
    see also turnover; wage labour
Labour Code, 134n, 135n, 137n,
    150n, 152, 152n, 233n
labour demand, 220, 257–60
    female, 257–60
labour force, *see* employment; female
    labour force participation
    see also male employment; female
    labour force participation;
labour markets, 26–7
labour recruitment, *see* employers
land, 93n, 265
landlordism (petty), 107, 111, 116
landowners, 116
language skills, 133, 136, 208, 221,
    232, 293
Lapu-Lapu, 2, 29, 32, 35, 36, 43, 45,
    56, 71, 72, 77–9, 88–92, 100–3,
    110–12, 136–42; *see also* Mactan
laundry, 95, 113, 191
    in home, 95, 113
    in hotels, 180, 185, 287
Law Promoting Social Equality for
    Women (Costa Rica), 307n
Legaspi, Miguel Lopez de, 73
legislation, 38, 40, 307–8, 309, 311, 313

Letter of Intent, 55
Lévi Strauss, Claude, 17
Leyte, 194, 201, 238, 239
lifecycle, 5, 109, 111, 115, 148, 149, 150, 170, 191, 264, 284
Lim, Alfredo (Mayor of Manila), 65n
links (migrant), 36, 118–22, 123, 124, 155–60, 197–9, 237–42, 264, 265, 273–4, 298; *see also* remittances
literacy, *see* education
'live-in' workers, 104, 118, 174, 175, 187, 192, 200, 201, 209; *see also* employment; tourism
livelihood strategy *see* household
livestock, 116
loans (to Philippines from abroad), 47, 49, 50, 51, 54–5, 58, 59
lone parent *see* household head; household structure
Luzon, 2n, 6n, 8, 32, 63, 64, 164, 238, 259, 265

Macapagal, Diosado (President), 48, 49
Macapagal Arroyo, Gloria (Senator), 40
Mactan, 60, 76, 77–9, 88
    Export Processing Zone, 60, 78, 88–9, 102, 110–12, 119, 130–42, 260, 262, 263n, 284
    Export Processing Zone Authority, 78, 134, 138
    International Airport, 76, 78
    see also Lapu-Lapu
Madras, 100n, 281n
mail order brides, 34, 40, 41, 308
maize, 116
Malaysia, 34, 46, 168n, 312
malnutrition, 68
managers, 135, 136, 141, 142, 145, 147, 167, 173, 180, 184n, 216, 220; *see also* employers
Mandaue, 72, 74, 119, 121, 156
manicures/manicurists, 107, 190, 192, 219; *see also* beach vending; employment; informal sector

Manila, 2n, 31, 64n, 65, 67, 70, 76n, 80, 105, 116, 120, 121, 155, 195, 198, 212, 218, 259, 275; *see also* National Capital Region
manufacturing, *see* export-manufacturing, industrialisation
Marcos, Ferdinand, 24, 38, 45, 48, 49–52, 66, 67, 70, 211, 310
Marcos, Imelda, 38, 50, 51
marijuana, 236
marital status, 95–6, 100, 103, 160, 163, 164–5, 199, 203–7, 222, 242, 245–8
    as factor influencing eligibility for employment, 137, 138, 143, 149, 175–6, 221
marriage, 14–16, 20, 25, 95–6, 100, 102, 103, 105, 109, 123, 124–7, 137, 149, 150, 160–5, 168, 170, 176, 203–7, 245–8, 250, 254, 271–2, 295
    to foreigners, 225, 246, 247–8, 250, 252, 295
    see also consensual union; husbands; mail order brides; penpal schemes; spouses; wives
martial law, 50, 51, 60
massage parlours, 216, 218, 231, 232; *see also* sex work
masseuses, 190, 192, 213, 231, 241; *see also* beach vending; employment; sex work; tourism
maternity leave, 40, 68, 137, 176, 206
meat, 115
mechanisation
    in agriculture, 54
    in industry, 131, 133, 171
    see also employers; employment; technology
Medan, 35n
Medicare, 68, 134, 152
medicine, *see also* antibiotics; health care; Social Hygiene Clinic
Medium Term Philippine Development Plan, 39, 41, 55–6, 80; *see also* Philippines 2000

methodology, 305–6, 318–23
Mexico, 23, 64, 134, 137, 148, 178, 208, 261n, 277, 281n, 284n, 285, 301, 319
Middle East, 34, 46, 80, 122
migrants, 31–6, 258–65, 322
  in Boracay, 93–4, 120–2, 176, 193–7
  in Cebu, 84, 109–10, 116–19, 157–60, 177, 193–4, 197, 237–42
  among factory workers, 32, 155–60
  among sex workers, 32, 237–42
  among tourism workers, 193–200
  in Lapu-Lapu, 89–90, 119–20
  origins of, 32, 84, 89–90, 93–4, 118–20, 155–60, 237–42
  return (from abroad), 123–4
  see also links; migration; remittances
migration
  approaches to gender and, 30–1, 257–65, 278–80
  distance of, 36, 197–8, 240, 241, 264, 265
  family, 117–22, 158, 196, 199
  female, 30–6, 155–60
  effects on migrant source areas, 122–4
  gender-differentiated, 30–6
  histories of individuals, 117–18, 120–1, 159–60, 193–202, 237–42
  independent, 32, 156–7, 199
  international/overseas, 33–4, 37, 123–4, 197, 225, 230, 247, 248, 252, 265n, 295, 310–11
  labour, 32, 117, 119, 155–7, 158, 199, 240, 276–7
  male, 32, 155–60
  marriage, 30, 32, 36, 118, 122
  permanent, 119, 122
  reasons for, 30–1, 36
  return, 122, 238, 240
  rural-urban, 31–3, 117, 261n, 322
  urban-urban, 158–9

  see also age; employment; household; household structure; links; migrants; mobility; remittances
Military Bases Agreement (1947), 48
Mindanao, 2n, 6n, 64, 89, 116, 155, 158, 238
Mindoro, 194, 195, 198, 205
mistress, 13, 125–6
mobility
  demographic, 197, 265, 277
  occupational, 167–71, 206, 207–8, 263, 263n, 291, 293, 294–7
  horizontal, 167, 291, 294–7
  vertical, 167, 291, 294–7
  socioeconomic, 164, 291
mothers, 6, 11, 98, 99, 152, 161, 164, 170, 199, 202, 203, 246, 271–2
mothers-in-law, 98
Multilateral Assistance Initiative (MAI), 55
multinationals, 1, 25, 130–42, 315, 317; *see also* export-manufacturing; export processing zones
Muslims, 6n, 46, 63

National Capital Region (NCR), 67, 70, 71
National Commission on the Role of Filipino Women (NCRFW), 37, 38, 39
National Democratic Front (NDF), 52
National Economic and Development Authority (NEDA), 40, 58, 70, 72, 80
National Endowment for Democracy Fund, 51
National Federation of Labour (NFL), 174n
National Power Corporation (NAPOCOR), 57n
National Statistics Office (NSO), 49
Negros Occidental, 72, 158, 238, 239
Negros Oriental, 72, 90, 122–4, 238
New People's Army (NPA), 52
non-governmental organisations (NGOs), 41, 42, 315–16, 322

Norway, 236
    sex industry in, 227n, 236n, 237n, 289n
nuclear family *see* household structure
nutrition, 68, 69; *see also* food

occupational mobility, *see* mobility, promotion
official data sources, *see* census
oil, 46
Olongapo, 218, 238, 239, 250, 251, 259, 316
Omnibus Investments Code, 71
one-parent household, *see* household head; household structure
Osmeña, Emilio (Governer of Cebu province), 73
Osmeña, Tommy (Mayor of Cebu City), 73
out-migration, 31–3, 36, 122–4
outwork, 107, 109, 134–5, 147–8; *see also* piece rates; subcontracting
overseas contract workers (OCWs) 33–4, 310–11; *see also* migration

Pagsanjan, 64n
pakikasama (concession), 15
Palawan, 64
Panglao Island, 64
Panos Institute, 235
parents, 15, 96, 99, 105, 156, 159; *see also* household; mothers; fathers
patriarchy, 38, 168, 245, 251, 252, 291, 292, 298, 300, 302, 303
peasants, 42, 52n, 54
pedicab-driving, 110, 189; *see also* transport
Pematang, 35n
Penal Code, 14n
'penpal schemes', 239, 239n, 250; *see also* mail order brides
People Power, 32
Peru, 21
Philippine Aid Plan (PAP), 55
Philippine Development Plan for Women (PDPW), 38, 39–41, 308, 309

Philippine Export Development Plan (PEDP), 56, 63
Philippine National Police (PNP), 81, 138, 219
Philippines 2000, 41, 56, 309, 310
piece rates, 24, 70, 107, 108, 134–5, 153–5
pig-breeding, 85, 98
Pinatubo, 47, 48n
pineapple, 50
pimps, 216
planning, 38, 39, 42; *see also* development planning
plantation *see* agriculture
'pleasing personality', 144, 182–4
police, *see* Philippine National Police
population, 38, 66–7
portering, 178, 181n; *see also* employment; hotels; tourism
poverty, 57, 67, 73, 117, 299; *see also* household; recession; structural adjustment
power, 9–11, 124–7, 294–5
    female, 9, 10, 124–7, 294–5, 297–302
    male, 124–7, 224, 227
pregnancy, 139; *see also* childbirth; maternity leave
primary sector, *see* agriculture; mining
promotion, 142, 164, 167, 292, 293, 295–7; *see also* employers; mobility
property, 39
prostitution, *see* employment; entertainment establishments; sex work
Puerto Rico, 28, 138, 277, 301
Puerto Vallarta, 261n, 301

racism, 226, 251; *see also* ethnicity
Ramos, Fidel, 40, 45, 55–7, 66
rape, *see* abuse; sex work; violence
rattan, 75, 130–2, 145–7, 154–5, 158, 152; *see also* furniture industry
raw materials, 48, 145; *see also* imports
recession, 19, 22–3, 46–7, 54–5, 57–9, 115–16
    effects on households, 22–3, 57–9, 115–16, 284–5

household responses to, 57–9, 115–16, 284–5

see also debt; household

reciprocity, *see* kin; kinship; links; remittances

regional inequality, 70–2; *see also* economic development

relatives *see* kin, kinship

religion, 15, 16, 95, 105; *see also* Catholic Church; Catholicism

remittances, 34n, 36, 46, 109, 118, 119, 123, 156, 157, 159, 160, 194, 195, 199, 241, 264, 268, 273–4; *see also* links

renters, 84, 89, 93, 107; *see also* land-lordism

reproduction, 4, 6–9, 109, 277

definitions of, 6–9

women's roles in, 6–9, 284

see also childcare; domestic labour

reproductive rights, 38, 308, 308n; *see also* abortion; contraception; family planning

'Rest and Recreation' (R & R), 2n

restaurants, 93n, 112, 113, 121, 172–88, 322, 323

retail, *see* commerce

rice, 58, 115, 116, 316; *see also* agriculture; farming

rubber, 50

salary, *see* earnings, income

SAMAKANA, 42

Samal, 64

Samar, 155, 156

San José, 261n

sanitation, 68–9

sari-sari store, 85, 104, 106, 107, 108, 109, 110, 111, 112, 113, 120, 191, 192, 196

Saudi Arabia, 102

saving (of money), 109, 110, 164, 191, 197, 204, 205, 269, 296, 297; *see also* income; earnings

Scandinavia, 105

schools, *see* education

seamstress, 113; *see also* sewing

Second World War, 45, 55, 218

secondary cities, *see* intermediate cities

secondary sector, *see* construction; export-manufacturing; industrial-isation

secretarial work, 178

Seoul, 76n

separation, 14, 15, 18, 100n, 165; *see also* divorce

service charge (in hotels), 186–7, 193, 207, 294; *see also* fringe benefits

services (employment), 24, 107, 109, 110

services (public), 107, 110

sewing, 113, 141, 287

sex, 13, 214, 223–7

sex ratio, 32, 36

sex tourism, 2, 24, 38, 63–5, 77, 172, 211–55

sex trade (international), 25, 64–5, 211–55, 313–14

sex work, 2n, 24, 29, 36, 72, 77, 211–55, 313–14

attitudes of society towards, 243–4, 250–5

attitudes of women involved, 248–51

intermediaries in, 217–18, 251

occupational hazards in, 25, 63, 233–7, 245, 248–9, 292–3

see also employment; men; migrants

sexual harrassment, 180

sexuality, 12–13, 124–7, 210, 229, 279, 280, 282, 288–91, 297–302

female, 12–13, 124–7, 254

male, 12–13, 124–7, 224–7, 287

manipulation of in employment, 179–81, 185, 213–19, 225–7, 254, 287, 288–91

Sexuality Transmitted Diseases, *see* AIDS; disease

shabu (drug), 236, 236n, 244n

shame, 15n, 140, 246, 247, 248, 250, 273, 276, 279, 282, 290

shanty town, 67; *see also* housing; irregular settlement

shelter, *see* housing

shipping, 73, 212, 231n
shipyard engineering, 56
shoe industry, 106
shops, 113, 173, 184; *see also*
    commerce
siblings, 8, 104, 156, 195, 269; *see also*
    brothers; links; migrants; remit-
    tances; sisters
Singapore, 34, 46, 76n, 105, 312
Siquijor, 72
sisters, 104, 156, 162, 199, 203, 253;
    see also siblings
skills, 139, 143, 144, 145, 148, 149,
    162, 168, 179, 208, 293, 296,
    297; *see also* language
Social Hygiene Clinic, 314
    in Cebu, 213, 220, 233n, 322
social security, 40, 58, 67–8, 134, 135,
    152, 154, 162, 174, 186, 187
    GSIS, 68
    SSS, 68, 152, 154
solo parent *see* household head;
    household structure
sons, 7, 33, 163, 165
South Korea, 46, 53, 78, 131n, 133n,
    137, 139, 255, 312
Southeast Asia, 7, 28, 33, 62, 65, 66,
    73, 129, 133n, 136, 220n, 250,
    314
Spain, 45
spinster, 12, 16
spouses, 7–18, 39, 105, 162, 200
squatters, 67; *see also* owner-occupiers
Sri Lanka, 100n, 312
stabilisation programmes, 47, 57–9
state, 307, 308, 317; *see also* government
statistics, *see* census
status, 226n
    female, 8, 27–9, 306–10
structural adjustment, 22, 47n, 57–9;
    see also debt; household;
    recession; stabilisation
    programmes
students, 51, 113
subcontracting, 24, 70, 107, 134–5,
    143, 145, 147–8; *see also*
    outwork; piece rates

Subic Naval Base, 63, 212, 238, 239
subsistence, *see* agriculture; household
    survival strategies
sugar cane, 48
survival strategies, *see* household
Suzuki, Zenko (Prime Minister), 64,
    313
sweatshops, *see* outwork; subcontracting

Tagalog, 9
Taipei, 76n
Taiwan, 28, 33, 46, 53, 63, 64, 73, 76,
    78, 133n, 169n
Taiwanese, 63, 130
tax, 71, 186, 308n
taxi drivers, 107, 181n, 189, 217
teachers, 194
Tebing Tinggi, 35n
technology, 131, 140, 149, 167, 170
    foreign, 170
    see also mechanisation
Telok Free Trade Zone, 168n
tenant, *see* housing; landlordism;
    renters
tenant farmers, 54
tertiary sector, *see* commerce; services
textiles, *see also* garment industry
Thailand, 33, 46, 171n, 235, 255, 312
theoretical approaches to household
    formation, *see* household
theoretical approaches to
    migration/gendered migration,
    see migration
timber, 75, 316
tips, 186–7, 231; *see also* service charge
Toledo, 74
tourism, 2, 24–5, 29, 63–6, 172–210
    in Boracay, 79–81, 172–210
    business-oriented, 76, 173, 212
    in Cebu, 76–7, 172–210
    as development strategy, 1–2, 63–6
    international, 2, 29, 63–6,
        172–210, 212, 313–14
    pleasure/sun-and-sea, 77, 79–81,
        172–3, 177
    as source of foreign exchange, 1–2,
        63–6

see also Boracay; Cebu; Department of Tourism; employment; hotels; restaurants; sex tourism; shops
tourists, 24, 208, 322
   female, 208–9, 230, 292
   interaction with workers, 208–9
   male, 220, 227–30
Trade Union Congress of the Philippines (TUCP), 51, 52
trading, *see* commerce; informal sector
training, 133–4, 136, 137, 143, 168
tranquilisers, 236
transport, 107, 110, 112, 189
Turkish (men)
   as clients of sex workers, 223, 224, 225

underemployment, 57, 69–70
unemployment, 57, 69–70, 112, 113
unions, 51–2, 135, 137, 138, 174, 186, 308; *see also* ALU; KMU; TUCP; worker organisation
United Kingdom, *see* Britain
United Nations, 310, 311, 312
United Nations Decade for Women, 8, 37, 311–12
United Nations Development Programme (UNDP), 56, 315
United States, 23, 34n, 45, 47, 52, 53, 55, 64, 76, 78, 122
   investment in Philippines, 47n, 49, 53
   military bases in Philippines, 48, 63, 212, 213n, 239, 250
   see also Angeles; Clark Air Base; Olangapo; Subic Naval Base
university, 90, 167n, 248; *see also* education
urban primacy, 67, 72
urbanisation, 17, 18, 66–7, 285
USSR, 171n
utang na loob (inner debt of gratitude), 15, 98

vegetables, 115, 119
Vietnam, 75, 171n
village home, 159, 238, 264, 265

violence (domestic), 12–14, 41, 124–7, 271
virginity, 12, 126, 250; *see also* marriage
virgins, 12, 223; *see also* sex work
Visayas, 2, 35, 36, 42, 72–81, 83–128, 149
   Central, 12, 36, 43, 45, 64, 71, 72–9, 84, 155, 198, 238
   Eastern, 36, 72, 155, 194, 198, 238
   Western, 43, 45, 64, 71, 72–80, 93, 194, 238

wage, 70, 79, 107, 133, 133n, 134, 137, 150–5, 168–9, 186–8, 192–3, 230–2, 262, 298
   minimum, 79, 107–8, 112, 134n, 150–4, 169, 174, 175, 186, 191, 207, 262, 309
   rises, 56n
   see also earnings, piece rates
waiters, 182, 184
waitresses, 181, 195, 201, 202; *see also* hotels; restaurants
welfare, 58, 67–9, 134; *see also* health care; household; social security
widowhood, 18
widows, 99, 242, 243
wickerware *see also* crafts; furniture industry
wife-beating, *see* violence
wives, 7–16, 39, 123, 156, 163, 164, 170, 269–70; *see also* spouses
Womanhealth Phil Inc, 42
women, *see* daughters; employers; employment; female labour force participation; gender; household head; mother; spouses
Women's Action Network for Development (WAND), 42
women's groups, 37–8, 41–2, 309, 311
women's movement, 37–8, 41–2
women's organisations, 37–8, 41–2, 309, 311
wood products, 130, 145–7, 161; *see also* furniture industry

work experience, 137, 143, 159, 168, 191
worker organisation, 51–2, 135–7, 138; *see also* unions
Worker Survey, 320–1
World Bank, 46, 47n, 49, 51, 54, 55, 57

World Tourism Organisation (WTO), 315

Yakuza (Japanese mafia), 218, 218n

Zamboanga, 238
Zimbabwe, 284n, 285